Predicting Outcomes in United States-Japan Trade Negotiations

Predicting Outcomes in United States-Japan Trade Negotiations _____

The Political Process of the Structural
Impediments Initiative

Norio Naka

QUORUM BOOKS   Westport, Connecticut
London

Library of Congress Cataloging-in-Publication Data

Naka, Norio.
    Predicting outcomes in United States-Japan trade negotiations :
the political process of the structural impediments initiative /
Norio Naka.
        p.   cm.
    Includes bibliographical references and index.
    ISBN 1–56720–005–2 (alk. paper)
    1. Protectionism—Japan.   2. Competition, Unfair—Japan.
3. Nontariff trade barriers—Japan.   4. Physical distribution of
goods—Japan.   5. Japan—Commercial policy.   6. Export marketing—
United States.   7. Foreign trade promotion—United States.
8. United States—Commerce—Japan.   9. Japan—Commerce—United
States.   I. Title.
HF2366.N35   1996
382′.0952073—dc20   95–24916

British Library Cataloguing in Publication Data is available.

Library of Congress Catalog Card Number: 95–24916
ISBN: 1–56720–005–2

First published in 1996

Quorum Books, 88 Post Road West, Westport, CT 06881
An imprint of Greenwood Publishing Group, Inc.

Printed in the United States of America

The paper used in this book complies with the
Permanent Paper Standard issued by the National
Information Standards Organization (Z39.48–1984).

10 9 8 7 6 5 4 3 2 1

Contents

Tables   vii

Preface   ix

Abbreviations   xix

1. Introduction   1

2. Overview of the SII Process and Its Agreements   15

3. Theoretical Framework and Research Design   31

4. The SII as a Means of *Gaiatsu:* The Perspective of Government
   as a Unitary Rational Actor   47

5. Quantification of Interactions between Governments:
   Pressures and Negotiations   67

6. The SII as a Site of the Transgovernmental Coalition of Subunits   95

7. The U.S. Agencies' Concerns: Content-Analysis of the SII Meeting
   Records   137

8. The SII as Part of Transgovernmental Coalitions
   among Top-Level Policy-Makers   149

9. The SII as Part of Transgovernmental Elite Policy Networks
   of Working-Level Officials   191

10. Conclusion: Findings and Implications   221

Appendices

Appendix A: The Coding Method for "Performative Structure"
                Content-Analysis   232
Appendix B: The Coding Method of Key-Word Content-Analysis   234
Appendix C: Tables   236

Bibliography   239

Index   257

Tables

3.1	Four Approaches and Analytical Concepts	39
5.1	Percentages of the Seven Categories in All Indexes	71
5.2	Percentages of the Seven Categories, Excluding Descriptions	71
5.3	Percentages of the Seven Categories from Both Sides (the United States and Japan)	71
5.4	Percentages of Demand, Criticism, and Suggestion with the Subject the United States or Japan in Pressure in *Nikkei* Indexes	73
5.5	Percentages of the Seven Categories in All Indexes	75
5.6	Percentages of the Seven Categories, Excluding Descriptions	75
5.7	Percentages of the Seven Categories from Both Sides (the United States and Japan)	75
5.8	Percentages of Demand, Criticism, and Suggestion with the Subject the United States or Japan in the *Nikkei* Indexes and the *Wall Street Journal* Indexes	78
5.9	The Number of Indexes of Seven Categories with the Subject the United States or Japan, and Ratios between Them in the *Nikkei* Indexes	78
5.10	The Number of Indexes of Seven Categories with the Subject the United States or Japan, and Ratios between Them in the *Wall Street Journal* Indexes	78
5.11	Coded Result of All *Nikkei* Indexes with the Key-Words of Issue Areas (May 1989-June 1990)	82
5.12	Percentages of Six Issue Areas in All *Nikkei* Key-Word Indexes, in the U.S. Subject Indexes, and in the Japanese Subject Indexes	85
5.13	Ordered Percentages of Six Issue Areas in All *Nikkei* Key-Word Indexes, in the U.S. Subject Indexes, and in the Japanese Subject Indexes	85

5.14   Coded Result of All *Wall Street Journal* Indexes with
        the Key-Words of Issue Areas (May 1989-June 1990)   87
5.15   Percentages of Six Issue Areas in All *Wall Street Journal*
        Key-Word Indexes in the U.S. Subject Indexes, and in the
        Japanese Subject Indexes   88
6.1   Coalition Map of the U.S. and Japanese Governmental Subunits   116
7.1   The Length of Speeches of Officials and Their Agencies in the
        Three SII Meetings   142
7.2   The Length of Speeches of Each Agency in Six Issue Areas,
        Opening and Closing Statements of the Three SII Meetings   143
7.3   The Percentage of Speeches Made by Each Agency in Six Issue
        Areas, Opening and Closing Statements of the Three SII
        Meetings   144
7.4   The Percentage of Speeches Made by Each Agency within the
        Context of the Total Speeches of the United States or in those
        of the Japanese Team in Six Issue Areas, Opening and Closing
        Statements in the Three SII Meetings   145
10.1   The Levels of Japanese Concessions in Five Issue Areas and
        Explanations   224

Preface

This book was written out of three motivations: first, to find an alternative way of international trade negotiations against the backdrop of an ongoing bitter dispute between the United States and the Japanese governments; second, to investigate the process of crisis control when the fate of the world trading regime is seriously threatened by a rise of economic nationalism in economically leading nations; and third, to suggest a more systematic way to study U.S.-Japanese trade negotiations based on international relations theories with empirically testable propositions, hoping to acquire a better understanding of the outcomes of international trade negotiations.

The Clinton-Hosokawa Summit meeting of February 11, 1994, was perhaps the first time in the history of the U.S.-Japanese trade negotiations in the last two decades that the leaders of the two governments made no effort to hide open disagreement on the trade issue. The new trade talks, the Japan-United States Framework for a New Economic Partnership were initiated by the Miyazawa government and the Clinton administration in June of 1993. Since then the talks had been deadlocked because of a long bitter "metaphysical debate" regarding the definition of "objective criteria" to measure the degree of openness and progress of liberalization in the Japanese market.[1]

From the beginning, the talks were poisoned by the issue of "numeric targets." For the U.S. government, "numeric targets" (objective criteria, benchmark, standards, or goals) mean "specific numerical sales goals for Japanese import markets" with specific dates in specific sectors.[2] However, the U.S. government rejected the notion of "market share." With the memory of the 1986 Semiconductor Agreement in which the desired goals of foreign sales were interpreted by the U.S. government as a firm market share commitment, the Japanese government rejected any specific quantitative targets on foreign sales as managed trade measures.[3]

Considering that the numeric targets issue is highly charged with an "ideological" tone regarding the nature of the Japanese economic system and its market (i.e., whether or not the Japanese economic system is fundamentally different from other Western style market economies)[4] and a zero-sum game-like conflict of interest (i.e., market share), it is no wonder that the Framework Talks had not been able to produce meaningful agreements for a long time. Even after the United States dropped its demands for the numeric targets and acknowledged "a fundamental error" in its negotiation tactics of "failing to recruit Japanese allies to join in demands for Tokyo to open up markets,"[5] it took another four months to reach a partial deal. While the U.S. and the Japanese government reached agreements on three priority issues, such as government procurement of telecommunication and medical equipment, insurance, and flat glass, disputes on auto and auto parts was not solved by September 30, 1994. Consequently, the U.S. government started a one-year investigation of the auto parts market under Section 301 of the 1974 Trade Act, which might lead to sanctions at the end of investigation if unfair trade practices were identified.[6]

The September 30 agreement was said to be a "small deal leaving big distrust" because the agreed areas cover only a tiny portion of the $60 billion U.S. trade deficit with Japan, and both sides were suspicious about the way the other side interpreted ambiguous wording of "objective criteria" in the agreement.[7] A long stalemate marked by ill feeling and distrust finally resulted in an unusual agreement on auto and auto parts in June of 1995. While the U.S. government boasted the success of verifiable numbers in the significant increase of auto and auto parts sales within years, the Japanese government announced that it had nothing to do with the "estimated numbers" unilaterally made by the U.S. government.[8] Thus, the question of how to interpret "objective criteria" still remains even after the supposedly final agreements.

The overall process of the Framework Talks reveals Clinton administration officials' problems in their trade policy goals, strategy, and tactics. Trade negotiation processes were hampered by a number of factors. Clinton administration officials were too occupied with *gaiatsu* (foreign pressure) politics toward Japan because of their simplistic view of Japanese foreign economic policy-making.[9]

Another factor was the Clinton administration officials' apparent ignorance about Japanese internal policy-making processes as well as the trans-governmental process through which the U.S. and the Japanese government could reach mutually acceptable agreements in trade negotiations. In particular, the Clinton administration does not seem to realize what factors, other than pressure, influence particular policy outcomes (agreements) in U.S.-Japanese trade negotiations.

To assess the apparent problems of the Clinton administration's Framework talks and its demands for "numeric targets," it is useful to compare those talks with an alternative approach, the United States-Japan Structural Impediments Initiative of 1989-1990 (SII), which is not well known among American policy-makers and scholars. Analyzing SII is important for several reasons. First, the principles and policies of the SII agreement, which aim at making the Japanese economy more open, transparent, and fair, have had (and continue to have) a major impact on Japanese policy-makers, business leaders, commentators, and the general public, as to perceptions and attitude.[10] Second, the SII approach is consistent not only with market forces and the aspirations of the majority of the Japanese people but also with the development of a rule-based multilateral trade regime under the General Agreements on Tariffs and Trade (GATT) and the World Trade Organization (WTO). Third, knowing what factors contributed to making successful trade agreements allows both scholars and policy-makers to understand the reasons for the different degrees of concessions in the SII issue areas. An examination of why the Japanese government conceded more in some issue areas rather than in others, will help U.S. policy-makers successfully conduct future trade negotiations. The analysis in this book focuses on three main questions: (1) Why did the Bush administration pursue the SII approach, a "rule-based approach," rather than take a "results-oriented approach" of demanding from Japan "appropriate sectoral import levels" as recommended by forty-five business leaders of the Advisory Committee for Trade Policy and Negotiations (ACTN) in the early spring of 1989?[11] (2) Why did the U.S. and Japanese government agree to such unusual agreements as the SII, which tried to change Japanese domestic economic institutions and business practices as well as some of those in the United States? (3) What important factors contributed to the different degrees of Japanese government concessions in SII issue areas?

The second motivation for this book was to investigate the process of crisis control when the fate of the world trading regime is threatened by a rise of economic nationalism in economically leading nations. From the viewpoint of the present, it is too easy to underestimate the magnitude of the U.S.-Japanese trade crisis of 1989, triggered by the FSX aircraft dispute and the implementation of the Super 301 provision of the Omnibus Trade and Competitiveness Act of 1988 (the 1988 Trade Act), and followed by numerous trade and investment disputes throughout 1989 to the spring of 1990.[12] In the early spring of 1989, policy-makers viewed the fate of the world trading regime and future of U.S.-Japan relations quite differently from we view now. Bush administration officials feared the 1988 Trade Act with its Super 301 provision could be a second Smoot-Hawley, which could trigger trade wars and a major recession, ending in a collapse of the multilateral trading regime under GATT. For U.S. and Japanese policy-makers, the early spring of 1990 was the especially critical period in which a burst of hair-trigger tension might have brought about a breakdown in U.S.-Japanese relations and an introduction of managed trade.

The wisdom of hindsight is of little use for the policy-makers who struggled to avoid such a worst-case scenario in the critical time of recent international economic history. Many disputes between the United States and its trade partners adequately demonstrate that as long as the structure of the present world system consisting of economically interdependent but politically sovereign nations remains, there is always a possibility of exchanging trade sanctions and "trade wars" regardless of scale, despite the institutional framework of the GATT/WTO. If such trade wars between major economic powers escalate into large-scale trade conflicts, operation of a world trading regime would be greatly hampered. Dazzled by growing economic interdependence, many tend to underestimate these possibilities. The 1989 trade crisis reminds us of these possibilities. In spite of technological and institutional development for the movement of money, goods, human resources, and corporations, the world trading regime could dysfunction or even collapse if the members of the system do not effectively cooperate with each other to maintain it.

Policy-makers can learn much from the broadly conceived SII process on how to control threats of trade crises caused by the rise of economic nationalism in economically leading nations. The 1989 crisis was effectively managed by the act of balancing unilateral actions, bilateral negotiations, and multilateral discussions. These three processes worked together to further the development of a world trading regime. The important point here is that despite some experts' expectation, none of these three processes can completely eliminate the other processes. Like it or not, the game of political bargaining to acquire economic gains for a nation's own favor in distributive economy and international economic rule-making will continue in a combined context of unilateral action, bilateral negotiation, and multilateral discussion, providing that the structure of the present world political-economic system remains. Therefore, the question is how to properly combine unilateral, bilateral, and multilateral modes of action to effectively solve trade disputes and major trade crises when they occur, rather than to choose which mode of action. In sum, just as studying the Cuban Missile Crisis of 1962 brings about many lessons about how to control a major crisis in which two military super powers confronted to each other on the verge of military-security system breakdown, studying the SII process reveals great insights into the issue of how to manage crisis of world trading regime in time of clashing economic nationalism between two major economic powers, the combined GNP of which accounts for almost 40 percent of the world GNP.

The third motivation for this book was to suggest a more systematic way to study the processes and outcomes of U.S.-Japanese trade negotiations, which may be useful for analyzing other types of international trade negotiations. Previously, most studies on the political process of U.S.-Japanese trade negotiations used the case study method often combined with economic analysis of data. As a result, although past studies on U.S.-Japan trade negotiations brought about important insights which potentially had significant policy implications, the state of the art essentially remained compilations of case studies without systematically tested propositions based on clearly defined international relations theories. Nor did those studies compare a variety of explanations based on different international relations theories for varying degrees of Japanese government's concessions.

Not only methods but also implicit and explicit theoretical frameworks used in most past studies on bilateral trade negotiations seem to have remained the same. For the analyses of bilateral trade negotiation processes, often-used theoretical frameworks are the "iron triangle"-like *sei-kan-zai* elitist model, the "patterned pluralist" model[13], or the bureaucratic dominance model—depending on the relative importance imparted to political actors, such as ministerial bureaucrats, the ruling party (the Liberal Democratic Party or the LDP), or business organizations and other types of pressure groups (e.g., agricultural cooperatives). According to these theories, policy outcomes of the Japanese government in trade negotiations are mainly results of bargaining among ministerial bureaucrats, LDP politicians, and business corporations and trade organizations (or agricultural cooperatives), although the relative significance of initiatives made by these political actors varies from case to case.

Furthermore, many past studies rely too much on the terms which the authors of those studies think uniquely characterize the Japanese policy-making process in explaining policy outcomes of the government in U.S.-Japanese trade negotiations. Those commonly used terms include *gaiatsu* (foreign pressure), *gyōsei shidō* (administrative guidance), *nemawashi* (building informal consent among the parties concerned), *kyōchō* (cooperation with consent), *batsu* (cliques and factions), *honne to tatemae* (true intention and publicly stated policy), *kuromaku* (behind-the-scene bosses) and so on. The net result of all these tendencies in the field of the political process of U.S.-Japanese trade negotiations is the accumulation of many single case studies and some comparative studies about particular trade issues, describing relevant government organizations and activities of political actors against background economic conditions, more or less based on a notion of tripartite policy making among LDP politicians, ministerial bureaucrats, and business organizations, characterized by a uniquely Japanese way of conduct.

To go beyond this state of affairs, a more systematic method to describe, explain, and possibly "predict" U.S.-Japanese bilateral trade negotiation processes and their outcomes was sought. The method used by Graham T. Allison in his landmark study on the Cuban Missile Crises of 1962 seemed a good candidate for that purpose. Allison described and explained some of major questions about the Cuban Missile Crises from the perspectives of three conceptual models—the rational actor model, the organizational process model, and the governmental politics model.[14] As research proceeded, however, it was found that although Allison's method is an example of great sophistication and mastery, further development is necessary for the purpose of systematic research on the political process of SII. The need for modification of Allison's method in part stems from the fact that his method was developed for the analysis of "actions of a government" in the military-security area in which communications and contact of persons between the governments are limited, especially in a crisis situation. To the contrary, the degree and scope of communications and personal contact in the area of international trade negotiations, especially among allies, are extensive. The "system" of a government is very much open; and therefore there is ample room for transgovernmental coalitions. Since transgovernmental coalitions are becoming predominant features in international trade negotiations, models which are used for analyzing international trade negotiations should be able to include the process of these coalitions.

Some features of development of Allison's method are as follows. First, a developed method is more thoroughly defined in terms of the level of analysis for each conceptual model than Allison's. The levels of analysis for Allison's three models are seemingly self-explanatory, although he did not use the term "the level of analysis." However, Allison was not thorough with the level of analysis in his second model, using both the level of analysis of organizations and that of persons.[15] In this book, the level of analysis for organizations and that for persons are clearly distinguished from each other. Since organizations and persons represent different levels of aggregation of social entities, this distinction helps a great deal when conducting systematic research.

Second, emphasis is put more on such categories as policies (or policy positions) of political actors, power relations, and transgovernmental coalitions among those actors than on organizational routines in Allison's second model. In my understanding, not organizational routines per se but the policies (or policy positions) of the organizations which are affected by their organizational routines, in relation to the policies (or policy positions) of the other governmental organizations which are also affected by routines of those organizations, that are important in understanding governmental actions. The above-mentioned categories serve as common categories which can be used for both the second and other conceptual models in this book and for analyzing policy outcomes across two conceptually different phases of policy-making processes. These two phases are the processes of making national policy outcomes and those of making international negotiation outcomes (agreements). Although Allison concentrated on analyzing and explaining the national policy outcomes as actions of a government, this research attempts to explain both national policy outcomes and international trade negotiation outcomes which are rather the results of interactions between the governments. Because these two analytically different phases of the policy-making process are in actuality interwoven, common categories which can be used for analyzing both phases provide great utility.

This book adds to the development of U.S.-Japanese trade negotiation and decision-making research. By using four systematically layered conceptual models with different levels of analysis emphasizing transgovernmental processes, this book tries to achieve a more systematic understanding of the political process of SII, thereby enhancing the power of describing, explaining, and predicting the outcomes of international trade negotiations.

Many people have kindly assisted me in conducting this research. Without their help, I could not have finished this research. I am most grateful to my dissertation advisor at Purdue University, Dr. Harry R. Targ, for his valuable advice, patience, and personal encouragement. Not only did Dr. Targ intellectually stimulate me in many ways, he also proofread and edited my dissertation, out of which this book was born. I would like to express my gratitude to Dr. Silvo Lenart, a member of my dissertation committee, for helping my research greatly with his expertise on content analysis and statistics. My sincere gratitude also goes to Dr. Robert A. Scalapino, Robson Research Professor of Government Emeritus and Director Emeritus, Institute of East Asian Studies, for his valuable comments on the manuscript in spite of his busy schedule. Many arguments in the book was clarified because of his advice.

I owe special gratitude to those who gave me their precious time in interviews. Part of my research could not be done without their assistance. Those people include former chief negotiators S. Linn Williams, John B. Taylor, Richard T. McCormack, James I. Rill, and other officials working in the U.S. and Japanese governments. (I am grateful to two former chief negotiators, Charles H. Dallara and J. Michael Farren, for their willingness to accept my interviews although it turned out that their busy schedule did not make this possible.)

Purdue University deserves my thanks for funding part of my research. The initial idea of the research was conceived when I was funded by David Ross Summer Grant in 1990. My appreciation also goes to the Political Science Department for allowing me to stay at Purdue University as a post-doctoral scholar in the fall of 1994. I would like to express my deep gratitude to former Director Mary Elizabeth Berry, Director Andrew Barshay, and the Center for Japanese Studies of Institute of East Asian Studies for giving me a wonderful opportunity to continue my research as a visiting scholar at the University of California, Berkeley. I also would like to thank Dr. Gregory W. Noble, my host professor at the Center for his input, as well as the Political Science Department of the University of California, Berkeley for accommodating my research. Knowing the faculty and staff of the Center and Institute of East Asian Studies has been one of the most joyful experiences of my life. The University with its excellent facilities and kind staff provided me a comfortable atmosphere in which I could complete the manuscript.

I must also thank many people for their direct and indirect help and advice. Those people include Dr. Harvey Marshall, a member of my dissertation committee at Purdue University; Dr. Lawrence V. Gould, Jr., my former advisor at Fort Hays State University; and the late Dr. Shukichi Nakamura and Dr. Masahiro Yamaguchi, my former teachers at Chiba University. I am grateful to Publisher Eric Valentine and to Quorum Books of the Greenwood Publishing Group, Inc. for giving me an opportunity to publish my research. I am thankful to Kirsten Lindquist, a graduate student at Purdue for editing the dissertation, to Pat Steele for copyediting the manuscript, to Wendy Sereda for proofreading the final manuscript, and to Production Editor Bridget Austiguy for the processing and final checking.

Finally, from my heart I thank my wife Hitomi, my parents Eimori and Hide Naka, my relatives, and friends. Without their help and support, I could not have continued my study abroad. Nor could I have published this book.

NOTES

1. The *Wall Street Journal* (*WSJ*), 5/25/94, p. A10. *Asahi Shinbun* (*Asahi*), 2/13/94, p. 1. Articles of *Asahi* dated after June 30, 1990, are from *Asahi Shinbun* (International Satellite Edition, New York), and ones dated before June 30, 1990, are from *Asahi Shinbun Shukusatsu-ban.*

2. Refer to *WSJ* 5/25/94, p. A2, and the *Christian Science Monitor* 5/25/94, p. 8.

3. See such articles as *WSJ* 4/19/93, p. A3; 6/13/93, p. A13; 7/5/93, p. A8; *Asahi* 1/5/94, p. 11; and The *Economist* 2/19/94, p. 25.

4. For example, refer to U.S. Trade Representative Micky Kantor's remarks "The markets in Japan aren't making decisions. There are artificial practices which do not allow market forces to work," *WSJ* 6/30/93, p. A7. Japanese officials refused to accept a so-called "revisionist view" that the Japanese capitalist system differs from other Western capitalist systems. For the Japanese view, refer to, for example *Asahi* 2/13/94, p. 7.

5. *WSJ* 5/25/94, p. A2.

6. Refer to such articles as *WSJ* 10/30/94, pp. A2, A8; *Asahi* 10/2/94, p. 7; The *Japan Times Weekly International Edition* (*JT*) 10/10/94—10/16/94, pp. 1, 3.

7. *Asahi* 10/3/94, p. 3; 10/2/94, p. 7; *JT* 10/10/94—10/16/94, pp. 1, 3.

8. *Asahi* 6/29/95, p. 1; 7/25/95, p. 4; 8/24/95, p. 11.

9. For example, see Deputy Secretary of the Treasury Roger C. Altman's article (1994), "Why Pressure Tokyo?" *Foreign Affairs* 73 (3), pp. 2-6. Also refer to B. Anne Craib (1994), "The Making of Japan Trade Policy in the Clinton Administration."

10. For example, refer to Prime Minister Murayama's policy speech, *Asahi* 1/21/95, p. 2; the article of Yu Hayami, Representative Caretaker of Keizai Doyukai (Committee for Economic Development), "Kaikaku o gyaku modori sasenai tameni," *This is Yomiuri*, May 1994, pp. 74-81; and Keidanren (Federation of Economic Organizations), "Following Through on the Structural Impediments Initiative," *Economic Eye* Autumn 1991, pp. 23-27.

11. The Advisory Committee for Trade Policy and Negotiations, *Analysis of the U.S.-Japan Trade Problem* (February 1989), pp. xvi-xviii.

12. On the account of the "1989 trade crisis," refer to such articles as "Bōeki sensō e totsunyū shita nichi-bei tsūshō masatsu," *Sekai Shūhō* 3/10/90, pp. 26-29; S. Linn Williams (former SII chief negotiator), "Kagami no naka no nichi-bei kōzō kyōgi," *Shūkan Daiyamondo* (*Daiyamondo*) 3/14/92, pp. 80-82; 3/21/92, pp. 110-114.

13. Ellis S. Krauss and Michio Muramatsu (1988), "Japanese Political Economy Today: The Patterned Pluralist Model."

14. Graham T. Allison (1971), *Essence of Decision: Explaining the Cuban Missile Crisis.*

15. See ibid., p. 87, and refer to p. 256. The same confusion in the levels of analysis is also found in his later article with Morton H. Halperin (1972), "Bureaucratic Politics: A Paradigm and Some Policy Implications," p. 384.

Abbreviations

JAPANESE GOVERNMENT

EPA	Economic Planning Agency
JFTC	Japan Fair Trade Commission
Kantei	The Residence of the Prime Minister
LDP	The Liberal Democratic Party
MAFF	Ministry of Agriculture, Forestry, and Fisheries
MFA	Ministry of Foreign Affairs
MHA	Ministry of Home Affairs
MITI	Ministry of International Trade and Industry
MOC	Ministry of Construction
MOF	Ministry of Finance
MOJ	Ministry of Justice
MOT	Ministry of Transportation
NLA	National Land Agency
NTA	National Tax Agency

U.S. GOVERNMENT

CEA	Council of Economic Advisers
EPC	Economic Policy Council
OIA	Office of International Affairs of the Treasury
TPRG	Trade Policy Review Group
TPSC	Trade Policy Staff Committee
USTR	Office of the United States Trade Representative

OTHERS

G-2   Group of Two (the United States and Japan)
G-7   Group of Seven Industrialized Nations
GATT   General Agreement on Tariffs and Trade
OECD   Organization for Economic Cooperation and Development
WTO   World Trade Organization

Predicting Outcomes in United States-Japan Trade Negotiations

1 Introduction

The United States-Japan Structural Impediments Initiative of 1989-1990 represents an example of bilateral trade negotiations. The SII has quite different characteristics from previous approaches as a means to solve trade imbalances between the United States and Japan. There have been numerous U.S.-Japanese trade frictions over steel, cars, textile, color TVs, and semiconductors. Previously, means used for managing trade imbalances were such measures as orderly marketing agreements; voluntary export restraints (VERs), compensation duties, trigger-price mechanisms for steel, quotas, market shares for semiconductors, and Japanese market liberalization measures.[1] These are mainly "border measures," concerning tariffs, the quantity of traded goods, and formal government regulations *between* the nations.

Yet, for the first time, the SII actually focused in a comprehensive manner on the domestic rigidities which impede the development of international trade and balance of payment adjustments. No international trade negotiation between sovereign states is as comprehensive as the SII except the Rome Treaty (and subsequent treaties) aiming at European economic integration. In the expression of Under Secretary of State Richard T. McCormack, one of the chief negotiators for the SII, "never before have two governments been charged by their leaders with addressing the entire range of domestic issues that affect their international economic interaction."[2]

When the SII talks began in September 1989, both countries claimed structural impediments to trade and balance of payments in the other country's economy. U.S. officials identified structural impediments to trade and balance of payments adjustments in six areas of Japanese economy: (1) saving and investment patterns, (2) land policy, (3) distribution system, (4) exclusionary business practices, (5) keiretsu relationships (interlocking ties among independent corporations), and (6) pricing mechanisms. Japanese officials suggested structural impediments in the seven areas of the U.S. economy: (1) U.S. saving and investment patterns, (2) corporate investment activities and supply capacity, (3) corporate behavior, (4) government regulation, (5) research and development, (6) export promotion, and (7) workforce education and training.

After year-long intensive negotiations, the Japanese government agreed to concessions. They agreed to spend 430 trillion yen (approximately $3 trillion) for public investment over the following decade, and to change laws affecting land prices and supplies. The coordination period for opening large retail stores would be shortened from the present average of six years (and up to ten years) to one and a half years. Antitrust law enforcement would be strengthened. Additionally, an attempt would be made to make keiretsu more open and transparent as well as to continue efforts to eliminate price difference between domestic and foreign markets. The U.S. government also agreed to make commitments to reduce its federal deficit and modify antitrust requirements for joint production ventures. The United States also agreed to study corporate behavior, eliminate unnecessary government regulations which impede the development of trade, and take action to promote exports. Finally it agreed to spend more money on research and development, workforce education, and training.[3]

Since the SII agenda covers systematic barriers across all sectors of the Japanese economy, many of which are deeply rooted in Japanese tradition, culture and society, the SII was often referred to as the beginning of the third "opening of the country" (kaikoku), the complete process of which may take a decade or more. The first opening of the country began when U.S. warships, led by Commodore Perry arrived at Tokyo Bay in 1853, to force the feudal Tokugawa rulers to open their country, culminating in the collapse of the entire feudal system, the Meiji Restoration. The second opening of the country was General MacArthur's occupational rule after the defeat of militarist Japan in 1945. Under the rule of General Headquarters of the Allies from 1945 to 1951, Japan's authoritarian economic and political system, often referred to as a "semi-feudal militaristic system," was dramatically transformed into a liberal democratic capitalist system, at least in form if not in substance. The SII is the third opening of the country, according to critics, comparable to the first and the second reforms in its scale. For example, in Taichi Sakaiya's view, the SII is an attempt to change Japan from a producer-oriented "bureaucrats-led business-government cooperation system" (kanryō shidō gata kyōchō taisei) to a consumer-oriented liberal economic system.[4] Yusuke Edo calls the SII the "second black ship," analogous to Perry's warships, since it is trying to change the economic-seclusionist structure of the Japanese economy (keizai teki sakoku).[5]

For the United States, the SII agreements are "a compilation of the important steps that the administration has taken and plans to take to maintain a strong competitive economy and to ensure American economic health and leadership in the years to come."[6]

In June 1993, the follow-up stage of the SII formally ended, leaving a major impact on Japan. To date, there have been some major changes, including at least seven major law amendments (e.g., the Large Store Law, the Tax Law, the Land Lease and House Lease Law, the Antimonopoly Law, the Company Law, the Securities and Exchange Law, and the Foreign Exchange and Foreign Trade Law), dozens of new regulations, new Ministerial ordinances, the publications of new guidelines, and the enactment of a new law (the Administrative Procedure Law).[7] These formal changes are also reflected in perceptional and attitudinal changes among members of government officials, of ministerial advisory committees, and of large corporations and trade organizations like Keidanren (Federation of Economic Organizations).[8] The Murayama LDP-Socialist coalition government proposed policies similar to those of the Hata and Hosokawa government, using the same terminology as those used in the SII agreement, such as references to a "consumer-oriented" economy, domestic demand-led growth, elimination of price differentials between domestic and overseas markets, further deregulation, strict enforcement of antimonopoly law, public works spending for the improvement of the "quality of life," and so on.[9]

In the meantime, the United States had also experienced some regulatory changes, such as the introduction of the metric system for federal government procurement, a new gas tax, and the executive line-item veto, although a balanced budget amendment could not pass the Senate.[10] Some structural reforms were begun with the Bush administration. The Clinton administration started some of structural reforms pledged by the Bush administration in the SII talks.[11] The current Republican-majority Congress seems to be pursuing some of the reform policies outlined in the SII agreement. The SII process influenced the momentum of these reform efforts in Japan and the United States, which might be considered part of broadly conceived worldwide political and economic reform efforts in 1989 and 1990.[12]

As for U.S.-Japanese trade relations, "The Japan-United States Framework for a New Economic Partnership" was announced in June 1993. In spite of the highly contentious issue of "numeric targets," the initial organizational characteristics of the new talks resembled those of the SII in terms of (1) its goals, (2) "the basic principle of two-way dialogue," (3) a combination of macroeconomic and market-opening measures to solve structural issues, (4) the interagency working group structure, (5) negotiators from subcabinet levels, and 6) the assessment of the progress in biannual meetings of the heads of each government (political intervention). Sectoral issues, which were discussed in the separate talks in the Bush administration, were simply included in the new framework. The item of "economic harmonization" was also on the agenda. With all these organizational characteristics, the Framework talks initially seemed to be a continuation of the SII framework, except for "quantitative and qualitative criteria."[13] Unfortunately, the potentials of those organizational characteristics were not well-cultivated by the Clinton administration officials who focused too much emphasis on "objective criteria" to guarantee "results of a sales increase," which later brought about the stalemate in the bilateral negotiations.

Nevertheless, the issue of structural differences between the United States and Japanese economies remains, which is one of the sources for bitter trade disputes from time to time. Therefore the issue of how to harmonize their differences continues to be on the agenda toward the next century until structural differences are no longer obstacles to economic interactions of two nations.

PREVIOUS RESEARCH

Despite the important impact of the SII on the ongoing reform processes and its unique characteristics as a means to solve trade friction, few facts about SII are known, much less explanations about events in the SII negotiation process. Although there are many descriptive or normative essays and articles in Japanese magazines and newspapers (and some in English), few academic studies on the SII have been done. In both English and Japanese, most studies on the SII to date have been written from either an "economic point of view" including macroeconomic analysis, macroeconomic policy coordination, and structural adjustment, or the perspective of "comparative economic institutions" (and its variation, a "harmonization of economic institutions" approach).[14] Among those studies, *Japan's Economic Structure: Should It Change?* edited by Kozo Yamamura remains the only major work on the SII in English, to date. But the articles in this book, like many other articles in Japanese, are mostly about the problems of Japanese economic institutions and business practices, not about the political process of the SII.

There are only six articles which study the political aspects of the SII.[15] The articles of Ouchi, Kusano, and Igarashi are analytical descriptions without a theoretical basis. Although Mastanduno's attempt to understand the Bush administration's SII initiative in terms of "loss avoidance" gives us some insights, his description and explanation lacks consistency, by using several approaches here and there, such as the logic of "loss avoidance," "bureaucratic politics," and "two other factors."[16] Moreover, one wonders how one analyst can claim that Bush administration officials' act of framing for the SII initiation was "loss avoidance," while the other analyst suggests that the same act can be understood in terms of "utility maximization."[17] In sum, "logic" is not a substitute for empirical research on concrete policies of political actors and dynamics among those actors, out of which national policy outcomes and international agreements are generated.

Schoppa's study with its theoretically conscious approach was an important first step for further systematic research on political aspects of the SII. However, his study has some serious problems. First, some of his assertions are not based on hard evidence and are simply incorrect. For example, Schoppa stated that five SII issue areas were given "essentially equal billing" by the Bush administration and that the U.S. government applied "similar external pressure" across the SII issue areas.[18] As shown later in this book, available evidence suggests this assertion is not correct. The U.S. government did not put a similar level of pressure on the Japanese government in all five issue areas. Consequently, the different levels of U.S. pressures influenced the negotiation results greatly.

Second, his assessment of the degrees of U.S. success in each issue area seems based on inadequate information and is not held with close scrutiny. By using multiple criteria and a chief negotiator's own assessment, this book suggests that the U.S. government was most successful in the saving-investment issue area and was successful in both distribution system and land policy areas. The different assessment of the degrees of negotiation success requires reconsideration about possible explanations.

Third, what is meant by the notion of "participation expansion" is not always clear. Certainly, the formal SII process highlighted U.S. agencies as visible new actors and helped open up the domestic policy process to those new actors.[19] Also it is true that the U.S. government consciously tried to make coalitions with some Japanese ministries by introducing a multiagency structure of SII framework and gain support from the media and Japanese public through extensive public relations. However, it is not certain that the nature of the Japanese policy-making process regarding SII is characterized as "participation expansion." For example, in the Japanese budget-making process, the Ministry of Finance (MOF) is certainly a dominant actor due to its legally mandated jurisdiction, expertise, and historical legacy. But MOF, however dominant, shares power with other political actors, that is, other ministries and the ruling party (the LDP) in many ways.[20] Contrary to what is meant by the notion of "participation expansion," that is, the state of affairs in which some political actors who were previously absent in the policy-making process become involved in the process by resorting to influence on outcomes, all relevant domestic political actors are already in the process as ever. What the SII changed was *not* the scope of elite participation by bringing new political actors into the budget-making process, but the balance of power by generating new coalitions among political actors which were already in the process. In this sense, Fukai's characterization seems more accurate than that of Schoppa. "Various actors in the process tried to use the pressure generated by the [SII] negotiation to defend or expand their own interests, causing a shift in the balance of power between and within the major policymaking circles."[21]

Furthermore, the SII politicized all five issues, raised public awareness on each issue, and provided specific alternatives which were not clearly recognized by the Japanese government. The attitude of the public, strongly influenced by the media campaign, was generally supportive of U.S. demands.[22] But one is not sure this is the case of "expanded participation at the public-level" as Schoppa suggests. The general support of the media and public for U.S.

demands created the "background condition" in which policy-makers including ministerial bureaucrats and LDP politicians should or could act toward the directions that the U.S. government demanded. "Consumer interest" was widely mentioned by the media and commentators. But, the "public" remained unorganized and consumer groups remained "quiet."[23] Rather, specific contents of SII agreements in five issue areas were the results of compromise among relevant political actors, each favoring particular policy positions, because of, in some cases, or in spite of the public mood in other cases, as had occurred in the past.[24] Therefore, there are several questions to be answered here, which Schoppa did not mention: (1) whether or not support of the general public often shown in public polls means "participation expansion" even when the general public is not organized and therefore cannot resort to systematic influence on policy-making process, (2) whether or not the effect of "participation expansion" between at the elite and at the mass level are the same, and (3) what the relationship is between them, and which factors explain variations in policy outcomes.

Additionally, the way Schoppa utilized his presumed variables (because he never use the words "variables") is arbitrary and therefore questionable. For example, his criteria for U.S. success in using "participation expansion strategy" is whether or not "latent support for foreign demands" in Japan exists at the elite or mass level, or both.[25] In the cases of public works spending and the Large Store Law, U.S. strategy was successful because of "latent support for U.S. demands" in Japan, while in the cases of exclusionary business practices and the keiretsu issue areas, the same strategy was not successful because of lack of such support. However, he never asked whether or not "latent support" existed in the land policy issue area, other than mentioning high level "politicization" and "fixed public attitudes."[26] As a matter of fact, there was a great deal of support for U.S. demands in the land policy issue area both at the elite and mass levels.[27] But again, even with strong support from both Japanese elites and the mass public with which the U.S. government successfully induced the Japanese concessions, the actual content of agreements in land policy were the results of compromise among relevant organizational actors. Furthermore, his presumed variable of possible existence of "latent support" cannot explain the variation between antimonopoly law and the keiretsu issue if "latent support" of the Japanese people was equally lacking for both issue areas.

Since Schoppa used several concepts with qualifications, one is never sure that the negotiation outcomes in the five issue areas were the result of which factors: participation expansion among the elite and/or the public, latent support for foreign demands before negotiations started, or support for U.S. demands from "outside usual circles."[28] Furthermore, policy positions *inside* "usual" policy-making circles are not much accounted for by Schoppa. In actuality, they had decisive influence on policy outcomes.

With respect to the application of "alternative specification," one also encounters a serious question. The issues, such as the need to improve the

Japanese people's living conditions through public investment for social infrastructure and housing and the delay of opening new stores under the Large Store Law were already "recognized local problems" before the SII, while both exclusionary business practices and keiretsu issues were paid little attention by policy-makers and commentators when the SII began.[29] Then, how one can claim the strategy of "alternative specification" had "no significant impact" on the saving-investment area in addition to the keiretsu area, while the same strategy led to some "consideration" in both distribution system and exclusionary business practices areas.[30]

In sum, considering the difficulty identifying (if not measuring) what exactly "participation expansion" is at elite and public levels and the degrees of impact of "alternative specification" on each issue area, as well as the inconsistency in applying some of his concepts to the SII case, Schoppa's method is not reliable for explaining the variations in SII issue areas.

Problems of Schoppa's approach seem in part to stem from confusion in levels of analysis, which is also the case for other writings on the SII, including both academic and nonacademic. Hitherto writings dealing with the SII had one thing in common: none of them pays serious attention to the level of analysis. They use all sorts of levels of analysis, such as world system, national governments, governmental subunits, and individuals, for describing and explaining events throughout the SII process. As a result, many of those writings provide inadequate, even contradictory, interpretations of the events throughout the SII. For instance, many interpretations of the purpose of the SII abound. For some, the SII is a means for the United States to "contain" Japan (*nihon fūjikome*), that is, a means to deal with the economic threat from Japan.[31] In this kind of interpretation, U.S. demands on Japanese public works spending is comparable to the reduction of naval arms under the Washington Treaty of 1922. The analogy is obvious; the Washington Treaty tried to "contain" Japanese naval power, while the SII tries to "contain" the expansion of Japanese industrial and financial power.[32]

For others, the purpose of SII is "to reform Japanese economic structure" which threatens the survival of U.S. industries in a time when economic power is more prominent than military power.[33] Soichiro Tahara believes that the U.S. goal of SII shifted from reduction of the trade deficit in the fall of 1989 to "reforming Japan" (*nihon kaizō*).[34]

Yamamura also believes one of two main goals of the U.S. administration in SII is "to change those parts of Japan's economic structure that are . . . incongruent with maintenance of the liberal world trade regime."[35] Therefore, the SII negotiations focused on "the real agendas," that is, necessary changes in Japan's economic structure. The Japanese agenda for the United States was placed on the negotiation table "only to make it easier for the Japanese to participate."[36] Takeshi Sasaki takes a view similar to that of Yamamura: "Japan did designate a list of American structural problems in the SII talks, but this was just for the sake of appearance."[37]

For Mitoji Yabunaka, the SII was a practice of "harmonization of economic institutions" between the United States and Japan.   As economic activities become globalized, differences in economic institutions and business practices become obstacles for smooth economic transactions.   In the SII, the United States and Japanese governments tried to harmonize their economic institutions. Indeed, structural problems in both countries, U.S. and Japan, are seriously discussed under the recognition of the "two-way" characteristics of SII, although the degree of discussion and commitments are not exactly the same because of different degrees of government regulations.[38]

As noted above, even such basic things as the purpose of the SII are interpreted in various ways among different writers.   One major issue regarding the SII is how to assess the characteristic of the "two-way street."   The official definition of the SII is "to identify and solve structural problems in both countries that stand as impediments to trade and balance of payments adjustment with the goal of contributing to the reduction of payments imbalances."[39]   The notion of a "two-way street" recognizes that *both* the U.S. system and the Japanese system have structural problems to be corrected.   The simultaneous correction of these structural problems in both countries will reduce the trade deficit and current account imbalances.

In spite of the official characterization of SII as a "two-way street" and the fact that U.S. officials repeatedly refer to the "two-way street" nature of the SII, no study ever seriously attempts to assess the actual extent of this notion. Except Yabunaka's brief description of U.S. officials' responses to Japanese criticism of the U.S. system, virtually all studies focus on the Japanese side of the issues.   This paucity of research on the intentions of U.S. officials and the extent of the "two-way street" in the policy-making process exists despite Yabunaka's reference to the words of a U.S. delegate that "we also need *gaiatsu* in order to implement policies which will ask our people for sacrifice, [therefore] it is very good that Japan stresses the reduction of the federal deficit."[40]

THE PURPOSE OF RESEARCH AND OUTLINE

The main purpose of the research is to investigate the entire political process of the SII by using a theoretical framework with clearly defined conceptional models and levels of analysis in order to answer two major "puzzling" questions and an additional question.[41]   Why did the U.S. government initiate the SII? Why did the U.S. and the Japanese governments reach an SII agreement? What factors contributed to the different degrees of Japanese government concessions in five SII issue areas?

Further, the research will assess the actual extent of the "two-way street" nature of the SII.   There will be many ways to do this assessment, such as examining the ratio of items on the U.S. and Japanese agendas, the amount of time spent on discussions by each side,[42] the perceptions and intentions of U.S. and Japanese officials, the numbers of changes in laws and regulations, and actual changes in business practices resulting from legal and institutional changes in both countries.

This research will assess the "two-way street" hypothesis by focusing on U.S. administration officials' perceptions and intentions. Instead of directly answering the big questions of whether or not the Japanese system will change or whether the U.S. and the Japanese economic systems will converge, this book, as a first step, attempts to reveal U.S. and Japanese officials' perceptions and intentions concerning how to solve structural problems in their own economies as well as in that of the other. In order for the system to change, key policy-makers' perceptions and attitudes need to change. Thus, when one finds perceptional and attitudinal changes among policy-makers, one could expect changes in policy-making processes over time, in regulations and laws, and eventually changes in institutions and practices. As a result of those changes in both countries which policy-makers consciously promote according to what they learned from the other system, some similarities in economic institutions and business practices may emerge. Perhaps those processes can be more aptly referred to as "convergence by direct learning" rather than some older notion of "convergence" which is a quasi-automatic process characterized by the logic of capital accumulation and technological development.[43] This book reveals the process of "direct learning" between U.S. and Japanese working-level officials throughout the SII negotiation and its implications.

The outline of the book is as follows. Chapter 2 describes some major events in the SII process and introduces the important features of SII agendas and agreements. Chapter 3 presents a theoretical framework and the basic research design. An approach used in the book is inspired by Graham T. Allison's method in *Essence of Decision*, but with further developed features. The theoretical framework for the research may be referred to as "a systematically layered multidimensional approach," for it systematically combines four different models with different levels of analysis. The method used in the research is a detailed case study supplemented by content analysis.

In Chapter 4, the entire process of the SII is described and explained from the perspective of the government as a rational unitary actor. The simplest image derived from this model is that the U.S. government initiated major policies in the SII and put pressure on the Japanese government for concessions. Thus, the SII is a means of *gaiatsu* to press Japan into making some concessions.

Taking a closer look, what emerges is the picture of an "imperfect three actor game" among the U.S. administration, the Congress, and the Japanese government, each as an independent political actor with their own political goals, in terms of making coalitions and pressuring one another.

In Chapter 5, based on the model of the government as a unitary actor, the *Nihon Keizai Shinbun* (*Nikkei*) indexes and the *Wall Street Journal* indexes on the events (excluding editorials and analytical articles) are coded and analyzed.

This portion of the analysis is used to assess which government initiated what kinds of policies and with what levels of strength. The second content-analysis of indexes is conducted to examine the pressure level in each issue area. The analysis results show that the different levels of Japanese concessions in five issue areas are associated with the different levels of U.S. pressures, with some exceptions which can be explained by other models.

In Chapter 6, the SII process is described and explained from a perspective that uses the model of the transgovernmental coalition of subunits. Here, policies in the SII agreements are seen as resulting from transgovernmental coalitions among governmental subunits as political actors. It is shown that the different levels of Japanese concessions are related to the size and strength of transgovernmental coalitions among subunits.

In Chapter 7, to know which agencies took a lead in which issue areas in the discussions of the SII meetings, the reconstructed meeting records of the SII are content-analyzed based on the second model. The analysis of the SII meeting records also reveals the same results as those of the Nikkei indexes.

In Chapter 8, the reality of transgovernmental coalition-making among top-level policy-makers in the U.S. and Japanese governments is described. Top policy-makers' personal relations and their close cooperation are stressed as important factors for successful international trade negotiation results. Overall, it is found that the different negotiation results in SII issue areas are influenced by the size and strength of the transgovernmental coalition among top-level policy-makers.

In Chapter 9, the characteristics of the SII are analyzed from the view that the SII is part of elite policy networks among working-level officials. From this perspective, the SII is seen as a transgovernmental policy coordination/policy-making/policy implementation by "another bureaucratic structure" (i.e., working group) in order to manage the problems of economic interdependence. Using available materials and interviews, the existence of elite policy networks between U.S. and Japanese working-level officials is described. The different degrees of concessions across the issue areas are explained here by the levels of "common views" or "perception gaps" among the U.S. and Japanese working-level officials.

Chapter 10 discusses research findings and their theoretical and practical implications for future trade negotiations.

NOTES

1. Macroeconomic policies are another type of measure to influence trade imbalances.

2. Press conference by senior administration officials on April 5, 1990. See The *Congressional Quarterly Weekly Report* (*CQWR*) 4/7/90, p. 1100.

3. *Joint Report of the U.S.-Japan Working Group on the Structural Impediments Initiative*, June 28, 1990 (hereafter *the Final Report*).

4. Sakaiya (1990), "Kokunan! rinri-kan no henkō o semaru beikoku."

5. Yusuke Edo (1990), *Nich-bei Kōzō Kyōgi no Yomikata*, p. 269. See also Takeshi Igarashi (1990), "Nichi-bei kōzō kyōgi no imi towa nanika," pp. 21-22.

6. McCormack at press conference, April 5, 1990, *CQWR*, p. 1100.

7. For the details of formal regulatory changes, see *First Annual Report of the U.S.-Japan Working Group on the Structural Impediments Initiative*, May 22, 1991; *Second Annual Report of the U.S.-Japan Working Group on the Structural Impediments Initiative*, July 30, 1992. Also refer to Eiichi Furukawa (1991), *Bei-Nichi Bōeki Hakusho* for the progress in implementation of commitments of the U.S. and the Japanese governments, pp. 134-193.

8. For example, see the articles of *Asahi*, on business practices 2/7/92, p. 2; on the Company Law, 3/12/93, p. 9, and 6/23/93, p. 3; on cross-shareholding, 6/8/93; on the openness of trade association, 8/21/92, p. 2; on the Administrative Procedure Law, 11/23/94, p. 2; on the Antimonopoly Law, 3/16, 17, 18, 19/93, each p. 5. Among these changes, nothing is more conspicuous than the recent new activism of the Japan Fair Trade Commission (JFTC). Refer to Noboru Honjo (1994), *Saishin Dokusen Kinshi-hō Kiiwaado*. Hideto Ishida (1994), *Kamitsuita Banken, Dokkin Seisaku Kyōka no Nami o Norikiru*. Assistant Attorney General James F. Rill, a SII chief negotiator, expressed his view that SII contributed to "significant improvement in the increased status of JFTC, greater enforcement of antitrust law, and increased recognition over the importance of antitrust law." Interview, 10/7/92, Washington, D.C.

9. Refer to Prime Minister's policy speech, *Asahi* 1/21/95, p. 2. Prime Minister Hata's policy speech, *Asahi*, 5/11/94, p. 8. Prime Minister Hosokawa's policy speech, *Asahi* 8/24/93, p. 6.

10. *West County Times* (Richmond, California) 4/19/95, pp. 1B-2B.

11. Bergsten and Noland (1993), *Reconcilable Differences?*, pp. 211-212.

12. Contrary to the political and economic reform movements in Eastern Europe in 1989 and 1990, the moves toward system reform in Japan and the United States through the SII are not well recognized. Rather, the SII is understood in the context of "a new conflict within capitalism" after the Cold War ended. For example, refer to Chalmers Johnson (1991), "History Restarted: Japanese-American Relations at the End of the Century." Islam (1990), "Capitalism in Conflict." Bush administration officials viewed the SII process as part of the 1989-1990 worldwide change. See Carla Hills' statement, "the call for managed trade comes at an inappropriate time in world history and is extraordinarily short-sighted. We are witness to a remarkable new era of openness and change around the world and Japan is a part of it." ("Japan Must Follow Through on Trade Commitments," Speech before the Japan Society, 6/18/90, p. 6.) Also refer to John Taylor's testimony, the Senate Finance Trade Subcommittee Hearing of March 5, 1990 (hereafter SH 3/5/90), p. 16.

13. "Joint Statement on the Japan-United States Framework for a New Economic Partnership, July 10, 1993." See also *Asahi* 7/11/93, p. 1, 2; 9/8/93, p. 11.

14. The analyses from the macroeconomic point of view include Naotatsu Hosaka (1990), "Kōzō chōsei kyōgi no seiji keizaigaku"; Heizo Takenaka (1991), *Nichi-bei Masatsu no Keizaigaku*; Naoko Ishii (1990), *Seisaku Kyōchō no Keizaigaku*, pp. 297-326. The studies from a comparative economic institutions perspective are such works as Kozo Yamamura ed. (1990), *Japan's Economic Structure: Should It Change?*; Yusuke Edo (1990), *Nichi-bei Kōzō Kyōgi no Yomikata*; Takehisa Awaji (1990), "Dokkin-hō no unyō

kyōka to songai baishō seido"; Masayuki Funada (1990), "Kakaku mekanizumu to torihiki kankō"; Shin Kisugi (1990), "Dokkin-hō no unyō kyōka—kachō-kin"; Kenji Sanekata (1990), "Ryūtsū seido"; and Toshimasa Tsuruta and Soshichi Miyachi (1990), *Posuto Kōzō Kyōgi*. The harmonization of economic institutions approach include Mitoji Yabunaka (1990), "Nihi-bei kōzō mondai kyōgi"; Mitsuo Matsushita (1990), "Nichi-bei kōzō mondai kyōgi to keizai seido chōsei." For more details of literature review, refer to Norio Naka (1994), *A Multidimensional Approach to the United States-Japan Structural Impediments Initiative* (Unpublished Dissertation, Purdue University), Chapter 3, "Review of Previous Research."

15. Hiroshi Ouchi (1990), "Masatsu kara keizai chōsei e"; Toshiko Igarashi (1991), "Amerika kara mita nichi-bei kōzō kyōgi"; Atsushi Kusano (1991), "Bush seiken-ka no nichi-bei kōzō kyōgi,"; Shigeko N. Fukai (1992), "The Role of 'Gaiatsu' in Japan's Land policymaking"; Michael Mastanduno (1992), "Framing the Japan Problem"; and Leonard J. Schoppa (1993), "Two-level Games and Bargaining Outcomes."

16. Mastanduno, op. cit., pp. 252, 258, 261.

17. Mastanduno, ibid., p. 263.

18. Schoppa, op. cit., pp. 355, 366. The pricing mechanisms area was dropped from the investigation because it was a less independent area than the other five areas.

19. But even this characterization should be understood with some qualification because U.S. agencies were not entirely "new actors" and domestic policy-making process was not entirely closed to outsiders. What SII process made was to make U.S. agencies more visible and to make domestic policy process more fluid.

20. For Japanese budget-making process, refer to such works as John Creighton Campbell (1977), *Contemporary Japanese Budget Politics*; Yukio Noguchi (1991), "Budget Policymaking in Japan."

21. Fukai, op. cit., p. 2.

22. Refer to the public poll results in *Nihon Keizai Shinbun* (*Nikkei*) 3/27/90, pp. 1, 3, in which the large number of 47.4 percent supported the U.S. demands, exceeding the nonsupport of 39.5 percent. (Articles of *Nikkei* are from *Nihon Keizai Shinbun Shukusatsu-ban*.)

23. Refer to *Asahi* 3/26/90, p. 1, "Consumer groups which are supposed to gain the greatest benefit [from reforms suggested by SII agendas] have remained quiet."

24. See *Asahi* 4/3/90, p. 2.

25. Schoppa, op. cit., p. 373.

26. Ibid., pp. 375, 379.

27. There seems to have been no nationwide poll on the degree of support in SII issue areas. However, the results of a public poll on the presidents of 107 major Japanese corporations are quite informative. In that poll, the overwhelming majority, about 95 percent, supported U.S. demands on land policy "entirely" or "basically." (*Nikkei* 3/29/90, p. 1.) Also refer to poll results of fifty attendeeds in a symposium sponsored by Paburikku Choisu Kenkyū-kai on 6/16/90, which might be interpreted as giving support for U.S. demands at the mass level. Although the forms of the questions are somewhat different, the patterns of support for U.S. demands are similar between the poll results at the symposium and those of *Nikkei*, except for keiretsu. That is, the highest support of about 67 to 95 percent was found in land policy and the distribution system, the medium-level support of 51 and 46 percent in exclusionary business practices, and the low-level support of 20 to 30 percent in the saving and investment

patterns area. In the area of keiretsu, a majority (80%) of corporate executives did not support the United States, while 48 percent of the symposium attendees supported the United States, exceeding non-supporters of 35 percent. See *Kōkyō Sentaku no Kenkyū*, 16, 1990, pp. 38-39. According to the results of the public poll on economic structural adjustment held in 1989, of 2,331 people, the highest percent of the general public thought that high land prices and high distribution costs were two major reasons for high commodity prices in Japan and therefore needed reform. This is consistent with the results of the above-mentioned two polls. Refer to Naikaku Sōri Daijin Kanbō Kōhō Shitsu, ed. (1989). *Seron Chōsa Nenkan*, p. 109. Providing that the former two polls reflect the level of support for U.S. demands at the (business) elite and mass levels (with margin of errors), the relatively low-level support in the saving and investment patterns area puts Schoppa's simple assertion in question and requires alternative explanations. Although one may argue that the general public and many elites supported a "cause" of U.S. requests for higher level of public investment but not for the heavy-handed specific demand of government budget spending, more sophisticated and reliable explanations can be sought.

28. See Schoppa, op. cit, Table 1 and pp. 374-382.

29. Refer to *Shūkan Tōyō Keizai* (*Tōyō Keizai*) 9/30/89, pp. 14-15. Kensetsu Daijin Kanbō Seisaku-ka (1990), *Nichi-bei Kōzō Mondai Kyōgi to Kenchiku Gyōsei*, pp. 49-50. Kazumitsu Sakata (1991), "Daiten-hō to ōgata ten mondai."

30. See Schoppa, op. cit., p. 375 and pp. 382-383. Schoppa himself seems to have some troubles to identify the degree of success of a "alternative specification" strategy. Compare the op. cit. article of 1993 with his 1992 article "Gaiatsu and the Japanese Policy Process." The former is a revision of the latter.

31. Yoshihiro Tsurumi (1990), "Nihon no kanryō tōsei keizai o mote amasu amerika," pp. 20-23.

32. Refer to *Nikkei* 11/9/89, p. 1; 1/1/90, p. 9. Also refer to an anonymous discussion of Japanese middle-level bureaucrats in *Chūō Kōron*, June 1990, pp. 145, 152.

33. For example, see Edo op. cit., preface and p. 63.

34. Soichiro Tahara (1990), "Nichi-bei anpo ga omocha ni sare dashita," pp. 169-170.

35. The other goal is to increase access to Japanese market and help reduce the U.S. trade deficit through elimination of the trade impeding effects of Japan's economic structure. See Yamamura ed. op. cit. Introduction, pp. 1-2.

36. Yamamura cd. op. cit., pp. 3-4.

37. Sasaki (1990), "SII and the Ticking Legacy," p. 37.

38. Mitoji Yabunaka (1991), *Taibei Keizai Kōshō*, pp. 194-198, 204-205. (Hereafter, all references are from this 1991 book.)

39. "Joint Statement by President Bush and Prime Minister Uno on Economic Issues, July 14, 1989."

40. Yabunaka, op. cit., p. 205. The expression "*gisei o shiiru*," which is translated into "ask for sacrifice" here, literally means "force sacrifice" in Japanese. Hereafter, quotations from the Japanese sources are my translation.

41. Mastanduno, "That the United States and Japan agreed to engage in the SII, much less to reach detailed agreement, might be considered puzzling," because no previous trade negotiation between them is "as comprehensive, and as intrusive domestically, as the SII," op. cit., p. 236. The SII is also "puzzling" because it creates "demands for

changes that could be accomplished only by a broad social revolution that is highly unlikely." See the *New York Times* (*NYT*) 3/16/90, p. A1+.

42. For example, Takenaka cites a report that most discussion time in the third (February) and the fourth (April) sessions in 1990 was spent on Japanese side issues, asserting that U.S. demands to Japan overwhelmingly exceeded Japanese demands to the U.S., in spite of official "two-way street" structural adjustment. See Takenaka, op, cit., pp. 286-287.

43. For "convergence by direct learning," refer to Koji Taira (1990), "From Americanization of Japan to Japanization of America in HRM/IR," pp. 470-472.

2   Overview of the SII Process and Its Agreements

THE BEGINNING OF THE SII

The SII was not initiated peacefully, based on a prearranged agreement between the United States and the Japanese governments to achieve economic integration between the two economies. It was born in the midst of the second "major foreign policy crisis"[1] of the Bush administration after the first crisis of the FSX aircraft issue in a time of "the highest level of trade tension since the war."[2] Bush administration officials feared they were witnessing the collapsing liberal international economic order. Michael Mastanduno, working in the Office of the United States Trade Representative (USTR) in the spring of 1989, observed that the passage by Congress the Omnibus Trade and Competitiveness Act of 1988 (the 1988 Trade Act) with its Super 301 provision raised "the spectre of a second 'Smoot-Hawley'" among administration officials, which could culminate in the demise of the multilateral trade regime under GATT.[3]

This observation is supported by the remarks of administration officials. The chairman of the Council of Economic Advisers, Michael J. Boskin, warned at that time that resorting to the Super 301 would cause not only a recession in the United States but also a worldwide recession, and even a "trade war."[4] Under Secretary of State McCormack recalled that, "We were not ready for a full-scale trade war with Japan at that time."[5] McCormack often used the analogy of the 1920s for the United States to the 1980s for Japan.[6] Assistant Secretary Charles H. Dallara, chief negotiator from the Treasury Department, said at the end of the first plenary meeting of the SII, "Our efforts in the SII may not be the best ones, but [they] could be the last ones that the U.S. and Japan can do constructively."[7] As the SII talks proceeded, Japanese policy-makers also started seeing the SII as "crisis control" (Foreign Minister Taro Nakayama) to avoid a possible backlash in the United States and even a break-down of the U.S.-Japanese relationship.[8]

But many facts surrounding the SII are not yet fully known, much less do we have an explanation or understanding of these facts. The words of a new trade talk on structural impediments was publicly announced for the first time by the U.S. government on May 25 1989, when the Bush administration named Japan, along with India and Brazil, as unfair trade practice priority countries under the provision of Section 301 of the 1988 Trade Act. Frustrated with the administration's lack of enthusiasm in dealing with the huge trade deficit with Japan (at its peak $55 billion out of the total U.S. trade deficit of $138 billion in 1986),[9] Congress passed the Trade Act in the summer of 1988. The Section 301 of the act, with its so-called Super 301 provision, required the U.S. Trade Representative to identify priority trade-liberalizing practices and countries based on the National Trade Estimate Report, and then initiate negotiations to eliminate these unfair trade practices in 1989 and 1990.[10]

The 1989 National Trade Estimate Report lists more than thirty Japanese trade barriers, more than any of the other thirty-four nations and two regional trading bodies. These barriers include the complexity and rigidity of Japan's distribution system and the Large Store Law, keiretsu (an interlocking corporate grouping), patent protection, services, and market restrictions along with more traditional trade barriers such as tariffs, quotas, standards, and government procurement practices.[11]   Under the unfair trade designations, Japan was charged with restricting U.S. exports in the areas of supercomputers, commercial satellites, and processed lumber. While the Bush administration specified only three priority-negotiation items, it proposed to the Japanese government a separate but parallel negotiation covering more broad structural barriers to trade, such as rigidities in the distribution system, dango (bid-rigging), market share allocation, group boycotts, and pricing mechanisms, in addition to other macroeconomic issues.[12]

The Bush administration's decision was widely interpreted as "walking a fine line between heated cries to battle by congressional trade hawks and equally urgent calls for restraint by dedicated free traders," and also as resorting to "a congressionally mandated swipe at Japan, but delivered the blow gently—in the hope that Tokyo would not feel compelled to counterpunch."[13]   While the Japanese government officially protested to the U.S. government over the unilateral Super 301 designation, which was, in the Japanese government's view, a violation of the rules of GATT, it showed a positive posture by accepting the U.S. proposal for structural talks with the condition that structural barriers to trade in both countries should be discussed.[14]

After some preliminary discussions by working-level officials, the SII was officially launched by President George Bush and Prime Minister Sosuke Uno at the time of the Paris Summit on July 14, 1989.   According to the joint statement, the purpose of the SII talks was "to identify and solve structural problems in both countries that stand as impediments to trade and balance of payments adjustment with the goal of contributing to the reduction of payments imbalances."[15] They also agreed to establish a joint interagency working group which would undertake these talks and present a joint final report to the heads of the governments within a year, with an interim assessment in the spring of 1990.[16]

In the summer of 1989, the interagency structure of the SII talks was created. The SII working group includes five departments and one agency from the U.S. government and three ministries and two agencies from the Japanese government on a regular basis. These include three co-chair agencies—State, Treasury, USTR—and Commerce, Justice, and the Council of Economic Advisers (CEA) on the U.S. side, and three co-chair ministries—Foreign Affairs (MFA), Finance (MOF), International Trade and Industry (MITI)—and the Economic Planning Agency (EPA) and the (Japan) Fair Trade Commission (JFTC) on the Japanese side. In the actual meetings, more agencies, several from the U.S. government and eleven ministries and agencies from the Japanese government, were brought in to discuss issues, such as construction, land, patents, and agriculture, depending on their jurisdiction.

THE SII AGENDA AND AGREEMENTS

During the summer of 1989, U.S. officials and the Japanese officials worked on their own agendas for SII, and then exchanged official agendas with each other before the first formal meeting of September 4 and 5. These "highly unusual agendas by any standard for international negotiations between two sovereign states"[17] revealed what U.S. and Japanese officials considered to be structural impediments to trade and balance of payments adjustment in the other country. The American officials identified Japanese structural impediments in six broad areas which block U.S. (and other countries') exports to and investment in the Japanese market. The Japanese officials suggested structural impediments in the U.S. economy, which in their view dampen competitiveness of U.S. corporations and make the reduction of the trade deficit difficult. The reasons for suggesting these structural impediments in these six areas are the following:

Structural Impediments in the Japanese Economy Identified by the U.S. Government

1. Saving and Investment Patterns

> A nation's current account balance is, by definition, equal to the difference between national savings and domestic investment. In Japan, its external surplus is equal to its excess of domestic savings over investment. The level of public investment in Japan has been declining as a percentage of gross national product (GNP) over the past several years, while the government budget surplus has been rising. On the other hand, Japan's social infrastructure lags behind other industrial countries, not compatible with its huge economic size. An increase in public investment by the Japanese government will reduce

the saving-investment gap (i.e., oversaving and underinvestment) in Japan, and eventually thereby reduce the Japanese trade and current account surpluses. An increase in governmental spending on public works will also benefit American firms and raise the standard of living of the Japanese people.

2. Land Policy

Japanese land-use policies work to prevent external adjustment through the saving-investment mechanism. For instance, current land-use policies and tax laws discourage the conversion of agricultural land for other purposes, resulting in a reduction in the supply of land for residential and business investment, and reduced consumption of housing-related consumer durables, some of which are imported. Additionally, high land prices discourage new business entries, both domestic and foreign, to the Japanese market. At the same time, existing businesses in Japan benefit from the rising land prices, which increase the value of corporate assets and enhance their ability to borrow against collateral. The Japanese government should remedy these impediments through more neutral tax and regulatory policies.

3. Distribution System

Problems in the Japanese distribution system are excessive regulation, inadequate infrastructure, and anti-competitive practices. These factors tend to work against new market entrants, both foreign or domestic. In the complex many-layered system, prices of goods are raised at each level. Elimination of these barriers will reduce the prices of both foreign and domestic products, and will provide more opportunities for imported products. In particular, the Large Store Law (the LSL), which in actuality requires large retail stores to acquire consent from small- and medium-sized local stores for opening new shops, should be changed. (Currently, the coordination processing period for opening new stores takes, on the average, six years up to ten years.)

4. Exclusionary Business Practices

Some exclusionary business practices, such as bid-rigging, market share arrangements, or price-fixing, are clearly violations of Japanese antimonopoly laws, while other practices the U.S. government cites as structural impediments may not be strictly illegal. Nonetheless, they seem to have the effect of excluding foreign firms from the Japanese market. Exclusionary business practices broadly include four categories: (1) practices that are covered by principles of antitrust law, (2) government-business relations, (3) procurement practices of private firms, and (4) the patent system. Collusion and cartelization in Japan's market are commonly found. The Japanese government bears considerable responsibility for exclusionary business practices by Japanese companies, for these practices have been shaped over decades by governmental regulations, the promotion or tolerance of cartels, and practices of administrative guidance. The enforcement of antimonopoly law should be substantially strengthened and the procedure more transparent. The Japanese government should change the way of administrative guidance.   Patent procedures also should be streamlined.

5. Keiretsu

Keiretsu ties are networks of formal and informal ties through links with procurement practices, cross-shareholding, and many personal ties among independent Japanese companies. Keiretsu relationships facilitate preferential group trade at the cost of outside suppliers, foster exclusionary business practices, and discriminate against foreign investment, especially mergers and acquisitions. Thus, keiretsu ties pose barriers to foreign firms' attempts to penetrate the Japanese market. To remedy the structural-impediment effect of keiretsu, the Japanese government should strengthen requirements for public disclosure on business information and restrict cross-shareholding. Shareholders' rights should also be strengthened through changes that enhance firms' accountability to shareholders.

6. Pricing Mechanism

Because of the existing market rigidities in Japan, foreign goods generally cost more in Japan than abroad. These price gaps are much too large to be explained by transportation costs alone. Price differentials provide us with a barometer by which the presence of structural barriers in Japan to market competition can be measured. All of the above-mentioned actions for addressing structural barriers would help reduce the excessive prices of foreign products, and would increase the scope and volume of foreign goods imported into the Japanese market.[18]

Structural Impediments in the U.S. Economy
Identified by the Japanese Government

1. Saving Investment Patterns

U.S. dissaving or low-level savings in the public sector (i.e., federal deficit) and the decreasing saving level in the private sector are the essence of the problem in causing huge current account imbalances. In other words, the very nature of the U.S. economy—over-consumption and under-saving—should be changed. To improve current account imbalances, the U.S. government should reduce its federal deficit level and raise the saving level in the private sector.

2. Corporate Investment Activities and Supply Capacity

Investment in equipment is necessary to raise the supply capacity and competitiveness of U.S. corporations. U.S. corporations, however, do not seem to invest enough to balance the supply capacity. U.S. antitrust laws seem too rigid, which, as a result, discourage U.S. firms' investment activities. Recent moves to restrict foreign investment is counterproductive for raising supply capacity. The cost of capital for businesses in the United States is high and can be lowered. Practices of hostile take-over and leveraged buy-outs (LBOs) pressure corporations financially, causing shortages in investment for new equipment.

3. Corporate Behavior

U.S. corporations often seem not to make corporate strategies from long-term perspectives. They often behave myopically. Factors such as the level of management salary linked to short-term profit and a tendency to provide high dividends to stockholders, foster the practices which emphasize short-term achievement. This, in turn, weakens U.S. corporate competitiveness. The United States needs to seek ways to remedy these problems in business practices.

4. Government Regulation

The United States has many regulations, like the Coordinating Committee for Multilateral Export Controls (COCOM) regulation, which seem to impede the growth of international trade. Reviews of outdated regulation and subsequent deregulation are necessary to enhance U.S. export competitiveness. Many import restrictions not only impede international trade but also weaken U.S. corporations' competitiveness.

5. Research and Development

To strengthen U.S. competitiveness in industry, efforts in research and development, in both public and private sectors, are necessary. In reality, however, research and development, useful for growth in industry, is less than adequate. Ways to help research and development in the private sector can be sought through various tax incentives. Adoption of the metric system in scientific and industrial-production areas is also advisable.

6. Export Promotion

From the Japanese point of view, U.S. corporations do not seem to make enough efforts to promote exports. It is suggested that the U.S. government take steps to encourage and support export efforts in the private sector.

7. Workforce Education and Training

To strengthen industrial competitiveness, good workforce education and training are necessary. There seems to be many ways to improve the level of the workforce through quality education and job training in schools and individual corporations.[19]

The United States-Japan SII Working Group had five formal meetings, either in Tokyo or Washington: (1) September 4-5, and (2) November 6-7 in 1989, (3) February 22-23, (4) April 2-5, and (5) June 25-28 in 1990. The Working

Group published two reports, the Interim Report after the fourth meeting of April 5 and the Final Report on June 28, 1990.   Since the Final Report contains a wide range of items, including implementation of concrete measures, plans for drafting new laws and regulations in the future, policy statements, and affirmation of principles, many of which are by no means trivial, it is not possible to describe all the contents in limited space.   The majority of the Final Report is highlighted below.

Japanese Government's Commitments

1. Saving-Investment Patterns

> To reduce the shortage of investments relative to savings and to the size of the Japanese economy and the current account surplus, the "Basic Plan for the Public Investment," was made, which plans to spend about 430 trillion yen (approximately $3 trillion) for public investment from fiscal year (FY) 1991 to 2000 with an emphasis on improvement in the "living environment and cultural functions."   In addition to this, the long-term plans for eight categories of social overhead capital would be formulated with the positive and specific targets, for some of which concrete yen figures will be developed by the end of FY 1990.

2. Land Policy

> To facilitate efficient utilization of land, the Japanese government is now conducting a comprehensive review of the land taxation system, which includes a review with a view to addressing the deferment system of payment of the inheritance tax and the fixed assets tax, and possible strengthening of the special land holding tax on idle land. Based on the report made by the Sub-Commission on Land Taxation, the Japanese government will submit the necessary legislation to the Diet by the end of FY 1990 so that new policies are to be implemented from FY 1992. Some important amendments of the City Planning law and the Building Standards Law concerning deregulatory measures were already enacted. Amendment of the Land Lease Law and the House Lease Law, which is being reviewed and will be ready by as early as the end of FY 1990, will be submitted to the Diet without delay.

3. Distribution System

> In order to ensure rapid entry of cargo imports to the domestic distribution system, the Japanese government will accomplish the goal of 24 hours clearance of entry procedures by 1991. The deregulation measures include the immediate shortening of the coordination processing period for opening stores (less than one and a half years), exemption of coordination procedures for an increase up to a 100 square meters of the floor space for import sales, exemption of such procedures for a 10 percent increase of the existing floor space or of 50 square meters, and relaxation of business hours. Amendment

of the Large Store Law aiming at further shortening of coordination processing period (about one year) will be submitted to the Japanese Diet during the next session.   The law will further be reviewed within two years after the amendment, including a possible removal of regulations in specific geographical areas. The government will promote deregulation in such areas as premium offers, tracking licensing, and liquor sales licensing by necessary law amendments and other measures, and introduce a new package of comprehensive import expansion measures.

4. Exclusionary Business Practices

In order to enforce the Antimonopoly Act, the (Japan) Fair Trade Commission will take such measures as resorting to more formal actions and criminal penalties. For this purpose, the Japanese government increased the number of personnel by 20 percent and the number of offices for violation detection and investigation. To examine accusation procedures, a liaison-coordination was set up between the Ministry of Justice (MOJ) and JFTC in April in 1989. A bill revising the Antimonopoly Act to raise the surcharges against cartels will be submitted to the next session of the Diet.   JFTC will implement the recommendations made by the study group on the effective use of a private damage remedy system. MOJ is considering an increase in the maximum fine for bid-rigging. The average patent examination period is to be shortened to twenty-four months within five years.

5. Keiretsu

The JFTC will strengthen its monitoring over transactions among keiretsu firms to determine whether or not the cross-shareholding has the effect of restraint on competition. If such effect is found, the JFTC will take necessary measures including restriction of cross-shareholding and ordering transfers of shares. The JFTC will publish guidelines by the end of FY 1990, which will clarify the criteria for enforcement of the Antimonopoly Act, and it will conduct close analyses of various aspects of keiretsu groups, regularly every two years. By reexamining and amending relevant laws, including the Securities and Exchange Law and the Company Law, the disclosure requirements on keiretsu groups will be strengthened and shareholder's rights enhanced.

6. Pricing Mechanism

The Government-LDP Joint Headquarters for Adjustment of Price Differentials between Domestic and Overseas Markets was established to implement the six policy pillars and fifty-two measures to remedy the price differentials in December 1989. The Japanese government will continue domestic and overseas price surveys and the dissemination of information to consumers and industries. Survey results will be submitted to the SII follow-up process and discussed with regard to SII issues.

U.S. Government's Commitments

1. Saving and Investment Patterns

> To achieve the administration's two top budget priorities, that is, elimination of the federal budget deficit and reform of the budgeting process, policy measures were already initiated, which included the initiation of negotiations with congressional leaders (the Budget Summit) in June, ordering the sequester following the procedures in the Gramm-Rudman-Hollings (G-R-H) budget law in FY 1990, support for the Legislative Line-item Veto Act of 1989, a call for a constitutional requirement to balance the budget, and a proposal of constitutional line-item veto authority. The administration further supports improving the G-R-H budget law by extending and strengthening the law and additional reform measures, which the administration shall make best efforts to be implemented. To raise savings in the private sector, the administration has proposed the Savings and Economic Growth Act (SEGA), Family Saving Accounts (FAAs), enhanced Individual Retirement Accounts, and lower capital gains tax rates.

2. Corporation Investment Activities and Supply Capacity

> To facilitate productive investment, the administration has taken policy moves, including forwarding legislation to Congress which would reduce uncertainty about the treatment of joint production ventures under the current antitrust laws, endorsing the Product Liability Coordinating Committee (PLCC) Bill, which would contribute to uniformity in all fifty states and limit damage awards, preparing the final regulations for the implementation of the Exon-Florio provision of the 1988 Trade Act, and opposing the Bryant Bill, which requires registration and disclosure of foreign investment in the United States.

3. Corporate Behavior

> The Treasury Department is conducting a study on the effect of relationships between company owners and managers on long-term competitiveness, role of executive compensation in affecting company performance and competitiveness, and government barriers which adversely affect the long-term time horizons of investors. Government agencies and Congress already took measures to ensure prudent LBO lending practices.

4. Government Regulation

> The United States and its allies have agreed to streamline export controls of COCOM. The administration took measures to eliminate energy trade barriers and to promote import liberalization. These measures include the removal of legal regulatory barriers to the development of a project to export Alaskan liquefied natural gas (LNG) to the Pacific Rim and the announcement of the Steel Trade Liberalization Program.

5. Research and Development

> The president's FY 1991 budget calls for a record high of $71 billion for funding civilian research and development (R&D), an increase by 12 percent and revising the rules for Research and Experimentation (R&E). As part of efforts to raise U.S. competitiveness and exports, the adoption of the metric system for federal procurement is under consideration. The Interagency Committee on Metric Policy will develop a time table for specific actions in carrying out the objectives of metrication.

6. Export Promotion

> The president's FY 1991 budget proposed $159 million for the Commerce Department's export promotion plans. The president directed a new initiative to create the Trade Promotion Coordinating Committee (TPCC) chaired by the Secretary of Commerce. The TPCC will unify and streamline federal trade promotion activities for the first time.

7. Work Force Education and Training

> The president and the nation's governors agreed to launch a package of six national education goals. The administration proposed $24.6 billion for the Education Department budget (an increase of $500 million over total 1990 budget authority), and $4 billion for the Job Training Partnership Act (JTPA) in the president's FY 1991 budget.[20]

FIVE DIFFERENT STAGES OF THE SII

How to divide the stages of historical events is an essential part of theorizing. Toshiko Igarashi suggested seven different stages in the SII process, starting with May 25, 1989, the day of the Super 301 designation. Those seven stages are divided by the formal meetings, each representing the different nature of negotiation and activities of political actors. Although Igarashi's seven-division is a convenient way to understand chronologically different phases of the SII, her division is not based on a theoretical notion. Instead of seven divisions, the five divisions of SII process is suggested here. The five divisions include the preparation stage of SII before May 25, 1989, which is hardly paid attention by previous research. The five-divisions of the SII process represents distinctively different stages of the development rather than simple chronological sequences and provides latitude for explanations of any of four conceptual models in subsequent chapters.

The Early Preparation (Late Fall of 1988-May 25, 1989)

The first stage of the SII began in the late fall of 1988, after the 1988 Trade Act was enacted in the summer of 1988. Since the incoming administration was expected to faithfully implement the Super 301 provision, the administration had to find proper ways to deal with the bilateral trade issues with Japan. The U.S. government had already identified several problematic issues, which were later discussed in the SII, such as problems of Japanese patent protection, keiretsu, and the distribution system. The Japanese government suggested a joint study on the distribution system to determine whether or not it actually impeded imports. Furthermore, it asked the United States for prudence in implementing the 1988 Trade Act because the Act might give rise to protectionism.[21] During the same period, the idea of SII was emerging in the Treasury Department. When the SII initiation was being considered first by the Treasury Department and USTR, and later together with other departments, the U.S. administration sent an investigation team to Japan to study the distribution system, in March 1989. At the same time several congressional hearings were held on a national trade policy agenda and Super 301 designation. The Trade Policy Review Group and the interagency Super 301 committee were preparing trade policies. Finally, the cabinet level Economic Policy Council announced the decision of the Super 301 designation and proposed the SII on May 25, 1989.

During the same period in Japan, on the other hand, many policy issues discussed in the SII began to appear in government publications, such as in the report of the Provisional Administrative Reform Commission (e.g., relaxation of the Large Store Law). Ministries in the Japanese government, with their U.S. counterpart departments, were fighting for the leading position in trade policy in coming years.

The Latter Preparation Stage (May 26-September 3, 1989)

This stage includes several meetings. The United States-Japan sub-cabinet level talk was held in Ito City on June 13-14 to discussed how to deal with the Super 301 trade and the SII framework. The Japanese government initially refused negotiations on Super 301 trade items but showed a positive posture for possible "talks" on structural issues with the United States. To discuss a framework of new talk, Japanese and U.S. officials met at the New York Federal Bank in New York on June 28-29. In the meeting, Japanese officials officially requested three conditions for a new trade talk, which were subsequently agreed to by U.S. officials. Those conditions are first that a SII is not "negotiation" but "talk" of exchanging ideas and suggestions about structural problems, second that a SII talk should be "two-way street," discussing structural problems not only in Japan but also in the United States, and finally that agreements of SII in a final report should not be interpreted as

trade agreements defined by U.S. trade laws, which enables the U.S. government to resort to unilateral punitive action if it thinks the agreements are
violated.[22]   The SII was officially launched by President Bush and Prime
Minister Uno at the Economic Summit of seven industrialized countries in Paris
on July 14, 1989. During that summer the U.S. and Japanese officials each
were preparing their own SII agenda.

Defining Structural Impediments and Exchanging Views
(September 4, 1989-January 30, 1990)

The third stage includes the first and the second formal plenary meetings of
the SII, in which the U.S. officials and Japanese officials strove to define what
were structural impediments in each country and exchanged views on the other
system. Progress in the talks was slow. Frustrated with Japanese bureaucrats'
defensive posture about the issues suggested by the United States and their initial
contention that structural issues do not exist in the Japanese system, the U.S.
negotiation team began to make its own list of Japanese impediments and the
policies to improve them, which later became known as the 240-item list.

U.S. Demand for Change (January 31-April 5, 1990)

Officially, the SII was a "talk," not a "negotiation," in which the U.S. and
Japanese governments expressed their views on their own and the other's
system, and suggested ideas for improvement.   In the core-agency secret
meeting of January 31 in Bern, Switzerland, Japanese officials were struck by
the 240-item list, viewing it as the "second U.S. occupation policy."[23] From
then on, the nature of the SII had been changed, becoming a real political
negotiation aiming at real changes in Japan.
    In the third formal session on February 22-23, the U.S. team officially
presented three major demands to the Japanese team. These three demands were
the annual government's expenditure of 10 percent of GNP on public works over
the next ten years, a repeal of the Large Store Law, and an increase in cartel
surcharges by 10 percent of effected illegal sales. The third SII meeting was
reported as a failure; the talks reached a deadlock. In order to make an interim
report acceptable to both sides and good enough to persuade the Congress not
to enact tougher protectionist measures, President Bush and Prime Minister
Kaifu met in Palm Springs, California, in the effort to break the deadlock on
March 2 and 3. In that period, top-level policy-makers, working-level officials,
and agencies in the U.S. and Japanese governments, making transgovernmental
coalitions, struggled to draw concessions from each other.
    During this stage, the U.S. government put continuous pressure on the
Japanese government in the different issue areas. To avoid another Super 301

designation, the U.S. and the Japanese governments tried to produce an interim report with enough "blue print and down payment" (U.S. Trade Representative Carla A. Hills) before publishing the national trade estimate of 1990. After the fourth round of SII talks on April 5, the interim agreement was reached, which contained some significant Japanese government commitments to (1) formulation of new long-term plans on eight categories of social overhead capital including housing, sewers, parks, airports, and port facilities and a new comprehensive plan of public investment for the coming ten years with the specification of the aggregate amount of expenditures; (2) shortening of coordination processing period for opening stores under the LSL to one and a half years (from the current average six years), submission of amendment of the law to the Diet during the next regular session with the goal of further shortening coordination processing period to one year, and review of the law within two years with possible exemption of the law's application to specific geographical areas; (3) taking a comprehensive review on the land taxation system by the Government Tax Commission and submitting the necessary legislation to the Diet by the end of FY 1990, a review with a view to addressing the deferment system of payment of the inheritance tax and the fixed assets tax (results of which will be implemented from FY 1992), and a review to possibly strengthen the special land holding tax on idle land; and (4) increasing the number of personnel in the JFTC investigation department and creating new divisions, and revising the Antimonopoly Act to raise surcharges against cartels within the FY 1991. The interim agreement also contained the U.S. government's commitment to reducing the federal deficit and taking measures to increase private savings among others.[24]

For the U.S. and the Japanese governments, the Interim Report was a success, good enough to discourage the Congress from enacting tougher protectionist laws. Both governments were relieved, for they could avoid the worst possible scenario—a breakdown of the U.S.-Japanese relationship and an introduction of managed trade measures.

Constant U.S. Demand for GNP-Ratio Public Works Spending
(April 6-June 28, 1990)

Since the "real deadline"[25] for the SII and three priority trade negotiation items (satellites, wood products, and super computers) was April, the time of another Super 301 designation, the Japanese government put the maximum concessions into the interim report. Therefore, from the Japanese point of view, the report was considered to be final. What remained was simply to add flesh to the interim agreements.

However, for the U.S. officials, "the interim report is just that, an interim report. The final report is due in July, but there is still much to be done."[26] In the final stage of the SII, the U.S. team again began to demand a public works spending of 10 percent of GNP, which the Japanese government vehemently refused to accept. One of the major questions in the SII processes was why the U.S. negotiation team brought in the issue of 10 percent of annual GNP spending on public works after the interim agreement was reached. For the Japanese government, the issue of public works spending was already over, because, in its view, the U.S. government agreed that the public works spending would be given in the form of the total amount over ten years, not in the form of GNP ratio; therefore there was no need to discuss the 10 percent of GNP issue again. Then why was the 10 percent of GNP public works spending issue brought in again? This is one of the questions to be answered.

NOTES

1. Mastanduno, op. cit., pp. 240-241.

2. S. Linn Williams to look back the spring of 1989. Testimony before the Subcommittee on Oversight of Government Management of the Committee on Governmental Affairs, May 8, 1991. *Oversight of U.S. Trade Policy with Japan*, p. 5.

3. Mastanduno, op. cit., p. 239.

4. *Newsweek* 6/5/89, pp. 48-49.

5. Interview, Washington, D.C., 10/7/92.

6. See for example, testimony before SH 3/5/90, pp. 12-13. NHK Shuzai-han (NHK) (1990), *NHK Supesharu Dokyumento Kōzō Kyōgi*, p. 250.

7. NHK, ibid., p. 270.

8. *Nikkei* 3/10/90, p. 1. Also refer to Yabunaka, op. cit., p. 167.

9. U.S. Department of Commerce, *U.S. Foreign Trade Highlights 1992*, pp. 6, 27.

10. See Public Law 100-418, Omnibus Trade and Competitiveness Act of 1988, 23 August, 1988. Also refer to U.S. State Department, "The 1988 Trade Bill" (Special Report No. 180, 1989).

11. USTR, *The 1989 National Trade Estimate Report*, pp. 97-114.

12. *Nikkei* 5/26/89, pp. 1-2; *WSJ* 5/26/89, pp. A1, A7; *NYT* 5/26/89, pp. A1, D5.

13. *Time* 6/5/89, p. 50.

14. *Nikkei* 5/26/89, p. 1.

15. "Joint Statement by President Bush and Prime Minister Uno on Economic Issues" (July 14, 1989).

16. Ibid.

17. Yamamura ed., op. cit., p. 1.

18. This is the summary from Charles Dallara's written testimony for SH 3/5/90, pp. 43-47. Both Williams' testimony on exclusionary business practices and McCormack's testimony on the distribution system are referred from the same hearing, pp. 6-8, pp. 12-13, and p. 21, respectively. Also refer to *Nikkei* 9/1/89, p. 5. for the detailed explanations of U.S. agenda.

19. This summary is based on the newspaper article *Nikkei* 9/2/89, p. 1, and the description of Yabunaka, op. cit., pp. 156-158.

20. Summary from *the Final Report*. Many Japanese side commitments were realized by the end of the three year follow-up stage of the SII, while U.S. commitments are still on the way to implementation.

21. See *Nikkei* 10/21/88, Evening edition (E), p. 1; 10/25/88, p. 13.

22. Michihiko Kunihiro, a chief negotiator from MFA, interview article in *Chūō Kōron* 11, 1989, pp. 94-95. See also Glen S. Fukushima (former USTR official) (1992), *Nichi-bei Keizai Masatsu no Seijigaku*, pp. 205-207.

23. NHK, op. cit., p. 100. In actuality, the 240-item list was informally handed in to three Japanese chief negotiators each by Under Secretary of Commerce J. Michael Farren when he flew to Tokyo for other business trip before January 31, 1990. See Williams, *Daiyamondo* 5/30/92, p. 829.

24. *Interim Report and Assessment of the U.S.-Japan Working Group on the Structural Impediments Initiative*, April 5, 1990. (Hereafter, *the Interim Report*.)

25. Fukushima, op. cit., p. 216.

26. McCormack at the press conference of April 5, 1990. *CQWR* 4/7/90, p. 1100.

3   Theoretical Framework and Research Design

THE LEVEL OF ANALYSIS PROBLEM AND THE ROLE OF MODELS

The procedures, such as choosing a proper level of analysis, abstraction, aggregation of data, or unit, and controlling some variables in order to examine the effects of other variables, are already standard for quantitative analysis, but not always for conducting a case study.

When people write, they usually follow "ordinary usage" of a daily language, and forget many assumptions, unspoken rules, and the levels of abstraction. For our daily conversation and writing, this custom is useful for convenience sake, that is, for the economy of daily language communication. Thus, in our daily usage, statements from the White House, the State Department (or any departments), members of the cabinet (or sometimes even senior officials), are equated as "policies of the U.S. government."

Unfortunately, this is the way that many case studies are still conducted. In their case studies, many scholars freely raise and lower the different levels of abstraction and use evidence which seems to support their contentions without paying attention to the levels of analysis. But for the purpose of theory building and empirical hypothesis-testing in social science, one needs a clear consciousness of the level of analysis problem, because explanations at one level of analysis and those at other levels are not readily exchangeable,[1] and explanations from a viewpoint of the government as a unitary rational actor are not always descriptively correct.[2] Therefore, not only for quantitative research but also for case studies, choosing one level of analysis and fixing that level throughout the entire description, explanation, and prediction on the social events are the first step for more reliable and credible analysis, that is, for more systematic accumulation of knowledge.

In addition to the levels of analysis problem, one needs to understand the role of models in social science in conducting case study. Conventionally, social scientists develop theories or models to try to demonstrate how they are superior to others in explaining events. At the outset, this research was designed to critically analyze the unidirectional notion of *gaiatsu* and to demonstrate how the SII political processes were interactive, as Schoppa did. However, it was discerned that major initiations, at least at the official level in the SII, came from the U.S. government. Upon further examination of and reflection on the data, it was understood that explanations at one level of analysis do not *falsify* explanations at other levels of analysis. In social science research one has to deal both with "empirical reality" and abstraction, or the level of analysis. A traditional state-centric paradigm is a good example of this duality. In this view, international relations are most of the time politics between states or governments. Communication channels are usually limited to the official realm through foreign ministries and professional diplomats. However, if one compares today's numerous communication channels between two governments, such as Japan and the United States, with those of twenty or thirty years ago, one finds a dramatic increase in the numbers of communication channels employed not only by foreign ministries but also by all sorts of other governmental agencies. So, as a matter of "empirical reality," one can refute a simplistic view of the state-centric paradigm, which most of the time focuses on formal official communication channels employed by foreign ministries and not on many unofficial and informal channels employed by many agencies and individuals.

But, even in contemporary international relations, if one wants to examine the numerous official communication channels between the governments as unitary legal entities, the state-centric paradigm can be useful. On the other hand, while the transnational politics model may be more useful today to examine various relations between governments than twenty years ago, that model can also be used to research relations between the governments of twenty years ago, by focusing on activities of informal subgovernmental units and individuals. This research project is sensitive to the levels of abstraction that are used, that is, which levels of abstraction or the level of analysis can be chosen for specific research purposes. What Alex Inkeles says about the role of models in social science seems quite inspiring:

In my opinion, there is no such thing as a right or wrong sociological model. There are richer and poorer ones. There are the more sensitive and less sensitive. There are those which are more appropriate to one time or place than another. All have a piece of the truth, but it is rare that any one model is really adequate to the analysis of a richly complex concrete historical case.[3]

If explanations at one level of analysis do not *falsify* explanations at other levels of analysis and any one model is rarely adequate to analyze many phases of reality, then combining several conceptual models with different levels of analysis will be much better than relying on any single model. Thus, this book will use, so to speak, a multidimensional approach to research the process of the SII, inspired by Allison's method to study the Cuban missile crisis, with further developed features.   Allison uses three conceptual models, with sets of assumptions and levels of analysis, in order to describe, explain, and predict the occurrence of events in the Cuban missile crisis. It is Allison who sensitizes us to the issue of our "conceptual lens" in seeing reality.[4]   He masterly demonstrates how different conceptual models describe, explain, and predict social events.   This kind of approach can be referred as a "systematically layered multidimensional approach," since different models are not simply juxtaposed to each other. (This could result in "model relativism.") Allison systematically layers his conceptual models from the level of analysis of "the government as a rational unitary actor," to that of "the government as a conglomerate of semi-independent organizations," and finally to that of "the government as a group of top policy makers."

A similar approach is also found in Robert Keohane and Joseph Nye's *Power and Interdependence*. Keohane and Nye combine different explanations deriving from different models for regime change; that is, from the economic process model, to the overall structural model, to the issue structure model, and finally the international organization model.[5] They say, "Because of the drawbacks of a single complex synthesis, it is better to seek explanation with simple models and add complexity as necessary,"[6] with different levels of abstraction.

The merits of this approach are obvious: it first sensitizes us to our own conceptual models and their sets of assumptions. Second, it paves the way for a systematic comparison among different explanations of the same social events. If one knows on what level of analysis one's explanations are made, then one is likely to avoid confusion in explaining the same events at another level of analysis.

One can choose any level of analysis: international system, national governments, subnational governmental units, divisions and sections in each governmental agency, groups in agencies, individuals, and even individual's perceptions. There is no definitive way of grouping levels of analysis. For example, at the subgovernmental units of analysis, one can choose the U.S. administration and the Congress, and explain national foreign economic policies as results of dynamics between them.   Or, one can choose various federal agencies in the administration and treat Congress like one of these agencies with its own priorities and power resources. Fixing the level of analysis is for the purpose of theory building and research, not for any other a priori reason. As long as the level of analysis is consistent, research results are meaningful.

For the study of the SII, three levels of analysis are chosen: (1) the national government, (2) governmental subunits, and (3) persons. Although Allison confines his scope of analysis to the realm of national decision-making processes, his method can be expanded to the international level.[7]

A SYSTEMATICALLY LAYERED MULTIDIMENSIONAL APPROACH
FOUR CONCEPTUAL MODELS

The Government as a Unitary Rational Actor

The method of the systematically layered multidimensional approach is as follows. To describe, explain, and possibly "predict" the process of the SII, first a "model of the government as a unitary rational actor" is introduced.[8] In this model, the U.S. administration and the Japanese government are each treated as a unitary rational actor, calculating and choosing policy options. The level of analysis is the national government. Particular national policy outcomes are results of the calculation of government as a rational unitary actor. The government chooses certain policies among options and selects means to realize these policies in relation to the ultimate national trade policy goals. In the SII process, this model is useful to investigate the direction of policy initiatives and degrees of pressure the U.S. administration exercised to gain certain concessions from the Japanese government in the different SII issue areas.

In this model, the SII is seen as a means of foreign pressure or *gaiatsu* to which the U.S. government resorts. The strength of this model is that it reveals the hard reality of international political economy. That is, in spite of all sorts of fancy words, such as "international cooperation," "policy consultation," and "mutual adjustment," an adjustment in the international political economy is made by bargaining among nations which are posited in particular power relations.   The more powerful nations force the weaker nations to pay adjustment costs, and hegemon or the leading country enforces rules with its own judgment and forcibly creates a new international regime with less powerful nations.[9]   This model provides the most parsimonious way to "predict" bargaining outcomes between nations with uneven power resources.

The Transgovernmental Coalition of Subunits

In the second model, the "transgovernmental coalition of subunits model" is used to study the SII process. From the viewpoint of model, the SII is seen as a site for transgovernmental coalitions.[10] In this model, political actors are governmental subunits with their own policy priorities and goals. National policy outcomes are results of "turf-battles" among agencies, each of which has its own organizational outputs resulting from standard operating procedures (SOPs), organizational programs, and repertoires.[11] However, policy outcomes (agreements) in the SII are combined results of three elements: first, organizational outputs of subunits in the government; second, results of "turf-battles" among governmental subunits which have their own organizational outputs; and third, transgovernmental coalitions of governmental subunits across the national boundary. Although these elements are conceptually distinguished from each other and therefore are analyzed in order, they are constantly conditioning each other and are not necessarily sequential.[12]

The Transgovernmental Coalition of Top-Level Policy-Makers

In the third model, the "transgovernmental coalition of top-level policy-makers" is used. To fully understand the occurrence of some events in the SII, one needs to investigate the interactions among individual policy-makers because decisions of individuals cannot be deduced from any higher levels of the social aggregation. Organizational or sociological variables can give researchers great *references* for policy-outcomes in the decision-making process. But it is decisions (policy positions) of individual policy-makers that are *relevant* to producing specific policy outcomes in particular decision-making dynamics.[13] Thus, in the third model, instead of organizations dictating to individual policy-makers, decisions of individual policy-makers are the point of reference.

In this model, the level of analysis is individual persons, not institutions like the national government or governmental subunits, and political actors are top-level policy-makers in the government. In the viewpoint of this model, national policy outcomes are mainly results of "pulling and hauling" among top-level policy-makers in the government. However, policy outcomes in the SII process are made through the various degrees of transgovernmental coalitions among top-level policy-makers in the cabinet, Congress, and the LDP party.

The Elite Policy Networks of Working-Level Officials

Finally, in order to understand semi-institutionalized patterns of interactions among working-level (senior and middle) bureaucrats, the "elite policy networks of working-level officials model" is added. Here the level of analysis is of individual persons. But the focus is not on the cabinet-level policy-makers, but on working-level bureaucrats. The fourth model is distinguished from the third model for both theoretical and empirical reasons.

First, including all four types of Allison's political players in the category of individual actors necessarily makes the description more complex, and therefore less powerful in explanation.[14]   Ordinarily, top-level policy-makers are supposed to be engaged in "agenda-setting" and authoritative decision making among policy choices, while working-level bureaucrats tend to be engaged in "alternative specification."[15]   Throughout the SII process, the distinction between "political decisions" and "bureaucratic work" was often expressed by Japanese chief negotiators. For instance, Vice Minister of the Finance Ministry, Makoto Utsumi said in his opening statement at the first SII meeting that bureaucrats alone could not make structural reform possible, only politics could make it possible.[16]   After the third SII meeting, the necessity of political decisions by politicians in the government (cabinet members) was often expressed by Japanese SII negotiators, because the amount of budget spending, amending the LSL, and cartel surcharge increases, for example, required political decisions by the cabinet members.[17] Also, frequency of meetings are different between the cabinet level and the working level, reflecting those supposed functional differences.   For example, in the U.S. government, Economic Policy Council (EPC) cabinet-level meetings for SII were held only once every three months in which SII principals (chief negotiators) attended to report the progress of negotiations.   On the other hand, principals and their staffs met more frequently (e.g., twenty times in April and May of 1989).[18]

Second, the distinction between the cabinet-level policy-makers and working-level officials is particularly useful in understanding the characteristics and dynamics of Japanese policy-making, in which the LDP politicians in the cabinet positions or in the party share power with relatively independent Japanese ministerial bureaucrats.   Many studies on the Japanese policy-making process report ministerial bureaucrats along with politicians in power as major political actors.[19]   Distinguishing between the different roles played by bureaucrats and politicians in Japanese foreign economic policy-making produces a more discriminating picture of the trade negotiation process.

For some the above-mentioned reasons do not seem to necessitate a new model separated from the third model, because the level of analysis is persons for both.   The third and most positive reason for such a distinction is that the introduction of the fourth model opens a new way to look at the process of international trade negotiations, resulting in different policy prescriptions. This model highlights the relatively distinctive process of activities of working-level bureaucrats, characterized by formal and informal communications and contacts that cut across national boundaries to cope with the condition of economic interdependence.[20]   The elite policy networks model enables us to understand "another reality" of international political economy, that is, various transgovernmental   policy   coordination/policy-making/policy-implementation behaviors by working-level bureaucrats in transgovernmental policy networks, including bilateral and multilateral fora.

There are some aspects of the SII that are well understood from the perspective of transgovernmental elite policy networks, which some view as international organizations in the broadest sense.   For instance, Nye and Keohane use the term international organization to refer to multilevel linkages, patterns of elite networks, norms, and institutions.[21]   In their view, when patterns of policy coordination become regularized, "transgovernmental elite networks are created, linking officials in various governments to one another by ties of common interest, professional orientation, and personal friendship."[22]

Other scholars believe that the elite policy networks are a better approach to the study of international organizations trying to cope with the reality of economic interdependence.   For example, after conducting research on domestic bureaucrats' activities, Raymond Hopkins found that within the U.S. government bureaucrats, whose mandates are primarily "domestic," are also responsible for the promotion, monitoring, and regulation of a wide range of activities, which are international in scope. He suggests that as the distinction between foreign and domestic policy becomes blurred, the concept of international organization should be broadened: international organizations include "these officials who are part of the organizational networks that perform international functions, whether they are formally in international or domestic bureaucracies, within governments or in the private sector."[23] He argues that some mid-elite officials, recognizing interdependence among states, use formal and informal networks of intra- and intergovernmental coordination, ranging from information sharing to collaboration in management. In his view, these "networks of interconnected behavior among middle-level officials have been, and will continue to be, an important force in performing international management tasks."[24]

Hopkins further argues that in many issue areas, such as food, energy, finance, communication, the environment, and technology diffusion, global management occurs "de facto in decentralized but occasionally coordinated frameworks."[25]   Such frameworks, he continues, might be considered "incipient regimes" or "institutional patterns of behavior and expectations."[26]

Transgovernmental policy networks and policy coordination are also extensively researched by C. Robert Dickerman who examines the relationship of three Scandinavian countries and that of the United States and Canada. Instead of viewing these networks as international organization, Dickerman describes these relations in such terms as "transnational decision-making and decision-implementing networks," or "dual domestic/external (i.e., transgovern-mental) administration."[27] According to him, many domestic bureaucrats (and politicians alike) at many levels in three Scandinavian countries have day-to-day direct contacts over telephone and through mails in addition to formal and informal international meetings. They develop transnational collegiality, form transnational coalitions, and often coordinate domestic policies.

Although many studies point out "turf-battles" among Japanese ministries and U.S. federal agencies in transgovernmental trade negotiations or trans-governmental bureaucratic politics,[28] there seems no study that examines patterns of interactions among U.S. and Japanese working-level bureaucrats through which important policy agenda and alternatives are developed and day-to-day management of the international economy is conducted. Throughout the SII process, these working-level officials had extensive contact by telephone, fax, and mail in addition to many formal and informal bilateral and multilateral meetings. These officials "often discussed the details of policies by telephone."[29] "Real progress [in making agreements] was made by telephone conversations and private discussions."[30]

However conspicuous, many agendas in the SII were not only already but also continuously discussed by working-level officials in the elite policy networks of Organization for Economic Cooperation and Development (OECD) and Group of Seven (G-7) macroeconomic policy coordination fora. The large part of ideas in the SII initially came from officials who were part of the broad trans-governmental macroeconomic and structural adjustment elite policy networks of OECD, G-7 Economic Summit, and G-7 Finance Ministers and the Governors of the Central Banks.   Furthermore, the SII contributed to expanding and deepening transgovernmental elite policy networks by bringing officials from many domestic agencies and facilitating communication among them. The SII process promoted "collegiality" between U.S. and Japanese working-level officials and improved the level of knowledge not only about others' systems but also their own systems.   In this sense, the SII itself is seen as creating an "epistemic community" ("broad vision of relationship between the U.S. and Japan") and an international regime ("fundamental rules of capitalism")[31] in general, in the antitrust law issue area, in particular.   All in all, the SII process in the form of bilateral negotiation is an effort to strengthen a multilateral trade regime, rather than act as an alternative to it.

The four models, with their levels of analysis, political actors (focus of analysis), analytical concepts, and the factors that influence policy outcomes are summarized in Table 3.1.

RESEARCH DESIGN AND THE PROPOSITIONS

The method used in this research is a detailed case study combined with content-analysis. The book describes and explains events in the process of the SII with each conceptual model, based on data from Japanese and English newspaper articles, journal articles, former officials' memoirs, government documents, videotapes, and interviews. The fourteen U.S. officials who were interviewed are of different ranks of former and present officials from six departments.[32] Those officials include four former U.S. chief negotiators, such as the Under Secretary of State Richard T. McCormack, Deputy U.S. Trade Representative S. Linn Williams, Assistant Attorney General James F. Rill, and Member of President's Council of Economic Adviser John B. Taylor.

The key Japanese officials were not interviewed due to limited time and resources.   But also, this book is more concerned with U.S. officials' perceptions of the SII and the extent to which the "two-way street" existed, which was rarely mentioned in journals or newspapers nor scholarly journals. However, former officials' memoir-like works and interview articles in Japanese journals are greatly utilized as major sources of information.[33]

Before discussing propositions, it is necessary to assess the degree of Japanese government concessions in five issue areas. The Final Report covers various specific issues, some of which have potentially more important policy implications than others.   Moreover, the potential impact on the Japanese economy of policy measures from five issue areas can be short term or long term or both. For example, the shortening of a coordination processing period

Table 3.1
Four Approaches and Analytical Concepts

Approach	Level of Analysis	Political Actors & Focus of Analysis	Analytical Concepts	Factors that influence Policy Outcomes
1. The government as a rational unitary actor	National government	1) U.S. government Japanese government 2) U.S. administration U.S. Congress Japanese government	National trade policy goals Policy options Means Choice based on rational calculation	Power relations between national governments (Pressure of the stronger state and receptivity of the weaker state)
2. The transgovernmental coalition of subunits	Governmental subunits	White House U.S. Departments Congressional committees Kantei Ministries Party (LDP)	Organizational Routines Goals SOPs Programs Repertoires National turf battles Transgov'tal coalitions	Transgovernmental coalition of subunits
3. The transgovernmental coalition of top-level policy-makers	Persons	Cabinet-level policy-makers Congressional leaders Party leaders	National and transgovernmental bargaining among top policy-makers in position Personal ties between top policy-makers	Transgovernmental coalition of top-level policy-makers
4. The elite policy networks of working-level officials	Persons	Working-Level officials in transgovernmental policy networks	Transgovernmental policy coordination/policy-making/policy implementation Communication channels Sharing information Perceptions Collegiality	Common views on the the issues through sharing information & knowledge

for opening new stores under the LSL may have more immediate effect on economic activities than an increased cartel surcharge.[34]   However, the strengthened antitrust regime can have more impact on Japanese corporations' economic activities than the former in the long run.[35]   Also, although the initial stage of SII ended in June 1990 with the announcement of the Final Report, the follow-up stage of SII lasted for three years. During this period, some major progress was made in such areas as antimonopoly law and land policy, including the increased surcharge of 6 percent on the illegal cartel sales, the raised maximum criminal fine of 100 million yen on antitrust violation of cooperations, and the land tax reforms with two "breakthroughs."[36]   Those changes are as significant as the amendment of the LSL. Therefore, one cannot easily tell in which issue areas the U.S. government was more successful.[37]

Despite those difficulties, assessing the degree of U.S. success in *five* Japanese-side SII issue areas is attempted, for any comparison necessarily sacrifices some qualitative differences.[38]   More precisely, assessment of the degree of U.S. negotiation success is here to be made in terms of "commitment making" *at the time of issuing* the Final Report, rather than of actual economic effect of such commitments later on. Assessment of the degrees of U.S. success (or Japanese concessions) in five issue areas is based on the following criteria: (1) whether or not the agreements contained the specific numeric expressions and dates, (2) how close the final agreements are to the original U.S. demands,[39] (3) how the U.S. negotiators assess the agreements, and (4) how the other sources assess the agreements.[40]

Assessment on the degree of U.S. success in five issue areas according to the above criteria is as follows. The Japanese government made high-level concessions in the saving-investment patterns area, a large specified amount of budget spending over ten years. Second, a medium-level concession was made in the distribution system, resulting in the immediate shortening of the coordination processing period for opening new stores from the current average of six years to one and a half years with the exemption for coordination procedure for the increased size of certain floor space, submission of law amendment in the next Diet session, and review of the LSL two years later with a possibility of partial repeal of the LSL in specific geographical area. Third, a low-level concession in the exclusionary business practices was made, along with a commitment to submit a bill to amend the Antimonopoly Act to raise the surcharges against cartels to the next session of the Diet, but no specific numbers for cartel surcharge increases. Fourth, the lowest level of concessions in the keiretsu, that is, only the general commitment on an increased disclosure system, issuing guidelines, and study reports, was made.

Assessment of the degree of U.S. success in the land policy issue area is not as clear-cut as other areas and needs some explanation. Although the U.S. government could not realize the initial suggestion of reducing the sales tax on land trade with specific numbers, it gained major progress in the area. Even at the time of the Interim Report, the Japanese government made significant policy commitments to changing the taxation system on agriculture land within urbanization promotion areas of the metropolitan area.   These included addressing the deferment system of payment of the inheritance tax, the fixed assets tax, and a possible special land-holding tax on idle land, with specification of some time schedule.   The Japanese government could not realize those policies, in spite of several attempts in the past.   With respect to the special land-holding tax, the Japanese government commitment even exceeded the initial U.S. demand.   Although the Sub-Commission on Land Taxation of the Government Tax Commission had just started in April 1990, and the specifics of reforming the land tax system were left to the final recommendation of the sub-commission, the above-mentioned commitments, which were essentially in line with U.S. demands, were already de facto policies by the time of the Final Report.   Those policies were significant tax system changes in two decades and would not have been realized without the SII as they were.[41]   However, the U.S. government could not realize one of the initial demands in land policy, that is, reduction of the capital gains tax on land sales.   Instead, the Japanese raised the capital gains tax on land sales, which is "exactly opposite to the American demand."[42]   While Japanese officials generally agreed to the "basic American formula . . . a return to the market to increase the supply of land,"[43] they not only opposed reducing the capital gains tax on land sales but increased that type of tax.   With all these considerations, it can be said that the level of Japanese government concession in the land policy area was medium, and that the United States was as successful in the land policy area as in the distribution system.[44]

In any political process, such factors as different degrees and content of political power, pressure, coalitions, and perceptions are found working with and influencing each other.   One can find these factors in international trade negotiations as well, and they can be measured and analyzed in various ways. One way to study the effects of these factors on trade negotiation outcomes is to make propositions, which can be thought of as logical components of the conceptual model, and then to test these propositions.   The general proposition to be tested in this research is shown below:

The levels of Japanese concessions in the SII issue areas are related to at least four factors: (1) the levels of U.S. pressure, (2) the size and strength of transgovernmental coalitions among governmental subunits participating in trade negotiations, (3) the size and strength of transgovernmental coalitions among top-level policy-makers, and (4) the level of common perception between U.S. and Japanese working-level officials.[45]

Although those four factors are interrelated and not mutually exclusive, nonetheless they require analytically different explanations to be tested by different procedures, different conceptual models, and different levels of analysis. In the research, the different levels of Japanese concessions in five issue areas (i.e., the high-level concessions in saving and investment patterns, the medium-level concessions in the distribution system and in land policy, the low-level concession in exclusionary business practices, and the lowest-level concession in keiretsu) are tested by a case study combined with content-analysis and different conceptual models. For this purpose, four specific propositions for research are also suggested:

P1. The different levels of Japanese concessions in five issue areas are associated with the different levels of U.S. pressure at the level of analysis of the national government.

P2. The different levels of Japanese concessions in five issue areas are associated with the size and strength of transgovernmental coalitions among U.S. and Japanese agencies at the level of governmental subunits.

P3. The different levels of Japanese concessions in five issue areas are associated with the size and strength of transgovernmental coalitions among top-level policy-makers at the level of persons focusing on top-level policy-makers.

P4. The different levels of Japanese concessions in five issue areas are associated with the levels of common perceptions between U.S. and Japanese officials at the level of persons focusing on working-level officials.

The first proposition is tested by the case study of Chapter 4 and the content-analysis of *Nikkei* indexes in Chapter 5. The second proposition is tested by the case study of Chapter 6, supplemented by content- analysis of the reconstructed SII meeting records in Chapter 7. The third proposition is tested by the case study of Chapter 8. The fourth proposition is tested by the case study of Chapter 9.

NOTES

1. J. David Singer (1961), "The Level-of-Analysis Problem," p. 29.

2. Allison, op. cit., pp. 246-247.

3. Alex Inkeles (1966), "Models and Issues in the Analysis of Soviet Society," p. 3.

4. Allison, op. cit., p. 2.

5. Robert Keohane and Joseph Nye (1977), *Power and Interdependence: World Politics in Transition*, pp. 58-60.

6. Ibid., p. 58.

7. Allison himself mentions this possibility. See "Applied to relations between nations, this model [the governmental politics model] directs attention to intra-national games, the overlap of which constitutes international relations.", op. cit., p. 149. Also refer to p. 178.

8. For discussions of the three requirements (description, explanation, and prediction) of an analytical model, see Singer op. cit. Singer makes an important point that "the primary purpose of theory is to explain and when descriptive and explanatory requirements are in conflict, the latter ought to be given priority, even at the cost of

some representational inaccuracy" (p. 22). There seems a tradeoff relationship among these three requirements of an analytical model. The purpose of this book is *not* to describe every detail of all the events in the SII as historians usually intend, but to explain major events by describing relevant aspects of the events as parsimoniously as possible.

9. In Akio Sakai's view, the reality of "international policy coordination" in the macroeconomic adjustment process is that "the United States led economic policy coordination with the intent to transfer the responsibility of external imbalances on the shoulder of the other countries, while retaining its own macroeconomic policies and keep its own economic structure" (1991), *Nichi-bei Keizai Masatsu to Seisaku Kyōchō*, p. 255. Also refer to Strange's criticism about the nature of international regimes. "All those international arrangements dignified by the label regime are only too easily upset when either the balance of bargaining power or the perception of national interest (or both together) change among those states who negotiate them" ([1982], "Cave! hic dragones: A Critique of Regime Analysis," p. 487).

10. For theoretical discussions about transgovernmental politics, refer to such works as Keohane and Nye ed. (1972), *Transnational Relations and World Politics*, (1974), "Transgovernmental Relations and International Organizations," and (1977), *Power and Interdependence*; and Karl Kaiser (1971), "Transnational Politics: Toward a Theory of Multinational Politics." From a perspective of transnational or transgovernmental politics, several studies on U.S.-Japanese trade negotiations were already done. Some well-known studies are I.M. Destler, Haruhiro Fukui, and Hideo Sato (1979), *The Textile Wrangle*; Atsushi Kusano (1983), *Nichi-bei Orenji Kōshō*; and Yoichi Funabashi (1987), *Nichi-bei Keizai Masatsu*. However, these studies generally use all sorts of levels of analysis, including individuals (top policy-makers, bureaucrats, and persons from the private sector), factions and groups, institutions (the government as a whole, ministries, and departments), and interest group organizations. Because of this feature, these studies are rich in description but less powerful in explanation.

11. For these concepts, refer to Allison, op. cit., p. 83.

12. This is a modification of Allison's second model, in which the outputs of the organizations constrained by organizational routines are the center of the analysis in his second model.

13. It seems that the distinction between *reference* and *relevance* in analyzing social events is not always made by social scientists who are satisfied with only studying various organizational and sociological variables, or "logic" of occurrence of social events. To understand particular policy outcomes in policy-making processes, one has to know both factors of *reference* (various organizational, institutional, and sociological variables, or "logic") and *relevance* (specific policy positions and decisions of political actors in particular policy-making dynamics of coalition-making among relevant political actors). However, more often than not, social scientists treat *references* as if they were *relevances*. Particular policy outcomes are results of the *configuration of coalitions* among relevant political actors favoring specific policy positions in various degrees of strength which may be influenced by many sociological and organizational variables. Knowing only *references* is a half way to meaningful understanding of the process of producing policy outcomes.

14. As to individual political actors or players, Allison suggests four types: (1) chiefs (president and cabinet-level officials), (2) staffers (the immediate staff of each chief), (3) indians (the political appointees and permanent government officials), and (4) ad hoc players ("congressional influentials," members of the press and interest groups, and surrogates for each of these groups) (op. cit., pp. 164-165). Later, Allison and Halperin introduced the distinction of "senior players" and "junior players," see op. cit., p. 384.

15. John Kingdon (1984), *Agendas, Alternatives, and Public Policies*, pp. 3-4, 33-35.

16. NHK, op. cit., p. 249.

17. *Tōyō Keizai* 3/10/90, p. 40. Refer to Deputy Minister of MFA Koji Watanabe's remarks in *Gaikō Fōramu* 5, 1990, p. 25.

18. Williams, *Daiyamondo*, 4/11/92, p. 93.

19. For example, refer to Chalmers Johnson (1982), *MITI and the Japanese Miracle*. Chihiro Hosoya et. al. (1989), *Nichi-bei-ō no Keizai Masatsu o Meguru Seiji Katei*, Chapters 1 and 5.

20. Keohone and Nye (1974), op. cit., p. 93. In their article, Keohane and Nye did not discuss the issue of level of analysis. However, it seems that in their discussion the level of analysis for "transgovernmental coalition" is governmental subunits and that for "transgovernmental policy coordination" is individuals (working-level bureaucrats).

21. Keohane and Nye (1977), op. cit., pp. 54-55.

22. Keohane and Nye, (1974) op. cit., p. 46.

23. Raymond Hopkins (1976), "International Role of 'Domestic' Bureaucracy," p. 406.

24. Ibid., p. 406.

25. Ibid, p. 408.

26. Ibid.

27. C. Robert Dickerman (1976), "Transgovernmental Challenge and Response in Scandinavia and North America," pp. 215, 337.

28. For example, refer to Pempel's observation, "Now on many issues, particularly those related to foreign economic policy and security matters, Japanese policy-making is becoming truly a transnational process" ([1987], "Unbundling 'Japan, Inc.'," pp. 149-150.

29. A Treasury Department official, interview, Washington, D.C., 10/8/92.

30. Williams, interview, Washington, D.C., 10/6/92. These pictures of simultaneous or parallel discussions by telephone conversations among officials outside formal meetings contradict a conventional image of international negotiations based on the state-centric view. In its simplified view, formal government delegates sit in the formal meetings, go back home after the meetings to consult key domestic decision makers, and come back again to the formal meetings to exchange concessions. The state-centric view does not necessarily exclude possibilities of informal or secret conversations behind the scene, though. It seems that relatively recent developments of inexpensive and efficient telephone, fax, and computer networks fundamentally have changed the way international trade negotiations are conducted, which are also transgovernmental policy-making.

31. Williams, interview of 10/6/92. On "epistemic communities" refer to John Gerald Ruggie (1975), "International Responses to Technology: Concepts and Trends," pp. 570-571. According to him, epistemic communities are one of interrelated roles which grow up around an epistem, a dominant way of looking at social reality, a set of shared symbols and references, mutual expectations and a mutual predictability of intention

through which political relations are visualized. Also refer to Peter M. Haas' definition, "A epistemic community is a network of professionals with recognized expertise in a particular domain and an authoritative claim to policy-relevant knowledge within that domain or issue-area" (1992), "Introduction: Epistemic Communities and International Policy Coordination," p. 3.

32. Among fourteen interviews, ten were conducted in Washington D.C. from October 6 to 9, 1992, and four were conducted by telephone. Some officials were interviewed more than once. For the details about interview method, see Naka, op. cit., p. 86.

33. These include Koji Watanabe, chief negotiator for Foreign Ministry (1990), "Chūkan hōkoku torimatome kōshō o oete" (interview article); Mitoji Yabunaka, Director of the Second North America Division of the North American Affairs Bureau of Foreign Ministry, one of the participants in the SII meetings including the secret meetings (1991), *Taibei Keizai Kōshō*; Nihon Hōsō Kyōkai (Japan Broadcasting Association)'s detailed documentary, (1990), *NHK Supesharu Dokyumento Kōzō Kyōgi Nichi-bei no Shōtōtsu*; S. Linn Williams (1992), "Kagami no naka no kōzō kyōgi" a series of articles; Glen Fukushima, former Deputy Assistant USTR for Japan and China (1992), *Nichi-bei Keizai Masatsu no Seijigaku*.

34. The number of both application and opening of new retail stores (including Toys R Us and other U.S. toy stores) increased significantly after the relaxation of the LSL. Refer to *Tōyō Keizai* 4/28/90, p. 48, and *Asahi* 1/29/94, p. 11; 2/13/94, p. 15.

35. Williams has the same view as the writer's. "Strengthened antitrust law enforcement has an important long-term effect." Telephone interview, 6/9/94.

36. Fukai, op. cit., pp. 3, 16, 17.

37. In my view, the value of the SII process with the 240-item list and the Interim and Final Reports is not limited in how much specific U.S. demands were materialized. Rather, its value lies in its "thoughts" (Williams, *Daiyamondo* 5/30/92, p. 830), its character of the "authoritative source for U.S. originated Japan reform plan for 1990s" (*Asahi* 3/23/90, p.1), or the "agenda setting and alternative specification function" (Schoppa, op. cit. [1992], pp. 17-18).

38. According to Williams, the pricing mechanism issue was adopted for political consideration, to gain political support from the Japanese people for SII because a price differentiation issue is easy to understand for anybody, and it was not initially considered as an independent issue area.   Indeed, the U.S. government did not ask specific economically significant demands in this area (Williams, *Daiyamondo* 4/11/92, p. 93. Also refer to the 240-item list in *Asahi* 3/23/90, p. 11). For this reason and scarcity of references, the pricing mechanism is dropped from proposition testing although the findings of this book are applied to that issue as well.

39. The original U.S. demands in the 240-item list, the specific eighteen-item list for an interim agreement, and the specific twenty-five-item list for the final agreement are compared with the agreements in the Final Report. (See *Asahi* 3/23/90, pp. 1, 11; *Nikkei* 3/20/90, p. 1; 6/9/90, p. 1.)

40. For example, see Bergsten and Noland, op. cit., pp. 211-212.

41. Refer to NHK, op. cit., pp. 146-149; *Nikkei* 3/12/90, p. 3; *Asahi* 6/23/92, pp. 1, 8, 9. For the effect of SII on the land policy, refer to Fukai, op. cit., "The Role of 'Gaiatsu' in Japan's Land Policymaking."

42. Fukai, op. cit., p. 7.

43. Ibid., p. 2.

44. Williams mentioned both the distribution system and the land policy as successful areas for the U.S. See *JEI Report* No. 1 (January 1991), p. 8. Williams' assessment of the issue areas is almost the same as the writer's. According to Williams, "the U.S. team made *the most significant success* in the saving-investment patterns area. Macroeconomic measures have both short-term and long-term economic effect; *major success* in the distribution system area to improve market access, which also has both short-term and long-term effects; *some important concessions* in exclusionary business practices, which have long-term effects in terms of stronger antitrust enforcement and the role of antitrust law. The U.S. team was *least successful* in the keiretsu area. As to the land policy, the U.S. team did not initially think it was successful because the criteria for success [for the United States] was to suggest policies that the Japanese government initially did not want; many policies the U.S. suggested in the land policy area were the ones that the Japanese government wanted to enact anyway. But the land policy area later turned out to be a *successful area*" (Telephone interview, 6/9/94). As shown in the subsequent chapters, SII agreements of all five issue areas contain both types of policies; those that the Japanese government initially did not want but accepted because of U.S. pressure, and those that the Japanese government already wanted to but could not promote because of opposition from many parties concerned in the domestic arena.

45. Sizes of transgovernmental coalitions are measured and presented quantitatively, while strength of such coalitions is not measured but shown rather qualitatively by using such terms as "strongly support" or "weak support" based on the case study analysis. The levels of common perceptions are suggested based on qualitative analysis of the reconstructed SII meeting records and other sources.

4   The SII as a Means of *Gaiatsu:* The Perspective of Government as a Unitary Rational Actor

EXPLANATIONS FOR SII INITIATION BY FUKUSHIMA AND MASTANDUNO

Identifying when the historical events started is an important question and depends on one's theoretical assumptions. The formal launching of the SII on July 14, 1989, by President Bush and Prime Minister Uno at the Paris Economic Summit, may be less important than the date that the words of the "broad initiative to alter structural impediments to trade" or "*kōzō mondai kyōgi*" (structural problem talk) publicly appeared for the first time on May 25, 1989.[1] To date, studies on the SII begin by mentioning the day of the Super 301 designation as the day the SII process started. Thus, for Schoppa "The Structural Impediments Initiative began in May 1989 as a compromise devised by the Bush Administration to satisfy the minimum demands of a restless Congress eager to step up pressure on Japan while avoiding an open break in relations with one of America's most important allies."[2] Many moves and events related to the SII before May 25 are treated as episodes. According to Mastanduno: "The idea of a structural initiative had been floating around the bureaucracy."[3] From the perspective of the first model, the fact that the SII was proposed on May 25, as an administration initiative outside of Super 301, is important because the official government decision is a reflection of relations in which the national governments are posited to each other.

The strength of the government as a unitary actor model lies in its "analytical ability" to persuasively explain the conduct of the governments, with minimum information.[4] Based on publicized governmental policies, this model describes and explains how and why the SII was proposed as a result of a "conscious choice" of the government. The government decisions are seen as "rational value-maximizing behavior" under the constraint of certain circumstances.

The simplest version of this model takes the view that the stronger state or government (the United States) initiated foreign economic policies, for whatever reasons, in the form of pressure on the weaker state or government (Japan) to advance its own national interest, either economic or political, or both. There are all sorts of variations based on this simplest model. For example, the SII was initiated by the U.S. government because Japanese technological, industrial, or monetary power had become a "threat" to the United States, and therefore, the United States felt the need to "contain" or "reform" Japan. For those who held this belief, the importance of distinguishing between these terms "containing" or "reforming" Japan do not make any difference. However illogical this may be, this is the interpretation that is held by some commentators.[5] The underlying assumption is that since the Cold War is over, a zero-sum game like economic competition looms larger and Japan now is an economic rival of the United States. To deal with Japanese economic power, the United States needs to confront this power, either by putting limits on Japan (e.g., a mandatory annual reduction in trade surpluses or market shares of imports) or by forcing Japan to change its economic institutions and business practices which are not compatible with the rules of the liberal world trade regime so that the Japanese economic threat is removed forever. The SII is one of the vehicles for achieving this goal because whatever the form may be, international trade negotiations are places in which the national self-interest of nations clash with each other in mutually competing economic and power relations.

A more sophisticated view, based on the model of government as a unitary rational actor, recognizes the institutional differences and their policy stances between the U.S. administration and the Congress. This view treats the U.S. administration and the Congress as independent political actors and explains the reason for the SII initiation in terms of intense struggle between the two. Glen Fukushima's interpretation of the SII initiation is based on this model, although his description and explanation are not entirely consistent in the level of analysis.

According to Fukushima, faced with the huge trade deficit with Japan, Congress pressed the Bush administration to name Japan as a "priority negotiation country" under the Super 301 provision of the 1988 Trade Act. Considering domestic political situations, the Bush administration could not alienate Congress by not designating Japan under Super 301. On the other hand, the Japanese government warned the Bush administration that there was a possibility of a deterioration of relations between the two countries if a Super 301 designation was imposed upon Japan. To solve this dilemma, the administration decided to take measures to satisfy both Congress and the Japanese government, or to minimize the dissatisfaction of both. Thus, the administration designated Japan as a priority negotiation country under Super 301 to satisfy Congress, but selected only three priority trade negotiation items which the Japanese government could solve relatively easily. The SII was the "price for compromise."[6] The administration chose to designate three items—commercial satellites, super computers, and wood products. These three trade items were chosen because their scope was limited to the narrow governmental jurisdiction, and consistent with the negotiation areas of the GATT Uruguay Round (governmental procurement, tariffs, and standards). But, sensing a danger of a congressional backlash by designating only three trade items (and by not designating Japan as a whole, nor broad structural barriers such as the distribution system, keiretsu, and weak antitrust laws as some congressmen insisted), the Bush administration proposed the SII at the same time that it announced the Super 301 designation.[7]

Another political motivation for the Bush administration's need to compromise was that it wanted to "tie" Congress not to make a political move so that it could concentrate on the GATT Uruguay Round in 1989 and 1990. In this sense, the SII was a useful tool to "buy time" for the administration by diverting congressional attention away from the U.S.-Japan bilateral problem to multilateral trade issues.[8]

Mastanduno provides another typical explanation for the SII initiation based on the government as a unitary rational actor model.

They [Bush administration officials] conceived of the SII as a means to avoid short-term tactical and long-term structural losses. In the short term, the SII enabled officials of the executive branch of the United States government to deflect what they perceived as a challenge from the legislative arm to their control over the formulations and substance of trade policy. Executive officials believed that without the SII, Congress was likely to adopt measures which would jeopardize the successful completion of the Uruguay Round of multilateral trade negotiations under the General Agreement on Tariffs and Trade (GATT)—the administration's top priority in trade policy—and drive American policy in the illiberal direction of managed trade. The SII was also viewed as a means to preserve the multilateral trading system over the long run. Bush administration officials believed that Japan was a potential system wrecker, that its domestic political and economic structures and practices were fundamentally incompatible with those of other advanced industrial states. The considerable trade and payments imbalance between the United States and Japan was a symptom, and a politically explosive one of that incompatibility. The failure to transform Japan would lead ultimately to the demise of the multilateral system.[9]

Mastanduno wrote this paragraph entirely through "reasoning" without providing any evidence based on official government statements or administration officials' remarks. Since Mastanduno was in the USTR office in 1989, perhaps he knew Bush administration officials' thoughts. That Mastanduno did not provide hard evidence does not necessarily mean his reasoning is unreliable. To the contrary, one is more likely to find pieces of evidence to support Mastanduno's reasoning in analyzing the situation in which the Bush administration was positioned. But, because "the government as a unitary actor" is an abstract construct, identifying government's "objectives," "choices," and "means," by one way of reasoning cannot *falsify* identifying those by an other way of reasoning, unless these "objectives," "choices," and "means" are suggested based on exactly the same empirical methods, analyzing the exactly the same sources.

Describing and explaining the events between the national governments by using the first model is always problematic, since it is possible to collect pieces of information from various sources, such as official White House announcements, presidential speeches, State Department policy statements, or Cabinet members' remarks, and then construct these evidence as "government policies," "objectives," and "choices" through coherent reasoning and logic. But, there is no credible way of *falsifying* one reasoning by another way of reasoning. By taking an example from State Department statements (or Japanese Ministry of Foreign Affairs announcements), one can test this. How much is official "U.S. government's policy" and how much is "State Department's policy" which is in actuality contradictory to policies of other departments. There seems to be no standardized way of making a distinction between "official U.S. government policy" and "each department's own interpretation" of "official U.S. government policy." Therefore, what one can do is to make interpretations, which are sound in analysis, rich in insight, and persuasive in explanation on "objectives," "choices," and "means" of the government, based on available sources.

For this chapter, the process of reconstruction was done in multiple steps: (1) all available sources, such as official government policy statements, policy-makers' speeches, remarks, interviews in newspapers and magazines, and congressional hearings were read; (2) next, my interview results were examined; (3) "the largest common denominator" among the statements expressed as government policy was found; and (4) "government goals," "options," "choices," and "means" in foreign economic policy were constructed and the SII was characterized in relation to these "goals," "options," "choices," and "means."

WHY DID THE U.S. GOVERNMENT INITIATE THE SII?

Many commentators, such as Fukushima and Mastanduno, believe that the SII was solely the administration's response to pressures from both Congress and the Japanese government; therefore, SII was a compromise to satisfy both of them. However, an investigation of the events in the fall of 1988 and the early spring of 1989 reveals that the SII emerged from the competing initiative-making relationship among the Bush administration, Congress, and the Japanese government regarding "comprehensive talks" on structural issues.

Although the SII, as seen today, no doubt originated in the U.S. administration, similar ideas were found in the activities of Congress and the Japanese government. According to a senior Democratic congressional staff member, the earliest idea about a "broad talk" with the Japanese government including structural problems emerged in Congress. When the Super 301 provision of the 1988 Trade Act was drafted, Congress believed that some kind of broad talks with the Japanese government were necessary. Section 1306 of the 1988 Trade Act, in the form of resolution, noted that since trade problems with Japan "cannot be effectively resolved through narrow sector-by-sector negotiations," the president should propose a "special summit" with the Japanese prime minister to address trade and other economic issues.[10] Reflecting the spirit of the 1988 Trade Act, with its Super 301 provision, which may usher "a new era in trade policy marked by a more prominent congressional role,"[11] Congress suggested that the "special summit" meeting should include members of Congress from both political parties, appropriate officials of the executive branch, representatives of all political parties in Japan and Japanese government officials.[12] With its own political goals, such as taking a more assertive role in U.S. trade policy-making and bringing down an unprecedented $50 billion trade deficit with Japan in the interest of U.S. domestic industries, Congress was interested in making "broad agreements" with the Japanese government which included trade, defense, and foreign aid.[13]

Aware of the congressional moves, the Japanese government had its own idea of a new "comprehensive framework" or "comprehensive consultation panel" headed by foreign ministers of both governments, in which subcabinet officials would discuss broad issues of macroeconomics, foreign aid, the Third World debt, and environmental problems.[14] The idea of a new consultative panel was officially proposed by the Japanese government at the Bush-Takeshita summit meeting of February 2, 1989. The Japanese government made this preemptive initiative to avert the implementation of the Super 301, while strengthening a cooperative "G-2 relationship" with the U.S. administration in many economic issues. In the Summit meetings, the Japanese government pledged Japan's expansion of domestic demand and promotion of structural adjustment, while the U.S. government promised to reduce the federal deficit.[15]

While neither the newly begun Bush administration nor the Japanese government was interested in the congressional proposals, the Bush administration was cautious of the Japanese government's proposal because a new comprehensive panel might be used "to gloss over trade problems created by long-established business practices—such as Japan's arcane distribution system."[16] In a time of increasing need for closer economic and political cooperation, including G-2 cooperation between the United States and the Japanese government on the global agendas on the one hand, and growing congressional assertiveness and frustration on the other hand, the Bush administration was looking for a proper policy among possible options to realize its national trade policy goals in the spring of 1989.

When the government is viewed as a unitary rational actor, it is assumed that the government has coherent national foreign policy objectives, and that national policies are chosen to realize these objectives. In order to know what the U.S. foreign economic policy objectives were in the spring of 1989, it is reasonable to start by examining the USTR's report to the Congress, *National Trade Policy Agenda* for 1989.[17]

According to this report and U.S. Trade Representative Carla Hills' testimony, the national trade policy goal of the U.S. administration in 1989 was "to open markets and create an ever-expanding trading system based upon equitable and enforceable rules."[18]   For this goal, the U.S. administration put top priority on the successful completion of the Uruguay Round, which was the largest and most ambitious of this kind, including the areas of agricultural products, intellectual property, investment, and services. The U.S. administration would concentrate on the Uruguay Round by putting "the majority of our resources in the next two years" into it.[19]

With respect to bilateral initiatives, there are three major bilateral trade concerns: the implementation of free-trade agreements (the U.S.-Canada and the U.S.-Israel), the European Community (EC) 1992 process, and Japanese trade barriers. Although the huge bilateral trade deficit with the Japanese is a "cause for concern," the trade deficit has more to do with macroeconomic factors than with trade measures. However, even though the overall trade deficit reduction will be achieved by macroeconomic measures, reducing the trade deficit with Japan can also be done by removing barriers to the free market and strengthening the multilateral trade regime, but not by managed trade measures.[20]   With regard to the unilateral trade initiative, the U.S. administration would implement the Super 301 provision of the 1988 Trade Act, which would provide the United States with an important leverage for Uruguay Round objectives.   Yet, it was necessary "to coordinate our policies and actions," therefore requiring a "creative use of the legal tools provided us under U.S. trade law."[21]

Almost all the clues as to the reason why the U.S. administration initiated the SII are found in the report of the national trade policy agenda and subsequent discussions between Hills and congressmen, although the name of the SII did not appear yet at that stage of national trade policy discussions. Based on those broad policy directions in pursuing national trade goals mentioned above, the broad structural talks were proposed on May 25, 1989. The specific reason why the administration initiated the SII was explained by Hills at another hearing of the House Ways and Means Committee on June 8, 1989. According to Hills, the Super 301 of the 1989 Trade Act was a congressional mandate that should be implemented.   In implementing that law, three specific trade priority negotiation items were selected according to four criteria: (1) the potential for U.S. exports, (2) the pervasiveness of the barriers, (3) the need expressed by private sectors to bring particular barriers down, and (4) the compatibility with multilateral goals. The SII was suggested outside of the Super 301 for such areas of long-standing structural barriers as the Japanese distribution system and anticompetitive laws, since a "rigorous time frame might not be conducive to constructive negotiations."[22]

Essentially, the same line of argument was expressed by Hills to the Japanese Trade Minister, Hiroshi Mitsuzuka, at the OECD ministerial meeting on May 30, 1989, and in an interview published in *Nikkei*. Hills said that if the U.S.

administration had not designated Japan under the Super 301, Congress would have enacted tougher trade laws, giving the U.S. administration no leeway. The three trade negotiation priority items were chosen specifically so that the Japanese government could liberalize them relatively easily. Elimination of Japanese structural barriers served the ultimate goal of creating a new trade order for the 1990s through the strengthened GATT. Japan's continuous import expansion through correction of trade barriers was the key to promoting GATT negotiations. Trade expansion should be achieved by measures stressing "market rules," not by the managed trade measures that Congress was trying to take.[23]

As noted above, the SII was proposed by the U.S. administration as a rationally chosen action among possible choices under certain constraints, which ultimately would serve for realization of national trade goals. These constraints were the impending problem of how to reduce a $50 billion bilateral trade deficit, the necessary implementation of legally mandated action by the Super 301, the necessity of keeping a good bilateral relationship with Japan, and the need for the successful completion of GATT (for which the administration should avoid abuse of a unilateral action). The U.S. administration had to avoid a possible full-scale trade war with Japan when the Super 301 was fully imposed on Japan, while there was a need to deal with Japan's economic system, which seemed immune to exchange rate alignment, resulting in the continuing large trade surplus.[24]

Under those constraints, the U.S. government considered three possible ways to implement the Super 301 provision: (1) only list unfair trade practices, (2) separately list unfair trade practices and unfair trade practice countries, and (3) list unfair trade practice countries and their unfair trade practices.[25] Congress insisted upon the second option to name Japan as a whole. But, the Bush administration finally chose the third option, supplemented by the SII, a separate but parallel talk, aiming to discuss structural trade barriers. While the SII, in a sense, is "an alternative to Super 301 process,"[26] it also is a part of "a comprehensive package" of a broader strategy "to create an ever-expanding multilateral trading system based upon clear and enforceable rules" for the benefit of all nations.[27]

One of the ways to strengthen the multilateral trading system is to change some of the Japanese economic structures and business practices, which from time to time seem incompatible with those of the world trading system. In October 1989, Deputy U.S. Trade Representative S. Linn Williams told a Japanese interviewer that, "our purpose is to integrate Japan into the world trading system. Japan is now integrated into the world trading system only as an exporter. We think Japan is not fully integrated into the world trading system as an importer of manufactured goods and capital goods.[28]

The theme of "integrating Japan into the world trading system" was one of the main ones in the Senate Finance Committee Hearing of March 5, 1990. For example, Under Secretary of State McCormack said "[Japan's] economic practices . . . prevent Japan from becoming a full participant in the free trading system of the world."[29]   Assistant Secretary of the Treasury Dallara called Japanese trade practices "economic schizophrenia in which it integrates its export sector into the world economy and in doing so tries to be fully supportive of the open world trading system while it appears to hold a different standard to its own markets."[30]   Therefore, by eliminating Japanese structural barriers to trade and investment, Japan would become more integrated in the world trading system, which in turn would strengthen the multilateral trading system.

But, the U.S. administration had another reason to start the SII: to counter protectionist moves influenced by revisionists' views in its own country, in particular in the Congress.[31]   Like the unilateral action of Super 301 implementation, managed trade measures that Congress was then moving toward were antithetic to the policy goals of the Bush administration. The multilateral world trade regime would be further weakened if Congress, backed by domestic industries, enacted such measures. Against the growing sentiment that Japan with its different economic system from its Western counterpart was becoming an economic competitor and that strong "results-oriented approach" was necessary,[32] the Bush administration wanted to promote "the operation of free and competitive markets" in the United States as well as in Japan.[33] In Hills' interview, this notion was clearly discernible: "Japan is an export superpower, but as to imports, Japan is like a developing country, hurting consumers interest . . . If Japan opens its market, this helps open the closed part of the U.S. market."[34]

This two-pronged trade policy goal of the SII for the Bush administration was repeated by administration officials on many occasions. For example, in the Senate hearing of July 20, 1989, Senator John Heinz (R-Penn.) insisted upon, "results, bottom line oriented trade—which means, numbers each year that have been negotiated . . . negotiations that result in annual decrements of the deficit one way or another."[35] Under Secretary of State McCormack resisted taking the managed trade measures insisted upon by Senator Heinz, while asserting the clear need to persuade Japan to modify its trade practices which would jeopardize the future of the world trading system.[36]   The importance of preventing managed trade was also stressed by Member of President's Council of Economic Advisers John B. Taylor in the Senate hearings of March 5, 1990.

The SII approach is superior to a managed trade approach, which would require the U.S. Government to attempt to achieve different patterns of imports and exports than would be dictated by private markets. Unlike managed trade, SII is in keeping with the trend to freer markets that has accelerated remarkably throughout much of the world during the last year. Indeed, it would be ironic and disturbing to the nations of Eastern Europe if the United States, the nation that has been the leader in moving toward freer trade and more open markets in the postwar world, were to turn toward managed trade at this critical juncture.[37]

In sum, the strength of the first model is, first that it makes us understand the large picture of national trade policy goals, policy options, choices, and means, and second, that it visibly demonstrates relationships among the large institutional political actors, that is, the U.S. administration, the Congress, and the Japanese government in light of their goals, policy options, choices, and means. The U.S. administration proposed the SII for two reasons: to counter the congressional initiative to introduce protectionist measures—managed trade, while to try to change some of the Japanese trade barriers and integrate Japan into the world trading system. These interrelated aims served the ultimate national trade policy goal of strengthening the GATT multilateral trade regime.[38]

WHY DID THE U.S. GOVERNMENT AND THE JAPANESE GOVERNMENT REACH THE AGREEMENTS IN THE SII?

After defining structural impediments in both countries and exchanging policy ideas for those impediments in the first and second formal SII meetings in September and November, 1989, real negotiation began when the U.S. and Japanese governments discussed the 240-item list at the secret meeting of January 31, 1990, in Bern, Switzerland. In this meeting, the U.S. government prepared two lists: the list of measures which would be taken by the United States and the list of those to be taken by the Japanese government. (Later, the content of the two lists were formally presented in the third SII meeting of February 1990). The Japanese side list contained measures attacking the heart of the post-World War II Japanese system. From then on, the SII changed its character from a "mere talk to an unprecedentedly important" negotiation.[39] The three major U.S. demands in the 240-item list were an increase of Japanese government spending on public works by an annual 10 percent of GNP over the next ten years to fill the gap between domestic savings and investment; a repeal of the Large Store Law, which became the symbol of the closed nature of Japanese market for many American exporters; and an increase in administrative surcharges on illegal cartels to remedy anticompetitive practices of Japanese corporations at the cost of foreign companies. Because of the Lower House election held in February 18, 1990, the Japanese government could not publicly discuss these demands and therefore could not offer any policy concessions at the third SII meeting of February 22-23 in Tokyo. The third meeting of SII was reported as a failure and the SII negotiations became deadlocked.

Meantime, Congress held hearings on November 6 and 7, 1989, and February 20 and March 5, 1990, during which witnesses expressed an increased skepticism about the effectiveness of the SII, and members of Congress began threatening the administration with a possible introduction of Super 301 measures on some of the issues being discussed in the SII negotiation.[40] Congress relentlessly asked the administration such questions as "how much would the U.S. trade deficit with Japan actually be reduced and over what period of time" and would the realization of a "level playing field for U.S. business" become reality.[41] These sentiments were repeatedly expressed with an increasingly hawkish stance to introduce managed trade measures that would "set simple targets in categories where trade relationship ought to be in one year, in two years, and in three years."[42] The political pressure was near to reaching a "breaking point" in the Congress.[43]

The U.S. administration and the Japanese government held the summit meeting at Palm Springs on March 2 and 3, 1990, to break the deadlock of the SII. Congress introduced a new bill that would expand the president's power to retaliate against unfair trade practices on March 28 and 29.[44] After intensive efforts on the part of both governments, an Interim Report was announced at the end of the fourth formal meeting on April 2-5, 1990, in Washington, D.C. The Japanese government agreed to make three major commitments: spending a specific amount of its budget in the form of a total amount over another ten years, shortening the coordination processing period under the Large Store Law from the current average of six years to one and a half years, and increasing the cartel surcharges in the antimonopoly law.

The Interim Report was well accepted among U.S. policy-makers. Consequently, the U.S. administration removed Japan from another designation as a priority country under the Super 301 in April, 1990, in spite of some congressional opposition.[45] Between the Interim Report of April and the Final Report of June, the issue of the annual GNP 10 percent spending on public works became a major contention between the two governments. The Japanese government refused the U.S. demand for public works spending with a ratio of GNP but finally agreed to the 430 trillion yen spending for ten years.

The first model provides answers for questions of why the U.S. government and the Japanese government reached agreements during the most critical period of the SII by using such categories of national trade policy goals, policy options, and means to realize the chosen policy. By using this model, results of international negotiation are explained in terms of national self-interest and power relations.

Most clues for explanations are found in the departing remarks of President Bush and Prime Minister Toshiki Kaifu at Palm Springs. According to President Bush's remarks, in the spring of 1990, the U.S. administration became more aware of the necessity to forge a global partnership with Japan to deal with the "great changes in the world from Eastern Europe to Panama to Cambodia."[46] The U.S.-Japanese security relationship had become more important to ensuring peace and prosperity as democracy and free markets spread all over the world. But the United States still had a huge $49 billion bilateral deficit with Japan, which aggravated the "mood" in the United States. The United States and Japan had to put their economic relationship on a "solid foundation" if both countries were to achieve the full promise of bilateral relations. To this end, the SII had to succeed in reducing the bilateral trade deficit. Reduction of the trade deficit "not by restricting U.S. markets or managed trade, but by further increasing U.S. exports to Japan" that the SII tried to achieve, is necessary for greater worldwide cooperation between two countries and a future trilateral cooperation among the United States, Japan, and the EC.[47]

The political goals of the U.S. administration during this time were also clearly expressed by Secretary of States James A. Baker before the Senate Foreign Relations Committee Hearings on February 1, 1990.

Today, we are building an extensive global partnership with the Japanese, focused on sharing responsibilities to foster world stability and growth . . . We regard the Structural Impediments Initiative process as critical to stimulating the structural adjustments necessary to sustain our global partnership.[48]

For the U.S. government, the SII is a means of smoothly integrating two economic superpowers, the United States and Japan.[49] According to one source, Bush said that we should not make Japan a destabilizing power in East Asia by isolating Japan through protectionist measures or Japan-bashing.[50] To achieve this national trade policy goal, the administration chose one option, that is, to demand visibly effective concessions from the Japanese government in some areas good enough to persuade the Congress, instead of pursuing Japanese concessions in all 240 items to the limit.[51] The means to achieve this were "pressure" through the summit meetings and a congressional threat. But, the U.S. government did not want to push the Japanese government too far because Japan was now "financing not only U.S. budget deficit but also to bankroll a foreign policy agenda that Washington cannot afford.[52] At the Summit meetings, the U.S. government specifically expressed the concern about a possible decrease in Japanese purchases of U.S. Treasury bonds, due to recent increases in discount rate and low stock prices.[53]

On the other hand, the Japanese government also had good reasons to reach agreements. While the FSX dispute created doubts on the Japanese side as to the U.S. intentions in treating allies, the widely publicized opinion poll result—a majority of Americans (68%) now think that the economic threat from Japan is more serious than the military threat from the Soviet Union—raised a real alarm among Japanese policy makers.[54] Thus, for the Japanese government, consolidating bilateral relations by reaffirming Japan-U.S. security arrangements was an urgent necessity for continuous U.S.-Japan economic relations and assuming a leading role in the coming years.[55] In the early spring of 1990, the Japanese government had a real fear of a complete breakdown of U.S.-Japanese military-security relations as well as economic relationship. For example, after criticizing the "dangerous idea" of anti-Americanism, Secretary-General of the Liberal Democratic Party Ichiro Ozawa said "if the U.S.-Japan relation was cut, the Japanese economy would collapse in a day" in his speech at the party meeting.[56] During the same period, Former Prime Minister Takeshita spoke in the general conference of the Takeshita Faction, stating that "Whatever changes occur, the U.S.-Japan Security Treaty relation should not be jeopardized." After the Palm Springs meeting, Foreign Minister Taro Nakayama asserted that trade issues became a "matter of crisis control," and that this was a hair-trigger situation in which Japan had to act.[57]

In addition to this, the Japanese government also feared a possible demise of the free trading system. In his speech to the National Diet on March 2, 1990, Prime Minister Kaifu expressed his government's urgent concern; "the world economic order is also at an important watershed. The rising pressures of protectionism today threaten the very survival of the free trade system that has sustained our postwar prosperity . . . The maintenance and strengthening of the multilateral free-trade system is one of the important issues confronting the world economy today."[58] This sense that the free-trading system is now facing "major trials" and "the issue of how to sustain this system is an urgent one" was shared among the policy-makers across the government.[59] Thus, reaching meaningful agreements in the SII good enough to deter the Congress from exacting tougher protectionist laws was also important for the Japanese government.

There was another reason why the Japanese government was forthcoming with the U.S. demands. During the early spring, the yen was becoming weaker. To stabilize the yen, the Japanese government needed the U.S. government's help. The Japanese government asked the reluctant U.S. government for macroeconomic policy coordination, to prevent the rapid depreciation of the yen in the foreign exchange market.[60] In his departing remarks, Prime Minister Kaifu explicitly mentioned this issue, "Japan-U.S. cooperation in exchange markets" twice, despite the fact that it was not included in the initial meeting agenda.[61]

For all of the above-mentioned political and economic interests, the Japanese government could not reject the U.S. demands, even though it believed the major factor causing the U.S. trade deficit was the U.S. federal deficit and the problem of competitiveness. But the Japanese government could not accept all of the U.S. demands either, for it might cause inflation without budgetary control, alienate medium and small shop owners (important electoral supporters for the LDP government), and produce resentment from industries because of stronger antitrust laws.

At the same time, the Japanese government did not have much power leverage to influence the U.S. government.[62] The Japanese suggestion of a "punitive clause" in the case that the U.S. government failed to reduce its federal deficit was rejected, although the U.S. government knew reducing the federal deficit was the single most effective short-term measure for reducing trade and current account imbalances. At last, what the Japanese government decided was to make some concessions in the key areas as seen before, while *hoping* the United States, for its part, would promote structural adjustment.[63] In sum, from the viewpoint of the first model, reaching the SII agreements was a result of a compromise between the U.S. government and the Japanese government dictated by economic and political self-interest in uneven power relations.[64]

Also from the viewpoint of the first model, the U.S. government's reintroduction of the GNP ratio issue after the Interim Report can be explained in terms of the administration's conscious choice under specific conditions. In the U.S. administration's view, the bilateral trade deficit was an obstacle to achieving real U.S.-Japanese global partnership in the new global context of the collapsing communist regimes of Eastern Europe and the rapidly destabilizing world politics in the spring of 1990. The trade deficit had to be reduced, and it was the macroeconomic measures that could actually reduce the trade deficit. This was the reason why the U.S. government insisted upon the issue of GNP ratio public works spending again, after the interim agreement was reached.[65]

Indeed, the strong U.S. concern with reducing the trade deficit was already expressed by a high-ranking State Department official in the fall of 1989: "Whether or not wiping out the anti-Japanese resentment centering around the Congress is possible depends on how much the trade deficit is actually reduced; the key is whether or not the $50 billion deficit can be reduced to some $20 billion. In the past, the focus was on [burden sharing in] defense and foreign aid, from now on that includes public works spending."[66] Therefore, demanding public works spending to reduce the trade deficit was one of the medium or long term national foreign policy goals, comparable to demanding burden sharing and the increase of foreign aid in the past.

Another widely reported interpretation was the following: since Japan surpassed the United States in annual investment for industrial equipment in 1989 for the first time in history, the fearful U.S. government could not ignore the consequence of Japanese massive industrial investment, which could create another export drive, resulting in a further decline of U.S. industry. To cut the "vicious cycle of Japanese massive industrial investment and export drive," the U.S. government demanded that the Japanese public works spending increase. This would take away money from new investment in the private sector.[67]

In any case, the reason why the U.S. government brought the GNP ratio public works spending issue onto the agenda, which the Japanese government believed was settled at the time of reaching the Interim Report, was explained in terms of a conscious choice by the national government as a unitary rational actor. All in all, for the U.S. government, the SII in the spring of 1990 was "an important framework in which the underlying causes of trade imbalances can be removed," and therefore "Continuing success on SII can help us move away from trade disputes, thus allowing us to focus our efforts on more positive activities as we continue to develop a global partnership between our two countries."[68]

FURTHER CONCEPTUAL UNDERSTANDING:
AN "IMPERFECT THREE-ACTOR GAME"

The way that the first model presents how governments reach agreements in international negotiations is as follows. National governments having long-term and short-term political and economic goals with calculated self-interests meet each other in certain power relations. The U.S. administration and the Japanese government shared many long-term and short-term political and economic interests. In relation to Congress, both the U.S. administration and the Japanese government had a common interest in preventing the enactment of tougher protectionist laws and managed trade measures, in particular.

The common goal of the SII negotiators—to prevent enactment of tougher protectionist measures including those of managed trade—was explicitly expressed by both U.S. officials and Japanese officials in the opening statements of the first SII meeting of September 4, 1989. Fukushima witnessed the statement made by the Japanese official at the beginning of the first formal meeting of the SII.

I still vividly remember the words of a Japanese official at the first day of the SII on September 4, 1989. "The chief objective of the SII is to make 'comprehensive measures' which can be sold to the outside world, especially to Congress." These words impressively and exactly express what we are going to do. As a matter of fact, the U.S. administration and the Japanese government are going to cooperate in the SII in order to eliminate possibilities that Congress enacts protectionist laws as a measure to deal with the bilateral trade and investment problem. The U.S. administration and the Japanese government viewed the SII as a joint work.[69]

Both the U.S. and Japanese chief negotiators expressed the common goal of the SII for them in their opening statements. "There is a dangerous idea in America that since Japan is different, contain it. But Japan is changing over the years. We can show these changes. We should not only criticize each other" (Michihiko Kunihiro, deputy minister of Foreign Affairs Ministry). "The idea that Japan is different is not a constructive one. If the U.S. government takes this kind of idea, that will be a big obstacle to the talks" (Naomichi Suzuki, vice minister of Trade Ministry). "The Congress thinks the exchange adjustment effectively worked to correct current account imbalance with EC but did not work with Japan. I don't think Japan is a different country and can't be changed by ordinary ways. Japan is now facing a similar problem as the United States faced in the 1920's and 1930's" (McCormack). "Every issue we take here is good for Japanese consumers. It is rather the Japanese that use the logic that Japan is different from the U.S. We think Japan is an equal ally for the United States" (Williams)[70] Therefore, it is apparent that the U.S. administration and the Japanese government tried to cooperate with each other against Congress, which at that time was taking the view that since the Japanese economic system was different from other Western capitalist economies, demanding market shares and a mandatory reduction of trade surplus was the way to deal with such a system. This situation is already pointed out by Clyde V. Prestowitz.

> To persuade the Japanese to make concessions, we had to try to frighten them by suggesting that, despite our best efforts, we might not be able to restrain the Congress. Implicitly we were linking ourselves in common cause with the Japanese and creating a false sense that free-traders on both sides were fighting against the black hats in Congress. The negotiation thus changed direction: originally a matter of U.S. government requests, it became one of mutually calibrating just how much action would be necessary to keep Congress leashed. Instead of a negotiator, the U.S. trade team became an advisor to the government of Japan on how to handle the U.S. Congress.[71]

However, the relationship among the U.S. administration, Congress, and the Japanese government has never been conceptually understood. What emerges through the SII process is more of a picture of an "imperfect three-actor game" rather than that of two national governments directly clashing with each other. There are structural bases for this conceptualization. Since the U.S. government is a divided government, it is quite possible that one branch of the government forms a transgovernmental coalition with foreign governments against another branch of the government. The executive branch of the U.S. government represents a nationwide constituency, while Congress represents the state and local district constituency. Because the whole is not the sum of the parts, the executive branch can actually represent different interests from those of Congress. Therefore, transgovernmental coalitions with other governments are formed not only because the executive branch puts priority on preserving the multilateral trade regime as part of the larger goals of strengthening political and military-security ties of the free world (or preference for laissez-faire policies), but also because it represents structurally different interests from those of Congress.

Throughout the SII process, the U.S. administration tried to resist or avert managed trade pressure from Congress, at the same time it used the pressure from the Congress as a power leverage to press the Japanese government for concessions.[72] In the meetings of the SII, the U.S. administration often used pressure from Congress as a power leverage against the Japanese government, while emphasizing a common interest with the Japanese government in preventing managed trade measures.[73] On the one hand, the Japanese government was often resentful of heavy-handed U.S. pressure and resisted the U.S. administration's "excessive demands," while at the same time it made a coalition with the U.S. administration against Congress. As the SII process continued, the U.S. administration in the position of coalition with the Japanese government tried to promote its own policy agendas, the "President's pro growth budget and the savings and education initiatives."[74] The expression of such coalition was, for example, found in President Bush' statement on the successful conclusion of the final round of the SII talks, which was announced when the administration was still negotiating with Congress in the "budget summit" in

June, 1990. "Removing structural impediments is a two-way street. As Japan tackles its structural problems, so must the United States. In particular, I look forward to working closely with the Congress on efforts to strengthen both public and private savings, and to reduce our budget deficit through the negotiations now underway."[75]

As noted above, three political actors representing different interests in the conflicting positions pressured, supported, and coalesced with each other. Congress pressured the administration to bring "concrete results" from the SII negotiation, while supporting the administration against the Japanese government to secure concessions from it. An interesting thing was that by insisting on its short-term goal of reducing the trade deficit, Congress was inadvertently in the same position as the Japanese government, which also insisted that the goal of SII was the reduction of the trade deficit, against the administration, which wanted to separate the SII from the issue of trade deficits at some point in the SII negotiation.[76] Thus, there was some element of a "de facto coalition" between Congress and the Japanese government. However, because the direct coalition and supportive relations between Congress and the Japanese government was weak or missing, the pressure and support game was imperfect.

Furthermore, the dynamic among the U.S. administration, Congress, and the Japanese government seems to explain some of the policy outcomes in the SII. According to one former official, "Congressional monitoring shaped the SII process unusually. The Congress asked for specific results with time tables."[77] With its own strong concern, but also due to persistent congressional pressure to produce concrete deficit reduction, the Bush administration brought in the settled matter of GNP ratio public works spending issue again after the interim report.[78] In the House Foreign Affairs Committee Hearings of April 19, 1990, congressmen repeatedly asked administration officials how much of the trade deficit would actually be reduced as a result of SII measures.[79] Part of the reason why the administration demanded repeal of the Large Store Law was because of a strong Congressional concern for the Toys R Us' fate—whether or not it could open a new store in Japan.[80] Because of those reasons, the Japanese government received the strongest U.S. pressure in the saving-investment issue area, and therefore yielded a high level concession in that area. The Japanese government felt the strong U.S. pressure until the Interim Report, but overall medium-level pressure in the distribution system area, compared with that in the saving-investment area, and therefore agreed to the medium level concession in that area.

In sum, the notion of an "imperfect three-actor game" is useful for understanding the dynamic among the U.S. administration, the Congress, and the Japanese government, that resulted in certain policy outcomes in some SII issue areas.

NOTES

1. *WSJ* 5/26/89, p. A7; *Nikkei* 5/26/89, E. p. 1.

2. Schoppa (1993), op. cit., p. 356.

3. Mastanduno, op. cit., p. 245.

4. Refer to Allison, op. cit., p. 251.

5. For the views about "reform" or "contain" Japanese economic system through SII, refer to *Nikkei* articles of 9/16/89, p. 5; 1/1/90, p. 9; 1/3/90, p. 1. Also refer to Tahara op. cit.

6. Fukushima, op. cit., pp. 199-200.

7. Ibid., pp. 200-201.

8. Ibid., pp. 201-202.

9. Mastanduno, op. cit., pp. 237-238.

10. *Nikkei* 5/21/89, p. 1. See Public Law 100-418, the Omnibus Trade and Competitiveness Act of 1988, August 23, 1988, Section 1306.

11. *CQWR* 5/20/89, p. 1170.

12. Op. cit. Public Law 100-418, the Trade Act of 1988, Section 1306.

13. *Nikkei* 1/28/89, p. 1; 5/16/89, p. 5; 5/21/89, p. 1.

14. *Nikkei* 1/28/89, p. 1.

15. *Nikkei* 2/3/89, p. 5; 2/4/89, p. 3; *NYT* 2/3/89, p. A5.

16. *Japan Economic Survey*, March 1989, p. 2. Also refer to *NYT* 2/3/89, p. A5.

17. The Office of the United States Trade Representative is part of the Office of the President and responsible for the formulation and administration of the nation's overall trade policy. The USTR directs and coordinates all multilateral and bilateral trade negotiations. The USTR is required by the Trade Act of 1988 to submit a national trade policy agenda to the Congress by March 1, 1989.

18. *National Trade Policy Agenda*, the hearings before the Subcommittee on Trade of the House Ways and Means Committee, February 28, 1989 (hereafter HH 2/28/89), p. 9.

19. Ibid., p. 53.

20. Ibid., pp. 11, 16, 51, 69, 72-73.

21. Ibid., pp. 11-19.

22. Hills' testimony before the Subcommittee on Trade of the House Ways and Means Committee, June 8, 1989 (HH 6/8/89), pp. 12, 21, 24.

23. *Nikkei* 5/31/89, p. 1; 8/13/89, p. 3.

24. Those are topics discussed in the hearing of the Subcommittee on International Trade of the Senate Finance Committee, July 20, 1989 (hereafter SH 7/20/89), *United States-Japan Structural Impediments Initiative* (SII).

25. *Asahi* 5/26/89, p. 2.

26. McCormack, interview 10/7/92.

27. Carla Hills, testimony before HH 6/8/89, pp. 7, 9, 12.

28. *Tōyō Keizai* 10/4/89, p. 101. Williams later clarified the theme of integration of Japan, saying that "Japan is not yet fully integrated into the world trading system in terms of amount and content of imports, pricing structure, and antitrust law." Interview, 10/6/92.

29. McCormack, testimony before SH 3/5/90, p. 13. Also refer to testimonies of Williams and Dallara in the same hearings, pp. 9, 11.

30. Dallara's testimony, *United States-Japan Economic Relations: Structural Impediments Initiative*, the joint Hearings of the Subcommittees on Asian and Pacific Affairs and on International Economic Policy and Trade of the House Foreign Affairs Committee, April 19, 1990 (hereafter HH 4/19/90), p. 145.

31. Such authors as James Follows, Chalmers Johnson, Clyde V. Prestowitz, and Karel van Wolferen are called "revisionists" for their view that the Japanese economic system is fundamentally different from other Western style capitalism, therefore, managed trade, not free trade, is the way to deal this type of system. See their joint article, "Beyond Japan-bashing" *U.S. News & World Report*, May 7, 1990, pp. 54-55. For influences of the revisionists' ideas on members of the Congress, refer to the cover story of *Business Week* (August 7, 1989), "Rethinking Japan," p. 52.

32. The report of the Advisory Committee for Trade Policy and Negotiations reflects this sentiment among U.S. business leaders. See *Analysis of the U.S.-Japan Trade Problem* (February 1989), which calls for a tough "results-oriented approach," pp. xvi-xviii.

33. Taylor, SH 3/5/90, p. 16. Also refer to Williams, *Daiyamondo* 3/28/92, pp. 94-95; 4/11/92, p. 92.

34. *Nikkei* 8/13/89, p. 3.

35. Heinz, SH 7/20/89, p. 19. Also refer to Heinz' view on the Japanese economy as "a capitalist developmental economy" by quoting Chalmers Johnson's term, p. 16.

36. McCormack, SH 7/20/89, p. 19.

37. Taylor, SH 3/5/90, p. 16.

38. Refer to Williams' view, "One can think of SII as the first step to create the world market by eliminating each country's structural barriers to trade and investment through multilateral negotiations." *Daiyamondo* 3/14/92, p. 81.

39. NHK, op. cit., p. 100.

40. For example, see the Hearings of the Subcommittee on the International Trade of the Senate Finance Committee, November 6 and 7, 1989 (HH 11/6-7/89), pp. 1-5; SH 3/5/90, p. 2. Also refer to *CQWR* 11/11/89, pp. 3041-3042.

41. Representatives Stephen J. Solarz and Toby Roth in the Hearings before the Subcommittees on Asian and Pacific Affairs and on International Economic Policy and Trade of the House Foreign Affairs Committee, February 20, 1990 (HH 2/20/90), pp. 2, 4.

42. Representative Sam Gejdenson, HH 2/20/90, p. 3.

43. Hills at a meeting of the Alumni Association on April 3, 1990. *CQWR* 4/7/90, p. 1054.

44. *CQWR* 3/31/90, p. 968.

45. *CQWR* 4/29/90, pp. 1252-1252; 5/15/90, pp. 1333-1334.

46. The departing remarks by President Bush, in *CQWR* 3/10/90, p. 785.

47. Ibid.

48. Baker, testimony before Hearings of the Senate Foreign Relations Committee, February 1, 1990, p. 101.

49. A presidential assistant, *Nikkei* 3/7/90, p. 1.

50. *Asahi* 3/2/90, p. 1.

51. Refer to an U.S. administration official's remarks, "It is necessary to demonstrate concrete results so that congressmen easily understand," *Nikkei* 2/24/90, p. 3.

52. *Business Week* 3/12/90, p. 37.

53. *Asahi* 3/18/90, p. 9.

54. See *Sekai Shūhō* (Rinji Zōkan-gō), March 10, 1990, pp. 26-29. Refer to *Business Week*/Harris Poll in *Business Week* 8/7/89, p. 51.

55. See the departing remarks made by Prime Minister Kaifu, *CQWR* 3/10/90, p. 786. Also refer to the Japanese government's suggestion to create a cabinet level consultation panel to strengthen the U.S.-Japan Security Treaty (*Nikkei* 6/9/90, p. 2).

56. *Asahi* 3/7/90, E.p. 2.

57. *NYT* 3/16/90, p. D2.

58. Ministry of Foreign Affairs, *Diplomatic Bluebook, 1990*, pp. 275, 278.

59. Ibid., p. 2.

60. *Asahi* 3/18/90, p. 9. See also *Business Week* 3/12/90, p. 36; 4/19/90, p. 22.

61. Op. cit. departing remarks of Prime Minister Kaifu, p. 786. See *Business Week* 3/12/90, p. 36.

62. Nothing is more eloquent than Former Vice President of LDP Shin Kanemaru's speech to the members of the Takeshita faction in expressing the uneven power relationship between the U.S. and Japan. "Japan depends on the United States, not the other way around. We owe the United States for the well-being we now enjoy" (*NYT* 3/24/90, p. D8). Also refer to *Nikkei* 3/23/90, p. 2.)

63. Refer to the wording of the departing remarks of Prime Minister Kaifu, op. cit., p. 786.

64. This includes a "secret deal" between the two governments. While the Japanese government asked the U.S. government for policy coordination in the exchange market to stabilize the yen, the U.S. government asked the Japanese government to keep buying Treasury bonds. Kaifu promised to use "administrative influence" on Japanese investors to maintain the level of Treasury bond purchases. This deal was not publicized after the Summit meeting and was revealed later by a U.S. private financial source. See *Asahi* 3/18/90, p. 9.

65. T. Igarashi argues that this was the reason the United States pushed for the GNP ratio expenditure on public works. See op. cit., p. 25.

66. *Asahi* 10/8/89, p. 9.

67. *Tōyō Keizai* 7/7/90, p. 42.

68. The White House, Office of the Press Secretary, "Statement by the President" (June 28, 1990).

69. Fukushima, op. cit., p. 212.

70. NHK, op. cit., pp. 248, 249, 250, 251-252.

71. Clyde V. Prestowitz (1988), *Trading Places*, p. 281.

72. The administration's resistance to managed trade pressure from Congress while at the time using congressional pressure as power leverage was quite apparent in discussions in many SII related hearings. For example, see the discussions of McCormack with Senator Heinz in SH 7/20/90, p. 19.

73. See for example, NHK, op. cit., pp. 250, 292-293, 303.

74. Taylor, HH 4/19/90, p. 109.

75. The White House, Office of the Press Secretary, "Statement by the President" (June 28, 1990).

76. See Williams, *Daiyamondo* 5/23/92, p. 108.

77. A former administration official, telephone interview of 11/13/92.

78. See Yabunaka, op. cit., pp. 189-190; Williams, *Daiyamondo* 5/23/92, p. 108.

79. For example, HH 4/19/90, pp. 139-142.

80. *Nikkei* 4/5/90, p. 5. See also Yabunaka, op. cit., pp. 173-174.

5 Quantification of Interactions between Governments: Pressures and Negotiations

SOME THEORETICAL QUESTIONS AND ASSUMPTIONS FOR THE CONTENT-ANALYSIS OF THE NEWSPAPER INDEXES

The simplest model, the government as a unitary actor, is useful for describing and explaining the larger picture of interactions between the two national governments. The greatest strength of the first model is its simplicity. It has the ability to explain outcomes of international trade negotiations as the results of interactions between nations which are treated like billiard balls, ignoring all other properties of the governments. Indeed, the SII process is generally described and explained by media and scholars alike in terms of "*gaiatsu* politics"; that is, the U.S. government put pressure on the Japanese government to change its economic institutions and business practices and spend some of its budget on public works.

In spite of the fact that laymen and scholars alike commonly use the term *gaiatsu* to describe and explain the larger picture of U.S.-Japanese interactions in international trade policy-making, the *gaiatsu* phenomenon is not well understood analytically. The term *gaiatsu* has become a convenient way to describe and explain changes in the Japanese government's foreign economic policy.[1] Thus, it is taken for granted that *gaiatsu* is analytically understood and there is no need for further exploration among Japanologists and laymen alike. Actually the issue of *gaiatsu* can be considered as broad a problem as the nature of interactions between two national governments, the United States and Japan, in the setting of international trade negotiations. The question of *gaiatsu* phenomenon can be answered as to which government resorted to what kinds of policies with what levels of intensity to bring about particular policy outcomes in international trade negotiations.

Gaiatsu phenomenon is about an issue of "political power," that is, the degree of influence in international trade negotiations. The nation which makes more policy initiations to bring about particular policy outcomes which it wants than the other does is considered to be more "politically powerful" than the latter. Therefore, the former usually prevails over the latter.[2] When a politically powerful country puts pressure on a less politically powerful country, the former usually gets some concessions from the latter. In general, the more pressure the country applies, the more concessions are wrung from the less politically powerful country.

To enhance the predictive power of possible bargaining results in international trade negotiations, one has to deal with two things: first, to identify which country is more politically powerful than the other, and second, to examine the relationship between the levels of pressure the politically powerful country resorts to and the levels of concessions it gains from the less politically powerful country. In this chapter, two kinds of content-analysis on newspaper indexes will be made.

The first content-analysis is the "performative structure" content-analysis. To identify the "politically powerful" government, the "performative structure" of policy initiations between the United States and the Japanese government is examined. Here a "politically powerful" government is defined as the one which pressures by making numerous policy initiations. Therefore, the more the policy initiations in the form of pressure are made, the more the government is politically powerful, by definition. On the other hand, the "less politically powerful" government is the one which responds more to the foreign government policy initiations rather than making its own initiations in trying to influence the other government. The forms of responses are reactive policy accommodation, activated internal policy-making activities of politicians, and the actual initiation or implementation of new domestic policies.

The second content-analysis is the "key-word" content-analysis. Once the politically more powerful government in the bilateral trade negotiations is identified, the next step is to know the relationship between the levels of pressure the politically powerful government resorts to and the levels of concessions it gains from the less politically powerful government. This was achieved by examining the frequency of key words. The frequency of key words with the subject word of either the U.S. government or the Japanese government are assumed to reflect both governments' "concerns" which are expressed to the other government in expecting some policy changes from it. Therefore, the frequency of appearance of certain key words can be used to measure the level of "pressure" which one government resorts to on the other government to do some policy changes.

In order to know which government initiated what kind of policies with what levels of intensity, event-related indexes on the SII (excluding editorials, analyses, and opinions) of newspapers are content-analyzed. The indexes used were 377 indexes under the subtitles *Nichi-bei kankei* (U.S.-Japan relations) and *Nichi-bei bōeki* (U.S.-Japan trade) in the monthly indexes of Japanese *Nihon Keizai Shinbun* and 32 indexes under the subtitle JAPAN in the *Wall Street*

Journal Index from May 1989 to June 1990. Those two papers were chosen because (1) they cover the most detailed stories on international trade and (2) they both are business and finance newspapers and are therefore considered as counterparts. Before proceeding, several theoretical questions should be answered.

Coding of the newspaper-article indexes in this chapter was based on two assumptions: first, that the government is a unitary political actor, and second, article-indexes reflect the "performative structure" of reality. The first assumption is made for research purposes. Here, for example, indexes with persons as subjects are treated as the expressions of the government. Take an index of "The U.S. Trade Representative demands a blueprint with actions by July" (*Nikkei*, 11/6/89). Even though the subject is a person (U.S. Trade Representative Carla Hills), this statement can be treated as an official government statement that makes demands upon the Japanese government in the form of pressure.

The second assumption is potentially more controversial. In making the assumption that the indexes reflect the "performative structure" of reality, one needs to answer three questions: first, how much does media coverage actually reflect the "performative structure" of reality; second, how much do brief newspaper-article indexes reflect the actual event-related articles which generally supply more complicated information;[3] and third, how much do those two newspapers reflect the reality of the world.

The answer to the first question is that with this method, one cannot distinguish "reality" from "media biases." Media biases always exist. Therefore, what our research reveals is actually the assumed "performative structure" of the government which appeared in the media coverage. The examination of media biases toward actual events, including the agenda-setting function of the press, is itself a subject for further investigation.[4] Here, one can simply argue that as long as research results obtained by this coding scheme are not greatly inconsistent with other evidence, these research results can be used as a "substitute" for "actual reality."

As to the second question, it can be said that if one has enough time and resources, content-analyzing actual articles (not indexes) using more detailed coding schemes is a better method to use. Coding actual articles is better since indexes generally contain simplified, even exaggerated information, which ignore the complexity of reported events. But, this necessarily offsets the merit of time and resource saving. Thus, within reasonable time and resource constraints, coding indexes is a good way to make inferences on rough "performative structure" between the governments.

The last question pertains to the issue of the universe versus the sample. Ideally, one can content-analyze the indexes on events from all or several randomly selected popular and elite newspapers, both in English and Japanese, and compare patterns among them. This should be done eventually. Research results here are therefore tentative, simply showing performative-structure patterns that appeared in two newspapers. This research is merely the first step toward more rigorous research. Therefore, research results should not be generalized beyond their scope.

Given those constraints, this way of coding two newspapers indexes, English and Japanese, has merit, since it produces sufficient inferences under reasonable time and resource constraints on the performative structure between the U.S. and the Japanese governments regarding the SII events.

PERFORMATIVE STRUCTURE OF INITIATIONS BETWEEN THE U.S. AND THE JAPANESE GOVERNMENTS

According to the grammatical structure of the sentences, that is, "*who does what to whom*," newspaper indexes are coded into seven major categories such as "pressure," "reactive," "policy-making activities," "policy initiation," "cooperation," "mutual initiation," and "description," along with some sub-categories. For example, the index, "The U.S. Government demands that the Japanese Government repeal the Large Store Law" is coded into "U.S., government, Pressure" (who=U.S. government, does=demand, what=repeal of the Large Store Law, to whom=Japanese government). Refer to Appendix A for a more detailed explanation of the content-analysis method.[5]

Nikkei Indexes

The raw scores of coding from *Nikkei* indexes appear in the Table C.1 in Appendix C. The actual 377 indexes (or articles in the newspaper) are coded into 400 entries because the indexes with two sentences with different subjects and themes are coded into two entries. Since only 5 percent of 377 indexes are coded into two entries, hereafter the words "indexes" are used to mean the raw scores of 400 entries. This will facilitate the intuitive understanding of the results. Analysis results are shown in Tables 5.1, 5.2, and 5.3.

Table 5.1

(1) Among the total 400 indexes, 130 begin with the U.S. subjects, such as "the U.S.," "the U.S. government," "U.S. official," or specific U.S. officials' names. Likewise, 156 indexes are about Japanese related subjects, government or persons. In Table 5.1, U.S. subject indexes (33%) and Japanese subject indexes (38%) are roughly equal. The 92 indexes, that is, 23 percent of the total are the indexes describing events without the subject being either the United States or Japan.

Table 5.1
Percentages of the Seven Categories in All Indexes

	U.S.	Japan	Total
1 Pressure	103 26%	25 6%	128 32%
2 Reactive All	3 1%	33 8%	36 9%
(Positive)	(1) (0%)	(24) (6%)	(25) (6%)
3 Policy Making	8 2%	65 16%	73 18%
4 Policy Initiation	0 0%	13 3%	13 3%
5 Cooperation	16 4%	20 5%	36 9%
(Subtotal)	(130) (33%)	(156) (38%)	(286) (71%)
6 Mutual Initiation			22 6%
7 Description			92 23%
Total			400 100%

Table 5.2
Percentages of the Seven Categories, Excluding Descriptions

	U.S.	Japan	Total
1 Pressure	103 33%	25 8%	128 41%
2 Reactive All	3 1%	33 11%	36 12%
(Positive)	(1) (0%)	(24) (8%)	(25) (8%)
3 Policy Making	8 3%	65 21%	73 24%
4 Policy Initiation	0 0%	13 4%	13 4%
5 Cooperation	16 5%	20 6%	36 11%
(Subtotal)	(130)(42%)	(156)(50%)	(286)(92%)
6 Mutual Initiation			22 7%
Total			308 99%

Table 5.3
Percentages of the Seven Categories from Both Sides (the United States and Japan)

	U.S.	Japan
1 Pressure	103 79%	25 16%
2 Reactive All	3 2%	33 21%
(Positive)	(1) (1%)	(24) (15%)
3 Policy Making	8 8%	65 42%
4 Policy Initiation	0 0%	13 8%
5 Cooperation	16 12%	20 13%
Total	130 99%	156 100%

(2) See total in the table. Among the first (Pressure) to the sixth (Mutual Initiation) categories, Pressure occupies the largest number (32%), which exceeds the sum of Cooperation and Mutual Initiation (15%). This result may reflect the situation of the intense exchange of pressure and counter-pressure, including unilateral demands, criticisms, and suggestions, between the two governments from May 1989 to June 1990.[6]

(3) See the United States and Japan. Among the "U.S." and "Japan" indexes, U.S. pressure is reported as the largest (26%), followed by indexes reporting Japanese internal policy-making process activities (16%).

(4) If one compares between the U.S. government-related indexes (U.S.) and those of the Japanese government (Japan), there is a clear contrast. First, there are more indexes expressing the U.S. pressure on Japan (103), than indexes expressing the Japanese pressure on the United States (25).

(5) Regarding the unilateral actions in the form of either Pressure or Cooperation, the U.S. government initiated more (119 = 103 + 16) than the Japanese government does (45 = 25 + 20).

(6) In the Reactive category, there are more indexes expressing Japanese reaction or responses to the U.S. government policy initiations (33) than the U.S. government's to the Japanese's initiations (3). Among the Reactive indexes, there are 24 Positive for the Japanese government, implying that the Japanese government responded to the U.S. government accommodatingly most of the time, while the U.S. government responded only once out of three times.

(7) On Policy Making, the Japanese internal policy-making processes seem more active (65) than those of the United States (8). Again this could be a reflection of media biases. Since any national newspaper knows more about domestic policy-making processes, it reports them more than a foreign country's policy-making processes.

(8) On Policy Initiation, there are 13 indexes on the Japanese side reporting the implementation of new SII-related policies which include taking policy measures, starting new regulations, and drafting new laws, while there is no index reporting the U.S. government's implementation of SII-related policies. This is an indication that the Japanese government actually implemented some of changes in regulation and policy measures during the one year SII process.

Table 5.2

Table 5.2 shows the percentages of 308 indexes, excluding Description. All of the above-mentioned characteristics are found in Table 5.2. Since Description indexes are excluded and now all indexes have the subject words (the United States, Japan, or the United States and Japan), the percentages of each category in Table 5.2 are the narrowly interpreted percentages for "performative structure" of initiations of both governments.

Table 5.3

(1) Within each side, the United States-related indexes (U.S.) report more about Pressure (79%), while Japanese-related indexes (Japan) report more about the domestic policy making process (42%).

(2) It is interesting to note that among the Japan-related indexes the second largest number (21%) is Reactive, the Japanese reaction to the U.S. initiations. Although differences are slight, the number for Japanese Reactive (21%) is larger than Pressure (16%), which is also larger than Cooperation (13%). This could be an indication that the Japanese government was actually more busy responding to the U.S. policy initiatives than making its own policy initiations to be presented to the U.S. government.

Table 5.4

Even within the pressure category, 76% of Japanese acts of pressure are made in the form of "Suggestions," while only 52% of U.S. pressure are made in the form of "Suggestions," with 38% in the form of "Demand."[7] With the analysis in Table 5.2, this can be interpreted as the U.S. government resorting to more pressure on the Japanese government than the Japanese government did on the U.S. government.

Table 5.4
Percentages of Demand, Criticism, and Suggestion with the Subject the United States or Japan in Pressure in *Nikkei* Indexes

	U.S.	Japan
Demand	39 38%	4 16%
Criticism	10 10%	2 8%
Suggestion	54 52%	19 76%
Total	103 100%	25 100%

Wall Street Journal **Indexes**

For comparison, 32 SII event-related indexes from the *Wall Street Journal* (*WSJ*) were content-analyzed. The 32 indexes were coded into 34 entries. See Table C.2 in Appendix C. There are some differences as well as similarities in the index distribution patterns between the two papers. In my view, some differences are results of different concerns between the U.S. and the Japanese newspapers.

Table 5.5

(1) See the total in the Table 5.5. Among seven categories, Description is the largest (32%). The sum of Cooperation and Mutual Initiation is (44%), while Pressure is (15%). Although Reactive is the largest among six categories (excluding Description), the distribution of categories is more even than that of *Nikkei*, in which the Pressure category is excessively large.

(2) See the United States and Japan. Reactive, that is, the indexes reporting Japanese responses is the largest (18%), followed by the indexes reporting U.S. pressure (12%). This result seems to reflect the U.S. newspaper's concern: Japanese responses rather than its own government pressure.

(3) Other traits are similar to those in the Nikkei index. There are more indexes expressing U.S. pressure on Japan (4) than indexes expressing Japanese pressure on the U.S. (1).

(4) Regarding the unilateral actions in the form of either Pressure or Cooperation, the U.S. government initiated more (6 = 4 + 2) than the Japanese government did (3 = 1 + 2). Here the "initiation ratio" between the United States and Japanese is 2:1. In other words, in the *WSJ* case, the U.S. government initiated unilateral actions 66.6 percent of the time (i.e., 6/9), while in the *Nikkei* case, 72.5 percent of the time (i.e., 119/164). Although one does not have to stick with the precise number, the fact that indexes note that the United States makes some kind of policy moves in U.S.-Japanese bilateral trade negotiations roughly 70 percent of the time does not contradict the observations already made by many.

(5) In the Reactive category, there are more indexes expressing Japanese reaction or responses to the U.S. government policy initiatives (6) than the U.S. government's to the Japanese government (0). Among the indexes in the Reactive category, the Japanese government responded to the U.S. government accommodatingly most of the time (5 out of 6 times).

(6) On Policy Making, there is an index reporting Japanese internal policy-making processes, while there is no index regarding the U.S. policy-making.

(7) On Policy Initiation, there are few indexes reporting Japanese policy implementation, while no indexes reporting U.S. policy implementation. This result is the same as that of *Nikkei*.

Table 5.5
Percentages of the Seven Categories in All Indexes

	U.S.	Japan	Total
1 Pressure	4 12%	1 3%	5 15%
2 Reactive All	0 0%	6 18%	6 18%
(Positive)	(0) (0%)	(5) (15%)	(5) (15%)
3 Policy Making	0 0%	1 3%	1 3%
4 Policy Initiation	0 0%	3 9%	3 9%
5 Cooperation	2 6%	2 6%	4 12%
(Subtotal)	(6) (18%)	(13) (39%)	(19) (57%)
6 Mutual Initiation			4 12%
7 Description			11 32%
Total			34 101%

Table 5.6
Percentages of the Seven Categories, Excluding Descriptions

	U.S.	Japan	Total
1 Pressure	4 17%	1 4%	5 22%
2 Reactive All	0 0%	6 26%	6 26%
(Positive)	(0) (0%)	(5) (22%)	(5) (22%)
3 Policy Making	0 0%	1 4%	1 4%
4 Policy Initiation	0 0%	3 13%	3 13%
5 Cooperation	2 9%	2 9%	4 17%
(Subtotal)	(6) (26%)	(13) (57%)	(19) (83%)
6 Mutual Initiation			4 17%
Total			23 99%

Table 5.7
Percentages of the Seven Categories from Both Sides (the United States and Japan)

	U.S.	Japan
1 Pressure	4 67%	1 8%
2 Reactive All	0 0%	6 46%
(Positive)	(0) (0%)	(5) (38%)
3 Policy Making	0 0%	1 8%
4 Policy Initiation	0 0%	3 23%
5 Cooperation	2 33%	2 15%
Total	6 100%	13 100%

Table 5.6

Table 5.6 shows the percentages of 23 indexes, excluding Description. All of the above-mentioned characteristics also are found in Table 5.6. Since Description indexes are excluded and now all indexes have the subject words (the United States, Japan, or the United States and Japan), the percentages of each category in Table 5.6 are the narrowly interpreted percentages for "performative structure" of initiations of both governments which appear in the *Wall Street Journal* (*WSJ*).

Table 5.7

(1) Within each side, the United States-related indexes report more about Pressure (67%) than other categories. This result is similar to that of *Nikkei* (79%). While U.S.-related indexes in the *WSJ* have a large number for Cooperation (33%), *Nikkei* has a relatively low number of Cooperation (12%). The reason for this is that *Nikkei* reported several Congressional Hearings. Indexes on these Hearings are coded into Policy Making in the United States or U.S. responses to the Japanese suggestions, that is, Reactive. Thus, the distribution of indexes is more even in *Nikkei* than in the *WSJ*. However, both *Nikkei* and the *WSJ* have a distribution which is polarized; both Pressure and Cooperation have large numbers.

(2) Within the Japan-related indexes, Reactive is the largest (46%), followed by Policy Initiation (23%), which seems a reflection of the U.S. paper's concern: how the Japanese government responded to the U.S. demands and make policy changes.

SIMILARITIES IN CODING RESULTS OF *NIKKEI* AND THE *WSJ*

As seen above, there are different distribution-patterns between *Nikkei* indexes and *WSJ* indexes. However, these differences seem to be a result of the Japanese newspaper's and U.S. newspaper's different concerns. Naturally, the Japanese newspaper is more concerned about U.S. pressure and the internal policy-making process as a result of U.S. pressure; the U.S. newspaper is more concerned about Japanese government responses and actual policy changes than its own government's pressure on the Japanese government or policy changes in the United States. Therefore, the differences in the distribution patterns of the indexes do not necessarily contradict each other.

On the other hand, the two papers share important features in the index distribution: (1) the ratio of unilateral policy initiation (Pressure and Cooperation) between the U.S. government and the Japanese government is 2:1; (2) the U.S. government put pressure on the Japanese government more than the Japanese government did on the U.S. government; (3) the Japanese government responded more to the U.S. government's initiations than the U.S. government did to the Japanese government's; (4) The Japanese internal policy-making process regarding the SII was more active than that of the U.S. government; and (5) The Japanese government actually implemented more policies than the U.S. government did during the one-year SII process.

Tables 5.8, 5.9, and 5.10

The most interesting thing is the ratios between the U.S. government-related indexes and the Japanese government-related indexes in each category. First see Table 5.8. Within Pressure, indexes are subcoded into three types, Demand, Criticism, or Suggestion, depending on the type of verbs which presumably reflect different levels of pressures. Since the *WSJ* has only 5 indexes, the distribution of those three subcategories are somewhat different between *Nikkei* and the *WSJ*.

However, look at Tables 5.9 and 5.10. The total number of indexes in the Pressure category in *Nikkei* are 103 (U.S. side) and 25 (Japanese side); therefore, the ratio is about 80:20, which is the exact ratio for the same category in the *WSJ*. The ratios between U.S. and Japanese subject indexes for other categories are also similar between two papers. The ratio for Reactive in *Nikkei* is 9:92, while 0:100 in the *WSJ*; Positive response in *Nikkei* is 4:96, while 0:100 in the *WSJ*; Policy Making, 11:89 to 0:100; Policy Initiation, 0:100 to 0:100; Cooperation, 44:56 to 50:50. This result is encouraging since it seems to provide a strong support for this method of content-analysis. Although the total numbers of the coded indexes are vastly different, the ratio of initiatives, of pressure and of responses between the U.S. government and the Japanese government are very similar. If the same method is applied to several Japanese and English newspapers and similar results are obtained, then it can be said that this way of content analysis produces credible results to measure the "performative structure" (or simply "interaction relationship") portrayal of the two governments in the media. Then, as long as the results of content analysis are consistent with evidence from other sources, one could use these results as a substitute for the political power relations ratio. For example, it can be said that the pressure ratio between the U.S. government and the Japanese government is 80:20, or, the reactive ratio between two governments is 10:90. This indicator could be used to "predict" overall negotiation results when two governments with uneven political power meet in international trade negotiations. In the SII process, most concessions resulting in actual changes in regulations and budget policy were made by the Japanese government because of uneven political power relations.

Table 5.8
Percentages of Demand, Criticism, and Suggestion with the Subject the United States or Japan in the *Nikkei* Indexes and the *Wall Street Journal* Indexes

| | Nikkei | | : | Wall Street Journal | |
	U.S.	Japan	:	U.S.	Japan
Demand	39 38%	4 16%	:	0 0%	0 0%
Criticism	10 10%	2 8%	:	2 50%	1 100%
Suggestion	54 52%	19 76%	:	2 50%	0 0%
Total	103 100%	25 100%	:	4 100%	1 100%

Table 5.9
The Number of Indexes of Seven Categories with the Subject the United States or Japan, and Ratios between Them in the *Nikkei* Indexes

	U.S.	Japan	Ratio
1 Pressure	103	25	80:20
2 Reactive All	3	33	9:92
(Positive)	(1)	(24)	(4:96)
3 Policy Making	8	65	11:89
4 Policy Initiation	0	13	0:100
5 Cooperation	16	20	44:56
Total	130	156	45:55

Table 5.10
The Number of Indexes of Seven Categories with the Subject the United States or Japan, and Ratios between Them in the *Wall Street Journal* Indexes

	U.S.	Japan	Ratio
1 Pressure	4	1	80:20
2 Reactive All	0	6	0:100
(Positive)	(0)	(5)	(0:100)
3 Policy Making	0	1	0:100
4 Policy Initiation	0	3	0:100
5 Cooperation	2	2	50:50
Total	6	13	32:68

THE RELATION BETWEEN U.S. PRESSURE AND THE LEVEL OF JAPANESE CONCESSIONS IN FIVE ISSUE AREAS

The merit of the first model is that it treats the government as a single entity, ignoring all other aspects of the government. Thus, this model is useful for empirical research to investigate the nature of interactions between the national governments. This model tells us what happens when two nations meet in international negotiations. With other things being equal, the politically powerful government usually prevails over the less politically powerful government. A corollary of the argument is that when the politically powerful government puts pressure on the less politically powerful government, the level of concessions increases or decreases, depending on the level of pressure. That is, the more pressure the politically powerful government puts on the less politically powerful government, the more concessions it gets from the latter. Therefore, the different level of concessions in different issue areas depends on how much pressure the dominant nation puts on the other government in the issue areas. This theory assumes that there is a direct causal relationship between the level of pressure and the level of concessions obtained from other governments. Although the model with this assumption is very simple, it is useful for certain research purposes.

One of the important questions in the SII process is whether or not the U.S. government put the same level of pressure on the Japanese government, with the expectation of acquiring the same level of concessions in the five issue areas, saving-investment patterns, the distribution system, land-use policy, exclusionary business practices, and keiretsu. Schoppa asserts that the U.S. government put the same level of pressure on all the issue areas with the same level of priority. "All of these areas were given essentially equal billing in this Bush administration initiative linked to the aggressive 'Super 301' provision of the 1988 Omnibus Trade and Competitiveness Act."[8]

His assertion is not supported for several reasons. First of all, the U.S. government did not put "equal billing" on all SII issue areas. Certainly, the administration officials said in the congressional hearings, that these six areas (the five issue areas which are under examination here and the pricing mechanism) should be considered as a package with the same level of importance.[9] This is the reason why the final report contains policy measures covering all six issue areas. However, although the U.S. government *initially* did not or could not put "priority" on any particular issue areas, as a matter of fact it pursued specific negotiation items in some issue areas by "shifting emphasis" (Taylor).[10] As the SII negotiation proceeded, the U.S. government narrowed down the 240-item list into a specific eighteen-item list for an interim agreement, and a twenty-five-item list for a final agreement and handed in them to the Japanese government.[11] The U.S. government asked the Japanese government for the specific concessions in specific issue areas. Consequently, the Japanese government understood what the U.S. government wanted most.[12]

With respect to the pressure level, Schoppa also asserts that "the U.S. brought similar pressure to bear on Japan in all five cases—in all cases holding the implicit threat of Super 301 over the heads of the Japanese."[13] First, what is meant by an "implicit threat of Super 301" is not clear. Certainly, some congressmen and officials in USTR thought the Japanese distribution system, keiretsu, and exclusionary business practices should be negotiated under the Super 301.[14] However, it was reported that Carla Hills was against the idea of having a negotiation on the distribution system under Super 301, which consequently became the policy of the USTR.[15] Also, no government officials' statements (including those of congressmen) in congressional hearings, administration documents, and newspaper articles which stated that the saving-investment issue and land policy should be negotiated under the Super 301, is found.[16]

Second, careful reading of newspaper articles and other documents clearly suggests that the U.S. government as a whole did not put "similar pressure" on the Japanese government in all five areas. For example, in the second SII meeting, McCormack said, "raising the public spending level and promoting infrastructure building is the most important issue in the SII."[17] McCormack, Dallara, and Ambassador Michael H. Armacost repeatedly reminded Japanese officials that the goal of the SII was "to reduce the U.S.-Japan trade deficit."[18] In order to reduce the trade deficit, macroeconomic measures, that is, the Japanese government spending on public works to fill the gap between domestic savings and investment, should be pursued. This is the reason why the U.S. negotiation team persistently pushed the Japanese government in the saving and investment patterns area until the final moment.   According to Yabunaka, the Large Store Law became "so symbolic an issue that the result of SII is judged based on the outcome of that Law" by the time of an Interim Report.[19] Toward the Final Report, the "greatest focus was put on the total amount of budget for the public investment ten-year plan."[20] The strong evidence on the different levels of the U.S. concerns and goals is also found in the comments of the U.S. delegates in the Interim Report. In the comments, the U.S. delegation stated that a "principal objective of the SII talks" was "the reduction of trade imbalances and current account imbalances," along with the detailed assessment of the Japanese concessions and suggestions on further necessary actions in six areas.[21]

Later, when specifically asked if the U.S. government put the same level of pressure on five issue areas, Williams said no. He said the U.S. government put *the highest level of pressure* on the saving and investment patterns area, next on the distribution system and on exclusionary business practices, and then land policy and keiretsu. In order to give some idea of the levels of U.S. pressure, Williams suggested the U.S. pressure levels were 10 for the saving-investment patterns, 9 for the distribution system and the exclusionary business practices, and 6 to 7 for the land use and the keiretsu.[22]

Based on all available evidence, the following hypothesis is suggested: the U.S. government put different levels of pressure on the Japanese government in five issue areas, that is, high-level pressure on the saving-investment patterns, medium-level pressure on the distribution system and the exclusionary business practices, and low-level pressure on the land policy and keiretsu. Although there is much evidence that the U.S. government did not put the same level of pressure on five issue areas, let us begin the investigation by examining the extent of U.S. pressure on the Japanese government. The 153 indexes with explicit key words out of total 377 event indexes of *Nikkei* were content-analyzed. The first model is useful for this research. Here the initial assumption is that the intensity of the U.S. concerns, therefore of U.S. pressure is reflected in the amount of newspaper coverage.[23] (For the details of the coding method, see Appendix B.)

Coding Results of Key-Word Content-Analysis

Table C.1 and Table 5.11

(1) First see Table C.1 in Appendix C. Generally, the large numbers of indexes (articles) appear in the months in which the formal SII meetings were held, September and November 1989 and February, April, and June 1990. March and June 1990 have the highest numbers of coverage; in the former month the Interim Report was prepared and in the latter month the Final Report was issued.

See Table 5.11 and compare it with Table C.1. The same patterns are found in Table 5.11, except during September 1989. The suspected reason for the low numbers in September in Table 5.11 is that in the first month in which the SII talks started, both the U.S. and Japanese teams discussed the entire range of the whole SII agenda without specifically mentioning particular issue areas, reflecting the situation in which neither side set any priorities or emphases.

Table 5.11

(2) Except for the above-mentioned point, the key-word coding method reveals visible patterns of shifting focuses throughout the SII, which match the evidence from other sources, such as the three meeting records of the SII and T. Igarashi's observation.[24] From September 1989 to January 1990, the SII had been exchanging ideas on structural problems and desirable policy changes to those problems in both countries. Thus, the numbers of the key-word indexes are generally low. In the third meeting of February 22-23, 1990, the first concrete "U.S. demands" were presented; after that the number of key-word indexes increased.

Table 5.11
Coded Result of All *Nikkei* Indexes with the Key-Words of Issue Areas (May 1989-June 1990)

		5	6	7	8	9	10	11	12	1	2	3	4	5	6	Total	%
Public Works	U.S.			1	1			1			2	4	4	2	11	26	
Spending	Japan							1			1	7	2		11	22	
	Misc.					1					2		1	2	9	15	
	Subtotal	0	0	1	1	1	0	2	0	0	5	11	7	4	31	63	41%
Land Use	U.S.			1	1	1		1								4	
	Japan				1	2										3	
	Misc.					1						2			2	5	
	Subtotal	0	0	1	2	4	0	1	0	0	0	2	0	0	2	12	8%
Distribution	U.S.	1	2		1		1	1			1	4	3			14	
System	Japan				1							5	8			14	
	Misc.	1				1						2	1		2	7	
	Subtotal	2	2	0	2	1	1	1	0	0	1	11	12	0	2	35	23%
Exclusionary	U.S.	1	2		2			3	1			1	1			11	
Business	Japan			1			1		2		1	1				6	
Practices	Misc.											2	1		2	5	
	Subtotal	1	2	1	2	0	1	3	3	0	1	4	2	0	2	22	14%
Keiretsu	U.S.	1	1	1	1			2				1	1			8	
	Japan														1	1	
	Misc.											1			1	2	
	Subtotal	1	1	1	1	0	0	2	0	0	0	2	1	0	2	11	7%
Price	U.S.							2								2	
Differences	Japan							1								1	
	Misc.		2				1	2			1	1				7	
	Subtotal	0	2	0	0	0	1	5	0	0	1	1	0	0	0	10	7%
Total		4	7	4	8	6	3	14	3	0	8	31	22	4	39	153	100%

Number of Articles: Total 153; U.S. 65; Japan 47

The pattern of key-word indexes reflect the patterns of concerns or contentions as well. The U.S. government did not put a highly visible emphasis on public works spending from May 1989 to January 1990.[25] Then the issue became one of the major U.S. demands in the February meeting. After that, the issue received a great deal of attention, and finally reached the highest point in June 1990, proving to be "the most contentious issue of the negotiation."[26]

The land policy issue, which is generally referred to as the "land-use" issue in the Japanese media, was presented by the U.S. government in the first and the second meetings; and was given a low profile afterward.[27] The distribution system indexes are generally distributed over the entire period. The issue was one of the three most contentious ones. The State Department strongly pushed the issue. And it was a major concern for USTR at the time of the 1989 Super 301 designation. Furthermore, Hills and Williams repeatedly mentioned the Japanese distribution system as a trade barrier throughout the SII process. The issue was presented as one of the major U.S. demands in the February meeting and became the important issue strongly pushed by the U.S. government as it approached an interim agreement. The repeal of the Large Store Law became the much politicized issue in Japan during the time of making an interim agreement. This situation is reflected in the large numbers of indexes in the Distribution System in March and April 1990.

In addition to the Japanese distribution system, the issue of exclusionary business practices was a major concern for USTR, an issue which was repeatedly presented by USTR officials at the SII meetings. Thus, Exclusionary Business Practices spread over the period. The issue was among the three major U.S. demands in the February meeting, and therefore the numbers in the indexes increased in March 1990.

Although the U.S. government initially had as strong a concern about keiretsu as other issues and presented it in the first three meetings, it did not pursue it with the same emphasis as other major issues. The keiretsu issue became obscured as a negotiation topic because of the issue's complexity, the initial U.S. confusion, and the Japanese government's lack of interest in discussing the issue.[28] Again, this situation is reflected in Table 5.11.

In the first and the second meetings, the pricing mechanism issue (referred to as the "price differences" issue in Japan), was well discussed. The United States and the Japanese agreed to a joint research project but had a serious disagreement on how to publish and interpret the research results. But afterward, it lost its status as an independent theme to realize institutional changes and meaningful economic effects. Thus, after November, there were only a few Price Differences indexes.[29]

There is another interesting point in the distribution patterns of the issue area-related indexes. The subtotals for each issue area are roughly the same by February 1990, with a possible exception for the keiretsu. The subtotals are 10 for Public Works Spending (saving and investment patterns), 8 for Land Use, 10 for Distribution, 14 for Exclusionary Business Practices, 9 for Price

Differences, and 6 for keiretsu.   This seems to indicate that the U.S. government started the SII with the same level of concern for all six issue areas, that overall the same level of concern was held by the time the third meeting was held, although a smaller number for the keiretsu issue might suggest that the issue was already less pursued by the U.S. government by that time. When the "real negotiation" for an interim agreement started after the Bush-Kaifu summit meeting of March 2 and 3, the U.S. government began to discriminate among the issues by putting more pressure on saving-investment patterns, the distribution system, and exclusionary business practices.[30]

As seen above, the key-word coding provides a general map of shifting major "emphasis," and contentious issues throughout the SII process. Since it was the U.S. government that pointed out problems in these issue areas and persistently asked the Japanese government for "action," one can reasonably assume that the extent of the media coverage can be used as indicators for the level of overall U.S. pressure.

(3) Out of 153 indexes, the largest number is about public works spending (41%), followed by the distribution system (23%), exclusionary business practices (14%), with the other three areas having similar low levels (7%-8%). This result demonstrates that the first three issue areas were major points of concern in making SII agreements, with relatively low emphasis on the last three issues. Indeed, according to Williams, "the U.S. wanted to avoid too much involvement in this complicated political issue [i.e., the land policy] . . . and remained simply to suggest a constructive opinion from a viewpoint of average citizen."[31]   As to the keiretsu issue, "the content of the issue was very much changed between the initial pointing out and the time of making concrete suggestions."[32]   Eventually, the United States dropped its demand of releasing the cross-shareld stocks of big companies because "it is too much interfering."[33]

Table 5.12 and Table 5.13

(4) The number of indexes with the subject "the U.S. government," "U.S. officials," or the names of U.S. officials can be narrowly interpreted as the level of U.S. concern or pressure, because these indexes explicitly express U.S. concerns or demands in such sentences as "the U.S. demands that the Japanese government spend 10 percent of GNP for public works over ten years." See Table 5.12 and Table 5.13. The overall distribution of indexes with either the subject of U.S. or Japan is similar to that of all indexes. Also, the percentages of the three major areas of all indexes and those of indexes with the subject "U.S." are similar to each other. That is, among all indexes, 41 percent are for public works spending; 23 percent are for the distribution system; and 14 percent are for exclusionary business practices, while among the U.S. subject indexes, these percentages are 40, 22, and 17, respectively. If one uses these percentages for the U.S. subject indexes as indicators for the extent of the U.S.

Table 5.12
Percentages of Six Issue Areas in All *Nikkei* Key-Word Indexes, in the U.S. Subject Indexes, and in the Japanese Subject Indexes

	Public Works Spending	Land Use	Distri-bution System	Exclusio-nary Business Practices	Keiretsu	Price Diff.	Total
All	41	8	23	14	7	7	100%
U.S.	40	6	22	17	12	3	(100%)
Japan	47	6	30	13	2	2	(100%)

Table 5.13
Ordered Percentages of Six Issue Areas in All *Nikkei* Key-Word Indexes, in the U.S. Subject Indexes, and in the Japanese Subject Indexes

All		U.S.		Japan	
P.W.Spending	41	P.W.Spending	40	P.W.Spending	47
Distribution	23	Distribution	22	Distribution	30
Exclusionary	14	Exclusionary	17	Exclusionary	13
Land Use	8	Keiretsu	12	Land Use	6
Keiretsu	7	Land Use	6	Keiretsu	2
Price Diff.	7	Price Diff.	3	Price Diff.	2
Total	100%		(100%)		(100%)

concerns or pressure in the six SII issue areas, then one can make an inference that the U.S. government put most pressure on the public works spending issue, next on the distribution system and on exclusionary business practices (with slightly more on the distribution system), and then on keiretsu and on land policy (but more on keiretsu than land policy), and finally on pricing mechanism. Allowing a margin of error, these results seem to reflect well the level of the U.S. concerns and consequent pressure, which can be supported by evidence from the other sources.[34]

(5) The coding results also reveal several interesting points. Since these six issues were suggested by the U.S. government, and the Japanese government was asked to make changes, the indexes with the subject "the Japanese government" or the names of Japanese officials are interpreted as Japanese-side responses to the U.S. demands. Tables 5.12 and 5.13 show that generally, the

numbers of Japanese subject indexes are almost the same as those with the U.S. subject in the issue areas, suggesting that the similar level of importance was placed on the issues by both governments. However, there are more indexes with the subject "Japan" than the subject "the United States" in Public Works Spending and the Distribution System. This seems to suggest that the two issues were much politicized and many political actors were involved in these two issues in Japan, so that as a consequence, the Japanese subject indexes exceed the U.S.subject indexes.

In contrast, the number of Japanese subject indexes in Exclusionary Business Practices is less than that of U.S. subject indexes, suggesting that the Japanese government responded less to the U.S. government. The most interesting result concerns the keiretsu issue. The difference between the U.S. subject numbers and the Japanese subject numbers is the largest in keiretsu, 10 points. This seems to suggest that the U.S. side had relatively strong concern about keiretsu (perhaps the same as about the exclusionary business practices especially in the earlier stages of the SII),[35] but the Japanese government did not have much interest in the keiretsu issue for their own reasons; and therefore, it responded less to the U.S. request. Consequently, the U.S. government did not pursue further the keiretsu issue.[36] This may be interpreted as a "responsiveness gap" between the U.S. government and the Japanese government in our scheme from the viewpoint of the first model.[37] In the paradigm of the first model, where the different degrees of "responsiveness" or "receptivity" between the governments exists, there are different degrees of effectiveness of pressure. The reason why the Japanese government was less responsive to the U.S. pressure is often explained as a "tactical error" in effectively using pressure.[38]

In short, Tables 5.12 and 5.13 contain several pieces of information: First, they show the level of U.S. concerns and consequent pressure and the level of Japanese concerns. Second, they show that the level of U.S. concerns and the level of Japanese responses are almost same. Due to the strong U.S. concerns, and consequently pressure, the Japanese government responded to the U.S. concerns with almost the same level of intensity. Third, when there is a large difference between the level of U.S. concerns and that of the Japanese responses, this difference could be interpreted as a "responsiveness gap." Because of the "responsiveness gap" between them, the pressure from the United States did not force concessions from the Japanese government.

Table 5.14 and Table 5.15

(6) For comparison, the indexes in the *Wall Street Journal* were content-analyzed. But the results are not as telling as those of Table 5.8 deriving from *Nikkei* indexes, because of the small sample size of only 13. The numbers for Public Works Spending and the Distribution System are still two large numbers, but the ranking is reversed because of the strong U.S. concern about the opening of a Toys R Us store in Japan. There are no indexes with the explicit key-word,

Table 5.14
Coded Result of All *Wall Street Journal* Indexes with the Key-Words of Issue Areas (May 1989-June 1990)

		5 6 7 8 9 10 11 12 1 2 3 4 5 6	Total	%
Public Works	U.S.	1	1	
Spending	Japan	1 1	2	
	Misc.	1	1	
	Subtotal	0 0 0 0 2 0 0 0 0 0 0 0 0 2	4	31%
Land Use	U.S.		0	
	Japan		0	
	Misc.		0	
	Subtotal	0 0 0 0 0 0 0 0 0 0 0 0 0 0	0	0%
Distribution	U.S.		0	
System	Japan	3 1	4	
	Misc.	1 1	2	
	Subtotal	0 1 0 0 0 0 0 0 0 1 3 1 0 0	6	46%
Exclusionary	U.S.		0	
Business	Japan		0	
Practices	Misc.		0	
	Subtotal	0 0 0 0 0 0 0 0 0 0 0 0 0 0	0	0%
Keiretsu	U.S.		0	
	Japan		0	
	Misc.	1	1	
	Subtotal	0 0 0 0 0 0 0 0 0 0 1 0 0 0	1	8%
Price	U.S.		0	
Differences	Japan	1	1	
	Misc.	1	1	
	Subtotal	0 0 0 0 0 0 1 0 0 1 0 0 0 0	2	15%
Total		0 1 0 0 2 0 1 0 0 2 4 1 0 2	13	100%

Number of Articles: Total 13; U.S. 1; Japan 7

Table 5.15
Percentages of Six Issue Areas in All *Wall Street Journal* Key-Word Indexes in the U.S. Subject Indexes, and in the Japanese Subject Indexes

	Public Works Spending	Land Use	Distri- bution System	Exclusio- nary Business Practices	Keiretsu	Price Diff.	Total
All	31	0	46	0	8	15	100%
U.S.	100	0	0	0	0	0	(100%)
Japan	29	0	57	0	0	14	(100%)

"exclusionary business practices." Because of U.S. interest in the price differ-ence issue in Japan, which became one of the symbolic issues about the closed nature of the Japanese market, Price Differences counts for 15 percent.[39] Table 5.15 shows the distribution of all key-word indexes, that of the U.S. subject indexes, and that of the Japan subject indexes. Since there is only one index with the subject of the United States, Public Work Spending counts for 100%, while the Japan subject indexes are more evenly distributed.

Summary of the Findings

The results of the content-analysis support the proposition that the U.S. government put high-level pressure on the saving-investment issue, medium-level pressure on the distribution system and on exclusionary business practices, and low level pressure on the land use policy and keiretsu.[40]

The levels of U.S. pressure generally match the levels of Japanese concessions in the SII agreements and explain well the outcomes of trade negotiation in the three issue areas: high level pressure yielded the high level concessions in the saving-investment patterns; medium level pressure yielded the medium level concessions in the distribution system, and low level pressure yielded the low level concessions in the keiretsu area.

However, the negotiation outcomes in the exclusionary business practices and land policy areas do not seem to be straightforwardly explained by the pressure level. Regarding the exclusionary business practices area, two interpretations are possible. Although the levels of pressure for the distribution system and the exclusionary business practices are considered to be medium, the U.S. government actually put somewhat more pressure on the distribution system than on the exclusionary business practices. The data reflect these differences.

Consequently, the concession level in the distribution system is higher than that in the exclusionary business practices.

Another interpretation is that in spite of the similar level of medium U.S. pressure on the distribution system and the exclusionary business practices, the Japanese government made more concessions in the former (medium level), and less concessions in the latter (low level).[41] Why was this true? The answer should be found in other factors that are more complex than a simple level of pressure.

As to the land policy, the opposite is the case. In spite of the low level U.S. pressure on the Japanese government in the land policy issue area, why was the level of concession medium? The answers to both of these questions will be found in the following chapters.

IMPLICATIONS OF THE FIRST MODEL

The implication of the first model with our case study and content-analysis is sobering. First, in spite of all sorts of discourse in modern economics, there is no such thing as "world market" in the same sense that the integrated market exists within the national boundary in which the free movements of capital, goods, and labor with the welfare compensation mechanism are guaranteed. In the "world market," since the movement of labor is limited and a welfare compensation mechanism is lacking, negative consequences of market forces have to be managed by political bargaining between the national governments. Those negative consequences include trade imbalances, current account imbalances, unemployment, accelerated decline of old industries without sufficient adjustment time, and uneven growth. In Nakatani's expression, "To correct those imbalances due to free economic competition, there was no other way than to control the free competition [between two nations i.e., the United States and Japan]."[42] The first model exposes theoretical shortcomings of modern economics. It reveals that the "world market" is more of a theoretical construct than an empirical fact. In the world economy, restoring economic balances is made by political bargaining from time to time. In the political bargaining to remedy negative consequences of market forces, the stronger states ("politically powerful states" in our scheme) generally prevail over the weaker states in concession making.

Second, from the viewpoint of the first model, the SII is a means for the stronger state (the United States) to compel the Japanese government to implement its pledges and agreements with other G-7 nations. This notion is found in the remarks of both U.S. and Japanese officials. According to Sadayuki Hayashi, general director of the Economic Bureau of MFA, the remedies to correct the U.S.-Japan bilateral trade deficit were already written in the communique of the OECD ministerial meeting and G-7 Economic Summit: surplus countries, such as Japan, need to expand domestic demand and promote structural adjustment and market liberalization, while deficit countries, such as the United States, need to reduce the budget deficit and strengthen domestic production. However, the problem is that both countries are doubtful as to whether or not the other country will actually implement these policies. The SII emerged in such a situation for the United States and Japan.[43] According to David C. Mulford, under secretary of the Treasury Department, the recognized policies of the G-7 Economic Summit and Finance Ministers and the Governors of Central Banks were to raise savings in the United States, expand domestic demand in Germany, and increase domestic consumption and investment in Japan. Therefore, the U.S. government asked the Japanese government to set the target for GNP ratio public works spending.[44]

Because the international system lacks an enforcement mechanism, hegemon or the leading state, the U.S. government, forced the Japanese government to spend more money for public works so that bilateral trade and current account imbalances would be reduced and the global balance restored. The United States forced the Japanese government to "normalize" some procedures and the coordination processing period in the Large Store Law, which became too perverted to satisfy even a minimum sense of fairness, in addition to need to run the smooth operation of the internationally connected markets.[45] Also the Japanese government had to strengthen its antitrust law, which was considered lax according to the international standard of industrialized nations.[46] As a matter of fact, "normalization of operational procedure of the LSL," was Prime Minister Takeshita's pledge at the Toronto Summit in June, 1988.[47] Changing the Japanese economic structure from an export-oriented to a domestic-demand-led one had also been a Japanese international pledge since the Maekawa Report of 1986.[48] Japan's weak antitrust law had long been criticized by other industrialized countries.[49]

The point is that since the world system lacks central authority, international rules of economic activities are still developing, and the world market is imperfect, the adjustment of economic imbalances is done through political bargaining between national governments. Internal structural changes are made by the coercive actions of the stronger state. An international antitrust law regime is forcibly created by a policy initiation of the leading state.

The multilateral trade regime is also strengthened through the actions of the leading state. For example, in the fall of 1988, the U.S. government recognized that the implementation of the nine codes of the Tokyo Round, reducing nontariff barriers, had been "partially successful." However, the organization and enforcement powers of GATT were weak and nations tended to "selectively observe or stretch the GATT rules."[50] The U.S. government's efforts in the subsequent years were meant to remedy precisely those problems. In Hills' view, the U.S. administration's job was to reconcile the multilateral goals (strengthening and expanding the rules of the international trading regime) with bilateral objectives (advancing the U.S. trade interests) through a balanced mix of multilateral, bilateral, and unilateral means. In cases where multilateral rules are ineffective or nonexistent, unilateral action may be necessary to protect U.S. trade interests as well as to strengthen the rules of the multilateral trading system. Here, the U.S. interest as a leading nation coincides with the interests of the international system as a whole, since the United States acts as "a surgeon using a scalpel to remove these trade barriers and promote a healthier trading system."[51] Therefore, such policies as strengthening the GATT system into the World Trade Organization, coercively increasing Japan's public works spending, changing the Large Store Law, and creating an international antitrust regime through the SII negotiation, are no coincidence. From the viewpoint of the first model, they are all interpreted as part of the actions of the leading state to strengthen the world trading regime and restore a global economic balance.

NOTES

1. For example, see Kusano (1990), "kōzō kyōgi go no nichi-bei kankei." Takenaka, op. cit., pp. 286-287. The articles of *Nikkei* 4/3/90, p. 2; 4/13/90, p. 1.

2. An economically and militarily powerful nation may or may not be a politically powerful nation.

3. *Nikkei* indexes are copies of actual headlines which appeared in the paper, while the *Wall Street Journal* indexes are brief summaries of the articles.

4. Articles of *Nikkei* and the *Wall Street Journal* may reflect the "policy agenda for business communities."

5. For content-analysis, refer to such books as Ole R. Holsti (1969), *Content Analysis for the Social Sciences and Humanities*, and Robert Philip Weber (1990), *Basic Content Analysis*, 2nd ed.

6. Of course, this could be a reflection of media biases favoring confrontation aspects of the bilateral relationship.

7. Since the numbers of indexes between the United States (108) and Japan (25) are greatly different, simple percentage may not be a good indicator, other than a reference purpose.

8. Schoppa, op. cit. (1993), p. 355.

9. Refer to SH 3/5/90, pp. 19-20. According to Williams, the U.S. negotiation team did not or could not put "priorities" on particular issue areas for two reasons: interrelated nature of structural problems among SII issue areas and turf battles among the U.S. agencies. No agency wanted to sacrifice their own areas of responsible for other agencies' sakes (*Daiyamondo* 5/30/92, p. 829).

10. Taylor, telephone interview 6/29/93.

11. *Nikkei* 3/30/90, p. 1; 6/9/90, p. 1.

12. For example, see *Nikkei* 2/24/90, p. 3.

13. Schoppa, op. cit. (1992), p. 10. His revised article of 1993 repeated the same point. See op. cit. (1993), p. 366.

14. Fukushima, op. cit., p. 200.

15. *Nikkei* 5/26/89, E.p. 1.

16. For example, see Taylor's statement, "Some of the topics in the SII, such as the saving and investment issues, do not lend themselves well at all to actions such as Super 301" (SH 3/5/90, p. 25). Senator Baucus actually submitted the bill that bound the administration, if SII failed, to take a Super 301 investigation on such issues as the distribution system and exclusionary business practices, but the issue of land policy was excluded from investigation, because it did not seem suitable for such an investigation (*Nikkei* 5/16/90, p. 1). Williams, "It is difficult to imagine that such issues as saving-investment patterns and land policy can be a subject for Super 301 investigation, but the other issues, for example, anticompetitive practices, the distribution system, and shareholders' rights can be subject to such investigation, for good reasons" (*Daiyamondo* 5/16/92, p. 16).

17. NHK, op. cit., p. 296.

18. Ibid., pp. 278, 290-291. Also refer to Armacost's remarks to LDP politicians Kato, Chairman of Policy Affairs Research Council and Nishioka, Chairman of General Affairs, on March 22 and 23, regarding the importance of the public works spending issue and the Large Store Law (*Nikkei* 3/24/90, p. 2).

19. Yabunaka, op. cit., p. 173.

20. Ibid., p. 191.

21. See "Comments of the U.S. Delegation on the Interim Reports by the Japanese Delegation" in the Interim Report.

22. Williams, interview 6/9/94. Williams' characterization of the U.S.pressure level matches the description and usage of the verbs for the five issue areas in his articles of *Daiyamondo* 6/6/92, pp. 232-234; 6/13/92, pp. 84-87. Williams' assessment is almost the same as mine, which is expressed in "relative" terms (or in ordinal-scale), instead of "absolute" terms (or in numerical-scale).

23. For some methodological limitations and possible further improvement of key-word content-analysis, refer to Naka, op. cit., p. 157.

24. NHK, op. cit., pp. 248-304. T. Igarashi's "The level of concreteness in the U.S. demands" presents the observation similar to the result here. See op. cit., p. 25.

25. Refer to NHK, op. cit., p. 73. The Treasury Department and MOF kept a macro economic issue underplay for a while.

26. *WSJ*, 6/22/90, p. A5.

27. The land policy became a less-pursued area after the second meeting. Refer to *Nikkei* 2/25/90, Sunday edition (S), p. 13; NHK, op. cit., pp. 145-146.

28. Refer to Williams, *Daiyamondo* 5/2-9/92, p. 110. NHK, op. cit., pp. 285-287, 300-302.

29. See *Nikkei* 2/25/90, S.p. 13; 3/13/90, p. 5.

30. The discrimination among issues, with the different levels of "emphasis" (if not "priority") and pressure as time went by, is evident in Williams' articles, *Daiyamondo* 6/6/92, pp. 232-234; 6/13/92, pp. 84-87. However, "shifting emphasis" (Taylor) might have occurred in part because of the negotiation dynamics. The Japanese government asked the U.S. government to choose priority issues in order to conclude the negotiation with acceptable terms, in spite of the initial U.S. desire of not putting a "priority" on any specific issues (refer to Williams, *Daiyamondo* 5/30/92, p. 829).

31. *Daiyamondo* 6/13/92, pp. 85-86. In the other article, Williams states that land use is the "most politically delicate issue" and therefore U.S. officials "treated it with great

caution" (*Daiyamondo* 4/18/92, p. 106).   Refer to *Nikkei* 3/12/90, p. 3 for Japanese officials' understanding.

32. Williams, *Daiyamondo* 6/6/92, p. 232.

33. Ibid.

34. For example, refer to Williams; The distribution system with the LSL drew "much attention" and became a "politicized trade issue" because of the Toys R Us issue (*Daiyamondo* 6/13/92, p. 86).   According to Yabunaka, since whether or not the LSL was repealed became a concern for Congress due to the Toys R Us issue, the U.S. team asked the Japanese government for "drastic measures" (see op. cit., p. 174).   These statements suggest that Japanese concessions in the distribution system area was pushed more by the U.S. team than in the exclusionary business practices area, although the overall pressure level for both areas is medium, compared to that for the saving and investment patterns area.   Keiretsu is obviously a greater concern for the U.S. team than the land policy issue.   Williams explained strong U.S. concern about keiretsu and its problems in great detail, while mentioning the land policy issue briefly in his articles (see *Daiyamondo* 6/6/92, pp. 232-234; 5/2-9/92, pp. 110-111 for keiretsu issues; 4/18/92, p. 106; 6/13/92, pp. 85-86 for the land policy).

35. Refer to Williams, "For the U.S. side, the Large Store Law was one of the many issues, and the importance of the [LSL] issue was [initially] lower, compared to that of antitrust law and keiretsu issues" (*Daiyamondo* 6/13/92, p. 86).   Notice that Williams here is talking of the importance of exclusionary business practices and keiretsu issues for the U.S. team in the initial stage of SII, compared to the LSL issue, but not to the distribution system issue area as a whole.

36. For the different degrees of U.S. concern and Japanese concern about the keiretsu issue, see NHK, op. cit., pp. 285-287, 300-302.   For relatively strong U.S. concern about keiretsu, refer to Williams, *Daiyamondo* 5/2-9/92, pp. 110-111; 6/6/92, pp. 232-234.

37. Williams suggested different degrees of "Japanese responsiveness" for each issue (Interview 6/9/94).

38. An example of this logic may be found in Fukushima's article. Fukushima attributed the stalemate of the United States-Japan Framework negotiation to the Clinton administration's ignorance of using pressure "where, when, and how much" on the Japanese government, among other reasons.   In his view, "the [Clinton] administration does not know the iron rule of 'speak soft while carrying a big bludgeon' for the negotiations with the Japanese" ("Nichi-bei hakyoku maneku ba-atari taiō," *This is Yomiuri*, pp. 41-42).

39. The average prices of goods in Japan are 60% higher than those in the U.S. due to the complicated distribution system, informal business practices, and possible other barriers (*Nikkei* 7/6/89, p. 1).   Also refer to Under Secretary of Commerce Farren's testimony on pricing mechanisms and a joint price survey in SH 3/5/90, pp. 48-51.

40. Notice the difference in points between Saving-Investment Patterns and Distribution System (18), that between Distribution System and Exclusionary Business Practices (9), and that between Exclusionary Business Practices and the rest of three (6-7).

41. This is Williams' assessment: The U.S. government put the same medium level pressure on the distribution system and on the exclusionary business practices, but gained

less concession from the Japanese government in the exclusionary business practices (Interview 6/9/94). Also refer to *Daiyamondo* 6/13/92, pp. 85-87.

42. Iwao Nakatani (1987), *Bōdaresu Ekonomi*, p. 86. For negative consequences of market forces, refer to pp. 82-86.

43. *Nikkei* 8/28/89, p. 5.

44. *Nikkei* 6/14/90, p. 5.

45. In 1989, more than 100 Japanese large retail stores had been doing business in the United States, while no such U.S. retail stores opened in Japan (NHK, op. cit., p. 154). According to Edward J. Lincoln, Toys R Us opened 580 stores worldwide, including all of the major European countries and Southeast Asia. Japan is the only major country in which Toys R us has no store (HH 2/20/90, p. 6). Furthermore, the "abnormality" of the LSL includes (1) an unusually long coordination processing period dictated by informal procedures which have no legal basis, and (2) the fact that it virtually necessitates consent from local store owners for the terms of opening new stores (e.g. store size and business hours). The latter problem can be interpreted as a violation of capitalist market principle. In the words of Toys R Us Chairman, "The Japanese case is somewhat different from other countries. Everywhere in the world, to open new stores, we don't need permission from our competitors" (cited in NHK, op. cit., p. 166). Thus, the problem of the LSL is not so much the issue of different forms of national "zoning" laws regulating opening new stores as the issue of principle of capitalist market system.

46. According to Williams, Japan's antitrust law is behind the world standard of U.S. and EC (Interview, 10/6/92).

47. *Tōyō Keizai* 4/29/89, p. 13. For detailed policies in the declaration of the Toronto economic summit, refer to *Nikkei* 6/22/88, pp. 1, 4.

48. Refer to the remarks of Farren in the opening of the SII first meeting, "We are not going to raise new issues. The content of this talk is the same as the Maekawa Report. If Japan had faithfully implemented the Maekawa Report, this talk would not be necessary" (NHK, op. cit., p. 252).

49. See Williams, *Daiyamondo* 4/25/92, pp. 94-95.

50. U.S. Department of State (1988), "U.S. Trade Objectives in the Uruguay Round," p. 9.

51. Carla Hill's written testimony for the Senate Finance Committee of May 3, 1989. *Oversight of the Trade Act of 1988*, pp. 61-63. The notion of "law enforcement" under GATT rules is expressed by Representative Gejdenson in the SII related hearing. "To insist that the Japanese government make an effort to reform structural barriers to trade is not American imperialism. The United States has a responsibility as a key player in the international trading system to ensure that Japan is playing by the same economic and trade rules as everybody else" (HH 4/19/90, p. 60).

6   The SII as a Site of the Transgovernmental Coalition of Subunits

BASIC FEATURES OF THE SECOND MODEL

The first model describes and explains political events as if the unitary national government consciously chose policy options among possible alternatives to realize national trade policy goals. This way of thinking, which many of us, laymen and professional scholars alike, are accustomed to, is useful for providing an overview of the social events and for particular research purposes. However, the description and explanation of events from the viewpoint of the first model is not always accurate from another point of view or level of analysis.

Mastanduno, for example, believes the Bush administration proposed the SII "without a prior systematic assessment of its costs and benefits relative to the alternative means to reduce the trade and payments deficit."[1] Mastanduno's argument follows the assumption of the first model, which draws its analysis from official announcements of the SII and does not examine internal decision-making and negotiation processes. From this position, one may think that "the proposal for a non-Super 301 negotiation with Japan came first; the specific details—such as the inclusion of American impediments as well as Japanese ones—came later,"[2] because the announcement of the Super 301 came only at the last moment, May 25, 1989. Officially, there had been little or no hint that the Bush administration would propose the SII prior to May 25. Even at the time of the Super 301 announcement, it appeared that the top policy-maker, President Bush, decided and directed the secretary of state, the secretary of treasury, and the U.S. trade representative to organize a high-level committee for discussing structural problems with Japan.[3]

However, the fact is that the Treasury Department had already obtained an agreement, however informal, from the Japanese Ministry of Finance in the early spring to have talks which would include *both* U.S. and Japanese structural issues.[4] Moreover, the basic framework of the SII was extensively discussed between the Treasury Department and USTR by April. A more detailed SII framework was developed by more than twenty secret meetings of chief negotiators and their staffs from major departments in the administration during April and May, 1989.[5]

The first model assumes coherent national policy goals. However, throughout the SII process, it is apparent that different departments had different policy goals. The Departments of State and Treasury pursued the issue of reducing the trade imbalance through macroeconomic arrangements, while USTR stressed the market-access issue. Indeed, particular policy outcomes in the SII are results of the dynamics among U.S. departments and their coalition partner ministries in the Japanese government. The official definition of the SII itself is an expression of the compromise among the U.S. and Japanese agencies, each favoring different interpretations.[6] From the viewpoint of the transgovernmental coalition of subunits model, the process of the SII is described and explained differently from that of the first model. The following are the basic features of the second model.

First, when one lowers the level of abstraction, the national government no longer is a coherent entity acting as a monolithic political actor. At the level of governmental subunits, the government is rather "a constellation of loosely allied organizations" with their own organizational goals, standard operating procedures (SOPs), programs, and repertoires.[7] No metaphor is more eloquent in characterizing the government as a conglomerate of loosely allied organizations than Swanson's "Canadiana constellation."[8]

This description also was the case for the U.S. government's economic policy toward Japan. By March 1989, Robert Pear already had criticized the situation, declaring it to be "so decentralized, so confused, and uncoordinated" in which "each agency negotiates with the Japanese in isolation and tries to cut a deal on its own issue."[9]

As for the Japanese government, the situation was quite similar. The same writer, Pear, also reported that there are "the deep-seated rivalries among Japanese agencies" and a "myth of a homogenized Japanese negotiation position."[10] Each Japanese ministry had organizational goals and interests, often referred to as "shōeki" (ministerial interests) in Japanese politics, with its own representatives in Washington. Furthermore, they each have separate communication channels with the home ministry, which serve to bypass the formal channels in the Japanese Embassy.[11] Therefore, at the level of analysis of governmental subunits, it is possible to say that the Japanese government per se does not exist in the same sense that "the United States government per se does not exist"[12] in the formulation and implementation of U.S. policy toward Canada.

Second, the second model describes and explains the observed governmental actions in terms of organizational outputs. Governments' actions on policies are first results of established routines and, to a lesser extent, choices made by government leaders. In many cases, top policy-makers simply choose options among existing routines and programs,[13] since, as Theodore Sorensen said, "Presidents rarely, if ever, make decisions—particularly in foreign affairs—in the sense of writing their conclusions on a clean slate . . . They make choices, they select options, they exercise judgement. But the basic decision which confines their choices have all too often been previously made by past events or circumstances, by other nations, by pressures on predecessors or even subordinates."[14] Therefore, the explanatory power of Allison's Model II is derived from "uncovering the organizational routines and repertoires that produced the outputs that comprise the puzzling occurrence."[15]

From the viewpoint of the second model, many "puzzling questions" in the SII process are not puzzling at all. For example, T. Igarashi wrote that there was a peculiar "mismatch" between the goal (reduction of trade deficit) and means to achieve this goal (macroeconomic measures) in the beginning of the SII. To achieve the goal of reducing the trade deficit, the macroeconomic measures are most effective; but macroeconomic measures were kept out of the agenda by the "secret agreement" between the Treasury Department and the Ministry of Finance.[16] Thus, on the one hand, Igarashi describes a subgovernmental-level "secret agreement," but unconsciously explains it on the other hand by using the logic of rational choice at the level of analysis of the national government. By fixing the governmental subunits as the level of analysis throughout the description and explanation, "a mismatch between the goal and means" is not a mismatch at all, for several reasons. Firstly, according to the Treasury Department's organizational routine, macroeconomic issues for reducing global imbalances traditionally have been discussed in the multilateral G-7 and other fora; the SII is only a supplement to these fora.[17] Secondly, for the Treasury Department and MOF, the purpose of the SII was not directly to reduce the trade deficit, but to identify and solve structural issues through which the process of adjusting trade and balance of payments imbalances could be facilitated. The SII was designed as the application of the same philosophy and framework as the Yen-Dollar Talks, which did not include macroeconomic issues. Therefore, it is quite reasonable that the Treasury Department and MOF did not bring macroeconomic issues to the SII agenda.

Third, the second model tries to describe and explain national policy outcomes in terms of "turf-battles" among these semi-independent organizations.[18] Fukushima's characterization of three groups in the U.S. administration, with respect to trade policy-making, is already considered to be conventional wisdom. These groups are: a "trade group" (USTR and Commerce Department), generally favoring tough trade policy in the interests of U.S. industry; a "diplomat group" (State and Defense Departments, and the National Security Council), insisting that the military-security relationship with Japan is more important than mere commercial interest; and a "pure economist group" (CEA, the Office of Management and Budget, the Justice Department, and part of the Treasury Department), taking a strong position of laissez-faire and free trade.[19]

U.S. trade policies toward Japan are usually decided by interagency turf-battles among these three groups of federal agencies. The trade group generally takes the toughest position; the diplomatic group is "over-protective of Japan"; and the pure economist group maintains a stance based on "free market principles" while holding the "the balance of power" depending on the issues.[20]

In a similar manner, the Japanese government's foreign economic policy-making suffers from long-standing ministerial battles. The Japanese government's foreign trade policies are decided through "deep-seated antagonism" among the Ministry of Foreign Affairs, the Ministry of Finance, and other "domestic ministries," such as MITI and the Ministry of Agriculture, Forestry, and Fisheries (MAFF), representing the interests of industries and of farmers.[21]

The interagency turf-battles are the key to understanding some national policy outcomes. For example, the reason why the U.S. SII team insisted on Japanese concessions in three major issues, that is, public works spending, the repeal of the Large Store Law, and an increase in the cartel surcharge, was the fact that these three areas were three co-chair departments' (the Treasury, State, and USTR) responsibilities.[22] When the SII was first announced as an alternative to the Super 301, it was believed that the SII would provide a discussion on the removal of "the broader structural barriers" to trade.[23] But as the SII talks proceeded, the U.S. team put more emphasis on macroeconomic issues, since the State Department took a hard position on trade deficit reduction through macroeconomic measures and made a coalition with the Treasury Department and CEA.

Fourth, the second model emphasizes transgovernmental coalitions among governmental subunits cross-cutting national boundaries. The complex processes of "demands and concession-making" are made through transgovernmental coalitions. For example, MITI officials believed that the U.S. team initially did not think of demanding the repeal of the Large Store Law, but rather MOF and MFA had suggested that idea to the U.S. team. On the other hand, MOF officials thought that it was MITI that had suggested that the U.S. team demand an increase in public works spending.[24] The reason why MOF accepted the specification of the large amount of budget spending was the large transgovernmental coalition among Japanese ministries which favored large public works spending (MITI, MFA, EPA, MOC, MOT, MAFF), the Liberal Democratic Party, Kantei (the Residence of the Prime Minister), and the U.S. departments (State, Treasury, and CEA).

In sum, negotiation outcomes (agreements) in the SII were due to a combined process of analytically different phases of policy-making: first, organizational routine (Treasury Department's internal process); second, "turf-battles" among domestic agencies (secret coalitions between Treasury and USTR against other agencies); and third, transgovernmental coalitions across national boundaries (coalitions among U.S. and Japanese agencies). However, these phases do not necessarily follow one another. For example, after the initial discussion in the

Treasury Department, the Treasury Department acquired an informal agreement from MOF regarding the idea of SII, *even before* it went to USTR. Thus, as an organizational routine, the Treasury Department already had a contact with MOF, which was a form of a transgovernmental coalition against other domestic agencies, especially the State Department and the Commerce Department. Therefore, at the time of March 1989, a de facto transgovernmental coalition was made among the Treasury Department, USTR, and Japanese Finance Ministry against other domestic agencies, on both sides. The order to communicate and/or share information between agencies demonstrates the existence of such a coalition.[25]

GOVERNMENTAL SUBUNITS AS INSTITUTIONAL ACTORS

While the first step in research is choosing a level of analysis, identifying major political actors at that level of analysis is the second step. The question of who the major political actors are is never obvious, depending on one's theoretical framework. For example, it is conventional wisdom that during the long period of the LDP rule, Japanese economic policies had been made by ministerial bureaucrats, the LDP, and industries and large business organizations such as Keidanren, although the relative emphasis on who initiates policies most differs among scholars.[26] Because of this conventional wisdom, Schoppa uncritically assumes the role of Keidanren in his explanation of the result of the Large Store Law compromise. Schoppa cites the policy statement of Keidanren as evidence of "expanded participation" and "consensus" among major political actors in the process of relaxing the Large Store Law.[27] However, in spite of its policy statement favoring relaxation of the LSL, Keidanren did not play an important role resulting in particular policy outcomes regarding the LSL. Rather, it was the organizations of small and medium store owners that resorted to pressure and influence upon the MITI and the LDP, and thus became a part of the actual policy-making process for the LSL issue.[28] A public policy statement made by a large business organization like Keidanren does not necessarily mean the organization is "playing the role," "influencing ministerial decisions," or "building consensus," although there is no doubt that Keidanren's policy preferences created a positive atmosphere for ministerial bureaucrats and LDP politicians who tried to promote certain policies.[29] However, the crucial factors are the direct dynamics among dominant interested parties that is, MITI, LDP, the Cabinet Secretariat, and the interest groups of small- and medium-sized retailers. The industry plays an important role, but in the case of the LSL, it was the organization of small- and medium-sized shop owners, such as Zenkoku Shōten Shinkō Kumiai Rengō-Kai (All Japan Retail Stores Development Union Federation) and their umbrella organization Nihon Shōkō Kaigisho (Nisshō, Japan Chamber of Commerce), rather than Keidanren that made a difference.[30]

Although the activities of private organizations and interest groups are often important in understanding certain government policies, this book focuses on the political process of formal governmental actors for two reasons. First, unlike sector-specific trade negotiations in which a particular industry's interests are affected, and that industry usually plays a political role, private actors (interest groups) did not take much part in the SII, except the LSL issue. Second, the main dynamics resulting in the specific content of SII agreement are sufficiently found among the governmental actors. Thus, with little knowledge about the activities of private actors, the policy outcomes in the SII can be explained by the dynamics among the governmental actors. For example, the policy position of the LDP reflects that of the small- and medium-sized retail stores organizations. Therefore, if one knows the LDP's policy, one does not need to investigate detailed activities of private interest groups. In sum, the research focuses on the policies of the governmental actors not because activities of interest groups are less important but because focusing on the governmental actors is more parsimonious and sufficient for explaining the major policy outcomes in the SII. Now, let us list the relevant governmental political actors in the SII process.

On the U.S. side, six major agencies were the political actors at the level of the government subunit which conducted the day-to-day SII negotiation: The Department of State, the Treasury Department, USTR, CEA, Commerce Department, and Justice Department. The positions of the first three as co-chair agencies are the most important in order to understand the negotiation results. Additionally, congressional committees took part in influencing U.S. negotiation teams by having hearings.[31] In the expression of a former administration official, "Congressional monitoring shaped the SII process unusually. Congress asked for specific results with time tables."[32] Generally, the role the congressional committees played was to oversee the progress in the negotiation and to pressure the administrative agencies. Congressional committees did not engage in day-to-day substantive agenda setting.[33] However, some issues in the SII, such as the repeal of the LSL and public works spending to reduce the trade deficit were strongly pushed by some administration agencies because of strong congressional committees' concern.

Finally, the White House played the critical role in providing the momentum to proceed with the negotiations and to conclude them.[34] With its overarching political function to present "national policy" and exercise "political guidance," the White House (or the president as an institutional actor) played an important role from time to time, although it was not part of the "direct dynamics" among the negotiation agencies, which resulted in specific SII agreements. The White House played this role on four occasions: a tandem announcement of Super 301 and the SII of May 25, 1989, the orchestration of the Bush-Kaifu meeting of March 2, 1990, to give political momentum to the talks, the creation of an Interim Report, and the conclusion of the SII talk in June 1990 by initiating a compromise.

On the Japanese side, the three co-chair ministries of MOF, MITI, and MFA (with weighted influence) plus EPA and JFTC were important in conducting the negotiation.   In addition to those ministries which have administrative jurisdiction over the specific trade issues, the Cabinet Secretariat of Kantei and the Liberal Democratic Party are key institutions to understand the SII process. Although the role of Kantei is to coordinate and persuade all-too-powerful and semi-independent ministries to agree to policies, its role in the Japanese policy-making process is apparent, as representing the Prime Minister's policy stance at times.[35]   Perhaps, the SII was one of the rare cases in Japanese foreign economic policy making in which the leadership of Kantei was demonstrated for a variety of reasons seen later in this chapter and in chapter eight. The initiative of Kantei in making the SII agreements was clearly recognized by both LDP members and commentators.[36]   Since the Japanese political system is parliamentary, the policy of the party in power is the key for whether and what kinds of policies are adopted. From an institutional perspective, the Japanese government's economic policies are usually decided by the dynamics among ministries, the party (LDP), and the Cabinet Secretariat of Kantei.[37]

Although many studies already describe transgovernmental coalitions among U.S. and Japanese agencies in trade negotiations, this book tries to demonstrate some patterns of coalitions with organizational routines resulting in certain policy outcomes, based on the SII case.

WHY THE U.S. GOVERNMENT INITIATED THE SII FROM THE PERSPECTIVE OF THE SECOND MODEL

Against the backdrop of a $50 billion trade deficit with Japan, the initiation of the SII in the spring of 1989 was so sudden that for some people it was seen as an "illogical prescription for resolving the immediate trade problems" because it was like a case of "a patient with an acute condition turning to the traditional herbal medicines—medicines designed to gradually restore the body to balance when taken over a period of many years."[38] However, once one goes into the depth of organizational routine, one will find nothing "illogical" about advocating the SII. The very first time the idea of SII appeared in the Treasury Department was in the late fall of 1988 *before* the Bush administration formally started discussing it.[39] The SII was discussed in the Treasury Department as a matter of organizational routine. The SII was preceded by the other bilateral trade talks. The Treasury Department had engaged in the Yen-Dollar Talks with the Japanese Ministry of Finance from November 10, 1983 to May 29, 1984; Market-Oriented Sector Specific Talks (MOSS) from January 2, 1985, to January 1986; and the United State-Japan Structural Economic Dialogue from April 1986 to October 1988. Although the Structural Dialogue was not a trade negotiation but a discussion of exchanging ideas, it covered almost the same issues as the SII, such as Japan's land-use policies, the distribution system, savings rate, and the U.S. federal deficit.[40] The Treasury Department co-chaired the Dialogue with the State Department on the U.S. side.[41]

In a speech to the School of Advanced International Studies at Johns Hopkins University on December 5, 1988, Under Secretary of the Treasury David Mulford emphasized the merits of the "broad-based Yen-Dollar Talks," and compared it with a product-by-product approach, calling for a "more comprehensive approach" to resolve the trade imbalance.[42] The SII was designed by the Treasury as the fourth attempt to deal with U.S.-Japanese trade imbalances, after the Yen-Dollar Talks, MOSS, and the Structural Economic Dialogue. As a matter of trade liberation areas, the Yen-Dollar Talks were aimed at liberalizing the Japanese financial sector; MOSS, at several selected sectors; and the SII, at the entire Japanese economy.[43]

In January or February 1989, the Treasury Department had informal contact with the Japanese Ministry of Finance. The Treasury Department's suggestion was that a new initiative to "solve structural problems affecting the U.S. and Japanese global trade and current account imbalances" be started.[44] The MOF agreed to a proposal on the condition that in exchange for accepting structural talks, macroeconomic issues should not be discussed in the talks. (The MOF thought macroeconomic issues should be dealt with in the customary G-7 forum or in the bilateral Treasury-MOF consultation).[45]

At about the same time, USTR was examining results of past trade policies. One of the main conclusions USTR reached was that U.S. and foreign companies still did not have greater access to the Japanese market, despite the improved competitiveness of U.S. goods in price and quality, macroeconomic adjustment of the yen appreciation, and the relative lack of formal trade barriers. Therefore, there must be some structural rigidities or informal barriers in the Japanese market, which substantially restrict foreign competition.[46] In the USTR's view, the effects of structural rigidities are far too important to leave to dialogue, for these rigidities will further aggravate trade frictions unless they are addressed.[47]

However, from the perspective of the second model, the "trade origins of the SII" were rooted in long-term organizational routines of USTR.[48] The USTR's organizational tasks of foreign market liberalization progressed from the elimination of formal trade barriers (tariffs, quotas, and regulations) to informal barriers or "structural rigidities."[49] A possible new trade talk to further open Japanese markets was under consideration, among several other policy options.[50]

In March 1989, the Treasury Department spoke with USTR. The Treasury Department wanted to expand the Yen-Dollar Talks to areas other than the exchange rate issue, while USTR was considering broad-range trade talks dealing with structural problems of the Japanese markets, such as exclusionary business practices, antitrust law, and the distribution system. Finally, the Treasury Department and USTR reached a consensus that there needed to be new types of trade talks which were somewhat between the Yen-Dollar Talks dealing with macroeconomic issues and traditional product-by-product trade talks dealing with "microeconomic" issues.[51]

Then, the Treasury and the USTR began examining the possibility for new trade talks. Initially, the USTR insisted that Japanese *dango* (bid-rigging) issues should be discussed under Super 301. But during discussions, these issues became part of the SII agenda. Otherwise, the original SII idea already included five of six broad issue areas. By April, the basic format of SII was almost completed between the Treasury Department and the USTR.[52]

In the meantime, from the beginning of the new administration, the Commerce Department had been busy advocating a strong business-government partnership and a "results-oriented" approach.[53] The State Department, which had long been known to be "soft on Japan," by putting priority on maintaining military-security relations, had its own consultative mechanism on economic issues with its counterpart, the Japanese Foreign Ministry. The State Department and MFA had sponsored the biannual United States-Japan Economic Subcabinet, in which subcabinet-level officials from other departments were invited to attend. Some of the issues in the SII, such as problems in the Japanese distribution system, the LSL, and keiretsu, were already discussed in the Subcabinet consultation meeting of October 1988.[54] The State Department was considering MFA's proposal to create a new comprehensive consultative panel headed by the secretary of state and the foreign minister. A new proposed panel, which was announced at the February Summit of 1989, was initially thought to be the development of the existing Economic Subcabinet.[55]

The Treasury Department and the USTR first considered MITI and MOF as Japanese counterparts for the new trade talks on the Japanese side.[56] Indeed, MOF informed only MITI of the idea of the new trade talks. Therefore, in the early stage, only the Treasury and USTR on the U.S. side, and MOF and MITI on the Japanese side knew of the idea of the new talks.[57] As to the U.S. negotiation team, the Treasury Department and USTR thought that consultation with other departments was necessary because of the overlapping bureaucratic jurisdictions and the possible controversial nature of some items on the agenda.[58] Because the State Department was considering possible new talks by that time, the "turf-battles" between the State and the Treasury Departments over who would take a leadership role in the structural talks emerged.[59] Later, the State and Commerce Departments joined the process. The Justice Department and the CEA were asked to join the SII negotiation team for tactical reasons because the Japanese government usually chooses responsible ministries for trade negotiations which are considered counterparts to the U.S. departments. The counterpart ministry for the CEA is the Japanese Economic Planning Agency (EPA), which in the U.S. agencies' view would support many trade liberalization measures suggested by U.S. agencies. Since the issue of antitrust laws was on the agenda, the Justice Department was needed, whose counterpart is the Japanese Fair Trade Commission.[60]

From April to May, the chief negotiators and their staffs from six agencies—Treasury, USTR, State, Commerce, CEA and Justice—had about twenty meetings to select the issues for the SII agenda. There had been once twelve areas of SII; eventually, six areas were chosen for reasons that negotiation issues should not be too large or too small. The pricing mechanisms issue was chosen as an issue to gain political support from the Japanese people, for price differences were easy for the Japanese to understand, although the pricing mechanisms was rather a "measurement to indicate [the degree of serious impediments] in other areas than an independent issue."[61]

The Japanese Ministry of Foreign Affairs did not know about possible new talks. Although MFA wanted to have the Subcabinet Consultation meeting by the middle of May, before the Super 301 designation, the schedule for a meeting was undecided because of the delay of the nomination of relevant officials in the U.S. administration.[62] The MFA sensed moves toward a new trade talk one week before the May 25 announcement of Super 301.[63] Even at the time of May 23, it was reported that the Subcabinet Consultative meeting would be the forum to discuss the structural issues.[64] The MFA finally confirmed a new structural talk the day before that announcement, when Secretary of State Baker and Secretary of Treasury Nicholas F. Brady suddenly lunched together. The MFA wondered about the reason for this sudden lunch and found out that it was because of the new talks.[65]

During the same period, beginning with the Senate Finance Committee Hearings of January 27, 1989, to confirm Carla Hills as U.S. trade representative, the congressional committees continuously pressured the USTR to designate Japan as a Super 301 trade negotiation priority country, while supporting for assertive trade policies of the Commerce Department against other less trade-oriented agencies such as the State Department.[66] While the USTR was expected to carry tougher trade policies by congressional committees, it could not reveal the idea of SII until the final moment.[67]

As seen above, the idea of SII first emerged from organizational routine in the Treasury Department. With the agreement of the Japanese MOF (although informal, nonetheless it was an important political resource to take the lead), the Treasury Department went to USTR, which had its own idea of a new talk dealing with structural barriers, deriving from its organizational routine. The Treasury Department and USTR, making a coalition with MOF, and later MITI, tried to build a leading position in trade policy-making against other departments, in particular the State Department and the Commerce Department, in the new Bush administration.

However, once the Treasury Department's leading position was established with support from USTR, the interagency group, consisting of chief negotiators and their staffs, carefully proposed the SII framework to top-level policy-makers. The most important point from the perspective of the second model is that the SII was already a dominant policy program among the limited policy menus available for top policy-makers of the White House, since without semi-established policy programs, top decision-makers could not launch a new policy.[68]   As a result, on May 25, 1989, top decision-makers of the White House accepted the SII along with Super 301 measures, because the SII was already an ongoing program involving both the U.S. and Japanese bureaucratic agencies at the time of the Super 301 announcement.[69]

GOALS OF U.S. DEPARTMENTS

The main dynamics in the policy-making process which resulted in the particular content of SII agreements came from the organizational goals of each agency, especially of six core agencies on the U.S. side and five on the Japanese side which were directly responsible for international negotiation results. Among these core agencies, the three co-chair agencies on each side had weighted influence in the negotiation processes.

When the idea of SII was conceived in the spring of 1989, the U.S. team roughly divided responsible areas among six agencies, although these areas often overlapped with each other. The Treasury Department took a lead on saving and investment patterns issues, land policy, and the keiretsu.   The State Department focused on the distribution system; USTR, on exclusionary business practices; the Commerce Department, on pricing mechanism; and the Justice Department, on antitrust law working with USTR. CEA prepared the theoretical arguments for the saving-investment patterns.[70]

From the beginning, the six core agencies had different organizational goals, although they all shared the same sense of urgency that the U.S.-Japanese bilateral relations, U.S. international competitiveness, and U.S. trade policy were all in a tremendously difficult situation.[71]   The organizational goals for the major departments are found in the first SII-related hearings of the Senate Trade Subcommittee of the Finance Committee in which the State and the Treasury Departments, and the USTR attended.

The Treasury Department

For the Treasury Department, the goal of the SII was to identify and solve structural problems affecting the bilateral U.S-Japanese trade and current account imbalances, with the goal of contributing to the reduction of payments imbalances. [72]

However, in the early stages of the SII, the Treasury Department's position was somewhat ambiguous or inconsistent. On the one hand, the Treasury Department stressed the "potential impact of macroeconomic policy changes," compared with the modest effect of product-by-product trade negotiations. On the other hand, it seemed to downplay the significance of macroeconomic policy issues in the SII talk. The initial purpose of the SII was to "solve structural problems affecting the United States and Japanese global trade and current account imbalances" but with the "specific goal of contributing to a reduction in payment imbalances."[73] Therefore, the explicit goal of SII was *not* directly to reduce payment imbalances but "structural change,"[74] which might contribute to a reduction in payment imbalances in time. Because the global and bilateral payment imbalances reduction was done mainly by macroeconomic measures through multilateral macroeconomic policy coordination process within the G-7, the SII was only meant to complement that process, but not to replace it.[75] This ambiguity or inconsistency is understandable, given the fact that the Treasury Department and Japanese MOF agreed with each other that macroeconomic measures were not to be discussed in the SII talk. However, this agreement was not kept long because of the dynamics of the SII process. The "radicalization" of the Treasury, along with the "radicalization" of the State Department, although for different reasons, was the key to understanding sweeping results in the Japanese public works spending issue.

The Office of the United States Trade Representative

The organizational goal of USTR was "to open markets" on bilateral and multilateral bases. The USTR maintained that, in spite of a significant reduction in formal trade barriers, the Japanese market still was not accessible to foreign companies because of structural barriers which may originate in government policies and practices. Therefore, "our objective is change . . . that will make the Japanese economy more accessible to foreign goods and services and to the participation of foreign investors."[76]

The USTR's position represents the market access aspect of the SII. For the USTR, the SII was "an essential part of the overall U.S. trade policy toward Japan,"[77] which was also part of the larger goal of sustaining and expanding the multilateral trade regime under GATT. In the USTR's view, "major political problems" were created by the perception that the Japanese market was closed to foreign goods, particularly to capital goods in which U.S. companies have a comparative advantage.[78] Therefore, "only trade flows solve trade issues."[79]

The important point, from the USTR's view, was that the market access issue should be separated from the trade deficit issue, which was a result of macroeconomic factors. "Although the bilateral trade deficit has perhaps fuelled the political fire that causes us to address structural barriers at this point in time, we should be having this Structural Impediments Initiative even if we had a surplus with Japan."[80]

This basic position is repeated by Carla Hills and Williams on many occasions in which they suggested that 70 to 80 percent of the U.S. trade deficit is caused by macroeconomic factors such as the interest rate, saving levels, the exchange rate, and relative growth.[81] The USTR's main concern was with exclusionary business practices, including keiretsu and barriers in the distribution system which hinder the import of U.S. capital goods into Japan. In the summer of 1989, USTR wanted "the import expansion of capital goods rather than that of consumer goods through the amendment of the Large Store Law."[82] It is suspected that because of those statements, MITI believed that the idea of repealing the LSL had not originated with the U.S. agencies.[83]

The State Department

The traditional trade policy stance of the State Department has been "preventing trade and economic frictions from undermining political support for our [the U.S.-Japanese] relationship."[84] The State Department stressed the importance of the U.S.-Japanese bilateral relationship by using the term "an alliance."[85] For the State Department, "the wisdom of this [alliance] policy" is clear. It had kept the peace in Northeast Asia for four decades, provided a stable environment for the United States and neighboring nations in the region, and also promised economic integration between the U.S. and Japanese economies.[86]

However, there were some problems in this relationship, one of which was the "unsustainable trade imbalances."[87] Resolving the criticism of Japan from Congress, after all, depends on whether or not the trade deficit is reduced.[88] Unless the trade imbalance is significantly reduced, the full development of a stable U.S.-Japanese relationship is not achievable. Thus, the SII was important for "the continuing development of a healthy relationship between the United States and Japan."[89] For the State Department, the goal of SII was clear from the beginning: "to reduce our payments imbalance" in order to achieve the political goal of a stable U.S.-Japanese relationship.[90]

It is interesting to note that, although the State Department unambiguously stated the goal of SII, it did not mention the effective measures which were needed to reduce the trade imbalance, that is, macroeconomic measures. All that the State Department mentioned was rather about market access issues in the summer of 1989. The purpose of SII was "to address structural impediments which are rooted in regulations, laws and business practices in the Japanese economy" because in Japan, "the market is not working as it should."[91] However, it soon became clear that to reduce the trade deficit, discussing macroeconomic measures was unavoidable.

In the opening statement of the Senate Finance Committee Hearing, the State Department is the only department among three that explicitly mentioned the U.S. side structural issues, accounting for about 10 percent of its opening testimony.[92] However, by the fall of 1989, the State Department had begun to take a strong position on the bilateral trade deficit, persistently insisting upon public works spending by the Japanese government.[93] Therefore, the "radicalization" of the State Department already appeared in the early stage of

SII, compared with that of the Treasury Department, which "evolved" though the SII meetings.[94]

The Congressional Committees

The congressional committees, reflecting their own institutional concerns and domestic industries' interests, were another institutional actor which shaped the process of the SII. The congressional committees, such as the Subcommittee on International Trade of the Senate Finance Committee and the Subcommittees on Asian and Pacific Affairs and on International Economic Policy and Trade of the House Foreign Affairs Committee, had five SII related hearings: July 20, 1989; November 6-7, 1989; February 20, 1990, March 5, 1990; and April 19, 1990. Two hearings (November 6-7, 1989, and February 20, 1990), coincided with the second and the third official SII meetings in Washington D.C., and Tokyo, apparently intending to pressure the administration and the Japanese government.

From the first SII-related hearing of July 20, 1989, the congressional committees started monitoring the SII process. In that hearing, administration officials from the Treasury and State Departments, and USTR were under direct pressure to produce specific results from the SII negotiations.[95] The position of the congressional committees was unequivocally expressed: the SII was part of an effort to implement the Super 301 provision of the 1988 Trade Act to address structural barriers for increasing U.S. exports to Japan; Congress did not want another Structural Dialogue that "talk[ed] a great deal and accomplishe[d] very little"; Congress expected "results" from the SII, that is, a "concrete contribution to expanding the U.S. exports to Japan."[96] In the hearings of November 6 and 7, the representatives from the organizations of domestic industries were invited to express their concerns. Such organizations as the U.S. Chamber of Commerce, the National Association of Manufacturers, the American Electronics Association, the Alliance for Wood Products Exports, National Forest Products, the Automotive Parts & Accessories Association, and the National Forest Products Association expressed concerns that included problems in accessing the Japanese market (Japanese weak antitrust law, keiretsu, the Japanese patent system), Super 301 issues, and the SII. With those hearings, the congressional committees began pressuring the administration agencies by suggesting a possibility of drafting tougher laws to deal with structural issues if the SII failed.[97]

From the viewpoint of the second model, the specific demands on such issues as the repeal of the LSL and the public works spending issue made the congressional committees part of the broad transgovernmental coalition among the U.S. and Japanese governmental subunits.[98] For example, the congressional committees placed specific emphasis on the repeal of the LSL issue due to the Toys R Us issue, which was important to the Interim Report.[99] As to the Japanese public works spending issue, the congressional committees were part of a strange de facto transgovernmental coalition (e.g., State and Treasury Departments, MITI, and MFA) which insisted on the "short-term goal of the trade deficit reduction" against the agencies (USTR and MOF) which wanted to separate the trade deficit reduction issue from the SII.[100]

GOALS OF JAPANESE MINISTRIES

Like federal agencies in the U.S. administration, Japanese ministries also have long-standing organizational biases and goals. From the beginning, these ministries pursued their own organizational goals, actively seeking coalition partners among the U.S. agencies against other ministries. Then, the SII became a site for transgovernmental coalition making, a place where the various ministries could realize their own interests.

Ministry of Foreign Affairs

The Ministry of Foreign Affairs has long been known as "internationalist" since it always puts weight on maintaining a good bilateral U.S.-Japanese relationship over domestic industries' interests.[101] From the beginning, MFA insisted that the discussion on macroeconomic measures should be included in the SII agenda. In the MFA's view, the tension between the United States and Japan, which would jeopardize the U.S.-Japanese military-security alliance, was caused by the huge bilateral trade deficit. Thus, the purpose of having the SII was to correct the bilateral trade deficit. To make this correction possible, macroeconomic adjustment was necessary, including the reduction of the U.S. federal deficit. If the bilateral trade deficit was not reduced, anti-Japanese feelings would continue to arise in the American public, as well as among members of Congress, further exacerbating the deteriorating U.S.-Japanese relations.[102]

MFA's organizational routine was to support the ongoing bilateral and multilateral agenda, such as those of the OECD and the G-7 Economic Summit, as part of international economic and political cooperation to establish a solid presence among G-7 countries. For this goal, MFA generally supported deregulation, structural adjustment, and market liberalization measures.[103]

The Economic Planning Agency

The Economic Planning Agency is generally referred to as the agency of "economists" in the Japanese government. Although the EPA is not as powerful as three of the other giant ministries (i.e., MOF, MITI, and MFA), it brought some influence into the SII discussions by representing sound economic data and analysis. The EPA had a view similar to that of the MFA that the basic element needed to reduce the trade and current account imbalances was a macroeconomic adjustment, in both countries. This means the reduction of the federal deficit in the United States and an increase in domestic demand in Japan, along with an exchange rate realignment.[104] The EPA already published the report on price differentials between domestic and overseas markets in 1988 and pointed out the problems of government regulations.[105]

Ministry of Finance

In the Ministry of Finance's view, import promotion and reduction of Japanese companies' competitiveness, through the strong yen, was needed to reduce the trade deficit. In addition, domestic demand needed to be stimulated through low discount rates and deregulation, not through fiscal measures. Since the balanced budget was the top priority for MOF, the additional governmental spending was not possible. Too much governmental spending could cause inflation and spur an increase in trade surplus, if the already overheated domestic economy was combined with the weak yen.[106] Most importantly, MOF insisted that the Treasury Department promise not to discuss the issue of macroeconomic policies in the SII.[107] So, MOF tried to avoid macroeconomic discussions and pass the burden of concession-making to the shoulder of MITI.[108]

The Ministry of International Trade and Industry

The Ministry of International Trade and Industry has preferred to expand domestic demand through an increase in public works spending. The importation of U.S. capital goods would be sluggish unless domestic growth through fiscal stimulus was made. In MITI's view, the budgetary policy that stimulated domestic demand, rather than the repeal of the LSL, would help reduce the trade deficit.[109] For MITI, the repeal of the LSL may only have an effect on the import of consumer goods, an area in which the United States is not competitive.

TRANSGOVERNMENTAL COALITIONS PRODUCED BY THE SII

The different organizational goals and policy stances of core agencies from both governments were well-expressed in the opening statement of the first SII meeting of September 4, 1989. MFA pointed out two things. The basic way to reduce the deficit was through macroeconomic measures, and the SII was to contribute to this. Because the SII was a two-sided job, both the United States and Japan had to tackle their own problems.[110]

MOF said that the Yen-Dollar Talks was the first time that the United States and Japan dealt with structural problems, and both countries cooperated with each other. For the SII, it should be kept in mind that only politics make structural reform possible.[111] MOF did not say anything about macroeconomic issues or deficit reduction.

MITI stated that the central policy of balancing the current account was macroeconomic policy coordination. Although the SII did not deal directly with current account imbalances, the role of SII was to complement it.[112] MITI believed that structural adjustment of the Japanese economy was ongoing and structural issues should be tackled from the viewpoint of efficiency.[113]

The State Department emphasized that due to the closeness of the relationship, trade frictions occur, but trade frictions should not hurt the U.S.-Japanese cooperative relationship. Japan should change its exclusionary business practices and strive to be an import superpower.[114] Although the State Department did not explicitly mention macroeconomic measures in the opening statement, it later directly asked how much the Japanese budget for the next year would increase in what sectors, which MOF refused to answer by saying that the issue of macroeconomics was not included in the SII theme.[115]

The statement of the Treasury Department seemed "twisted" or somewhat ambiguous. The Treasury Department said that the SII was agreed to by the heads of the governments in order to clarify the existence of structural problems in both countries and solve the current account imbalance problems. In the Treasury Department's view, both countries have structural problems. Macroeconomic policy coordination was dealt with in the G-7 forum, and trade issues were dealt with in the traditional forum. However, discussing such issues as land policy and distribution systems in the SII talks would contribute to the improvement of the current account imbalance.[116]

For USTR, the SII was a talk to discuss the market access issue, even though the current account balance issue was a matter of macroeconomic policy coordination.[117] Like USTR, the Commerce Department stressed that Japan should become an import superpower.[118] CEA added that it wanted to approach the SII from a viewpoint of "government economic policy," that is, Japan should make an effort to enhance the economic interest of the world.[119]

The first "fight" in terms of different organizational goals occurred between the Japanese MOF and EPA, (not between U.S. agencies and Japanese agencies), when EPA emphasized that the issue of the current account balance was macroeconomic, and therefore, SII issues should be discussed from the viewpoint of macroeconomic policies, such as the correction of the strong dollar, expansion of domestic demand in trade surplus countries, and reduction of the U.S. deficit.[120] Instantly, MOF criticized EPA by saying that the issue of macroeconomic policies was not included in the mandate of the SII.[121]

As seen above, from the very beginning of SII meetings, each agency brought different organizational goals and interpretations in the SII process. After finding tremendous gaps between the U.S. and Japanese agencies in their analysis, policies and goals at the first meeting, U.S. agencies expressed their objectives in stronger terms at the beginning of the second SII meeting of November 1989. The Treasury "demanded" change in Japanese domestic investment patterns and reminded the Japanese ministries that the goal of SII was "to reduce bilateral imbalances."[122]   The State Department insisted on the reaffirmation of the SII goal agreed to in the Bush-Uno statement, that is, "to correct bilateral U.S.-Japan imbalances." Therefore in the State Department's view, the SII measures to be taken should be judged from the viewpoint of how effective they are to correct bilateral imbalances.[123]

Even after the secret meeting of January 31 in Bern, Switzerland, in which the concrete demands of U.S. agencies in the form of the 240-item list were shown, Japanese ministries could not move quickly to draft possible agreements which contained concrete actions. The main reason for this sluggish move was the Lower House of the Diet General Election on February 18. Japanese ministries and the LDP party alike were afraid to politicize SII issues. For instance, MOF did not want the LDP to take advantage of the public works spending issue, that is, promising more money for construction of roads and bridges in the local districts.   Under LDP pressure, MITI tried to avoid politically sensitive issues, such as repeal of the LSL, which would antagonize the organized interests of small and medium retail store owners (for those groups were some of the major supporters of the LDP), and an increase of cartel surcharges, which also could generate opposition from the industry.   Contrary to U.S. agencies' high expectations for the February 22-23 meeting after the victory of the LDP in the general election, the third SII meeting was disappointing, showing no sign of a possible compromise. In the U.S. agencies' view, the proposals the Japanese ministries showed in the meeting all were "only explaining and defending present policies" with no concrete further actions.[124] The U.S. agencies felt that the Japanese ministries did not have "adequate political guidance."   The Japanese ministries also felt that what ministerial bureaucrats could do had reached the limit, and the remainder of the job was left to politicians.[125]

To induce "political guidance" from the top in breaking the deadlock at the working-level negotiation, the White House initiated the summit meeting on March 2 and 3 in California. The proposal of this meeting was highly unusual in the ordinary sense of preparing diplomatic meetings. The White House directly telephoned Kantei at midnight, Tokyo time, by-passing official channels of MFA and other ministries. Ordinarily, official diplomatic meetings take at least one month to prepare. However, this summit meeting was set only a week in advance. Kantei instantly accepted the White House proposal even though it did not have any concrete policy offers.[126]

The initial response of the LDP party and Ministries to the White House proposal was not enthusiastic, for they did not know exactly how much and what concrete concessions would be necessary for an interim report. Even the major Japanese ministers representing their ministries, except MFA, did not attend the Palm Springs summit meeting of March 2-3, while the White House brought in Cabinet members representing the major departments.

However, from the viewpoint of the White House and Kantei, the Summit meeting was successful. The White House could turn to the "political guidance" of Kantei, which represented the political unit of the Japanese government. Kantei could now use the endorsement of the White House for taking a more assertive policy stance against the ministries and the LDP. Although there were still many disagreements, the cold atmosphere in the LDP generally changed and the resistance of ministerial bureaucracies weakened.[127]   The "hot line" between the White House and Kantei was strengthened.[128] In March and early April, the Cabinet Secretariat of Kantei was busy persuading the ministries and the LDP to make concessions for an interim report by raising the sense of crisis: "We must not make the U.S.-Japan relations be like that on the eve of a world war."[129]

During the early spring of 1990, just before the Interim Report was issued, the initial policy positions of relevant political actors on three major issues were the following.

The Large Store Law

State Department:

> Total repeal of the LSL and other forms of deregulation in the distribution system.

Kantei:

> "Improving operational procedures" (*unyō kaizen*) of the law is not enough. At least, "partial repeal" of the LSL, such as "exemption of the LSL regulation in the major urban areas" is necessary. Hopes for the total repeal of the Law after three years.

MITI:

> Has the policy of "Improving operational procedures" including the shortening of the coordination processing period for new store openings and abolishing local governments' regulations.   Inclines toward accepting necessary law amendment in the future.

The LDP:

> Absolutely opposes to repeal of the law because LDP supporters of small and medium store owners will be severely damaged. "Improving operational procedures" is enough. Resistant to even "exemption of the LSL application in the major urban areas."

Public Works Spending

Treasury Department:

> Public works spending should be raised up to the level of an annual 10 percent of GNP within three to five years. The implementation of the Fifteen-Year Infrastructure Construction Plan should be accelerated.

Kantei:

> Hopes to propose the target numbers for eight sectors in public works, such as housing and parks, by the time of an interim report, if the GNP ratio proposal is not possible.

MOF:

> Setting the GNP ratio target is not acceptable, because if this is done, the function of the budget as a means to control the business cycle will be lost. Proposing a concrete "public works expansion plan" is not possible by the time of an interim report. For a final report of July, proposing a multi-year public works plan including some numbers in eight sectors will be possible.

The LDP:

> Strongly supports the U.S. demand. The construction "policy tribes" are most supportive, demanding an increase in the government construction bond and an abolishment of the "budget ceiling" system.[130]

Regarding the case of the LSL, at first glance, the policy of MITI roughly fell between Kantei's position and the LDP's policy preference. This seems to support the Japanese bureaucrats' "add-and-divide-by-two solution."[131] That is, trade negotiation agreements are the results of a compromise between U.S. demands and the interests of domestic industries. Here, Kantei's policy position was closest to that of the United States because of its overall concern with maintaining good bilateral relations with the United States, including economic, political, and military security. The LDP party represented the interest of domestic industries and local districts. Ministerial bureaucrats have to respond to both, therefore, trade agreements are products of a compromise between U.S. demands and domestic interests. This formula is also applicable to the issue of increasing cartel surcharges. The exact policy preference of Kantei on that issue was not found. However, the known actors' policy positions are stated below.

The Cartel Surcharge Increase Issue

USTR:

> An increase in cartel surcharges by 10 percent of affected illegal sales. Major amendment of antitrust laws, including introduction of a private damage remedy system and strong enforcement of criminal prosecution.

Kantei:

> (Probably close to the position of U.S. agencies)

JFTC:

> Overall improvement of operational procedure of antimonopoly laws is sufficient. (Later, JFTC accepted an increase in cartel surcharges by amending the antimonopoly law).

The LDP:

> Opposes to amending the antitrust law, stronger enforcement, and an increase in cartel surcharges and more criminal prosecution.[132]

The "add-and-divide-by-two" scheme is a rule of thumb, which can be useful in predicting the major content of trade negotiations. However, that scheme is not applicable to the case of public works spending in which Kantei's policy position is somewhat between LDP's policy position (which is closest to that of the United States) and MOF. As a matter of fact, the actual process of making agreements is more complex and dynamic than the simple "add-and-divide-by-two" scheme. As to the antitrust law issue, JFTC did not announce the possibility of amending the laws until mid-March. Before that, although JFTC claimed it would strengthen its organization and law enforcement and draft new guidelines, it denied any possibility of amending the laws from time to time. The JFTC was so afraid of "the second failure" in its effort to strengthen the antitrust law that it could not take an initiative of proposing a surcharge increase by amending the antimonopoly law.[133]

But this time, it was rather MITI along with MFA, that first suggested a surcharge increase,[134] in part because "MITI could not offer many concessions in the LSL issue for an interim report."[135] Moreover, although the opposition to strengthening the antitrust laws, including an increase in surcharges, was in the air in the LDP, the opposition was not as well organized against this issue as it was against the repeal of the LSL. The discussion on the antitrust law issue was half-hearted, and the party itself was not well-consulted on the issue.[136]

Table 6.1
Coalition Map of the U.S. and Japanese Governmental Subunits[137]

Public Works Spending

Treasury	LDP	MFA	
State	Kantei	MITI	
CEA		EPA	←————————————→MOF
USTR		MOC	
		MOT	
		MAFF	

Large Store Law

State	Kantei	MFA	
USTR		MOF	←——→LDP←——→MITI
Treasury		EPA	

An Increase in Cartel Surcharge (March 1990)

USTR	(Kantei)	MITI	
Justice	MFA		←------------→LDP
State	JFTC		

An Increase in Cartel Surcharge (June 1990)

USTR	(Kantei)	
Justice	JFTC	←————————————→MITI
State	MFA	LDP

Land Policy

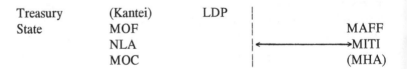

Treasury	(Kantei)	LDP	
State	MOF		MAFF
	NLA		←————————→MITI
	MOC		(MHA)

*Left-and-right arrows indicate relations of opposition.
*Kentei in the parenthesis indicate the presumed policy position.
*Dotted left-and-right arrows indicate weak or unorganized opposition.

Contrary to a simplistic way of explaining and predicting the policy outcomes in the major SII issue areas, such as the "add-and-divide-by-two" scheme, the configuration of the transgovernmental coalitions among subunits is more helpful in understanding the dynamics of the negotiation process. (See the coalition map of the U.S. and Japanese governmental subunits in Table 6.1.) The map shows the transgovernmental coalitions that produced major agreements in the Interim Report. The six U.S. agencies were naturally expected to be on the same side of the coalition. But, here only the U.S. agencies that strongly insisted on demands in the issue areas are presented. The relative location of agencies from left to right presents the presumed closeness of policy positions. As seen in the transgovernmental coalition map, the LDP, Kantei, and at least six ministries in the Japanese government supported the U.S. agencies' demands on the public works spending issue: a larger sum of the government budget for public works over ten years. Those governmental subunits and the LDP were in a broad coalition with the U.S. governmental subunits against the Finance Ministry, which resisted the large sum of governmental spending. The LDP expressed the most enthusiasm for such an expansionist policy. Because of the pressure from the large coalition, MOF finally gave in to this demand.

The case of the LSL was twisted in many ways. MITI initially thought that "normalization of the operational procedure" to shorten the coordination period from the current no-limit to one or one and a half years, would suffice.[138] In line with the idea of a possible future partial repeal of the LSL, Kantei's position was the closest to the U.S. agencies' position, which demanded the total repeal of the law. MFA, MOF, and EPA believed that major change in the LSL was necessary to satisfy the U.S. agencies and to promote reforms in the Japanese distribution system. The U.S. agencies with support from Kantei, MOF, MFA, and EPA, demanded the total repeal of the LSL.

The LDP was in a difficult position. On the one hand, it was under strong pressure from the small- and medium-sized retail stores organizations, which were against any major change of the LSL, whether it was a repeal or amendment of the law. Because of this pressure, the LDP initially opposed the total repeal of the LSL. The LDP members from the urban district were even against Kantei's idea of a possible compromise: a future partial repeal in the major cities. Indeed, the LDP was divided. On the other hand, the LDP gradually began to understand that keeping a good U.S.-Japanese relationship was important, therefore it could not completely concede to domestic interest groups by rejecting the U.S. agencies' demands. Finally, the LDP made a decision; it agreed to a partial repeal of the law.[139] As time went by, MITI was placed in a dilemma. The ministry was torn between its desire to "normalize" the LSL and to promote economic efficiency, and its other desire to maintain the basic framework of the LSL, keeping its control on the distribution system. At some point, MITI found that even the normalization of operational procedures was too difficult to achieve. MITI was pressured by both the LDP and the U.S. agencies with its Japanese allies, Kantei, MFA, MOF, and EPA.

Because of this peculiarly twisted configuration of transgovernmental coalitions, the SII agreement on the LSL issue was a compromise among three groups. With a policy of anti-repeal and a preference toward normalization of the coordination procedure, MITI was in a coalition with the LDP, against the U.S. agencies and its Japanese allies, Kantei, MOF, MFA, and EPA. Under U.S. agencies' pressure, MITI at some point considered the possibility of amending the LSL (not just a normalization of it through a ministerial ordinance) because it thought further concession was necessary, when the LDP was still stuck with the idea of normalization of the procedure in the present framework of the LSL.[140] But once the LDP leaned closer to Kantei's compromise plan, i.e., amending the LSL to further shorten the coordination period (one year) and a possible future partial repeal of the law in the major urban areas within two years, MITI resisted that policy.[141] Therefore, at the last stage just before an interim report, it was the LDP in a partial coalition with Kantei, other ministries, and the U.S. agencies, that was against MITI, pushing it towards the final compromise. But MITI, through a broader coalition with Kantei, other ministries, the LDP, and the U.S. agencies, was also able to achieve its original policy goals against domestic interest groups, of normalizing the LSL correcting coordination procedures and shortening the coordination period.[142]

Regarding the cartel surcharge issue, see the coalition diagram of March, 1990. Again, the U.S. agencies were in a position of coalition with JFTC, MFA (and probably Kantei) against the LDP. Unlike the case of the LSL, the LDP opposition against cartel surcharges was not well organized. MITI was initially reluctant to accept the idea to raise the cartel surcharge. But, because it was now one of the co-chair ministries and did not have much to offer in the other areas, MITI finally accepted the need to make some concessions, which the LDP could not accept.[143]

The difference in the LDP's positions toward the cartel surcharge increase issue and the LSL issue at the time of an interim report was found in the process of draft-making for the interim agreement. The "government draft" (seifu-an) was made by ministerial bureaucrats under the coordination of the Cabinet Secretariat. The draft already contained an increase in cartel surcharges, indicating that MITI accepted the policy change.[144] By the time that the party's Special Research Commission on Economic Adjustment meetings were held from March 27 to 30, the LDP was not well informed about the government policy on a cartel surcharge increase. Consequently, the LDP simply complained to the government for not adequately informing the party, although it was critical of the idea of strengthening the antitrust law. LDP opposition to the cartel surcharge increase was not yet organized.

On the contrary, in the same period, the LDP was busy opposing the repeal of the LSL, while not opposing a shortening of the coordination processing period by improving the operational procedures. Later, the LDP itself made a new move to make a further compromise through a partial repeal of the law, in spite of its initial opposition to the total repeal of the LSL, while there was no such move on the antitrust law issue.[145]

Regarding the land-use policy, the Ministry of Agriculture, Forestry, and Fisheries (MAFF) was reportedly not supportive of a new taxation on the agricultural land in the urban areas.[146] But the LDP was already on the same side with other agencies that preferred a reform of land taxation policy at the time of the Interim Report. Although the LDP was still afraid of antagonizing farmers, one of its major supporters, and was still cautious about going too far with new policies, it felt new policies were necessary to control land prices.[147] Regarding an introduction of a new landholding tax, MITI was against a such policy and Ministry of Home Affairs (MHA) was cautious of it. While the LDP recognized the necessity to introduce a new policy in controlling the high land prices, it tried to water down the initial proposal of a higher tax rate proposed by MOF and National Land Agency (NLA) later on.[148]

Making the Interim Report was a difficult task which required "political guidance" from both the White House and Kantei. Reportedly, the White House was trying to dampen "working-level dissatisfaction" to create a "political compromise."[149] Meanwhile, Kantei was striving to make concessions which would satisfy all relevant actors, that is, the U.S. agencies, responsible ministries, and the LDP backed by the industries. Finally, the Interim Report was reached through the configurations of transgovernmental coalitions among the U.S. and Japanese governmental subunits. Many actors were somewhat relieved. Kantei and the White House were happy, for they could avoid the major political setback which might result from the failure to make agreements. The Interim Report was good enough to sell to the congressional committees. The State Department and USTR gained points, for the coordination processing period for the opening of new stores under the LSL was now one and a half years, which made it a reasonably short time in which Toys R Us could open its first store in Japan.

Although the Treasury Department was not completely satisfied, it received a promise from MOF to increase public works spending in the form of the total sum with a specific ten-year plan. Since the Japanese agencies accepted a cartel surcharge increase, USTR was somewhat satisfied. Japanese weak antitrust law enforcement has long been a complaint of American corporations, as well as for congressional committees. Now USTR could show some progress in that area. Although the congressional committees were still skeptical about the SII, it was somewhat impressed by the Interim Report.[150]

Like Kantei, MFA was also relieved. The worsening bilateral relationship appeared to be halted. MITI was still disgruntled since the LSL became "a scapegoat" and the ministry was forced to pledge further concessions that it initially did not anticipate.[151] Nonetheless, the worst time was over for MITI. The compromise reached was a sum of positions of all relevant actors: the U.S. agencies, Kantei, MITI, and the LDP and its respective interest groups.

However, from the perspective of organizational routine, the concessions in the Interim Report can be considered as rather "minor." They are "minor" *not* in the sense that these concessions are unimportant, but in the sense that these concessions are in the line with the policy programs and repertoires of the bureaucracies which are constrained by preestablished procedures and budgets. The second model provides strong explanatory power for the land-use issues. Almost all policy measures in the land policy were already found in programs and menus of the organizational routines of relevant ministries. In Williams' expression, "Many policies the U.S. suggested in the land policy were the ones that the Japanese government wanted to do anyway."[152] As for the LSL, the basic ideas, such as shortening the coordination processing period to two years and other forms of deregulation, already appeared in MITI's advisory committee's report in June of 1989.[153] Although some concessions exceeded the original idea, these were few and minor. To use the comment of Mutsuki Kato, Chairman of the LDP Policy Affairs Research Council, the basic LSL framework was kept intact.[154] A repeal of the LSL, which was not in the MITI's original policy agenda, was not realized. In short, the U.S. agencies' demands mostly accelerated the existing policy programs and repertoires, and in some cases furthered the scope of implementation of such policies. But they did not dramatically alter these preestablished policy programs and menus.

From the perspective of organizational routine, the same thing could be said for MOF's concessions, however, to a lesser extent. MOF's goal of eliminating the "deficit bond" was achieved. Since the old Five-Year Public Works Plan was expiring in 1990, a new multi-year plan was needed. It was already decided in the Japanese government that the level of the public investment in the social infrastructure should be raised in a New Five-Year Economic Plan.[155] Because the pace of business had become somewhat sluggish, MOF already reached a "turning point" and had to make a new budgetary initiative.[156] Therefore, however conspicuous they may have been, MOF's concessions were not as dramatic as initially thought. Certainly new elements, such as a multi-year plan with a numeric budget target, were found in MOF concessions. But these elements could be considered as products of "incrementalism" from the perspective of the second model.[157]

As to antimonopoly law, there was not a policy menu of cartel surcharge increases in JFTC that the U.S. demanded, although JFTC already consulted many experts and conducted research on exclusionary business practices. JFTC recognized a need to clarify rules and regulations in the antimonopoly law and made a policy move to issue new guidelines by the fall of 1989 immediately after the first SII meeting.[158] For the keiretsu issue, there was no such recognition and policy moves in JFTC.

Therefore, in light of the second model with its emphasis on organizational routines of the bureaucracy, concessions in the interim agreement are "all changes that they want to make."[159] But the extent of availability of programs and policy menus conditioned the degree of concession-making, which in turn was affected by the configuration of national and transgovernmental coalitions.

RESURGENCE OF THE GNP RATIO PUBLIC WORKS SPENDING ISSUE

There were several developments after the Interim Report. First, MITI and the LDP became reluctant to raise the cartel surcharge to a level that could have hurt corporations' competitiveness.[160] The transgovernmental coalition in the area of the antitrust law changed in June of 1990. (Refer to the coalition diagram on an increase in cartel surcharge issue in June, 1990 in the map.) Here, the coalition was made between MITI and the LDP (backed by the industries) against other actors.[161]

In June 1990, closer to the Final Report, JFTC took a strong position, announcing that it planned to propose an amendment on surcharge increases in the next Diet session. The LDP became suspicious of JFTC's move to push its own agenda by using U.S. pressure. MITI also became cautious about any large increase in surcharges with a punitive nature. To neutralize the opposition from LDP and MITI, JFTC tried to go on with its own agenda in the committee under direct supervision of prime minister in Kantei.[162] Eventually the decision was made: a consultation committee on surcharge increases, headed by the chief cabinet secretary, was created to further discuss the appropriate level of surcharges.[163]

Then, between the announcement of the Interim Report of April 5 and that of the Final Report of June 28, three issues became the foci of concern: Japanese public works spending by annual percentage of GNP, the patent system, and follow-up mechanisms. The first issue, a GNP ratio public works spending issue, became "the most contentious issue" throughout the SII. The GNP ratio public works spending was again presented by the State Department, the Treasury Department, and CEA in the informal small group meeting in Hawaii on May 23-24, 1990.[164]

Initially, MOF refused to discuss the issue again. In the MOF's view, the GNP ratio issue was already over at the time of the Interim Report; the compromise was reached between MOF and the Treasury Department that public works spending would be shown in the form of the total amount of the budget, but not of GNP-ratio in the final report.[165] Since then, the U.S. agencies had taken a very tough position on the issue until the final moment in June. Some newspapers reported that MOF's "surpluses-are-good" argument (*kuroji yūyō-ron*) is the direct reason why the U.S. agencies took a hard-line position on the issue. According to these reports, MOF asserted that Japan's trade surplus was necessary because of the financial need for countries around the world, such as East European countries in the time of capital shortage in the 1990s. The U.S. agencies were critical of this argument and doubted the sincerity of MOF. In the U.S. agencies' view, MOF's "surpluses-are-good" argument undermined the exact premise of the SII, that is, both governments agreed to reduce the bilateral trade deficit.[166]

However, from the institutional perspective of the second model, that episode seems rather minor. MOF's "surpluses-are-good" argument might have hardened the U.S. agencies' policy stance on the issue, but it was not the reason or the "cause" of the U.S. agencies tough position. Arguably, this is true for several reasons from an institutional point of view. The State Department consistently pursued its organizational goal: a significant reduction of the bilateral trade deficit for political ends that would forge a "U.S.-Japan global partnership." Therefore, it continuously took "tough positions" on public works spending issues. The State Department believed that the most effective way to reduce the bilateral deficit was to ask the Japanese government to increase the budget of public works an annual percent of GNP. If the total size of the Japanese GNP grew large, then the specific sum of money that was pledged to be spent for domestic investment would not have a significant impact in reducing the saving-investment gap. As a result, the bilateral deficit would not be reduced in the coming years.[167]

The gradual "radicalization" of the Treasury Department occurred even before the Hawaii meeting. As mentioned before, the Treasury Department initially described the SII aims as attempting "to address structural practices that cut across the Japanese economy" with "the specific goal of contributing to a reduction in payment imbalance," without mentioning necessary macroeconomic measures.[168] Even in the speech of February 22, 1990, at the Japan Society, the under secretary of the Treasury repeated that the goal of SII was "reducing broad structural economic problems" which would help the multilateral G-7 economic policy coordination process. There was no mention of macroeconomic measures to reduce the Japanese saving-investment gap, that is, the spending of the government budget for public works.[169]

However, in the prepared statement for the March 5 Senate Hearing, the Treasury Department used "transitional expressions" regarding the U.S. goals in the SII. In the statement, the separate but interrelated goals of the SII—a "market access component" and "promoting trade and balance of payment adjustment, and of reducing our deficit and Japan's surplus"—are officially acknowledged.[170] Finally, in the prepared record of the April 19 House Hearing, reporting on the interim agreements, the Treasury Department clearly stated that the structural reforms under the SII involved a "mixture of macroeconomic and microeconomic changes."[171] Moreover, with respect to saving and investment patterns, "a principle objective of the SII talk is the reduction of trade imbalances and current account imbalances" by "setting a goal for a shift in these macroeconomic variables."[172] In short, for the Treasury Department, the GNP ratio public works spending issue was not entirely solved at the time of the Interim Report. The agreement on the total sum notation for public works spending was a temporary compromise for the sake of reaching the interim agreement, and the Treasury Department did not really stop pursuing its organizational goal of setting specific targets for macroeconomic measures.[173]

Just before the final SII meeting on June 24, 1990, the Treasury Department unequivocally expressed its policy stance: "Whether or not Japanese surplus is reduced is the question."[174] The Treasury Department suggested that the Japanese government make not only a ten-year public works plan, but also a five-year plan with a specific sum of money, although it did not insist on an annual GNP ratio spending if the investment was sufficiently large enough to be effective for surplus reduction.[175]

Reportedly, the reason for this strong position of the Treasury Department was that its federal deficit reduction plan experienced setbacks in the domestic arena, and a further exchange alignment for the weaker dollar was difficult because of the possibility of inflation. An increase in Japanese public works spending by 50 percent was the last resort for the Treasury Department to correct the bilateral imbalance.[176]

Although somewhat impressed by the Interim Report, the congressional committees were still stuck with their "own political objectives."[177] In particular, the congressional committees were interested in exactly how much the SII measures (specifically Japanese public works spending) would reduce the bilateral trade deficit. In the House Hearing of April 19, each administration official representing each department for the SII was persistently asked this question. The administration officials did not directly answer the question, except to say that the size of deficit reduction depends on many factors, and that the SII prescriptions are more medium- and long-term ones.[178] Reportedly, the congressional committees criticized the Treasury Department, claiming that it conceded too much to MOF.[179] Indeed, other U.S. departments also felt the constant pressure from the congressional committees.[180]

On the other hand, while MITI had kept an official posture of "prudence" on the public works spending issue, it was critical of MOF's "surpluses-are-good" argument.[181] MFA was also critical of MOF's position. In the Foreign Minister Summit meeting of June 16, 1990, MFA officially denounced the "surpluses-are-good" argument and reaffirmed the "Japanese government's basic policy that the correction of external imbalances is necessary." Although MFA did not support GNP ratio public works spending, it made public its policy to continue its efforts to reduce the bilateral deficit.[182] The State Department also strongly criticized MOF's argument and insisted on GNP ratio public works spending to reduce the huge trade deficit which was, in its view, politically unsustainable.[183]

Regarding the public works spending issue, the basic configuration of transgovernmental coalitions among subunits remained the same between the announcement of the Interim Report of April and that of the Final Report of June. As the final round of SII talks became closer, a GNP ratio public works spending was no longer an issue, but rather the total amount of public works spending over ten years was. The MOF initially proposed 415 trillion yen against the Treasury Department's 500 trillion yen for public works spending over ten years. During the four-day final meeting of June, the public works spending issue had been the most contentious one.

It was at this time that the White House tried to make a compromise for the sake of the larger political goals of maintaining good U.S.-Japan bilateral relations. The White House had reached out to each agency and persuaded each of them to conclude the negotiation by emphasizing the need to balance three pillars of the U.S.-Japanese relations: the military-security tie, global cooperation centering around foreign aid, and trade. In the White House's view, if the trade problem was not solved, this eventually would "spoil" the U.S.-Japanese relations in the other two areas.[184]

Meanwhile, the LDP and Finance Ministry prepared to compromise. The Treasury and State Departments visited Kantei in the early evening of June 28 to ask for a great increase on public works spending. Later, Kantei negotiated with the Finance Ministry for a possible addition of public works spending to conclude the negotiation through a "political decision." The final decision to compromise was made by the White House and Kantei. In the late evening of June 28, the White House and Kantei had a talk over the telephone, reaching an agreement by means of a "political decision" between them.[185]

However, from the viewpoint of the second model, the 430 trillion yen for public works was a compromise based upon a "power balance" among the U.S. agencies, Kantei, the LDP, MOF, and other ministries. The U.S. agencies' demand was 500 trillion yen; the LDP, 450 trillion yen; MOF, 415 trillion yen. The addition of 15 trillion yen was made by the "political decision" of Kantei. The final agreement was on the basis of the 430 trillion and the additional 25 trillion investment by the privatized former state corporations, such as the Japan Railroad (JR) and Nippon Telephone and Telegram (NTT). Thus, the amount which appeared in the letter in the final agreement was 455 trillion yen, which was the middle between the original U.S. agencies' demand and the initial MOF proposal, satisfying the LDP's appetite for "pork-barrel."[186]

CONCLUSION

From the viewpoint of the second model, the SII agreements were the results of a mixture of each agency's organizational routines, national turf-battles, and transgovernmental coalitions across national boundaries. The organizational routines of responsible governmental subunits often help us understand why certain policies of these subunits are proposed, and some of these policies are more likely to be pursued than others. But knowing only organizational routines is not enough because jurisdictions in trade policy-making often overlap, and therefore seldom, if ever, are trade policies decided by one agency. To understand how some policies are actualized, one has to understand the organizational routines and goals of multiple agencies and examine the matrix of those routines and goals. In the SII process, policy goals of governmental subunits were not made along national lines. Rather, the governmental subunits often supported the goals of subunits in the other government, which were similar to their own goals, against the goals of other subunits in their own government. Then, the particular configuration of transgovernmental coalitions resulted in the particular policy outcomes.

In this chapter, the second specific proposition was tested by a coalition analysis. (See the coalition map again.) The levels of Japanese concessions in four SII issue areas are associated with the size of transgovernmental coalitions. The simple numbers of governmental subunits in the winning coalition (the left side of the map) can conveniently predict the level of concessions: the large-sized coalition of 12, in the public works spending; the medium-sized coalition of 7, in the large store law; the medium-sized coalition of 6, in the land policy; and the small-sized coalition of 5, in the increase in cartel surcharge (June 1990). If the number of six U.S. agencies is treated as a constant, then the number of Japanese government subunits which supported the U.S. demands for their own reasons can predict the possible policy outcomes. The number of Japanese ministries in the saving-investment issue area is still the largest, 8; next, 4 in the distribution system; and 4 in the land policy. The 3 in exclusionary business practices in March 1990 explains why an increase in cartel surcharges was agreed to by the time of the Interim Report, while the 2 in the same area suggests why the concrete number of cartel surcharge increases that USTR and Justice Department wanted was not agreed to by the time of the Final Report.

Because of a lack of references, policy positions of governmental subunits on the keiretsu issue cannot be identified. However, it is suspected that the coalition size for keiretsu is small because the keiretsu was often referred to as one of the issues of antitrust law. The LDP was critical of both higher cartel surcharge and limiting cross-shareholding.[187] It seems quite possible that the coalition size for keiretsu is the smallest because even JFTC did not buy the U.S. argument for a need to restrict cross-shareholding, while JFTC supported the U.S. idea of a need to strengthen antitrust law and JFTC organization.[188]

The coalition map shows one important point: the LDP occupies the "strategic position" among governmental subunits in Japanese economic policy-making. Although the specific content of trade agreements was decided by power balances among the relevant subunits, it appears that whether or not the LDP is part of a winning coalition virtually conditions the extent of acceptance of the basic policy lines. More precisely, the location of the LDP in the coalition map indicates how much the Japanese government would accept basic policy lines in trade negotiations. In the saving-investment issue, the LDP is in the winning coalition, with the U.S. agencies supporting the larger budget on public works; therefore that policy was strongly promoted resulting in high level concessions. In the distribution system issue, the LDP is in the middle between the U.S. side coalition and MITI, against the repeal of the LSL but later taking part of the winning coalition with a possible future partial repeal in the urban areas against MITI's resistance; this situation contributed to creating the conditions in which the middle-level concessions were achieved. In the land policy area, the LDP is again in the winning coalition but as a weak supporter; therefore although new initiatives in land policy were accepted, these were not promoted as strong as policies in the saving and investment patterns area.

In the exclusionary business practices issues, the LDP generally disagreed to an increased cartel surcharge and stronger antitrust law enforcement. However, in March 1990, MITI, MFA, and JFTC initiated a policy of cartel surcharge increases, and the LDP was not well informed about the issue, only expressing frustration and general criticism about the new policy. But by June 1990, the LDP with MITI clearly opposed the large increase of cartel surcharges. Because of the LDP's opposition, the level of concessions in terms of acquiring concrete number figures remained relatively low. Likewise, the LDP was critical of the U.S. agencies' argument on keiretsu; therefore, the concession level was low.[189]

The size (and strength) of transgovernmental coalitions among the U.S. and Japanese governmental subunits provided a good reference for predicting the degrees of negotiation outcomes. The larger the size of the transgovernmental coalition, the higher the Japanese government concessions on the issues. Among the members of the winning coalition in the Japanese government, which supported the U.S. agencies' demands, the LDP was the key actor resorting to weighted influence in deciding whether and to what extent the basic policy lines were accepted.[190]

NOTES

1. Mastanduno, op. cit., p. 245.

2. Ibid.

3. See Hills' statement, *Nikkei* 5/26/89, p. 2.

4. NHK, op. cit., p. 72.

5. Williams, *Daiyamondo* 4/11/92, pp. 90, 92-93.

6. Refer to the opening statements of each agency in the reconstructed SII meeting records in NHK, op. cit., pp. 248-53. Also refer to Williams, *Daiyamondo* 5/22/92, p. 108.

7. Allison, op. cit., pp. 80-81, 87-88.

8. Roger Swanson, "The United States operates in the interaction, not as a unitary government but through a 'Canadiana constellation'—a number of loosely allied organizational components, arbitrarily considered as a grouping, which have functional or geographical responsibilities in matters directly or indirectly affecting Canada" ([1972], "The United States Canadiana Constellation, I: Washington D.C.," p. 184).

9. *NYT* 3/20/89, pp. A1, A8.

10. *NYT* 11/24/89, p. A12.

11. Ibid. See also *Asahi* 11/30/91, p. 9. Asahi Shinbun Keizai-bu (1974), *Keizai Seisaku no Butaiura*, pp. 207-217.

12. Swanson, op. cit., p. 184.

13. Allison, op. cit., p. 88.

14. Theodore Sorensen, *New York Times Magazine* 3/19/67, p. 167.

15. Allison, op. cit., p. 88.

16. Igarashi, op. cit., p. 25.

17. Refer to Mulford' statement, SH 7/20/90, pp. 4-5.

18. "Turf-battle" does not necessarily mean that the U.S. federal agencies fought with each other or that the relations among departments are always "conflictual." It simply means that each agency has its organizational goals, priorities, and preferences for policy measures; and that because of this, each agency bargains with other departments in the policy-making process. Even the departments which have main jurisdiction over particular issues need to acquire some consensus from other departments before the final policy decision is made due to overlapping legal and actual responsibilities. Refer to Williams, "the policy-making process of the U.S. government is horizontal" (*Daiyamondo* 4/11/92, p. 90).

19. Fukushima, op. cit., pp. 45-51. Prestowitz describes the positions of the U.S. department from a similar viewpoint. See *Trading Places*, pp. 268-271. Stephen D. Cohen's view of "trifurcated Japan policy" is also based on the same notion. See (1991) "United States-Japanese Trade Relations," p. 186.

20. Pear, *NYT* 3/20/89, pp. A1, A8.

21. Asahi Shinbun Keizai-bu, op. cit., p. 209. Alan Rix studied Japan's foreign aid policy from the viewpoint of "bureaucratic politics" among ministries. See (1980), *Japan's Economic Aid*.

22. Refer to Mastanduno, op. cit., p. 257.

23. For example, *NYT* 5/26/89, p. D5. Refer to Hills' statement of May 25, 1989, "In this negotiation [SII], the focus will be put on structural import barriers, such as the distribution system and the rigidity in the pricing mechanism" (*Nikkei* 5/26/89, E.p. 2).

24. *Asahi* 4/6/90, p. 1. See also NHK, op. cit., pp. 103-104. This notion, that is, that the complex interactive processes of demand and concession making (the understanding that even in the demand-making stage, the U.S. and Japanese agencies coalesced with each other), is somewhat different from that of Schoppa, which only focuses on the explanations for the concession-making stage of the SII (i.e., the reasons why U.S. *gaiatsu* worked in some areas but not in others).

25. Fukushima reported one episode (op. cit., p. 267): When he asked a friend in the State Department for the paper analyzing possibilities that the FSX agreement would be ratified in Congress, his friend said, "All right. It won't hurt to share this document with USTR, for it was handed in to the Japanese government last week." Fukushima commented that for the State Department, the Japanese Foreign Ministry is a far more trustworthy ally than USTR. This episode illustrates that the State Department shares information with MFA without telling other domestic agencies. The Japanese Finance Ministry also often expresses a "strong pipe" or "microcosmic relationship" with the Treasury Department. MOF officials often feel a closer relationship with the Treasury Department than other domestic rival agencies. See *Asahi* 11/30/91, p. 9; 7/10/93, p. 3.

26. For example, refer to Zenichro Tanaka (1981), *Jimintō Taisei no Seiji Shidō*; Shinkichi Eto (1974), "Nihon ni okeru taigai seisaku kettei katei"; Seisaburo Sato and Tetsuhisa Matsuzaki (1986), *Jimintō Seiken*.   Daniel I. Okimoto (1988), "Political Inclusivity: The Domestic Structure of Trade."

27. Schoppa, op. cit. (1993), pp. 378, 381.

28. See the numerous activities and lobbying efforts of thirteen large trade organizations of retail stores on MITI and the LDP, *Nikkei* 3/11/90, p. 13; 3/21/90, p. 5; 3/30/90, p. 3; 4/2/90, p. 1. *Asahi*, 4/6/90, p. 2; 4/7/90, p. 3. In contrast, there are no such newspaper articles reporting Keidanren's positive lobbying on MITI and LDP.

29. It is customary for Keidanren to announce its policy stance on the variety of economic issues. For example, see the recent announcement on deregulation, *Asahi* 9/2/93, p. 1. But such a policy announcement does not always have influence on the particular policy outcomes in certain issue areas. For example, Japanese agricultural policies are mostly decided by the dynamics among MAFF, LDP agricultural policy "tribes," and farmers' cooperatives. While Keidanren for a long time has preferred agricultural trade liberalization, it has had little influence on that dynamics.

30. Keidanren is an umbrella trade organization for big corporations, industrial organizations and various trade organizations, while Nisshō represents small and medium size retail stores and manufacturers in the local communities.

31. One can use the term either Congress or congressional committees, because from a theoretical viewpoint, they are the same. Here Congress is treated as one of the subunits in the overall U.S. government, not as a "large institution," that is, one opposed to another "large institution" (the administration) in the first model. However, the term "congressional committees" is preferred in this chapter for theoretical and empirical reasons. Theoretically, the term "congressional committee" is more consistent with groups in the level of analysis of the second model. Empirically, making laws and passing regulations by the Senate and House are considered as institutional acts by the Congress as a whole, while having committee hearings can be thought of as activities of congressional subunits. I choose the term "congressional committee" throughout the chapter to distinguish Congress as a "large institution" in the first model from that as "one of the subunits" in the overall U.S. government.

32. Interview, 11/13/92.

33. A former administration official, telephone interview 11/4/92.

34. According to Raymond J. Ahearn, U.S. trade policies are usually made in one of two ways: a decision is reached either through bargaining and the formation of a dominant coalition among agencies, or by presidential support, initiative, or arbitration. In his view, because many trade issues today are politically sensitive and divisive, presidential involvement is required to break a deadlock. See (1982), "Political Determinants of U.S. Trade Policy," p. 424.

35. In Japanese politics, "Kantei" ordinarily means the policy position of the cabinet secretariat including prime minister and chief cabinet secretary. For the prime minister's leadership and the role of Kantei, refer to Robert Angel (1988/89) "Prime Ministerial Leadership in Japan."

36. Refer to *Asahi* 4/3/90, p. 3; 4/7/90, p. 3; *Nikkei* 4/4/90, p. 2; 4/6/90, p. 3. Also see Williams, *Daiyamondo* 6/6/92, p. 235; Yabunaka, op. cit., p. 167. In the Nakasone government, Kantei demonstrated a political initiative to make the Comprehensive

Economic Measures (*Sōgō Keizai Seisaku*) in the effort to solve trade friction with the U.S. See Funabashi, op.cit., p. 33.

37. Throughout the SII process, this dynamic is expressed as "the triangular struggle among Kantei, the Party, and the ministries" (*Nikkei* 4/6/90, p. 3). For Japanese policy-making process and institutional actors, for example, refer to Seigen Miyazato and Kokusai Daigaku Nich-bei Kenkyū-jo (1990), *Nichi-bei Kōzō Masatsu no Kenkyū*, pp. 61-72. The dynamics of LDP factions is another factor. Although the dynamics among factions in the LDP is important, here I will focus on "formal institutional actors."

38. Sasaki, op. cit., p. 35.

39. A Treasury Department official, interview 10/9/92. See also Dallara, in NHK, op. cit., p. 70.

40. See William H. Cooper (1990), "Japan-U.S. Trade: The Structural Impediments Initiative" (CRS Report for Congress), pp. 5-6. According to the U.S. Embassy official Greenwood, there was nothing new about the topics on the SII agenda. All the issues, including land policy, have been discussed since the Structural Economic Dialogue of 1986. Cited in NHK, op. cit., p. 93.

41. NHK, op. cit., p. 68. See also Allen Wallis, "Structural Adjustment, Dialogue, and the U.S.-Japan Economic Relations" (State Department, Current Policy No. 924, March 1987), pp. 4-5.

42. Mulford's speech, "U.S. and Japan: Forging a New Relationship" (12/5/88, C-SPAN Video, ID: 14312 AB.) Some basic notions of the SII were expressed in this speech in explaining the organizational characteristic of the Yen-Dollar Talks, although he did not use the word "SII." In the interview of 10/7/92, a Treasury Department official pointed out the existence of this speech as the first public appearance of the idea of SII. No study on the SII has ever mentioned this speech, nor was it reported in any newspaper articles or government documents. The second model highlighting organizational routine enables us to find the existence of this speech.

43. See Mulford, SH 7/20/89, pp. 3-4. Also refer to "U.S. and Japan: Cooperation in World Economic Leadership" (Speech before the Japan Society on February 22, 1990) in *Treasury News* NB-680 2/22/90, p. 6.

44. Mulford, SH 7/20/89, p. 4.

45. NHK, op. cit., pp. 71-73; *Nikkei* 7/27/89, p. 5; 9/8/89, p. 5.

46. Williams, testimony before SH 7/20/89, p. 6. See also Williams, *Daiyamondo* 4/4/92, p. 113.

47. Williams, SH 7/20/89, p. 6.

48. Ibid.

49. Refer to Williams, SH 7/20/89, p. 6; *Daiyamondo* 4/4/92, pp. 111-113. I prefer the distinction between business practices as "informal barriers" and "structural barriers," for the sake of clarification. Distinguishing institutional arrangements or "structures" (e.g. weak antitrust laws, problems with the patent laws, a land tax system, keiretsu ties, the distribution system) from business practices (e.g. Japanese corporations' long-term procurement practices, the "buy Japanese" mentality) is useful for many reasons. But those barriers are not always distinguished by U.S. officials as well as others. Williams' "structural rigidities" include both informal business practices and structural barriers. As a matter of chronological fact, such structural barriers as Japanese weak antitrust law are the latest form on trade agendas for a bilateral trade negotiation.

50. For other policies under consideration in USTR in the late fall of 1988 and the early spring of 1989, refer to Mustanduno, op. cit., p. 243.

51. Williams, *Daiyamondo* 4/11/92, p. 90. According to a high-ranking official of USTR, a new talk is designed to be outside Super 301 because the strict time limit of Super 301 is not suitable for dealing with broad structural issues, such as exclusionary business practices, and the distribution system (cited in NHK, op. cit., p. 77).

52. Williams, *Daiyamondo* 4/11/92, p. 90; NHK, op. cit., pp. 77-78.

53. Refer to Commerce Secretary Robert Mosbacher's speech "America's Economic Security," May 8, 1989, *Vital Speeches of the Day* 55 (18), 6/1/89, pp. 554-556; Bruce Stokes, *National Journal* 8/12/89, pp. 2033-2034.

54. *Nikkei*, 10/21/89, p. 1.

55. *Nikkei* 1/28/89, p. 1; *NYT* 2/3/89, p. A. Also refer *Nikkei* 10/5/88, p. 1, for MFA's policy initiative to create a new panel to solve trade disputes.

56. Fukushima, op.cit., p. 205.

57. NHK, op. cit., pp. 78-79.

58. Williams, *Daiyamondo* 4/11/92, p. 91.

59. Fukushima, op. cit., p. 204.

60. Williams, *Daiyamondo* 4/11/91, p. 91.

61. Williams, *Daiyamondo* 4/11/92, pp. 92-93.

62. *Nikkei* 5/1/89, p. 5.

63. NHK, op. cit., pp. 78-79.

64. *Nikkei* 5/23/89, p. 5.

65. NHK, op. cit., pp. 78-79.

66. Those congressional committee hearings include the Senate Finance Committee hearings, January 27, 1989 (*Nomination of Carla Anderson Hills*), March 1; April 20; May 3, 1989 (*Oversight of the Trade Act of 1988*, Part 1-3), the House Trade Subcommittee of the Ways and Means Committee hearings, February 28; April 26, 1989 (*National Trade Policy Agenda*).

67. It was reported that USTR's tandem decisions of Super 301 and SII proposals were made with congressional approval just before May 25, although congressional committees initially wanted to remove certain structural barriers under Super 301. See *Nikkei* 5/21/89, p. 1; *CQWR* 5/27/89, p. 1242.

68. Williams describes the Super 301 designation and the SII as somewhat separate policies which were announced on the same day (*Daiyamondo* 5/16/92, p. 106). Williams' descriptions have some basis because Super 301 and the SII originated in different parts of the U.S. government and went through different policy-making processes in the administration bureaucracy. Refer to Williams, *Daiyamondo* 4/4/92, p. 113; 4/11/92, p. 90-91, and Fukushima, op. cit. p 44.

69. Williams, "By that time [May 25, 1989], both governments had reached an informal agreement to discuss structural issues" (*Daiyamondo* 5/16/92, p. 106).

70. Williams, *Daiyamondo* 4/11/92, pp. 91, 92. Also refer to SH 7/20/89, p. 10.

71. Williams, *Daiyamondo* 4/11/92, p. 92.

72. Mulford, HH 7/20/89, pp. 3-4.

73. Mulford, SH 7/20/90, pp. 4-5.

74. Ibid., p. 5.

75. Ibid., pp. 4-5.

76. Williams, SH 7/20/89, p. 7.

77. Ibid.

78. Ibid.

79. Ibid.

80. Ibid.

81. Williams, newspaper interview *Nikkei* 6/7/89, p. 5. Williams clearly stated that "As Ambassador Hills pointed out, U.S. trade deficit is mainly caused by macroeconomic factors such as saving rate, not by market barriers. Although the SII will contribute to macroeconomic adjustment and have an effect on reducing the trade deficit by 20 to 30 percent, the SII is not held for the reduction of trade deficit" (*Asahi* 7/9/89, p. 9). See also *Daiyamondo* 3/21/92, p. 111.

82. Williams, *Nikkei* 6/7/89, p. 5. The same point is repeated by Williams on the other occasion. See Williams interview, *Tōyō Keizai* 10/14/89, p. 102.

83. *Nikkei* 4/6/90, p. 1.

84. Richard Solomon, Assistant Secretary for East Asian and Pacific Affairs. Speech April 10, 1990 (State Department, Current Policy No. 1268), p. 1.

85. McCormack, SH 7/20/89, p. 8.

86. Ibid.

87. Ibid.

88. A State Department official, *Asahi* 10/8/89, p. 9.

89. McCormack, SH 7/20/89, p. 7.

90. Ibid., p. 8.

91. Ibid., pp. 8-9.

92. McCormack, "For our part, we must balance our fiscal budget, increase savings and investment . . . produce more competitive product . . . continue vigorous programs to promote U.S. exports" (SH 7/20/89, p. 8).

93. Refer to McCormack's speech of October 30, 1989 (State Department, Current Policy No. 1223). See also *Asahi* 10/8/89, p. 9.

94. The strong position taken by the State and Treasury Departments in the public works spending issue might be attributed to the policy stance of individuals rather than organizations. "Dallara and McCormack took the strongest position at the negotiation table, in spite of the fact that they both represented such departments as the Treasury and State which traditionary took a moderate policy stance (Williams, *Daiyamondo* 4/11/93, p. 92). However, explaining "radicalization" of two departments' positions from the viewpoint of the second model is quite possible, considering their organizational goals and routines. Indeed, the strong positions Dallara and McCormack took were consistent with two departments' policy positions at that time. Stephen D. Cohen offers a general clue for a recent "evolutionary phenomenon" of the policies of two departments; that is, "a narrowing in the gap [between State and Treasury] in their divergent perceptions of what international economic policy option in a given case will best serve the national interest" and "the State Department's increased sensitivity toward the greater presence of domestic economic strength in the contemporary definition of national security" ([1994], *The Making of United States International Economic Policy*, p. 47).

95. The same pattern was repeated in the March 5 and the April 19 hearings attended by chief negotiators from the Treasury, State, USTR, CEA, and Commerce, (and Justice on April 19).

96. Senator Max Baucus' opening statement, SH 7/20/89, pp. 1-2.

97. Senator Baucus, SH 11/6-7/89, p. 1; SH 3/5/90, p. 24.

98. Keohane and Nye suggest two types of transgovernmental coalitions: "potential coalition"(or "tacit coalition") and "explicit coalition." But, making a distinction between "potential" and "tacit" coalition is more useful for analytical reasons. To use their characterization, (1) a "potential coalition" is one between subunits in which subunits do not come into contact with each other but have common or complementary interests; (2) a "de facto tacit coalition" is one between subunits in which the independent actions of one member seem to serve the interests of the others and vice versa; and (3) an "explicit coalition" is one characterized by direct communication among the subunits. [See op. cit. (1974), p. 51.] Logically, only *actions* (i.e., taking the same positions or supporting for others' policies) can convert "potential" into a "de facto tacit" coalition, even without direct communication and sharing other resources. Here, the transgovernmental coalition includes the second and the third types because all subunit actors are already in the process of the transgovernmental trade policy-making.

99. Refer to discussions in HH 2/20/90 and SH 3/5/90. See also quotations from U.S. officials in Yabunaka, op. cit., p. 179.

100. Refer to Williams, *Daiyamondo* 5/23/92, p. 108. In that article, Williams did not specify which agency took the latter position. However, it is inferred that USTR took the latter position against such agencies as State and Treasury, which strongly insisted that the trade deficit reduction be achieved through macroeconomic measures, because Williams thought linking the trade deficit issue to the SII was a "mistake."

101. Haruhiro Fukui (1978), "The GATT Tokyo Round," p. 85. Also refer to *Asahi Janaru* 12/2/77, pp. 7-13.

102. NHK, op. cit., p. 83; *Nikkei* 7/27/89, p. 5; 9/8/89, p. 5. *Asahi* 3/4/90, p. 2.

103. See *Nikkei* 8/28/90, p. 5. Deputy Minister of MFA Michihiko Kunihiro in *Ekonomisuto* 9/5/89, pp. 10-12 and *Chūō Kōron* 11, 1989, pp. 92-101.

104. NHK, op. cit., pp. 252-253; *Nikkei* 9/8/89, p. 5.

105. *Nikkei* 7/6/89, p. 1; 10/16/89, p. 2. According to Williams, many documents which the U.S team used to analyze the Japanese market were made by the EPA (*Daiyamondo* 4/11/92, p. 91).

106. *Nikkei* 4/8/90, p. 1.

107. *Nikkei* 9/8/89, p. 5; NHK, op. cit., p. 83.

108. *Nikkei* 9/8/89, p. 5.

109. *Asahi* 4/6/90, p. 1.

110. Michihiko Kunihiro, NHK, op. cit., p. 248. Deputy Minister of MFA, Kunihiro participated in the preparation stage of the SII and in the first meeting. After the first meeting, Deputy Minister Koji Watanabe took over his position.

111. Utsumi, NHK op. cit., p. 249.

112. This statement is rather a repeat of the official definition of the SII. This is a sharp contrast to MITI's insistence in the later stage that the purpose of the SII is "to reduce the trade and current account imbalances." See Williams, *Daiyamondo* 5/23/92, p. 108.

113. Vice Minister of MITI Naomichi Suzuki, NHK op. cit., pp. 249-250.

114. McCormack, ibid., p. 250.

115. McCormack, Utsumi, ibid., pp. 268-269.

116. Dallara, ibid., p. 251.

117. Williams, ibid., pp. 251-252.

118. Farren, ibid., p. 252.

119. Taylor, ibid., p. 252.

120. Vice Minister of EPA Tsuneo Unno, ibid., pp. 252-253.

121. Utsumi, ibid., p. 74.

122. Dallara, ibid., pp. 278, 290-291.

123. McCormack, ibid., p. 290.

124. Williams, ibid., p. 303.

125. *Tōyō Keizai* 3/10/90, p. 40.

126. *Nikkei* 2/25/90, p. 1.

127. *Asahi* 3/5/90, p. 1; 4/3/90; *Nikkei* 3/5/90, p. 2; 3/10/90, E.p. 1; 4/7/90, p. 2.

128. *Nikkei* 6/17/90, p. 2.

129. *Asahi* 4/3/90, p. 2. The "activism" of Kantei is so well-noticed that some LDP politicians complained about Kantei's "forerunning" without enough consent from the party (*Nikkei* 4/4/90, p. 2).

130. *Nikkei* 3/30/90, p. 3; 3/28/90, p. 3; NHK, op. cit., pp. 294, 297.

131. *Nikkei* 3/28/90, p. 1.

132. *Nikkei* 3/21/90, p. 5; 3/27/90, p. 1; 3/28/90, p. 3.

133. *Nikkei* 3/17/90, p. 5. JFTC already experienced a major setback in an attempt to strengthen the antimonopoly laws in 1977, because MITI and industries strongly opposed amending the laws. Refer to NHK, op. cit., pp. 200-214.

134. *Asahi* 3/5/90, p. 3.

135. An administration official, interview 10/8/92.

136. *Asahi* 4/5/90, p. 9; *Nikkei* 6/13/90, p. 2.

137. The U.S. departments are based on NHK book (pp. 248-304) which expressed their concerns in the discussions of the issue areas in the SII meetings. The Japanese ministries are based on the newspaper articles, the NHK book, Fukai op. cit. p. 8, and Schoppa op. cit., p. 378. Information about the Commerce Department is so scarce that its policy positions are not identified in the map.

138. *Asahi* 3/17/90, p. 1.

139. The final LDP decision was left to the top executive members of the Party (*Nikkei* 3/30/90, p. 1).

140. *Nikkei* 3/30/90, p. 3.

141. *Asahi* 3/29/90, p. 1; 4/3/90, p. 3; *Nikkei* 4/4/90, p. 2.

142. Refer to Edo, op. cit., pp. 142-145. MITI initially wanted to normalize the LSL by issuing a ministerial ordinance in line with the policy of *90 Nendiai no Ryūtsū Bijon* (The Vision of the Distribution System in the 1990s) by September of 1989. But because of the strong opposition from interest groups, MITI could not achieve this goal.

143. *Nikkei* 3/17/90, p. 5; *Asahi* 3/28/90, p. 2.

144. *Asahi* 3/17/90, p. 1.

145. *Nikkei* 3/27/90, E.p. 1; 3/28/90, p. 3; *Asahi* 3/28/90, p. 2; 3/29/90, p. 1.

146. *Nikkei* 9/5/89, E.p. 1.

147. See *Asahi* 6/23/90, p.9; NHK, op. cit., pp. 135-150.

148. Refer to Fukai, op. cit., pp. 3-8.

149. *Asahi* 4/5/90, E.p. 2.

150. Refer to the opening statements of representatives (HH 4/19/90).

151. *Asahi* 4/6/90, p. 1.

152. Williams, telephone interview 6/9/94.   Also refer to Watanabe's remarks in NHK, op. cit., p. 279.

153. Refer to *Nikkei* 6/10/89, p. 3.   See also *90 Nendai no Ryūtsū Bijon*, pp. 181-182.

154. *Asahi* 4/7/90, p. 3.

155. Refer to remarks of Unno and Ozawa in NHK, op. cit., pp. 276, 277.

156. *Asahi* 4/8/90, p. 1.

157. On "incrementalism" in Japan's response to U.S. pressure, refer to Aurelia George (1991), "Japan's America Problem: The Japanese Response to U.S.Pressure," pp. 9-11.

158. Refer to *Nikkei* 9/3/89, p. 1.

159. An administration official, interview 10/8/92.

160. *Nikkei* 6/18/90, p. 12.

161. See *Asahi* 6/13/90, p. 2.

162. *Asahi* 6/13/90, p. 3.

163. *Nikkei* 6/26/90, p. 1.

164. *Asahi* 6/18/90, p. 1.

165. *Nikkei* 5/26/90, p. 5; *Asahi* 6/18/90, p. 1.

166. *Asahi* 6/7/90, p. 9; 6/18/90, p. 1.

167. Refer to the remarks of a high ranking U.S. administration official in *Asahi* 6/23/90, p. 1, although the article did not specify to which department this official belonged.

168. Mulford, SH 7/20/89, p. 4.

169. Mulford, op. cit., speech before the Japan Society 2/22/90, p. 6.   However, reportedly the Treasury Department was becoming more critical of Japanese investment barriers and the closed nature of the Japanese financial market than before (*Nikkei* 1/1/90, p. 9).

170. Dallara, SH 3/5/90, p. 43.

171. Dallara, HH 4/19/90, p. 101.

172. Ibid.   Also refer to the U.S. delegates' comments in the Interim Report, "A principle objective of the SII talks is the reduction of trade imbalances and current account imbalances of Japan and the United States."

173. See Williams *Daiyamondo* 6/13/92, p. 85.

174. Dallara, *Nikkei* 6/25/90, p. 1.

175. Ibid.

176. *Nikkei* 6/28/90, p. 3.

177. A former administration official, telephone interview 11/5/92.

178. HH 4/19/90, pp. 131-32, 138-42.

179. *Asahi* 6/7/90, p. 9.

180. Refer to such remarks as a U.S. official's: "430 trillion yen for public work over ten years is the minimum level in order to persuade Congress" (*Nikkei* 6/28/90, p. 3).

181. *Asahi* 6/8/90, p. 2; 6/9/90, p. 2.

182. *Asahi* 6/16/90, p. 1.

183. Ibid.

184. NHK, op. cit., pp. 224-226.

185. *Nikkei* 6/27/90, p. 1; 6/28/90, p. 1; *Asahi* 6/28/90, p. 1.

186. Refer to *Asahi* 6/28/90, p. 2; *Nikkei* 6/27/90, p. 3.

187. *Nikkei* 3/27/90, E.p. 1.

188. See NHK. op. cit., pp. 298, 301-302. Schoppa suggested that the Japanese business community, professional economists, and government bureaucrats including those of JFTC all defended keiretsu (op. cit. [1993], p. 364).

189. *Nikkei* 3/27/90, E. p. 1.

190. The U.S. SII team seemed to know that the key to obtaining a high-level of Japanese government's concessions was the LDP's decision. Refer to NHK, op. cit., p. 105.

7　The U.S. Agencies' Concerns: Content-Analysis of the SII Meeting Records

To know U.S. and Japanese agencies' concerns and areas of responsibility, and the relative "emphasis" of the issue areas in the overall SII discussions on the problems in the Japanese economy, I examined the length of speeches made by chief negotiators in the SII meetings by counting the numbers of lines in the reconstructed records of the SII meetings. "*Nichi-bei kōzō kyōgi gijiroku no kiroku*" (the Record of U.S.-Japan Structural Impediments Initiative Meeting Records) in the appendix of NHK Shuzai-han's *NHK Supesharu Dokyumento Kōzō Kyōgi* is a reconstructed record based on notes taken by Japanese officials in the SII meetings and NHK Shuzai-han's own interviews with these officials. I cross-referenced this record with other available sources and found it to be reliable.[1] In addition, I spoke via telephone with a producer at NHK. According to him, the person who reconstructed the record described it as a "big story" and highly credible (*shinrai-sei ga takai*). Since there are no official SII meeting records open to the public so far, the NHK records can be treated as a substitute for the official records until the official record is published some day.

The method of content-analysis here is simple: counting the number of lines of each speaker. (The numbers are rounded.) The assumption is that the length of the speech is positively associated with the extent of initiatives each agency took. I counted the length of individual speaker's speeches and calculated the percentages for each agency.

See Percentages in All Speeches of Table 7.1. The Treasury Department had the largest percentage in the total speeches (23.1%), followed by Japanese MOF (14.2%, indicated by MF), and then by the State Department (11.9%) and MITI (11.3%); finally by USTR (8.6%) and MFA (7.8%), with the lowest percentages of all other agencies. If Ambassador Armacost's speech (1.8%) is included in State Department count, then the percentage is 13.7. These numbers indicate the dominance of six co-chair agencies in the discussions: Treasury, MOF, State, MITI, USTR, MFA. It also shows the leading role of the

Treasury Department and its counterpart MOF to a lesser extent. Among the six agencies, the Treasury, MOF, State and MITI were the most dominant.

In Table 7.1, on the Japanese side, MOF occupies 32.0 percent of the time, followed by MITI, 25.2 percent and the by MFA, 17.6 percent. On the U.S. side, the Treasury Department's speeches occupied 41.7 percent, followed by the State Department, 21.4 percent (or 24.6% if Armacost's speeches included), and then USTR at 15.5 percent. This result again suggests the leading position of the four major agencies, the Treasury and State Departments, MOF, and MITI. This also suggests the weight of two major issues, saving-investment patterns and the distribution system, which were these four agencies' areas of responsibility.

In Table 7.2, as expected, the total number of lines for saving-investment patterns are large: 413 (175 + 238); for the distribution system, 272 (142 + 130); and for exclusionary business practices, 226 (63 + 163).[2] These results are consistent with those of the *Nikkei* indexes, in which the greatest number of indexes are found in the saving and investment issue area, and next, in the distribution system and exclusionary business practices areas (but more indexes in the former).

There may be cases that the length of speeches is not positively associated with the actual extent of concerns about the issues in trade negotiations. Some issues may be discussed in great length, not because these are greater concerns for negotiation parties but because they are technically complicated. However, in ordinary conditions (i.e., other things being equal), one can safely assume that negotiation parties will spend a longer time for the issues of greater concern. Indeed, the U.S. and Japanese agencies spent much time on Japanese saving and investment patterns issues by analyzing the details of the facts, and by suggesting, defending, and counter-suggesting necessary policies to be taken.[3] The U.S. agencies expressed their concern at great length about how to reduce the bilateral trade deficit. Due to the U.S. agencies' great concern about the issue of saving-investment patterns in the Japanese economy, the Japanese ministries also had to respond to U.S. agencies' questions and policy suggestions. As a result, the length of speeches in the saving and investment patterns area was the largest.

The same logic also can be applied to two other issues—the distribution system and exclusionary business practices. Overall, the length of the aggregated speeches of U.S. and Japanese agencies manifests the extent of relative "emphasis" (if not "priority" or "importance") of the issue areas in the SII discussions.

In short, the results of Table 7.2 regarding the relative "emphasis" of the issue areas are consistent with those of *Nikkei* indexes. In the first three plenary SII meetings, the greatest time spent was for discussing saving and investment patterns issues, and next for the distribution system and exclusionary business practices (the latter to a lesser extent than the former).

Table 7.3 shows which agencies took a lead in the total discussion of each issue area. For instance, in the saving-investment patterns area, the Treasury Department (38%) and MOF (40%) dominated the discussion 78 percent of the time. In the distribution system, the State Department (37%) and MITI (27%), with JFTC (11%, indicated by FTC), took the lead. Likewise, the Treasury Department took a lead by 67 percent in keiretsu; the Justice Department (38%) and USTR (31%) in exclusionary business practices; and the Commerce Department (49%) and MITI (36%) in the issue of pricing mechanisms.

Table 7.4 shows the percentage of speeches made by agencies from each side in the issue areas. These numbers can be interpreted as each ministry's jurisdiction over the issues on the Japanese side and departments' planned areas of responsibility as well as concerns on the U.S. side. On the U.S. side, the percentage of speeches matched each agency's planned responsible areas that were described in the Senate Hearings on July 20, 1989, and in Williams' article. According to that format, the Treasury Department was to take a "lead" in savings-investment patterns, working with CEA; in keiretsu; and in land use, with the State Department. The State Department was expected to take a "lead" in the distribution system; and then in land use, with the Treasury Department; and take part in price mechanisms with the Commerce Department. USTR would take a lead in exclusionary business practices.[4] The Commerce Department planned to play a leading role in pricing mechanisms. The Justice Department shared responsibility on antitrust law in exclusionary business practices with USTR.[5] The actual percentage of speeches of agencies in each issue area are as follows. In the saving and investment patterns, the Treasury Department spoke 66 percent of the time; and CEA, 14 percent. In keiretsu, the Treasury Department spoke 100 percent of the time. In land use, the Treasury Department spoke 69 percent; and the State Department, 31 percent. In the distribution system, the State Department occupied 78 percent of the entire discussions. In the exclusionary business practices area, the USTR shared responsibility of leading discussions (44%) with the Justice Department (53%). In the pricing mechanisms, the Commerce Department indeed took a leading role by speaking most of the time which was assigned to the U.S. team (92%), while the State Department took a small part (8%) as described above.

There is one important point which should be mentioned regarding the savings-investment patterns. The Treasury Department (66%) dominated the discussion supported by CEA (14%) on the U.S. side. The State Department also spoke for a considerable amount of time, 19 percent (i.e., the total of Armacost and McCormack). This supports the State Department's relatively high concern about the saving-investment patterns issue, which is consistent with the observations made in the case study.

On the other hand, the percentages on the Japanese side seem to show jurisdiction over the issues. For instance, in the area of the savings-investment patterns, MOF spoke 94 percent of the time, during which EPA spoke only 6 percent of the time, and other agencies not at all. Since these reconstructed records are of formal plenary sessions of the SII, it is quite possible that the agencies with official jurisdiction over issues mostly spoke in the meetings, and subsequently, only those official speeches were recorded. From the 94 percent, one can infer that MOF was powerful and monopolized jurisdiction over the budget issue.[6] In the land use area, four Japanese agencies, that is, National Land Agency, MOF, Ministry of Home Affairs, and Ministry of Justice, and MFA shared jurisdiction.[7] In the distribution system area, MITI had main jurisdiction over policy issues because of the LSL, while other ministries and agency (JFTC, MOF, Ministry of Transportation, and National Tax Agency) had some jurisdiction in the area.

There are several interesting points regarding keiretsu and exclusionary business practices. On keiretsu, MOF spoke 57 percent of the time on the Japanese side. This is because MOF is a counteragency to the Treasury Department and many of the issues were about financial keiretsu (e.g., problems of cross-shareholding, shareholders' rights, and foreign investment). In the exclusionary business practices issue, not JFTC but MITI, spoke 60 percent of the time. This means that MITI was the key in changing the antitrust law. As seen before, the case study suggested that a concession on the increase in surcharges was initiated by MITI, with MFA's support. The analysis results seem to support those of the case study results.

Tables 7.3 and 7.4 are useful for identifying which agencies took part in which discussions, and therefore what transgovernmental coalitions were possible. For instance, on pricing mechanisms, MITI was defensive about its position, asserting that there were no price differentials between domestic and overseas markets for most goods that MITI surveyed in August of 1989, while EPA was in the position of a "de facto tacit coalition" with U.S. agencies. In EPA's view, although the prices of goods in the domestic markets reflected the high yen, that reflection was not enough, and further policy measures were necessary.[8] EPA also supported U.S. arguments on macroeconomic issues against MOF.[9] In the exclusionary business practices, although three U.S. agencies, the Justice Department, USTR and the State Department, criticized Japan's weak antitrust law enforcement, they also supported JFTC's position in its efforts to strengthen organizational functions.[10] Contrary, MITI defended its administrative guidance and industrial policy.[11]

In addition to this data, the number of U.S. agencies which spoke in each issue area provides information about the extent of U.S. agencies' "concerns" and the political pressure they applied.[12] Because the SII meetings constituted international trade negotiation aiming at specific results, the extent of expressed concerns can be interpreted as the extent of the pressure on Japanese ministries and agencies to which U.S. departments resorted in the effort to acquire specific concessions from them. Take some short speeches in the records for example: "The problems of such tax system as asset tax are important structural impediments and should not be underestimated" (Dallara); "With respect to the issue of [improving] operational procedures in the Antimonopoly Law, the point is how much the deterrent power is expected from it" (Rill); "Why does it take five years to issue [liquor selling] licenses for large-scale retail stores?" (McCormack); "I am surprised to hear that the level of Japanese investment is high. But, the fact is that GNP ratio public investment is significantly decreasing, while the [budget] surpluses remain. Isn't the time arriving that investment for social infrastructures is necessary" (Dallara); "You said 10 percent [of GNP for public works spending] is a shock. But we did not bring that number from nowhere. Our suggestion is based on the calculated numbers in order to achieve the goals in public works in a certain period of time" (Taylor). "By the way, considering the coming of the aging society, I think an increase in public investment is urgent. Do you think it is? Also, we have great concern about how much public investment will increase for the next year and to which areas priorities will be given" (McCormack).[13] These speeches are different in their form of sentences, such as simple assertion, facts pointed out, question, or suggestion. But they are all the expressions of U.S. agencies' concerns by which these agencies expect some improvement in policies and therefore concessions from Japanese agencies. Thus, they can be interpreted as expressions of pressure that the U.S. agencies are exercising on the Japanese agencies.

See the total of the tables again. Four U.S. agencies, a large number, spoke in the saving-investment patterns issue area. Three U.S. agencies spoke in the distribution system and in the exclusionary business practices areas, while only one or two agencies expressed their concerns about the land use, the pricing mechanisms, and keiretsu issues. However, if Armacost is counted separately, assuming that he represented an independent organizational entity (the U.S. Embassy in Tokyo), the sizes of coalitions, and therefore pressures from the U.S. agencies, match the political pressure level measured by the frequency of key words in the *Nikkei* indexes for five issue areas. The largest coalition (5) was in the saving-investment patterns, the medium (4) for the distribution system, the medium but somewhat less (3) for the exclusionary business practices, and the lowest (2 or 1) for the land use and keiretsu issues.

These numbers show the size of the coalitions among U.S. agencies which felt compelled to express their concerns about the issue areas in one way or another, regardless of their initial areas of responsibility. Therefore, these numbers indicate the level of political pressure the U.S. agencies applied in the issue areas. More precisely, the level of U.S. political pressure in the issue areas here is measured by the number of U.S. agencies which expressed their concerns in the issue discussions.

Based on these content-analysis results, the following inferences are made. The U.S. political pressure in the saving and investment patterns area was the greatest, because five U.S. agencies, the largest number (if the U.S. Embassy is counted separately), expressed their concern about the issue of how much the trade deficit would be reduced, thereby pressing responsible Japanese ministries for the concession of a large sum of money for public investment.

Table 7.1
The Length of Speeches of Officials and Their Agencies in the Three SII Meetings

		I			II			III			Total Line	Percentage within Each Side		Percentage in All Speeches	
		Line	Agency Total%	Person %	Line	Agency Total%	Person %	Line	Agency Total%	Person %		Agency Total%	Person %	Agency Total%	Person %
MFA	Kunihiro	69	20.4	20.4	-	17.2	-	-	12.7	-	69	17.6	8.6	7.8	3.3
	Watanabe	-		-	51		17.2	22		12.7	73		9.0		4.0
MF	Utsumi	31	19.6	9.2	43	39.8	14.5	47	42.8	27.2	121	32.0	15.0	14.2	6.7
	Shinozawa	35		10.4	64		21.6	19		11.0	118		14.6		6.5
	Yoshida	0	0	0	11		3.7	0		0	11		1.4		0.6
	Sumiya	0	0	0	0		0	8		4.6	8		1.0		0.4
MITI	Suzuki	113	33.4	33.4	30	12.1	10.1	34	31.8	19.7	177	25.2	21.9	11.3	9.8
	Yokota	0		0	6		2.0	21		12.1	27		3.3		1.5
EPA	Unno	29	8.6	8.6	10	3.4	3.4	0	0	0	39	4.8	4.8	2.1	2.1
MHA	Endo	12	3.6	3.6	0	0	0	0	0	0	12	1.5	1.5	0.7	0.7
MJ	Terada	4	1.2	1.2	0	0	0	0	0	0	4	0.5	0.5	0.2	0.2
FTC	Itoda	28	8.3	8.3	17	5.7	5.7	22	12.7	12.7	67	8.3	8.3	3.7	3.7
NLA	Fujiwara	17	5.0	5.0	0	11.8	0	0	0	0	17	6.4	2.1	2.8	0.9
	Chinzei	0		0	35		11.8	0		0	35		4.3		1.9
MT	Tsuchisaka	0	0	0	12	6.8	4.1	0	0	0	12	2.5	1.5	1.1	0.7
	Sasaki	0		0	8		2.7	0		0	8		1.0		0.4
NTA	Hoga	0	0	0	9	3.0	3.0	0	0	0	9	1.1	1.1	0.5	0.5
Subtotal		338		100.1	296		99.8	173		100.0	807		99.9		(44.4)
State	McCormack	123	30.3	30.3	73	19.7	19.7	20	8.7	8.7	216	21.4	21.4	11.9	11.9
Treasury	Dallara	116	34.5	28.6	132	46.7	35.6	106	45.9	45.9	354	41.7	35.2	23.1	19.5
	Bestani	24		5.9	37		10.0	0		0	61		6.1		3.4
	Simpson	0		0	4		1.1	0		0	4		0.4		0.2
USTR	Williams	32	7.9	7.9	50	13.5	13.5	74	32.0	32.0	156	15.5	15.5	8.6	8.6
CEA	Taylor	13	3.2	3.2	25	6.7	6.7	10	4.3	4.3	48	4.8	4.8	2.6	2.6
Commerce	Farren	44	10.8	10.8	0	0	0	7	3.0	3.0	51	5.1	5.1	2.8	2.8
Justice	Rill	17	9.1	9.1	15	9.4	9.4	0	6.1	0	72	8.5	7.1	4.8	4.0
	Bodin	37		0	35		0	14		6.1	14		1.4		0.8
Armacost		17	4.2	4.2	15	4.0	4.0	0	0	0	32	3.2	3.2	1.8	1.8
Subtotal		406		100.0	371		100.0	231		100.0	1008		100.2		(55.6)
Total											1815				100.0

Table 7.2

The Length of Speeches of Each Agency in Six Issue Areas, Opening and Closing Statements of the Three SII Meetings

	I Japan	I U.S.	II Japan	II U.S.	III Japan	III U.S.	Total Japan	Total U.S.
Opening Statements	MFA 31(1) MITI 30(1) EPA 21(1) MF 12(1)	State 31(1) Treasury 22(1) USTR 18(1) CEA 9(1) Commerce 9(1)	MITI 18(1) MFA 13(1) MF 11(1)	Treasury 21(1)	MFA 14(1) MF 5(1)	USTR 29(1) Treasury 4(1) State 3(1)	MFA 58 MITI 48 MF 28 EPA 21	Treasury 47 USTR 47 State 34 CEA 9 Commerce 9
(Subtotal)	94	89	42	21	19	36	155	146
Saving Investment Patterns	MF 43(2)	Treasury 58(2) 10(1) CEA 4(1)	MF 86(5) EPA 10(1)	Treasury 52(3) CEA 25(1) Armacost 15(1) State 11(2)	MF 36(5)	Treasury 48(2) State 7(1) USTR 4(1) CEA 4(1)	MF 165 EPA 10	Treasury 158 CEA 33 Armacost 25 State 18 USTR 4
(Subtotal)	43	72	96	103	36	63	175	238
Land Use	NLA 17(2) MFA 14(6) MHA 12(1) MF 11(2) MJ 4(1)	Treasury 45(5) State 9(2)	NLA 35(1) MFA 27(3) MF 3(1)	Treasury 39(3) State 28(2)	(Record Omitted)		NLA 52 MFA 41 MF 14 MHA 12 MJ 4	Treasury 84 State 37
(Subtotal)	58	54	65	67			123	121
Distribution System	MITI 43(1) FTC 19(1)	State 73(2) Treasury 8(2) Armacost 7(1)	MT 20(2) MF 11(2) FTC 10(1) NTA 9(2)	State 18(5) Treasury 4(1)	MITI 30(2)	State 10(2) USTR 10(1)	MITI 73 FTC 29 MT 20 MF 11 NTA 9	State 101 Treasury 12 USTR 10 Armacost 7
(Subtotal)	62	88	50	22	30	20	142	130
Pricing Mechanisms	MITI 26(2) EPA 8(1)	Commerce 35(1) State 3(1)	(Record Omitted)		(Record Omitted)		MITI 26 EPA 8	Commerce 35 State 3
(Subtotal)	34	38					34	38
Keiretsu	(Record Omitted)		MF 7(2) FTC 7(1)	Treasury 44(1)	MF 19(3) MITI 7(1) FTC 6(1)	Treasury 50(2)	MF 26 FTC 13 MITI 7	Treasury 94
(Subtotal)			14	44	32	50	46	94
Exclusionary Business Practices	FTC 9(1) MITI 6(1)	Justice 37(2) USTR 8(1)	MITI 18(2)	USTR 50(2) Justice 35(2) State 6(1)	FTC 16(1) MITI 14(1)	Justice 14(1) USTR 13(1)	MITI 38 FTC 25	Justice 86 USTR 71 State 6
(Subtotal)	15	45	18	91	30	27	63	163
Closing Statements	MFA 24(2) MITI 8(1)	State 7(2) Treasury 7(1) USTR 6(1)	MFA 11(1)	Treasury 13(1) State 10(1)	MF 14(1) MFA 8(1) MITI 4(1)	USTR 18(1) Commerce 7(1) CEA 6(1) Treasury 4(1)	MFA 43 MF 14 MITI 12	Treasury 24 USTR 24 State 17 Commerce 7 CEA 6
(Subtotal)	32	20	11	23	26	35	69	78
Total	338	406	296	371	173	231	807	1008

143

Table 7.3

The Percentage of Speeches Made by Each Agency in Six Issue Areas, Opening and Closing Statements of the Three SII Meetings

	I Japan	I U.S.	II Japan	II U.S.	III Japan	III U.S.	Total Japan	Total U.S.
Opening Statements	MFA 17 MITI 16 EPA 11 MF 7	State 17 Treasury 12 USTR 10 CEA 5 Commerce 5	MITI 29 MFA 21 MF 17	Treasury 33	MFA 25 MF 9	USTR 53 Treasury 7 State 5	MFA 19 MITI 16 MF 9 EPA 7	Treasury 16 USTR 16 State 11 CEA 3 Commerce 3
(Subtotal)		100		100		99		100
Saving Investment Patterns	MF 37	Treasury 50 Armacost 9 CEA 3	MF 43 EPA 5	Treasury 26 CEA 13 Armacost 8 State 6	MF 36	Treasury 48 State 7 USTR 4 CEA 4	MF 40 EPA 2	Treasury 38 CEA 8 Armacost 6 State 4 USTR 1
(Subtotal)		99		101		99		99
Land Use	NLA 15 MFA 13 MHA 11 MF 10 MJ 4	Treasury 40 State 8	NLA 27 MFA 20 MF 2	Treasury 30 State 21	(Record Omitted)		NLA 21 MFA 17 MF 6 MHA 5 MJ 2	Treasury 34 State 15
(Subtotal)		100		100				100
Distribution System	MITI 29 FTC 13	State 49 Treasury 5 Armacost 5	MT 28 MF 15 FTC 14 NTA 13	State 25 Treasury 6	MITI 60	State 20 USTR 20	MITI 27 FTC 13 MT 7 MF 4 NTA 3	State 37 Treasury 4 USTR 4 Armacost 3
(Subtotal)		101		101		100		100
Pricing Mechanisms	MITI 36 EPA 11	Commerce 49 State 4	(Record Omitted)		(Record Omitted)		MITI 36 EPA 11	Commerce 49 State 4
(Subtotal)		100						100
Keiretsu	(Record Omitted)		MF 12 FTC 12	Treasury 76	MF 23 MITI 9 FTC 7	Treasury 61	MF 19 FTC 9 MITI 5	Treasury 67
(Subtotal)				100		100		100
Exclusionary Business Practices	FTC 15 MITI 10	Justice 62 USTR 13	MITI 17	USTR 46 Justice 32 State 6	FTC 28 MITI 25	Justice 25 USTR 23	MITI 17 FTC 11	Justice 38 USTR 31 State 3
(Subtotal)		100		101		101		100
Closing Statements	MFA 46 MITI 15	State 13 Treasury 13 USTR 12	MFA 32	Treasury 38 State 29	MF 23 MFA 13 MITI 7	USTR 30 Commerce 11 CEA 10 Treasury 7	MFA 29 MF 10 MITI 8	Treasury 16 USTR 16 State 12 Commerce 5 CEA 4
(Subtotal)		99		99		101		100

Table 7.4
The Percentage of Speeches Made by Each Agency within the Context of the Total Speeches of the United States or in those of the Japanese Team in Six Issue Areas, Opening and Closing Statements in the Three SII Meetings

	I Japan	I U.S.	II Japan	II U.S.	III Japan	III U.S.	Total Japan	Total U.S.
Opening Statements	MFA 33 / MITI 32 / EPA 22 / MF 13	State 35 / Treasury 25 / USTR 20 / CEA 10 / Commerce 10	MITI 43 / MFA 31 / MF 26	Treasury 100	MFA 74 / MF 26	USTR 81 / Treasury 11 / State 8	MFA 37 / MITI 31 / MF 18 / EPA 14	Treasury 32 / USTR 32 / State 23 / CEA 6 / Commerce 6
(Subtotal)	100	100	100	100	100	100	100	99
Saving Investment Patterns	MF 100	Treasury 81 / Armacost 14 / CEA 6	MF 90 / EPA 10	Treasury 50 / CEA 24 / Armacost 15 / State 11	MF 100	Treasury 76 / State 11 / USTR 6 / CEA 6	MF 94 / EPA 6	Treasury 66 / CEA 14 / Armacost 11 / State 8 / USTR 2
(Subtotal)	100	101	100	100	100	99	100	101
Land Use	NLA 29 / MFA 24 / MHA 21 / MF 19 / MJ 7	Treasury 83 / State 17	NLA 54 / MFA 42 / MF 5	Treasury 58 / State 42	(Record Omitted)		NLA 42 / MFA 33 / MF 11 / MHA 10 / MJ 3	Treasury 69 / State 31
(Subtotal)	100	100	100	101 / 100			99	100
Distribution System	MITI 69 / FTC 31	State 83 / Treasury 9 / Armacost 8	MT 40 / MF 22 / FTC 20 / NTA 18	State 82 / Treasury 18	MITI 100	State 50 / USTR 50	MITI 51 / FTC 20 / MT 14 / MF 8 / NTA 6	State 78 / Treasury 9 / USTR 8 / Armacost 5
(Subtotal)	100	100	100	100	100	100	99	100
Pricing Mechanisms	MITI 76 / EPA 24	Commerce 92 / State 8	(Record Omitted)		(Record Omitted)		MITI 76 / EPA 24	Commerce 92 / State 8
(Subtotal)	100	100					100	100
Keiretsu	(Record Omitted)		MF 50 / FTC 50	Treasury 100	MF 59 / MITI 22 / FTC 19	Treasury 100	MF 57 / FTC 28 / MITI 15	Treasury 100
(Subtotal)			100	100	100	100	100	100
Exclusionary Business Practices	FTC 60 / MITI 40	Justice 82 / USTR 18	MITI 100	USTR 55 / Justice 38 / State 7	FTC 53 / MITI 47	Justice 52 / USTR 48	MITI 60 / FTC 40	Justice 53 / USTR 44 / State 4
(Subtotal)	100	100	100	100	100	100	100	101
Closing Statements	MFA 75 / MITI 25	State 35 / Treasury 35 / USTR 30	MFA 100	Treasury 57 / State 43	MF 54 / MFA 31 / MITI 15	USTR 51 / Commerce 20 / CEA 17 / Treasury 11	MFA 62 / MF 20 / MITI 17	Treasury 31 / USTR 31 / State 22 / Commerce 9 / CEA 8
	100	100	100	100	100	99	99	101

The U.S. pressure in the distribution system and in exclusionary business practices areas was medium (but somewhat more in the former), because a medium-sized number of U.S. agencies expressed their concerns. Finally, the U.S. pressure in the land policy and keiretsu areas was low because only one or two U.S. agencies expressed their concerns about the issues (at least "strongly enough" to be recorded as official speech in the reconstructed SII records).

In sum, the content-analysis of the SII meeting records tells us useful information about which agencies took a lead in which specific issue areas as well as the extent of the political pressure measured by the number of U.S. agencies which expressed their concern in the issue areas. The results of the content-analysis are consistent with those in the case study.

NOTES

1. Other sources on the discussions in the SII meetings are the newspaper articles of *Nikkei* 9/5/89, p. 3; 9/6/89, p. 3; 9/10/89, S.p. 13; *Asahi* 11/8/89, p. 1; *Tōyō Keizai* 12/2/89, pp. 58-59; *Nikkei* 2/23/90, p. 5; 2/25/90, S.p. 13; Yabunaka op. cit., (1991), pp. 159-192; Policy Section Minister's Secretariat of Ministry of Construction (1990), *Nichibei Mondai Kyōgi to Kenchiku Gyōsei*, pp. 11-17; Sugiyama (1989) "Nichibei kōzō kyōgi to kyōsō-seisaku."

2. Since some records on land use, keiretsu, and pricing mechanisms are omitted, the numbers for these areas are not identified.

3. Refer to NHK, op. cit., pp. 253-256, 273-278, 293-296.

4. SH 7/20/90, p. 10.

5. See Williams, *Daiyamondo* 4/11/92, p. 93.

6. In Japan MOF is often called the "state in the state," *Asahi* 10/21/91, p. 2, Editorial.

7. MFA did not have legal jurisdiction over domestic land use policies. It is suspected that since MFA was a counteragency to the State Department, MFA was assigned to take part in the land use policy issue area. The role of MFA in that area is an example of how international trade negotiations not only make domestic economic issues "internationalized" but also make international economic issues "domestic." Because the issue of pricing mechanisms of domestic land is part of the broad issue of macroeconomic policies which affects trade and current account balances, and therefore can be subject to international macroeconomic policy coordination, MFA now obtains de facto jurisdiction over the domestic land policy issue area. (MFA has Economic Affairs Bureau (*Keizai-kyoku*) dealing with multilateral trade negotiations and international economic issues.)

8. Refer to NHK op. cit., pp. 264-265.

9. Williams, "EPA supported U.S. suggestions on macroeconomic issues" (Interview 10/6/92).

10. Williams, interview 10/6/92; *Daiyamondo* 4/25/90, p. 96. For three agencies' criticism of Japanese weak antitrust law enforcement, see NHK op. cit., pp. 265-266, 287-289, 298-299.

11. NHK op. cit., pp. 289, 300.

12. Here, the term "concerns" should not be confused with "interests." In many cases, persons and organizations have "interests" in the multiple issues, especially if they are interrelated to each other, like SII issues areas. But as a matter of "priorities" or "emphasis," persons and organizations have to choose some issues among many and present them as their "concerns" in various degree. The expression of "concerns" is a signal by which the sender of the signal wants the receiver of the signal to know which and how much concessions the sender expects from the receiver of the signal.

13. NHK, op. cit, pp. 259, 290, 284, 256, 296, 268.

8   The SII as Part of Transgovernmental Coalitions among Top-Level Policy-Makers

TOP-LEVEL POLICY-MAKER AS POLITICAL ACTOR

The SII process can be described from a perspective of top-level individual actors. This perspective is important, since only individual persons can make decisions, not the state, the government, nor governmental subunits. What are usually referred to as the "government's decisions" or "department decisions" are actually policy outputs from official policies of those institutions in which individuals of all ranks strive to promote their own ideas and proposals. Those outputs are the results of pulling and hauling through more or less regularized channels among key policy-makers, who have different views and power resources in various positions. According to Allison, the decisions and actions of governments are the "resultant of various bargaining games among players in the national government."[1]

While much of Allison's concern is with "intra-national" bargaining among key policy-makers in the foreign policy making process in his third model, he suggests possibilities of transgovernmental bargaining. "Thus players in one nation who aim to achieve some international objectives must attempt to achieve outcomes in their intra-national game that add to the advantage of players in the second country who advocate an analogous objective."[2] However, Allison's suggestion about "inter- and intra-national relations"[3] seems to refer to "de facto tacit coalitions." Indeed, the description of the "tenuous alliance" or "partnership" between President Kennedy and Chairman Khrushchev in the Cuban missile crisis was understood in this context,[4] since that tenuous alliance emerged between antagonists in an extreme crisis situation in the military-security realm, where communication is limited.

In the international economic realm, trade negotiations between allies allow more room for the creation of transgovernmental coalitions among top-level policy-makers. Throughout the SII process, transgovernmental politics among top-level policy-makers was pervasive, although there was more intra-government bargaining within the U.S. administration during the initiation stage of SII in the spring of 1989. Japanese Cabinet members were divided; some ministers formed a coalition with U.S. cabinet members and attacked others in favor of the U.S. demands. Indeed, top-level politicians finally produced the final agreements after pulling and hauling each other with allies in the other governments.

Before proceeding it is necessary to introduce the basic process of decision making concerning trade in the Bush administration and the Japanese government. According to Fukushima, there are three levels of formal decision making in foreign economic policy, and there are three decision-making bodies that work at each level: the Trade Policy Staff Committee (TPSC), which consists of director-level staffs from twelve to fifteen agencies; the Trade Policy Review Group (TPRG) consisting of under secretary and assistant secretary-level officials from the same trade related agencies of TPRG; and the Economic Policy Council (EPC), consisting of cabinet-level members. Formally, the president is the chairman of the EPC. However, the secretary of the treasury often resides as an acting chairman for the EPC in president's absence.[5]

In Fukushima's description, ordinarily, the TPSC, as the first stage of policy-making, discusses specific trade issues and makes proposals and lists of items to be discussed in trade negotiations for the TPRG. The TPRG reviews proposals and lists made by the TPSC and then submits its policy suggestions to the EPC. The EPC makes the final decision among alternatives. In urgent cases, the TPRG can make policy suggestions to the EPC without the TPSC's preparation. Also, the "rump group" of the TPRG, consisting of a few agencies, can have meetings to discuss specific trade issues when these issues are either politically sensitive or too difficult to reach a consensus in large meetings with many agencies.[6]

However, the policy-making process among working-level officials for the SII seems more fluid than this formalized three-step process for product-by-product negotiations. For example, within the USTR, policy drafts were developed by SII staffs, deputy assistant secretaries (DAS), and deputies. Drafts were often discussed and reviewed at three levels simultaneously.[7] The reason for this fluidity may be that some staff members and DAS participated in the SII negotiations and principals' meetings. Also, strong policy-making initiatives at the subcabinet level of principals are noticeable.[8] Finally, the principals attended cabinet-level EPC meetings to report on the progress of the SII, which were held every three months by the Bush administration.[9]

In the Japanese economic policy-making process, ministerial bureaucrats usually draft bills, in consultation with ministers and politicians of the LDP when necessary. Within each ministry, substantive policy issues are examined and policies are developed by division chiefs (*kachō*) and their subordinates. Although there are many levels of inter-ministerial meetings, the views of general directors (*kyokuchō*) of the bureaus or equivalent level "deliberaters" (*shingikan*), which are based on policies developed by division chiefs and their subordinates, usually represent the policies of the ministry in international trade negotiations. The inter-ministerial issues, which are not solved at the level of ministry, are coordinated by the cabinet secretary.[10]

In Japanese politics, the decision-making dynamics consisting of relevant political actors are expressed in many ways, depending upon one's focus, such as the relationships among ministerial bureaucrats, LDP politicians, Cabinet secretaries, or the relationships among ministers often representing ministerial interests, the LDP leaders (three top executives, influential members of "policy tribes" holding the important positions, and leaders of factions), and the chief cabinet secretary and Prime Minister.

The chief cabinet secretary (*naikaku kanbō chokan*) of Kantei is usually considered the prime minister's loyal assistant, representing the prime minister's policy position. Under the LDP rule, one of the most influential politicians customarily held the position of chief cabinet secretary, who was often among the top decision-makers of final decisions for major policies. The vice cabinet secretary (business affairs) is the highest ranking bureaucrat who is often in charge of policy preparations dealing with inter-ministerial issues for the Cabinet.[11]

As for the role of ministers, "most of the ministers act rather as representatives of ministerial interest, not interfering into other ministries' affairs."[12]   Within the Japanese government, the final decision of foreign economic policies are often made by the prime minister, chief cabinet secretary, and major ministers of four large ministries, that is, MOF, MITI, MFA, and MAFF. However, throughout SII process, pulling and hauling among Japanese ministers became more fluid than is ordinarily seen in Japanese politics. Because of the interagency structure of SII framework, many economic issues which before were separately dealt with became part of the broadly packaged issue of structural impediments. Consequently, ministers were pulled into the situation in which they could substantially "disturb" other ministries' affairs.

Within the LDP party, three top executives—secretary-general (*kanjichō*), chairman of the executive council (*sōmukaichō*), and chairman of the policy affairs research council (*seichōkaichō*) are often among those who make the final decisions. LDP politicians who constantly resort to influence in particular issue areas, such as construction, agriculture, transportation, are called "policy tribes" or *zoku*. Those politicians are often chairmen or influential members of Policy Affairs Research Council (*seimu chōsa-kai* or *seicho-kai*). In many cases, policy tribes create definite streams of policies among alternatives in the party. For example, the LDP's agricultural policies are dominated by agriculture and forestry policy tribes in the party.[13]

There are many patterns and variations of who initiates policies, who interacts with whom, and who exercises how much influence in particular decision-making processes.[14] However, to obtain sufficient explanatory and predictive power for particular policy outcomes in international trade negotiations, one can focus on configuration of transgovernmental coalitions among top-level policy-makers, instead of describing many initiations and interactions of numerous individuals at many ranks in policy-making process. Here the criteria for productive research is not so much "detailed historical description" as "parsimony of social science theory" in explaining and predicting outcomes of international trade negotiations.[15] In this chapter, the SII processes are described and explained from a perspective of top-level policy-makers in both governments.

WHY THE U.S. GOVERNMENT INITIATED THE SII: BATTLES AMONG TOP-LEVEL POLICY-MAKERS

When Carla Hills accepted the nomination for the position as U.S. trade representative, she faced a formidable task: an interpretation of the Super 301 provision of the 1988 Trade Act in a situation in which there was a lack of trust between the administration and Congress. In her confirmation hearings of January 27, 1989, Chairman of Senate Finance Committee Lloyd Bentsen (D-Texas) expressed criticism of past administrations for a lack of consultation and cooperation with Congress. Knowing "the special relationship" between the USTR and the Senate Finance Committee and the House Ways and Means Committee, Hills pledged close consultation with members of these committees on a regular basis, including formal and informal meetings, in order to realize a partnership between the administration and Congress in implementing trade policies. Hills was in a difficult position. While stressing the importance of successfully concluding the Uruguay Round in which she had a personal stake, she also promised to "faithfully implement" U.S. trade laws, including the Super 301 provision of the 1988 Trade Act. Although she knew the United States as a global leader preferred multilateral trade negotiations, she had to mention her "results-oriented approach" to the Japanese market: expansion of U.S. exports by lowering "hidden barriers" to U.S. products and services. As the U.S. trade representative she was required by law to report to Congress the national trade agenda by March 1, the national trade estimate by April 28, and finally, identify trade negotiations with priority countries and practices by the end of May. Hills spent much of the spring of 1989 making national trade agendas and identifying Super 301 practices and countries, while the interagency 301 committee and Trade Policy Review Group were also examining trade policy and Super 301 designations.[16]

Meanwhile, immediately before the scheduled summit meeting of February 2 in Washington, Secretary of State James Baker was informed through the MFA-State line that Prime Minister Noboru Takeshita planned to suggest the creation of a new U.S.-Japan comprehensive talk in which the heads of the State Department and the Ministry of Foreign Affairs, Baker and Uno, would take charge, with high-level officials discussing trade, security, foreign aid, and debt issues.[17]

On February 2, the first United States-Japan Summit meeting was held in Washington. Prime Minister Takeshita and President Bush met with each other and discussed general policy issues of close cooperation, such as Japanese domestic demand-led growth, further market openings, structural adjustment, U.S. deficit reduction, and bilateral trade deficit reduction through macroeconomic policy coordination. Prime Minister Takeshita officially proposed to President Bush a new high-level comprehensive talk to discuss impeding issues, particularly trade. In the meeting of foreign ministers, Secretary Baker and Foreign Minister Uno also discussed an idea of new subcabinet-level consultative panel to facilitate trade policy coordination. Baker said to Uno that appropriate institutional mechanisms already existed but he agreed to discuss the proposal further. In the meeting, Baker expressed a strong desire to use an alternative to foreign exchange alignment for reducing Japanese external imbalances, such as structural adjustment measures. Although admitting that the bilateral trade imbalances were improved by foreign exchange alignment, Baker was more concerned with whether or not the improvement was continuous. At the summit meeting and other subsequent meetings, Treasury Secretary Brady and Finance Minister Murata exchanged views on such issues as both countries' financial and monetary policies, G-5 and G-7 macroeconomic policy coordination, and Third World debt problems, but there was no talk about a structural impediments issue.[18] This seems understandable, for Baker and Uno were discussing a possible comprehensive talk which would include broad trade issues. Also it is inferred that Brady did not know at this stage that the SII was under consideration by working-level bureaucrats.

Since the proposal for a new bilateral talk appeared to be a Japanese preemptive initiative to avoid the Super 301 designation, key members of Congress saw the proposal as a "ploy" to avert the real trade issues. Chairman of Senate Finance Committee Bentsen urged President Bush not accept Takeshita's proposal for a new trade panel, since such an agreement might omit Japan from the list of priority countries.[19]

Meanwhile, influential members of Congress—many of them were members of the Senate Finance Committee and the House Ways and Means Committee—pressured Hills to name Japan under the Super 301 provision. Those congressmen, such as Chairman of the Senate Finance Committee Bentsen, Chairman of the Senate Finance Trade Subcommittee Max Baucus (D-Montana), Chairman of the House Ways and Means Committee Dan Rostenkowski (D-Illinois), and House Majority Leader Richard A. Gephardt (D-Missouri) told Hills that naming Japan under Super 301 was "essential to carrying out the law." They repeatedly warned Hills that a "firestorm" on Capital Hill would rise if Japan escaped from the Super 301 designation. Senator Baucus and Senator Danforth wrote a letter to Hills, stating that they would be amazed and alarmed if Japan were not designated as a priority country under Super 301. Seventy-two members of the House of Representatives even sent a jointly signed letter to Hills, asking her not to avoid the designation of Japan. Senator Baucus began advocating his own idea of a "comprehensive bilateral talk," including macroeconomic and monetary cooperation, in addition to the Super 301 designation, which could be applied to some structural issues of specific sectors such as the distribution system.[20]

Because of these pressures from members of Congress, Hills had many closed-door meetings with influential members of the Senate Finance and House Ways and Means Committees, although she did not give any clue as to which country and what practices would be on the Super 301 list in the congressional hearings in which she testified.[21]

For the time being, a serious division concerning foreign trade policies among administration cabinet members was emerging. On April 4, President Bush invited some of his cabinet members, such as Secretary Brady, CEA Chairman Michael Boskin, Chief of Staff John H. Sununu, and IBM Chairman John Akers, to Camp David to consult on foreign trade policy. Many of them suggested that it was wrong to take a hard-line position in trade policy. In the EPC meeting of April 28, when trade sanctions on the telecommunications issue was actually discussed, Hills and Mosbacher took a strong position, while some cabinet members strongly opposed tough measures. Eventually, Hills and Mosbacher succeeded in persuading those cabinet members.[22]

When May began, the divergence in views on Super 301 issues had intensified. On May 1, CEA Chairman Boskin took the issue to the public, describing an ominous scenario of another "trade war": "If we wind up with a series of these retaliatory measures with our trade partners . . . it will not only cause a recession in the United states, it will cause a worldwide recession."[23] In the middle of May, U.S. Ambassador to Japan Michael Armacost sent a cable addressed to Secretary of State Baker, stating that a designation of Japan under the Super 301 would prompt "an emotional outburst in Japan." Reportedly, Treasury Secretary Brady feared that foreign exchange and financial markets might become destabilized if the trade friction escalated. By mid-May, he became greatly inclined to support the idea of a "comprehensive talk" to discuss broad trade and structural issues. On May 24, the day before the Super 301 announcement, Brady suddenly lunched with Baker, where he officially informed Baker of the idea of a comprehensive talk on structural issues as an alternative to the Super 301. On the same morning, Senator Bentsen already had told President Bush that there would be an outrage on Capital Hill if Japan was not named.[24]

By that time, cabinet-level EPC meetings had already been held several times. But the EPC could not reach a final decision on the Super 301 issue. The Cabinet members were seriously divided between the "hard-liners" or "pragmatists" and the rest of the cabinet who preferred a "softer approach," warring about foreign policy repercussions and possible damage to the broad U.S. economic interest when the Super 301 was fully implemented. In the EPC meeting, Hills insisted on the application of Super 301 to Japan. Commerce Secretary Mosbacher supported Hills' position. They argued that the administration would damage its relations with Congress if it did not carry out the trade law. Agriculture Secretary Clayton Yeutter joined Hills and Mosbacher. Those three strongly insisted on the Super 301 designation, arguing that putting countries on the list was essential in signaling that the U.S. government was serious about taking retaliatory action. On the other hand, "free traders," CEA Chairman Boskin and Director of the Office of Management and Budget, Richard Darman were strongly against such action. In their view, naming Japan for protectionist trade practices would be hypocritical. Boskin pointed out the fact that the U.S. industries benefitted from import restrictions, reminding President Bush that he ran for president as a free-trader, while Hills admitted that U.S. quotas on agricultural imports such as sugar were a disgrace. Then Bush joked that "Maybe we ought to take actions against a whole bunch of countries—including ourselves."[25] The other members of the cabinet initially were in support of "free traders." Secretary of State Baker, Defense Secretary Richard Cheney, and Treasury Secretary Brady cautioned against a tough trade policy which could damage broader economic and political relations with Japan. As a compromise, Boskin and Darman proposed an idea of only designating "unfair trade practices," instead of naming both "practices" and "country." But this was rejected by some other members, for naming only "practices" violated the letter of the 1988 Trade Act. Then, Treasury Secretary Brady suggested the idea of "structural talks" which would deal with broad structural problems. Reportedly, Brady suggested a broad initiative in part because the Treasury Department needed Japanese cooperation in maintaining stable currency markets and dealing with third world debt problems.[26]

President Bush, as a "free-form passive accommodator,"[27] was listening to the arguments of both sides. Recognizing the reality of a Democrat-dominated Congress, Bush already had pledged "cooperation with Congress" in doing business, and expressed his willingness to use the Trade Act of 1988 positively to open foreign markets. In the end, Bush leaned toward tougher action advocated by the "pragmatists," by naming Japan.[28]

The details of the final decision, how and who advocated which policy, were not entirely clear. First, three specific products, such as supercomputers, forest products and commercial satellites, were selected to be designated. Reportedly, Hills herself was cautious against identifying the Japanese distribution system under the Super 301 because of the excessively rigid time framework of the Super 301. Second, three countries, Japan, India, and Brazil, were chosen because Baker and National Security Adviser Brent Scowcroft pleaded that Japan not be named alone. Third, the form of a new initiative, as "a means of limiting the number of formal charges on the Super 301 list," was discussed. According to the letter of Hills' Super 301 announcement, President Bush directed State Secretary Baker, Treasury Secretary Brady, and Trade Representative Hills to form a high-level panel, as a separate administration initiative, to negotiate with the Japanese government on issues of structural impediments.[29]

However, from the perspective of the third model, it appeared that the new initiative headed by three Cabinet members was a product of a compromise among them, that is, Hills with her statutory responsibility to identify Super 301 practices and countries; Brady as acting chairman of the EPC for the president, representing the Treasury Department which promoted the idea of SII beneath the surface for months; and Baker, the former treasury secretary, who successfully made the appreciation of the yen through the Plaza Accord of 1985 and the Louvre Accord of 1986 but who thought that he could help with the unfinished job of restoring the bilateral balance, now that he could consider U.S.-Japanese relations from a broader political viewpoint as secretary of state.

For the announcement of Super 301 designation and a separate administrative initiative on broad structural issues, all necessary issues were discussed in the EPC. Finally, a "brutal behind-the-scenes fight" among top policy-makers in the administration ended.[30] Hills announced the Super 301 designation and the SII on May 25.

BEGINNING OF THE POLITICS OF
TRANSGOVERNMENTAL COALITION-MAKING

Although there were some components of transgovernmental politics involved in the initiation of the SII process, such as Japanese Ambassador Nobuo Matsunaga's telephone call to National Security Advisor Scowcroft not to name Japan alone,[31] the initiation of SII was mainly a product of intra-governmental politics. In contrast, the processes culminating in the interim agreement and the Final Report were more accurately described as transgovernmental politics of coalition making among top-level policy-makers.

This process began with the visit of Foreign Minister Hiroshi Mitsuzuka of the newly formed Uno cabinet to Washington D.C. on June 26. Mitsuzuka met Treasury Secretary Brady, Commerce Secretary Mosbacher, and U.S. Trade Representative Hills on that day. Brady asked Mitsuzuka to positively tackle SII talks, since in Brady's view, the SII was suggested to avoid the application of Super 301 to many other items, which was an option that some people in the U.S. government preferred. Mitsuzuka showed his willingness to cooperate in the SII, while stating the official Japanese government's position that the unilateral Super 301 designation was regrettable, and that his government did not negotiate under threat of sanctions. Mitsuzuka invited Hills and Mosbacher to visit Japan so that they would know more about the real picture in Japan.[32]

Secretary Baker's concern from the beginning was more political: to develop a "global partnership" between the United States and Japan, which was first addressed in the speech at the Asian Society on June 26. In Baker's understanding, a new order was emerging in East Asia. The economic success of the nations of East Asia created both problems and challenges. In East Asia, rapid economic growth had been accompanied by "imbalances that threaten the integrity of the open trading system." Based on this recognition, Baker called for the creation of a new multilateral cooperation mechanism among countries of the Pacific Rim to "encourage the free flow of goods, services, capital, technology, and ideas."[33] Although Baker did not directly mention the SII in his speech, his persistent concern throughout the SII can be discernable. That is, Japan's huge external imbalances, which threatened the development of a true global partnership between the United States and Japan and the world free-trading system, had to be reduced.[34]

Meanwhile, the Japanese political landscape was dramatically changed. Takeshita's hand-picked successor Sosuke Uno resigned from a premiership of only sixty-eight days because the LDP lost its majority in the upper house of the Diet in the July election for the first time after thirty-five years in power. Since almost all key figures of the LDP, including the two factional leader and potential prime minister candidates Shintaro Abe, Kiichi Miyazawa, were tainted by the Recruit Stock Scandal, Toshiki Kaifu from the minor Komoto faction, was chosen by party bosses as a compromise candidate for prime minister. In particular, Kaifu was supported by Takeshita, who led the largest faction, *Keisei-kai*, in the LDP, and Shin Kanemaru, the former deputy prime minister and vice president of the LDP, now acting head of the Takeshita faction as the chairman.[35]

From the beginning of his government, Kaifu was handicapped by his weak power base in the party. Important policy initiatives were taken by key LDP members, such as General-Secretary Ichiro Ozawa and Chairman of the Policy Affairs Research Council Mitsuzuka. In dealing with policy matters, the first month of Kaifu's government was described as "the party initiates-Kantei follows."[36] Consequently, Kaifu began appearing directly to the Japanese public, stressing his role as the promoter of "political reform" and the people's quality of life based on valuing consumers' interests. Kaifu was the first prime minister who ever advocated "consumer-interest" as government's major policy goal.[37]

Kaifu's basic policy stance, to value consumers and promote a fairer society, was also expressed in his first official meeting with President Bush on September 2 and 3, 1989, in which promotion of a "global partnership" between the U.S. and Japanese governments was advocated. There, Kaifu pledged to promote structural adjustment, market access, and domestic demand-led growth in Japan, although he did not make a statement promising to make a "concrete interim agreement" by next spring, as Bush and some cabinet members expected. At the summit meetings, Kaifu told the U.S. policy-makers that his government's members would make the progress of the SII a priority, while reminding them that the SII was a two-way street, a joint effort; thus, the U.S. government had to strive to reduce the federal deficit and raise competitiveness. According to one of Kaifu's aids, Kaifu also asked Bush for consideration for the LDP's situation first, since the Lower House general election would be held before the fall election of U.S. House of Representatives in 1990. After the Lower House election, Kaifu could accommodate some of the U.S. requests.[38]

On the other hand, President Bush told Kaifu that the large trade imbalance had generated tension between the two countries. Bush specifically asked Kaifu for tangible results in the form of an interim report by the following spring. He stressed the importance of success in Super 301 negotiations and the SII, while saying, "I understand well how the Prime Minister has been under strong pressure from the Diet. But I am also under tremendous pressure from the Congress." Bush also mentioned the two-way street nature of SII and some positive prospects in his efforts to reduce the federal deficit. Bush repeatedly expressed his gratitude to Kaifu for his early visit to the United States.[39]

Many of Bush and Kaifu's performances throughout the summit meetings left the impression that they had a good "personal relationship."[40] This impression was crucial, since both Bush and Kaifu needed their counterpart's support to strengthen their weak power bases at home. The elections in 1990 were waiting for both of them. Bush needed a clear-cut success in the three Super 301 trade negotiations and the SII to restrain members of Congress from enacting tougher protectionist laws and draw their cooperation in promoting his own deficit reduction policies. Kaifu also needed Bush's support to consolidate his leadership position in the LDP and promote his own policy agenda of structural adjustment in the Japanese economy. They both shared common interests: prevent the deterioration of the bilateral U.S.-Japanese relationship, restrain the rise of managed trade measures, and promote world wide cooperation "global partnership" between the two countries. And the important aspect of the Bush-Kaifu meeting was that both of them emphasized the "two-way street" nature of the SII. They both privately and publicly stated that in order to reduce bilateral and current account imbalances which caused tension between the two countries and to promote necessary domestic structural changes, efforts in both countries were needed.[41] Since then, the "two-way street" nature of the SII had been repeated by Bush and Kaifu on many occasions.

At the summit meetings, Secretary Brady praised the Japanese for the $2.5 billion financing it was giving to Mexico as part of the Brady Plan for eliminating the Third World debt. In addition, he stated that SII was suggested against congressional insistence that the Super 301 be applied to structural issues. Moreover, he said that the SII was a good opportunity to demonstrate that trade frictions could be solved by bilateral talks, not by a unilateral action. Bush supported Brady's remarks at the meeting. On the other hand, Trade Representative Hills spoke for the Uruguay Round, emphasizing necessary cooperation in the Round between the two largest trade countries in the world.

Although Secretary Baker spoke about foreign political issues from Panama to Vietnam to Poland at the summit meeting, he and the new Foreign Minister Taro Nakayama also had a separate one and a half hour meeting in which they confirmed the necessity of mutual efforts in the SII. Baker told Nakayama that in order to avert the protectionist pressure from Congress, progress in the SII should be made by the spring of 1990 by both parties.[42]   Overall, the top policy-makers from both governments in the summit meeting confirmed the necessity of cooperation in order to proceed with the SII, while expressing their own concerns.

On the afternoon of September 1, after the summit, Kaifu met congressional leaders, Senators George J. Mitchell and Robert J. Dole and Representatives Thomas S. Foley and Richard A. Gephardt.   Those congressmen stressed the need to correct the trade imbalances and burden sharing in defense, while asking for meaningful progress in the SII.   Speaker Foley welcomed Kaifu's early visit and pointed out that the U.S.-Japanese relationship was the "most important bilateral relationship."   On the other hand, Gephardt told Kaifu that the Congress had a "special concern" about the progress of SII.   In response, Kaifu expressed his view that SII would be a "sincere and honest talk" which could make progress.[43]

JAPANESE CABINET MEMBERS' VIEWS ON THE SII

When the official SII talks began on September 4 in Tokyo, it soon became apparent that Japanese government cabinet members varied in their views on the character of SII and how they responded to the U.S. requests.   At the press conference after the cabinet meeting on September 5, Trade Minister Hikaru Matsunaga was very forthcoming, insisting on making concrete reform policies with specific dates for an interim agreement because of the strong U.S. interest in the SII and maintaining a good bilateral relationship.[44]   He later expressed his view to business leaders that Japan should take its own initiative to reform the economy, even without the U.S. pointing it out.[45]

In contrast, Finance Minister Ryutaro Hashimoto expressed a strong opinion that the SII was not a talk in which Japan submitted itself to the United States. While the United States expected the results by next spring for its own reason, the Japanese government should judge the SII by making its own initiative. Since the United States had pointed out many problems of the Japanese economic structures, Japan also should do the same with U.S. problems, said Hashimoto.[46]

Between Matsunaga's accommodating position and Hashimoto's "rejectionist" view, there were many variations among cabinet members.   Director General of Economic Planning Agency Sumiko Takahara pointed out the macroeconomic cause of trade imbalances, while welcoming joint price differentials research by the MITI and the Commerce Department, since, in her view, the definite research results were good for consumers.   Construction Minister Shozo Harada was quick to take advantage of the U.S. demands, saying that the U.S. suggestion about land and housing policies had some reasonable bases, and that the Ministry would begin examining the residential tax rate on agricultural lands

in urban areas.   In contrast to Harada, Agriculture Minister Michihiko Kano
expressed caution against the residential tax rate on agricultural lands in the
urban areas, and he then told other members that explaining the Japanese
situation to the United States was important because land-use conditions in the
United States and Japan were different.[47] These different views and attitudes
about the U.S. demands among the cabinet members persisted throughout the
fall of 1989 and were also found in the second Kaifu cabinet.   After the
February general election of 1990, differences among top-level policy-makers
often increased their intensity.

Meanwhile, to examine SII issues, the LDP started a policy affairs research
council, the Economic Structural Problems Council (*Keizai Kōzō Mondai Kyōgi-
kai*) chaired by Takeo Nishioka, the former education minister.   The initial
consultation between the government and the LDP was expected to start in late
September.   Senior staff members from three chair-ministries attended the
Council meeting to explain the SII issues and negotiation progress.[48] But, soon
the LDP set up a larger specialized body with sixty members to deal with the
SII issues. This new body, the Special Research Commission on Economic
Adjustment (*Keizai Chōsei Tokubetsu Chōsa-kai* or the Special Research
Commission) chaired by Toshio Yamaguchi, was technically under direct
supervision of the party-head Kaifu.   The Commission was expected to have
meetings three times a week to examine the SII agenda such as the distribution
system, price differences, and exclusionary business practices, and represent the
party's views on the these issues.[49]

The first meeting of the Special Research Commission was held on October
23 at LDP headquarters.   In the opening statement, Kaifu, this time as prime
minister representing the government, requested support and cooperation from
the LDP.   Kaifu made the same points he made before: the necessity to
harmonize Japan with international society to develop a free-market economy,
the importance of the U.S.-Japanese bilateral relationship, and the major goal
of the Japanese people—to create a "fair and spiritually rich society" and
improved quality of life. Kaifu emphasized how important it was for Japan to
initiate its own structural adjustments as well as the necessity to study the U.S.
structural problems for policy suggestions. In other words, he told the members
of the party that the SII was a fair and reciprocal effort for structural adjustment
in both countries.[50]

During the same period, subtly different concerns might be found among
some cabinet members of the U.S. administration.[51] For example, on the eve
of the first SII meeting, CEA Chairman Boskin welcomed a Japanese suggestion
on the need to improve the U.S. saving level, saying that "on this occasion
Japan can frankly say what it wants to say to the United States."[52] When
Boskin visited Japan to attend the public panel in Tokyo, he also met Kaifu at
Kantei.   According to the report, Boskin said that he took the Japanese
suggestions on such issues as the U.S. federal deficit, low savings rate, and

education problems seriously, while reminding Kaifu that solving Japanese structural problems was also good for Japan.[53]

Hills' concern was more about market access issues, in part because of her role as U.S. trade representative. In the fall of 1989, Hills visited Japan several times to discuss the Super 301 and opening construction market issues, often mentioning the SII and the exclusionary nature of Japanese distribution system which hindered opening new stores of Toys R Us.[54] In Japan, on the one hand, Hills as the chief U.S. trade negotiator constantly pressed Japanese policy-makers with single-minded demands for market opening, "commitment," "blueprint," and "down payment" on the SII by the next spring. At the same time, she expressed her support for free trade and criticized managed trade which was gaining favor among some quoters in the United States.[55] While Hills criticized weak Japanese antitrust law enforcement and suggested measures to improve foreign access into such Japanese markets as construction by taking stronger actions against anticompetitive practices, she urged Japan to play a "pivotal role" in maintaining the world free trading system.[56]

Hills' role as a "presser" on Japan to improve antitrust enforcement and open markets and "encourager" for Japan to become a responsible pivotal player in maintaining the world trading system against the rise of managed trade, generated a complicated spectrum of support among Japanese policy-makers.[57] In Japan, she energetically met Japanese cabinet members, the leaders of the political parties and business, including Prime Minister Kaifu, Foreign Minister Nakayama, EPA Director Takahara, Construction Minister Harada, Trade Minister Matsunaga, Posts and Telecommunications Minister Senpachi Oishi, Chairman of JFTC Setsuo Umezawa, LDP General-Secretary Ozawa, Keidanden Chairman Eishiro Saito, and Vice Chairmen Akio Morita and Takuji Matsuzawa. Some of these officials were forthcoming to Hills' requests; Matsunaga understood Hills' call for a "blueprint" and promised to make it by the summer of 1990.[58] Similarly, Foreign Minister Nakayama told Hills that with regard to the SII he wanted to satisfy both USTR and Congress.[59] Although EPA Minister Takahara had been supportive of a joint MITI-Commerce price research "from the consumer's point of view," she denied the idea of repealing the LSL in the meeting with Hills.[60] JFTC Chairman Umezawa told Hills about a plan for updating the antitrust law and publishing a new guideline for exclusionary business practices by next June, although he disputed the effectiveness of criminal prosecution and increased cartel surcharges.[61] In spite of Hills' strong request to meet with him, Finance Minister Hashimoto did not see her. The official reason was a mismatch of schedules. However, it was reported that Hashimoto was "angry about nosy U.S. demands," such as an increased spending on social infrastructure, which was suggested by the U.S. team at the second round of the SII session in November.[62]

Hills met Keidanren leaders, such as Chairman Saito, and Vice Chairmen Morita and Matsuzawa twice, in October and November. Although these leaders did not agree with Hills' criticism of keiretsu, they said they had been asking the Japanese government to reform land-use policies and the distribution system for a long time.[63]

It is evident there was a "spectrum" of willingness to accommodate U.S. requests among the Japanese cabinet and business leaders; some were very supportive, others were supportive of specific issues, and still others were "defiant."

THE BUSH-KAIFU SUMMIT AT PALM SPRINGS

Within hours of the collapse of the third round of the SII talks on February 23, President Bush telephoned Prime Minister Kaifu at midnight, Tokyo time. The telephone call came directly to Kaifu's room in Hotel Okura after Bush found Kaifu was not in the Kantei building. After congratulating him on the LDP's election victory, Bush invited Kaifu to Palm Springs, California to have a summit meeting on March 2 and 3 to discuss impending issues in the broad context between the two countries.[64] The telephone call was made based on Bush's "personal decision," intending to give "fresh impetus" to break the deadlocked SII negotiation.[65] Kaifu joyfully accepted Bush's invitation, except for the exact date of the meeting. He had to wait until the official nomination of the prime minister in the Diet and the formation of a new cabinet. When the Director of the North American Affairs Bureau of MFA Matsuura rushed to the hotel from his home, the telephone conversation between the two leaders was already over. The next morning, Kaifu informed key government and party leaders, such as Takeshita and Kanemaru, of the Bush telephone call.[66]

This "blitzkrieg decision of a summit meeting" opened an entirely new stage of the SII process.[67] The SII negotiation was completely deadlocked. The American SII officials expressed their dismay and criticized the Japanese team for only defending current policies which were already under way, without taking further actions.[68] The Japanese negotiators also saw the U.S. team's offers as less than adequate, while feeling that "all of the issues that can be solved by bureaucrats alone are past us; the questions that are left are political."[69]

Meanwhile, the bilateral U.S.-Japanese relationship was rapidly deteriorating; it was "the worst during the post-World War II period."[70] Polls in the United States showed a negative image of the Japanese, whose economic threats were now seen as greater than the military threats of the Soviet Union. Sony's purchase of Columbia Pictures and Mitsubishi's 51 percent share of stock of Rockefeller Center caused alarm and resentment of the "Japanese invasion." In Japan, a portion of the public raised criticisms of the U.S. interference in Japanese culture and domestic politics, fueling a nationalist backlash.[71]

The abrupt telephone call from the president of the United States suddenly placed Kaifu in the political spotlight, out of the obscure position created by the weak power base in his own party. Initially, Kaifu planned to visit the United States in late April or early May, while Takeshita, Kaifu's potential contender as a party leader but still a supporter of Kaifu for the time being, and Former Foreign Minister and Secretary-General of LDP Abe, Kaifu's chief rival and the leader of the second largest faction, had been showing their intention to visit the United States sometime in March.[72] Abe's relations with Kaifu had been bitter because of the exclusion of his proteges from Kaifu's cabinet. But, Bush's direct telephone call demonstrated the U.S. government's recognition of Kaifu as the head of government and party leader. Suddenly, Kaifu saw the chance to reinforce his leadership over other party leaders. In the words of a senior member of the Komoto faction from which Kaifu came, "Diplomacy gains points for domestic politics."[73] Since the Bush call was made at midnight, Kaifu could bypass all bureaucracies and party bosses' interference. Now Kaifu was able to get ahead of other major players, including bureaucrats and party influentials.[74]

In Palm Springs, Bush's personal support for Kaifu was demonstrated from the beginning, when Bush himself, along with Baker and other cabinet members, welcomed Kaifu at the Palm Springs Regional Airport, which was "unusual."[75] At the summit meetings, Bush asked Kaifu for "political guidance" as they moved toward the interim agreement. Bush had been under pressure from congressmen; twenty-six senators had already written Bush a letter about forest products.[76] Just before the summit, Senator Bentsen explicitly told Bush in his letter that "it is important that you be as direct as possible with the Japanese Prime Minister."[77] Bush reminded Kaifu of "the mood and concern" in the United States and the importance of solving Super 301 trade issues and breaking through the SII deadlock. He specifically requested strengthening antitrust laws, relaxing of the LSL, increasing public works spending, and liberalizing investment markets.[78]

Bush had a personal stake in the success of Super 301 and the SII negotiation, since a failure could jeopardize his plan to successfully conclude the Uruguay Round. Success would also ensure that the United States maintained a good bilateral relationship to forge a "global partnership" with Japan and a new "conceptual framework" (cooperative relationship among the United States, the EC, and Japan in the 1990s).[79] If the SII was not successful, all these plans, including his reelection, would vanish. Bush asked Kaifu for cooperation by saying that he did not want to be remembered in history as the president who failed to manage the U.S.-Japanese relationship.[80] Secretary Baker also emphasized the "critical importance of SII" to forge a world wide U.S.-Japanese cooperative relationship and avert protectionist moves.[81]

Recognizing a near-crisis situation in economic relations and its possible repercussion on the entire U.S.-Japanese relationship, Kaifu expressed his determination to "firmly tackle structural reforms of Japan as one of the top priorities" of his new cabinet."[82]

What the two leaders were doing was "crisis management" of bilateral economic relations. This management has several components. First, the two leaders were personally allied and supportive of each other against their opponents, that is, party leaders, members of the Congress, and even their own cabinet members. Whereas before Kaifu had been obscured by other powerful members in the cabinet and the party, now he was able to get ahead of those rivals. Since the finance minister and the trade minister were not there, Kaifu got the spotlight as the head of the Japanese government. In the reception, Bush said, "I want to cooperate with Toshiki for the coming many years."[83] Also in his departure remarks, Bush praised Kaifu's "outstanding leadership" and called him a "dynamic new leader" at the press conference.[84] Bush also demonstrated to members of Congress that he could manage the situation by invoking the political guidance of the head of the Japanese government.[85]

Second, the two leaders mentioned the two-way street nature of SII in their speeches; while Kaifu mentioned this in the form of hope, Bush explicitly expressed the two-way street.

But, let's face it, these talks are a two-way street. We Americans must increase our own savings, reduce our budget deficit, provide more incentive for our investors, strengthen our educational system, focus on producing goods of the highest quality. So our task is to make the American economy even stronger and even more competitive, and that is a task for America, not for Japan.[86]

Kaifu appealed to the Japanese people and industries to support his effort to successfully conclude the SII at the press conference after the first summit meeting on March 2.[87] Bush stressed the need to cut the federal deficit and raise the saving-level against the potential domestic opposition. Therefore, they both appealed to domestic interests for necessary concessions, although in different forms.

Third, they allied with each other to effectively dictate to bureaucrats. "We're facing some important deadlines, and the prime minister and I are calling on our officials to redouble their efforts to achieve meaningful interim and final results."[88] Kaifu's case is quite intriguing. He consciously combined the U.S. president's personal support with the support from the Japanese public to reinforce his power against ministerial bureaucrats to achieve the necessary changes. While emphasizing a "view to improving the quality of Japanese life, with further stress on the consumer-oriented economy," Kaifu said "I told the president of my determination to maintain such policies as expansion of domestic demand, improvement of market access and deregulation."[89]

From a personal point of view, the Palm Springs summit was a success for both Bush and Kaifu. They demonstrated strengthened personal ties, showing their determination to keep good bilateral relations and solve trade conflicts in a mutually constructive way "in the spirit of cooperation and joint efforts."[90] Together, they stood against the opposition in both countries by explicitly stating the two-way street nature of the trade problem, in the time of a crisis characterized by increasing nationalist sentiments.[91]

STANCES OF THE PARTY LEADERS

On Tuesday, March 6, after returning from the Palm Springs summit weekend, Kaifu attended a LDP-government liaison meeting which was regularly held at Kantei. In the meeting, Kaifu asked key party members for cooperation with his government in preparing an interim agreement.[92] Although the LDP General-Secretary Ozawa understood the importance of U.S.-Japanese bilateral relations and "global partnership," he maintained a posture of the party's general support for the Kaifu government in its efforts on the SII. Ozawa told Kaifu that because the SII was a diplomatic negotiation between governments, the government should take a lead and the party would support the government if necessary.[93] Chairman of the Special Research Commission Yamaguchi agreed with Ozawa when he said: "the government first will make a draft, the Research Commission will review the government draft and make suggestions."[94]

The timing was bad for Kaifu since LDP politicians, including leaders and rank and file, still were not enthusiastic with the attitude of "wait-and-see" as to how Kaifu handled such intractable issues as the LSL. During the election campaign, LDP politicians told one of their strong supporters—small and medium-sized retail store owners and their organizations—that the LDP would not repeal the LSL. There was a strong sense among LDP members that they could not betray those supporters after the election.[95] In addition to the fact that Kaifu came to power from a minor faction, there was another reason why many LDP members were cold toward Kaifu. To show a "clean image" of his government and willingness to achieve political reform before the Japanese people, Kaifu excluded the Recruit and Lockheed scandals-related politicians from his cabinet, two of whom were members of the Abe faction and the Watanabe faction. By doing so, Kaifu alienated these two factions.[96] Since Chairman of the Special Research Commission Yamaguchi was a member of the Watanabe faction, it is no wonder that he showed a reticent attitude toward Kaifu.[97] Similarly, Kaifu's motion to create a new organizational body sponsored by the government and LDP, which was announced just before his departure for Palm Springs, was officially denied by Yamaguchi and Ozawa.[98] Reportedly, the party leaders were cautious about Kaifu's own move to establish his own leadership based on U.S. support for him.[99]

Abe also had a reticent attitude toward Kaifu. When Chief Cabinet Secretary Misoji Sakamoto visited Abe's office, Abe suggested that the government should follow the procedure: first, make a policy draft, then ask the Party for support.[100] In contrast, Miyazawa, former vice president and the head of the Miyazawa faction, encouraged Kantei's leadership by endorsing the ideas for a policy draft which could satisfy both the Special Research Commission of LDP and the ministries. Miyazawa's words were interpreted as signaling support for Kaifu against the Abe and the Watanabe factions.[101]

However, within days the atmosphere of the party started to change when the grand old party boss and the acting chairman of the Takeshita faction Kanemaru made his support for Kaifu public before the party members. Although Kaifu failed to bring Kanemaru to his cabinet as deputy prime minister in charge of foreign economic policy without a portfolio, he succeeded in positioning Kanemaru as the chairman of the Road Policy Research Council (*Dōro Chōsakai*).[102] In a speech to the Takeshita faction's general conference, Kanemaru asked the members of the faction for extensive support for the Kaifu government. He also called for the party's all out support for a government facing a difficult diplomatic negotiation. Once Kanemaru made his support for Kaifu clear, the "bring-down Kaifu" move stopped and the party started moving forward in building a consensus.[103]

Another key person in the LDP was Takeshita. Even after he was forced to resign from the premiership due to the Recruit Stock Scandal, Takeshita exercised his covert and overt influence, with the ambitious intention to come back to power some day. Kaifu's premiership was made possible because of Takeshita and his faction's support. Since Kaifu owed Kanemaru and Takeshita his position as premier, he constantly kept in contact with them.[104] On March 9, just before leaving for the United States, Takeshita suggested the creation of a task force which would be able to effectively handle the interim report drafting. Accepting Takeshita's advice, Kaifu decided to set forth an interagency task force headed by Deputy Cabinet Secretary Nobuo Ishihara.[105] Indeed, this task force became the vehicle by which Kaifu succeeded in drafting the interim agreements and organizing consensus among the rival ministerial bureaucrats and party members.

The final preparations before the full move was for Kaifu to convene the Four-Cabinet-Member meeting. On March 10, Finance Minister Hashimoto, Foreign Minister Nakayama, and new Trade Minister Kabun Muto, representing three major ministries, met at the Hotel Okura to discuss how to prepare SII interim agreements. The four cabinet ministers were joined by Chief Cabinet Secretary Sakamoto and Vice Cabinet Secretary Ishihara. They affirmed the need for a timely response to the U.S. requests. Kaifu stated that President Bush claimed he needed Japanese cooperation to fight against protectionist trends among congressmen, and that Japan should respond positively to the president's requests so that the good bilateral relationship would be maintained. Foreign Minister Nakayama reminded the members that the Super 301 issues and the SII should be solved by any means because the U.S.-Japanese bilateral relation was now in a crisis situation. Finance Minister Hashimoto and MITI Minister Muto explained the progress of the issues under consideration in their Ministries and pledged cooperation.[106]

THE BAKER-TAKESHITA CONNECTION

On the U.S. side, perhaps nobody among cabinet members played as important a role in making progress in the SII process as Secretary Baker. Baker had kept a personal relationship with Takeshita, along with a strong knowledge of the "faction map" of the LDP.[107] Baker, in cooperation with Takeshita, succeeded in the appreciation of the yen through the Plaza Accord of 1985. In the U.S. administration, there had been a belief that the Uno cabinet was the second Takeshita cabinet and the Kaifu cabinet was the third. It was Baker who initially had the idea of inviting Takeshita to Washington, to help the progress of the SII by using Takeshita's influence as the "true owner" of the largest faction in the LDP.[108] Takeshita was thought to have enough influence over the party, ministerial bureaucrats and industries to make the necessary concessions.   Reportedly, President Bush's January letter of invitation to Takeshita during the election campaign was Baker's idea.[109]

When Ambassador Armacost delivered Bush's letter, Takeshita told him that since he had been out of government office, it would be better to invite Kaifu first. Since he scheduled a trip to Brazil in March to attend an inauguration ceremony, on the way there he would be able to stop in Washington, said Takeshita. In response, Baker and Bush worked together to create the scenario of the emergency Bush-Kaifu summit and subsequent Takeshita visit. In addition, Baker telephoned Takeshita several times during the February election campaign, asking him to visit to Washington.[110]

During his visit to Washington, Takeshita first met Baker. On Sunday afternoon, March 11, Baker and Takeshita played golf outside Washington, D.C. Afterward, they had a one and a half hour meeting at the same country club. Baker reminded Takeshita of the 1985 Plaza Accord and said that the SII was more urgent than the Plaza Accord. Then Baker gave the list of demands to Takeshita. The list contained the eighteen most important U.S. concerns out of a list of 240 negotiation items which was given to the Japanese team months before. Baker told Takeshita that without some kind of positive results in the interim agreements, it would be difficult to restrain members of Congress from taking protectionist measures. The discussion on each of the eighteen items was in-depth. With regards to the public works spending issue, Baker specifically asked for the annual 10 percent of GNP, saying that even if 10 percent of GNP was difficult, the closer to that percentage the better, so that congressmen would easily recognize the success. Takeshita declined to receive the list, saying he was not a negotiator. Baker responded, "Don't worry. Prime Minister Kaifu has the same list." Except for explaining the general progress being made by Ishihara's special task force, it was not clear how Takeshita answered Baker's requests.[111]

The next day, Takeshita and President Bush met. Bush treated Takeshita "like a real prime minister," spending an "unusually long time (more than one hour) for a person other than a head of government." In the meeting, Bush

called Takeshita "a well-respected leader in Japan," telling him that the bilateral
U.S.-Japan relationship and global partnership would be endangered if the SII
failed. Bush stressed the grave atmosphere in Congress and said, "I want to
fight against protectionism but I cannot do it alone. I need Japan's cooperation." Facing this plea from Bush, Takeshita promised support for Kaifu's
government from the party side.[112]

Baker met with Takeshita again, this time in the State Department on the
afternoon of March 12. Baker repeated his request that Japan demonstrate
concrete policies in an interim report and make an "effort to reduce external
surplus."[113]

Takeshita met Treasury Secretary Brady on the next day. Interestingly, Brady
told Takeshita that it was rather a feeling of unfairness than the trade imbalance
itself that was intractable. In Brady's understanding, the pressures in the United
States were caused by the problems of the exclusionary nature of Japanese
markets and business practices rather than the $50 billion trade deficit itself.
Takeshita interpreted Brady's words as meaning that a compromise would be
possible even without the GNP ratio target on public works.[114] If the report
was an accurate description of Brady's concern, then his were somewhat
different from Baker's at that time, at least as officially expressed words to
Takeshita.

Before leaving for Brazil, Takeshita had a brief talk with Hills at her request.
Hills expressed her expectation about Takeshita's ability to create a consensus
in domestic politics. Takeshita also met House Speaker Foley, pledging that
"once the Japanese government decided, it surely will implement its
policies."[115]

DIVERGENCE AMONG CABINET MEMBERS

The Takeshita-Bush meeting was a clear signal to members of the Japanese
government and the LDP as to the importance put on the SII by U.S. policy-
makers, particularly on an interim agreement. Since Takeshita had promised
that the government and the party in unison would tackle the SII issue with an
interim agreement in mind, all parties concerned recognized that the issue was
getting serious and that it was time to move forward. On March 13, the LDP
held two meetings, one of the Special Research Commission on Economic
Adjustment and one of the Antimonopoly Law Special Research Council to
prepare intra-party discussions.

Although the moves to build consensus in the party and government began,
Kaifu's cabinet members were still seriously divided. In the cabinet meeting of
March 13, Kaifu showed his resolve to make the necessary "political decision."
Foreign Minister Nakayama warned all parties concerned about the "hair-trigger
crisis" of bilateral relations and a serious threat of rising managed trade.
Attacked by all sides, frustrated Hashimoto requested that other Cabinet

members be careful when they expressed their "personal opinion" on the SII issues, and that they should not draw attention to other ministries' issues to distract attention from their own.[116]

On the LSL issue, Kaifu thought that some kind of expression suggesting "repeal" (*teppai*) of the law was necessary to satisfy the United States. Even if the total repeal was not possible, partial repeal in the major urban areas with a definite future date could be stated. As to the public works spending issue, Kaifu's policy stance, which was reflected in that of Kantei, was to show the target numbers in eight sectors, such as housing and parks if the GNP ratio presentation was difficult.[117]   Although Kaifu's exact view on the anti-monopoly law issue was not found in newspaper articles, it is suspected that his position was generally accommodative to the United States.

The policy position of Foreign Minister Nakayama, reflecting the policies of MFA, was probably closest to Kaifu's policy stance, favoring most the possible concessions due to the political consideration of bilateral relations.   In Yamaguchi's Research Commission meeting, Nakayama appealed to LDP politicians, stating that the SII was a "crisis control" measure for U.S.-Japanese relations and consistent with the long-term national interest.[118]

The ministers of the "domestic ministries" had different views.   Trade Minister Muto was resisting any major change in the LSL.   Before becoming trade minister, he was chairman of the League of Shopping District Dietmen (*Shōten-gai Giin Renmei*).   In early March, Muto revealed his view on the LSL, that improving the operational procedure of the LSL should come first; if it did not work, then a repeal could be considered.   But even the slightest hint of "repeal" was severely criticized by the organizations of small- and medium-sized retail shop owners.   Once his own ministerial officials officially denounced any possibility of repeal, Muto "corrected" his words within two days by denying any possibility of repealing the law.   He said that shortening the coordination processing period about two years by improving operational procedures would suffice.   Since then, Muto had become a forerunner of the "anti-repeal" of the LSL against Kaifu.   He even personally lobbied LDP leaders with his own idea of "anti-repeal" without telling Kaifu and the Deputy Cabinet Secretary Ishihara, who was in charge of making the government draft.[119]

Muto's position was openly criticized by Minister of Home Affairs Keiwa Okuda at the cabinet meeting.   In Okuda's view, American *gaiatsu* was a proper one because it intended to raise the quality of the Japanese people.   Therefore, improving the operational procedures of the LSL was not enough; amending the law, including a repeal, would be necessary.   Okuda's criticism in part reflected his ministry's view, and in part his personal friction with Muto.   MITI had often used the Home Affairs Ministry's own regulation as an excuse for a rejection of any major change in the LSL.   For example, at the meeting with Commerce Secretary Mosbacher on March 16, Muto told Mosbacher that without the LSL, the Ministry of Home Affairs would go out of control and use its own ordinance to regulate the local distribution system.[120]

Finance Minister Hashimoto's stance was criticized as "directly reflecting the Ministry's view with no flexibility." Hashimoto's initial idea was only to show some numbers in the Public Works Five-Year Plan by July, the time of the final report.[121] In contrast, EPA Director Hideyuki Aizawa had already told Kaifu that an interim report should contain some concrete ideas, such as public investment, which was relatively easy for the government to tackle. In addition, Aizawa said that the focus should be put on improving living conditions with the increased public investment. By the same token, Director of National Land Agency Moriyoshi Sato expressed his view after the cabinet meeting that public investment should go to land-use and that an increase in housing supply, through infrastructure construction, was necessary. Construction Minister Tamisuke Watanuki, like Harada in the first Kaifu cabinet, had been the most enthusiastic supporters of the U.S. ideas, saying that his Ministry had been seriously advocating the necessity of improving Japan's social infrastructures for a long time, which were far behind U.S. and European standards, and that more than ever, his Ministry would pressure the Finance Ministry to expand the public investment-related budget.[122] As seen above, cabinet members varied on SII issues. As the interim agreement became closer, some of them supported the U.S. demands to promote their own ministerial interests.

Meanwhile, LDP politicians were working on their own agenda among themselves and with U.S. cabinet members when opportunities were available. One of these opportunities was Commerce Secretary Mosbacher's visit to Japan on March 14 to discuss a joint MITI-Commerce export promotion program, including an exchange of trade missions, sponsoring trade events, market research, and investment information. Citing Toys R Us's plan to open a new store in Japan, Mosbacher insisted on a repeal of the LSL. Although Trade Minister Muto did not agree to the idea of repeal, he said that everybody thought it was wrong to take so long to open new stores.[123] In other words, while denying a repeal of the LSL, on the one hand, Muto tried to promote his own ministry's long-waited policy of normalization of the law against the opposition from domestic interest groups, in coalition with Mosbacher.

At the Ministry of Foreign Affairs, Minister Nakayama told Mosbacher that it was important to solve the SII issues for the U.S.-Japanese global partnership. Later, Mosbacher met Chairman of Keidanren Saito. He also gave a lecture to the Japanese public on such pending issues as the semiconductor and the distribution system.[124]

Perhaps Mosbacher's single most important activity in Japan was to visit the acting chairman of the Takeshita faction Kanemaru in his office. Since the February General Election of the Lower House, Kanemaru was emerging as the dominant figure along with his protege Ozawa in the LDP. Kanemaru now occupied a strategic position in party politics, chairman of Road Policy Research Council of LDP, which was the center of the LDP construction policy tribes. Kanemaru told Mosbacher that "I am the boss of the public-construction-work policy tribe. Even though the U.S. demand of 10 percent GNP is difficult to achieve due to budgetary conditions, 8 percent of GNP can be possible." Later, Kanemaru telephoned Kaifu, saying that "Make enough concessions to the U.S. as much as you can. The Party will support you wholeheartedly."[125]

Kanemaru's words to Mosbacher were not publicized until he himself later made them public at a general conference of the Takeshita faction. In his speech, Kanemaru revealed that he had told Mosbacher that the 8 percent of GNP on public works was necessary as a promise to the United States although the 10 percent of GNP target had some problems. Kanemaru strongly supported the idea of setting concrete targets, criticizing MOF's reluctance to offer concrete numbers.[126]

Kanemaru's influence on the LSL issue was also reported. Kanemaru told Muto that he was against a repeal of the LSL but was for the exemption of the law in major urban areas. Kanemaru's remarks created the "definite stream" regarding the LSL in the party. Kanemaru's protege Ozawa worked to create a consensus in the party along this line.[127] Kanemaru's policy position was closer to those of U.S. policy-makers than the initial policy position of Hashimoto, reflecting MOF's policy in the public works spending issue. Also Kanemaru's was closer to U.S. policy-makers' than those of many LDP politicians who were against even a partial repeal of the LSL in the distribution system area.

As the public work spending issue became the major sticking point, Finance Minister Hashimoto was expected to break the deadlock. Reportedly, Hashimoto was eager to make a "personal relationship" with Treasury Secretary Brady. Hashimoto had heard a great deal about Takeshita's story that when he was finance minister, he had built a personal relationship with the then Treasury Secretary Baker. Since Takeshita had told the press in Brazil that he would send Hashimoto to Washington to meet Brady, Hashimoto was looking for the right time to go.[128]

On March 23, Hashimoto and Brady met in Los Angeles to discuss possible policy coordination to stop the rapid depreciation of the yen and falling stock prices in the Tokyo stock exchange market. The meeting also was a preliminary meeting for the scheduled meeting of G-7 Finance Ministers and the Governors of Central Banks in Paris on April 7. The atmosphere of this meeting was not altogether amicable. While Brady asked for an increase in the Japanese public investment level up to 10 percent of GNP over a three- to five-year period, Hashimoto counter-proposed that the United States cooperate to stabilize the yen. To press Brady, even Hashimoto hinted at raising the discount rate, which Brady did not want. If Japan raised the discount rate, then the U.S. would have to raise its discount rate too to attract Treasury bond buyers, which in turn might cause recession.[129] Hashimoto was eager to stabilize Japanese financial markets because "his political future was at stake."[130]

However, Brady and Hashimoto seemed to reach a mutual understanding on the public works issue. Although Hashimoto rejected the GNP ratio targets on public investment, he suggested drafting a Ten-Year Public Works Plan with specifications for a total sum of the budget. It is not entirely clear to what extent Brady accepted this compromise. However, it was reported that because of the mutual understanding between Hashimoto and Brady, the public works issue was smoothly passed on the first day of the fourth round of SII meetings.[131]

THE FINAL MOVES OF KEY ACTORS TOWARD THE INTERIM REPORT: ARMACOST, PARTY LEADERS, KAIFU AND BUSH

Michael Armacost's role in the SII process is worth mentioning as his activities were an example of transgovernmental politics. As an ambassador to Japan, his intensive lobbying was well known among Japanese politicians and bureaucrats. Armacost himself later acknowledged that "As economic interdependence deepens, it is unavoidable for the governments and people to directly express their own interests in other countries' policy-making process. Since I don't have much money to pay for lobbyists [as the Japanese government pays in the United States], I have to rely on my own tongue."[132] Contrary to his predecessor, Mike Mansfield, who served for twelve years with a style of a "grand old diplomat," Armacost was a career bureaucrat in the State Department. He had served as a ambassador to the Philippines and as deputy secretary of state for political affairs before his appointment to Japan. As an active practitioner busily lobbying for U.S. interests in Tokyo, he was called one of the "Bush machine" along with Hills and Baker.[133] In his Senate confirmation hearing, he pledged to become "the embassy's senior commercial officer."[134] He participated in formal SII meetings and spoke eloquently of the need to reduce the Japanese external surplus. With good knowledge of Japanese politics from LDP factions to the Japanese Diet schedule, he set the goal to see all Japanese cabinet members.[135] Armacost's lobbying during the SII was so conspicuous that many acknowledged he deserved "considerable credit" for successfully reaching the Interim Report.[136]

Armacost's lobbying began with a courtesy meeting with the new prime minister Kaifu in August 1989, where he emphasized Japan's role to be an "import super power." Prime Minister Kaifu and Armacost agreed on the importance of the promotion of successful SII talks. Armacost later met Finance Minister Hashimoto, requesting an increased budget for public works, which was somewhat of a diverted issue in the first SII session, due to the MOF-Treasury agreement.[137] By the end of 1989, Armacost already met several cabinet members. He even had a "lunch lecture" with Yohei Mimura, chief caretaker of the Friday Club of the Mitsubishi Group, so that he could know more about the "reality of keiretsu."[138]

In the early spring of 1990, Armacost was tremendously busy lobbying influential people in the Japanese government and the LDP. He was quick to publicly praise the remarks of Trade Minister Muto that the LSL could fundamentally be reviewed for repeal, although Muto changed his mind later.[139] Armacost visited Mutsuki Kato, chairman of the Policy Affairs Research Council of LDP on March 22, and Takeo Nishioka, chairman of General Affairs of LDP on March 23, two of the three most influential positions in the LDP party, explaining the "foremost priority" of the public works spending issue and the LSL, among others.[140] Between March 27 and 28, Armacost met Home Affairs Minister Okuda, LDP Secretary-General Ozawa, and other party leaders such as Abe and Takeshita in order to discuss the prospects for an interim report.[141]

Armacost even proposed a formal discussion with the rank and file LDP members.[142] On March 27, Armacost and his staff met sixty politicians of the League of Japan-U.S. Legislators (*Nichi-bei Giin Renmei*) in the LDP headquarters. In his opening statement, he stressed that the important issue was whether or not Japan could reduce external imbalances through a change in the domestic system. In his view, Japan needed to harmonize its economic system with the world economic system and to raise the level of imports. Then Armacost responded to questions and criticism from LDP politicians of U.S. demands. Some criticism of the U.S. demands included the too much detailed demand list and a repeal of the LSL. LDP members repeated that since local shop owners were against repeal of the LSL, the LDP would lose the election again. Also in their view, the U.S. demands would not be readily effective in reducing the trade deficit. Interestingly, when Chairman of the League Shintaro Abe noted that people in the United States, in particular, those in Congress, were becoming emotional, Armacost answered that he himself was worried about that trend. In the meeting of the Foreign Affairs Research Council (*Gaikō Chōsa-kai*) of the LDP on March 6, Armacost gave a lecture, quite frankly stating the U.S. requests, and answered questions from the council members.[143]

In sum, throughout a year-long SII process, Armacost had lobbied the relevant people in "strategic positions" in Japanese policy-making, that is, prime minister, cabinet members, influential leaders as well as the rank and file of the LDP, important businessmen in trade organizations, and the media.[144] Armacost had deeply penetrated and was able to participate in the Japanese policy-making processes by lobbying influential people, in particular, in the government and the LDP. In the expression of one Japanese newspaper, he was engaged in consensus building or *nemawashi* among Japanese politicians.[145] The one article suggests several reasons for why Armacost engaged in this form of transgovernmental politics. First, he believed that the United States and Japan were allies in sharing global responsibility. Second, since U.S. policy-makers interpreted Kaifu's power-base as being weak, there was the simple necessity to buttress that weakness; and third, his personal style was as a practical, professional diplomat.[146]

When the LDP started intra-party discussions in the Special Research Commission on Economic Adjustment on March 27, it immediately became apparent that an intra-party consensus-building was extremely difficult. The meetings lasted for four days, and such issues as the LSL, public works, and antimonopoly law were discussed. Initially, Chairman of the Special Research Commission Yamaguchi began meetings with enthusiasm, in order to "input the party's view" into the government's draft. But he soon toned down, once he found that consensus building in the party was not possible. Although many party members at the Special Research Commission meetings were strongly in favor of expanding public works spending, they were against a repeal of the LSL and a strengthening antimonopoly law. Especially LDP members from the urban districts resisted any future partial repeal of the LSL in the major cities.[147] At the end of the fourth day of discussions, Yamaguchi and the commission members decided to leave handling of the issues to the LDP's four top executives, that is, President Kaifu, General-Secretary Ozawa, Chairman of the Executive Council Nishioka, and Chairman of the Policy Affairs Research Council Kato.[148] Ozawa's general support, although it was not enthusiastic, was a great asset for Kaifu, giving him a foothold in the party. While Ozawa was cautious of Kaifu's own initiatives to establish strong leadership by creating new organizational bodies, he began to have a view that Japan should "internationalize" its business practices because of its position in international society.[149]

Meanwhile, Chief Cabinet Secretary Sakamoto visited leaders of the LDP factions, such as Abe, Watanabe, Komoto, Miyazawa, and Kanemaru, to ask their support for Kaifu's effort, paving the way for the "Prime Minister's final political decision." With the draft made by Deputy Cabinet Secretary Ishihara, Sakamoto tried to persuade party members and resisting ministers, by saying that "we must not make the U.S.-Japan relation be like that on the eve of a world war."[150]

With all of those efforts by the Kantei staffs and support from party leaders, Kaifu finally succeeded in making a government draft (seifu-an) for interim agreements on April 2. Kaifu submitted the draft to the LDP's three top executives, Ozawa, Nishioka, and Kato. They were satisfied with the draft, which signaled that the party had accepted the Kaifu government policy.[151]

In the evening of the day before the fourth SII meeting, Kaifu telephoned Bush, saying that he had made the "maximum effort to put the package together in the government draft." Bush said that he expected a good interim report would be made.[152] Additionally, Kaifu sent former Ambassador Matsunaga as his "personal special envoy" to Washington on the day of the fourth round of the SII. Matsunaga brought Kaifu's personal message to President Bush. Matsunaga met with all of the major cabinet members and presidential aides, including Baker, Brady, Sununu, Hills, and Scowcroft, to tell them about Kaifu and his government's maximum efforts. He even visited congressional leaders, such as House Speaker Foley, Baucus, and Simpson, and telephoned more than ten influential congressmen. Since Matsunaga had substantial trust from the congressmen, officials of the administration welcomed Matsunaga's lobbying of congressional leaders.[153]

In the morning of April 6 at Tokyo time, a cabinet meeting had been scheduled because the agreements needed the formal approval from the cabinet as a government policy. In the evening of April 5 at Washington time, the U.S. and Japanese delegates reached interim agreements. The agreements were immediately reported to Kaifu's cabinet fifteen minutes before the cabinet meeting started at eight o'clock in the morning in Tokyo. The agreements were formally accepted by the cabinet.[154] That same day Bush telephoned Kaifu to praise his efforts and congratulate him on successfully reaching the Interim Report.

RAISING THE GNP RATIO PUBLIC WORKS SPENDING ISSUE AGAIN

When the Interim Report was announced, Japanese officials thought that the fundamental problems were already solved, and the peak of the negotiations was over. With this understanding, Prime Minister Kaifu made a statement to the Japanese people, saying that the SII was good not only for consumers and U.S.-Japanese relationship, but also for the world by preventing the rise of protectionism. He emphasized that the SII was a two-way street; even though there might be painful steps to implement some measures, the government needed understanding and help for a smooth implementation. Kaifu's public approval rating in the polls soared, reaching about 52 percent, which was among the highest of this kind (as opposed to 24% disapproval). Kaifu consolidated his leading position in the party and the government with solid support from the Takeshita faction on the one hand, and Bush's support on the other hand.[155]

Meanwhile, President Bush wanted to "repay friend Kaifu" for his effort, so that Kaifu could escape from political difficulty with his rivals in the Party. Bush's personal return to Kaifu was to drop Japan from the list of Super 301 designations.[156] When Japan was not named for the second year to Super 301 designation, Japanese government officials felt that the bilateral crisis was over, the only thing left was simply to "flesh out" the interim agreement. However, it soon became apparent that the "fundamental issues" were not yet solved, at least from the viewpoint of U.S. policy-makers. From the start of the informal Hawaii meeting on May 23, the U.S. team requested that Japan spend 500 trillion yen on public works over ten years: 200 trillion yen for the first five years and 300 trillion yen for the latter five years.[157]

On May 31, after the meeting of OECD Ministerial Council, EPA General Director Aizawa modestly expressed the view that Japan needed to maintain about 2 percent of GNP surpluses to finance East European countries and developing countries. Aizawa's remarks were, in part, a response to the OECD's calls for raising worldwide saving levels and reducing external trade imbalances. But Aizawa did not forget to mention that while Japan's overall surplus was decreasing, the surplus with the United States was not; this was the problem.[158]

Finance Minister Hashimoto went too far. Based on the Finance Ministry's advisory committee report, Hashimoto publicly announced, "The report strongly suggests the direction we are going to. The time has come to think about the appropriate level of surplus."[159]

Hashimoto's remarks immediately invited criticism from U.S. policy-makers as well as other Japanese cabinet members. Trade Minister Muto was the first among Japanese cabinet members who warned of the controversial nature of the "surpluses-are-good" view. Although Hashimoto modified his view within a week, after facing severe criticism from all sides, the seeds of suspicion and political anger were already planted.[160]

Treasury Secretary Brady pointed out that the "surpluses-are-good" argument should not be confused with the saving-investment balance issue; the surplus nations should strive for imbalance reduction.[161] President Bush telephoned Kaifu, reaffirming mutual efforts to bring about satisfactory final agreements. Bush urged Kaifu to use his influence to break a new deadlock, which was generated by Hashimoto's remarks.[162] Reportedly, Treasury Secretary Brady, Trade Representative Hills, and other cabinet members were planning to send letters to the Japanese ministers to "adjust their views" for making a final report.[163]

Three U.S. Senators—Baucus, Packwood, and Danforth—wrote a letter to Trade Representative Hills expressing their doubt about the Japanese officials' sincerity to reduce the surplus, among others. The letter demanded further progress, beyond the measures made in the Interim Report.[164]

BAKER'S INSISTENCE ON GNP RATIO PUBLIC WORKS SPENDING

So far, the sequence of events based on many newspaper articles is described. These articles, sometimes even citing Japanese officials' views, attributed the resurgence of the U.S. demand of GNP ratio public works spending to the MOF's "surpluses-are-good" view and Finance Minister Hashimoto's endorsement of that view.[165] However, the question remains: at the Hawaii meetings, the U.S. team *first* asked the Japanese team for a 500 trillion yen expenditure, roughly equal to 10 percent of the GNP. *In response*, a MOF official explained to the U.S. officials the "surpluses-are-good" view.[166] The sequence of speeches may be less important than the fact itself that the U.S. team expressed their "request" to the Japanese team at the meeting. The "surpluses-are-good" view may have made some U.S. officials angry and exacerbated the situation, but it was not the reason or "cause" for the tougher U.S. position. The U.S. negotiation policy was made *before* the negotiations. Here, what commentators of newspaper articles unconsciously did was to use the logic of the second model (MOF's resistance against U.S. demand on public works issue) and explain the events based on this logic, even though the explanation contradicts the actual sequence of events. The U.S. team came to the Hawaii meeting with the definite policy that Japan should spend a specific amount of the budget on public works.[167] Reportedly, the dispute over public works issue was resolved by a compromise between Treasury Secretary Brady and Finance Minister Hashimoto at the time of the Interim Report; that is, the amount of government spending for public works was to be shown in the form of a total sum, not of GNP ratio. Furthermore, dropping the GNP ratio demand seemed quite reasonable considering such views as CEA Chairman Boskin's: "You can't specify the annual amount of budget for public works. If you do so, the budgetary policy would become rigid."[168] Then why did the issue emerge again? Here the third model provides a another explanation for this.

First of all, it seems that Japanese and U.S. policy-makers differently understood the so-called "GNP ratio public works spending" issue after the announcement of the Interim Report. For U.S. policy-makers, the issue was not so much form as substance. Therefore, in their view, the U.S. request was in line with the "principles outlined in the interim report," while Japanese policy-makers literally interpreted it as a "new demand," which exceeded the initial agreement.[169]

Second, new policy debates might have occurred, which resulted in shift in policy goals among U.S. policy-makers. Initially, Hashimoto and Brady, as head of the agencies which have official jurisdiction over budgetary issues and macroeconomic policy coordination, reached a compromise on the public works issue at the time of the Interim Report. But this compromise was forced to be temporal because the overall configuration of pulling and hauling among U.S. cabinet members changed later. It is inferred that one of the cabinet members who contributed to this change was Secretary Baker.

NHK Spesharu Dokyumento Kōzō Kyōgi attributes the demand of the GNP-ratio public works spending to Secretary Baker. The NHK book suggests that Baker had a sense of caution against "Japan Money" becoming out of control, wandering all over the world.[170] However, the sudden fear and alarm about "Japan Money," triggered by Sony's acquisition of Columbia Pictures Entertainment and Mitsubishi Estate's control over Rockefeller Center in the fall of 1989, were found among many U.S. policy-makers as well as ordinary citizens; therefore that sense was not unique to Secretary Baker.[171] In my view, Baker's concern, which was shared by other State Department officials, seemed more specific. As already pointed out several times before, Baker thought the bilateral trade imbalance with Japan was the real problem that fanned the political flames for protectionist moves in Congress and anti-Japanese sentiment in the nation.[172] Therefore, the bilateral trade imbalance should be definitely reduced to eliminate these sentiment in both Congress and elsewhere so that worldwide U.S.-Japanese cooperation, "global partnership," can smoothly grow in 1990s.

Also it seems that Baker had another specific concern, which was first expressed by Under Secretary McCormack in October, 1989 and repeated in the SII meetings. Considering a "White House model" decision-making structure under Secretary Baker in the State Department, it can reasonably be inferred that McCormack's concern was the same as Baker's.[173] On October 30, 1989, in the Conference on U.S. Perspectives in Washington, D.C., McCormack expressed his strong concern about "Japan's massive current capital expansion plans," which would result in the problem identified by Kondratief, that is, the "potential for overcapacity in production to impact upon sustained economic growth," spurring Japanese corporations' export drive. MacCormack saw "parallels between Japan today and the United States of the 1920s."[174]

McCormack's concern was presented at the United States-Japan Economic Subcabinet meeting in Washington on November 3. To avoid a possible recession cause by the down sequence of massive investment, overcapacity, export drive, the Japanese government needed to direct the monetary flow into domestic public works.[175] He repeated the same point in the second SII meeting. "In Japan, against the backdrop of unprecedented money [supply] level, there has been active investment in the private sector. It would be advised that the government absorb the money in the private sector by taxation and transfer money and manpower from the export-related manufacturing sector to the domestic public works sector."[176] Here, the point is not simply reducing the bilateral trade deficit but reducing the trade deficit through the increased investment in the public works sector, *not* in the manufacturing sector, because investment in the manufacturing sector would further drive export. In other words, changing the Japanese economy from an "export-oriented" to a "domestic-demand oriented," from "manufacturing-centered" to "public work-centered" was desirable.[177]

Baker seemed to have the same concern as McCormack and strongly insisted on the GNP ratio public works spending.[178] According to the NHK book, the Treasury Department officials told MOF officials that "we can't do anything [for the GNP ratio issue]. If you are not happy with it, you can go and persuade Secretary Baker."[179] Since MOF officials did not have a strong relation with the State Department, they begged MFA officials to arrange a meeting to persuade Baker.[180] This was exactly what happened. Foreign Minister Nakayama and Secretary Baker were to meet in San Francisco on July 15.

In the meeting, Secretary Baker persistently asked for not only a proper way of expressing the aggregated amount of budget in the final report but also for the Japanese government's commitment to a GNP ratio spending on public works for ten years. He emphasized that the bilateral trade deficit was still so large that there was great concern about it. Unless the final report contained more progress beyond the level of the Interim Report, the domestic political situation might worsen. Baker particularly criticized the "surpluses-are-good" view, which generated suspicion among those who were critical of Japan. After handing in Kaifu's letter for Bush to Baker, Foreign Minister Nakayama denied the "surpluses-are-good" view as the official Japanese government policy. He stressed the continuous need to correct the bilateral imbalances. A "deep heated argument" between Nakayama and Baker lasted for three hours. Nakayama repeated that the Japanese government could not accept the GNP ratio notation for public works spending, while Baker continuously asked for concrete concessions on each SII issue. After both agreed to set up a follow-up mechanism and conclude the SII talks before the Houston Economic Summit of G-7 nations in July, the meeting was over.[181]

Returning to Japan, Nakayama announced in a press conference after the cabinet meeting of June 19, that "the persons who advocated the 'surpluses-are-good' view greatly hurt Japan's national interest; I definitely denied such an idea." He also hinted that the U.S. government might accept the total sum method instead of a GNP ratio on public works.[182] It is not exactly clear how much Nakayama and Baker reached a "mutual understanding" or a "deal" at the Foreign Ministry meeting. However, Nakayama later said at the Government-Party Top-Level meeting of June 25 that he and Baker had already cut a deal. Worrying about possible repercussions on bilateral relations, Chief Cabinet Secretary Sakamoto ordered Nakayama's words to be off-the-record.[183] At the press conference on June 19, EPA General Director Aizawa reported, without mentioning the source, that the secretary of state said he would not insist on the GNP-ratio notation, but he would not accept the Japanese offer either unless it contained considerable additions to the total amount of the budget.[184]

Meanwhile, in the United States on the same day that Nakayama hinted at a possible U.S. acceptance of the total sum method on public works in Japan, Hills answered the question from a Japanese reporter at the Japan Society that "I have not heard anything that the U.S. had dropped its request [of GNP ratio public works spending] to Japan."[185]

As the final round of the SII talks was approaching, the political moves in the LDP intensified. Kanemaru, now the chairman of the Consultation Meeting of Party Dietmen on Public Investment Promotion (*Tō Kōkyō Tōshi Suishin Giin Kondan-kai*), backed by the construction industry, was busy advocating the budgetary spending of 450 trillion yen on public works, which was roughly 8 percent of GNP. While top officials of the MOF were considering a possible addition of 20 to 30 trillion yen to the original 400 trillion yen, they strongly denied Kanemaru's 450 trillion yen figure.[186]

As the final agreement of SII approached, the basic configuration of coalitions among top U.S. and Japanese policy-makers remained the same as those from the Interim Report. While party leaders such as Kanemaru strongly favored the larger amount of public works spending, Finance Minister Hashimoto continuously resisted the U.S. demand. Kaifu, backed by Bush and other U.S. and Japanese cabinet members and LDP politicians, pushed Hashimoto for a compromise. Baker sent a letter to Takeshita on June 26 in which he requested the additional amount on public works, while asking Takeshita "to tell the U.S. points of requests to the leaders of each faction [of the LDP]."[187]

The last political lobbying of the U.S. policy-makers in the "total mobilization,"[188] was done to Former Secretary-General of LDP and Foreign Minister Abe when he visited Washington as a government special envoy to attend the celebration of the thirtieth anniversary of the United States-Japan Security Treasury on June 22. Bush, Brady, Baker, and Hills all met Abe, most of the time asking for further help to successfully conclude the SII, instead of discussing military-security issues which the Japanese side initially wanted. Bush expressed appreciation to Abe for his "support for Kaifu," which was not entirely true. As mentioned before, Abe, as the leader of the second largest faction in LDP, was not altogether enthusiastic in supporting Kaifu. Rather his concern was to become prime minister after Kaifu. Now Bush clearly demonstrated his support for Kaifu and asked Abe for his support for Kaifu. Abe promised U.S. officials that he would tell the U.S. view to the government and party officials.[189] In the press conference, Abe was assured that the U.S. government would not pursue the GNP ratio issue any more; rather the size of the total amount on public works in the final agreement was the issue.[190]

When the final round of the SII talks began on June 25, the public works issue was the most contentious issue, stuck in the same position without a prospect for any compromise for three days. Kanemaru spoke with Hashimoto, preparing for the Japanese government's final offer. On the evening of June 27, Armacost and Dallara visited Finance Minister Hashimoto to ask for an addition to the government offer. Subsequently, Kaifu and Hashimoto discussed the final compromise at Kantei.[191]

Finally, Kaifu telephoned Bush at midnight on June 27; Hashimoto telephoned Brady. Nakayama also explained about the amount of public works to Baker through Ambassador Murata. Over the telephone with Kaifu, Bush mentioned the announcement of his new policy to increase tax revenues: "I think you already knew my statement about tax."[192] For Kaifu, this was a good sign which could be used to persuade Hashimoto and MOF officials. The final compromise was reached through telephone conversations between Bush and Kaifu; a total amount of 430 trillion yen, consisting of the base of 415 trillion yen (Hashimoto's initial proposal to Brady) and the "flexibility range" of 15 trillion yen (Kaifu's "political decision"), depending on economic conditions.[193] Since the additional 25 trillion yen investment by privatized former state corporations, such as Nihon Telephone and Telegram and Japan Railroad was mentioned in the Final Report, the total public investment was 455 trillion yen, close to the number Kanemaru had been advocating. The final compromise was headlined as the political decision of U.S. and Japanese top policy-makers, President Bush and Prime Minister Kaifu.[194] The year-long transgovernmental politics of coalition making across national boundaries among the top-level policy-makers had finally ended.

CONCLUSION

From the perspective of the third model, the different degrees of concessions across the SII issue areas are associated with the size (and strength) of the transgovernmental coalitions among top-level policy-makers. Before discussing the findings, several points have to be made. First, the role of top-level policy-makers (president, prime minister, and cabinet members) may be qualitatively different between the presidential system of the United States and the parliamentary system of Japan with a tradition of strong bureaucracy. Also some cabinet members and party leaders may be exercising their influence unproportionately, for a variety of reasons, in the decision-making process in particular issues areas. The policy decision of such party leaders as Kanemaru and Ozawa in the distribution system area might be more important than that of Kaifu in reaching compromise because the extent of power they exercised for consensus-building in the LDP was different. In other cases, the insistence of certain policies by some members in the cabinet which consists of almost equally powerful people in terms of position and influence may make differences in policy direction, as of Hills' Super 301 designation.

With respect to transgovernmental coalitions, some coalitions are "stronger" than others in terms of their actual influence on trade negotiation outcomes. For example, the transgovernmental coalition of Baker and Takeshita might be more decisive than that of Bush and Kaifu in terms of bringing about specific policy outcomes, if not in terms of overall political effect to generate public support for a larger cause. Likewise, the quiet Baker-Takeshita coalition on public works spending in the saving and investment patterns issue area seems to be more substantial than Okuda's overt support for U.S. demand for repeal of the LSL and open criticism of Muto's policy stance in the distribution system area. Also, Kaifu's explicit support for repeal of the LSL, which was characterized by direct communication and contact with U.S. policy-makers might be less crucial than Ozawa's de facto tacit coalition with U.S. policy-makers. While Kaifu's communication and contact with U.S. policy-makers were direct as official head of the government, Ozawa (with guidance given by Kanemaru), rather acted by his own in consensus-building in the party toward the compromise of partial repeal of the LSL, which turned out to be the "definite policy stream" in the party.

Therefore, there are many qualitative differences in terms of substance or strength of transgovernmental coalitions in which top-level policy-makers with various power and influence interacted to each other. However, these differences are difficult to quantitatively demonstrate. Consequently, here I have to focus on one indicator which is useful to demonstrate the overall extent of transgovernmental coalitions—number of top-level policy-makers whose interests happened to coincide to each other for variety of reasons and therefore they posit themselves in the same side of policy spectrum, generating the configuration of broad coalitions cross-cutting the national boundaries. In turn, these transgovernmental coalitions influenced the outcomes of negotiation in one way or another.[195]

References to U.S. and Japanese top policy-makers' policy positions on each SII issue are incomplete.   Also congressional leaders' specific policy preferences, beyond their general support for reducing the trade deficit and Toys R Us' opening of a new store in Japan, and their effects on the policy outcomes is difficult to identify. However, a glance over the moves of the major cabinet-level players tells the overall picture. The transgovernmental coalition among cabinet members on public works spending (saving-investment patterns) was the largest, including Baker, Brady, Mosbacher, Bush (and Armacost), on the U.S. side, and Kaifu, Nakayama, Muto, Watanuki, Sato, and Takeshita and Kanemaru, two influential LDP leaders and bosses of the construction policy tribe in the party, on the Japanese side. Finance Minister Hashimoto was pressured by all those members. Director of EPA Aida may be somewhat between Hashimoto and the coalition members, expressing both intention to support and prudence.

For the LSL issue, the transgovernmental coalition seemed to be medium-sized. Among those who expressed their concerns about the issue were Hills, Mosbacher, Bush, Kaifu, Okuda, and probably Nakayama. On the Japanese side, Kaifu was the most enthusiastic in repeal of the LSL.   Reportedly, Kanemaru and Ozawa, standing between the advocates of repeal and Trade Minister Muto, added the necessary weight for a final compromise.

For the increase in cartel surcharges issue, such a coalition seems minimum. Initially, no Japanese cabinet members made positive remarks in support of amending the law regarding an increased cartel surcharge. JFTC Chairman Umezawa himself initially denied a possible legal amendment by early March of 1990, although he might have concealed his desire to strengthen the antitrust law for tactical reasons until the last moment. As the SII negotiation went by, Kaifu and Nakayama probably took a position supportive of the U.S. policy. Umezawa gradually expressed his willingness to strengthen antitrust enforcement by one way or another.[196] Because top-level policy-makers' remarks on land policy and keiretsu are rarely found, the exact policy positions of policy-makers on these issues cannot be identified.

Those results generally support the third specific proposition, that is, that the degree of Japanese concessions are influenced by the size (and strength) of the transgovernmental coalition among top-level policy-makers. Several points on transgovernmental coalition making among cabinet-level policy-makers are suggested. It can be said that when influential LDP politicians and many cabinet members for their own reasons supported the U.S. demands, a successful agreement was most likely. Second, when the cabinet members were divided on an issue the United States raised, that is, some were more supportive than others, there was room for the creation of new transgovernmental coalitions through which U.S. policy-makers could generate some influence and therefore expect some concessions from the Japanese government. Third, when there were only a few cabinet supporters (e.g., the cartel surcharge increase issue) or no supporters for U.S. demands (e.g., GNP ratio public works spending issue), the possibility for Japanese concessions was least likely.

NOTES

1. Allison, op. cit., p. 6.

2. Ibid., p. 178.

3. Ibid.

4. See ibid., pp. 212-213.

5. Fukushima, op. cit., pp. 42-43 and an administration official (interview 10/6/92).

6. Fukushima, ibid., pp. 43-45. Also refer to Williams' characterization of decision-making processes in the U.S. administration as "horizontal," which means that a responsible department needs consultation with and consensus from other departments, because of overlapping jurisdiction.   In contrast, decision-making processes in the Japanese government, in his view, are "vertical" (because ministries are so independent) (*Daiyamondo* 4/11/92, p. 90).

7. An administration official, interview of 10/9/92.

8. Refer to Williams, *Daiyamondo* 4/11/92, pp. 90-91; 5/16/92, p. 105.

9. Williams, *Daiyamondo* 4/11/92, p. 93.

10. A Japanese government official (interview 10/9/92, Washington D.C.). Also refer to such studies as Fukui, op. cit. (1978); Chihiro Hosoya et al. op. cit.; and Yasunori Sone and Masao Kanazashi (1989), *Bijuaru Zeminaru Nihon no Seiji*, pp. 145-48, 170-71.   Masao Sakurai (1989), "Formulators and Legislators of International Trade and Industrial Policy in Japan and the United States." See *Nikkei* 4/3/90, p. 1 for a kyokuchō-level meeting coordinated by the Vice Cabinet Secretary to prepare a government draft for an interim agreement.

11. For the roles of chief cabinet secretary and vice cabinet secretary (business affairs), refer to Miyazato and Kokusai Daigaku Nich-bei Kenkyū-jo, op. cit., pp. 63-65. See also *Asahi* 11/27/93, p. 4.

12. Miyazato and Kokusai Daigaku Nich-bei Kenkyū-jo, op. cit., p. 61.

13. For LDP policy tribes, refer to Takasi Inoguchi and Tomoaki Iwai (1987), *"Zokugiin" no kenkyū*. Sato & Matsuzaki, op. cit., Hidenori Itagaki (1987), *Zoku no Kenkyū*. For seichō-kai, refer to Nihon Keizai Shinbun-sha (1983), *Jimintō Seichō Kai*.

14. For foreign economic policy-making patterns, refer to Funabasi, op. cit. For example, the final decision of the additional public works spending in the Comprehensive Economic Measures was made by the general secretary of the LDP, the chief cabinet secretary, and the finance minister (Funabashi, p. 24). The decision-making process consisting of relevant institutional actors and individuals in positions for the Comprehensive Economic Measures of 1983 in the Nakasone government was a proto-type for the political process of the SII in many respects.

15. Historians are usually concerned about accurate *descriptions of unique historical events*, while social scientists are more concerned about *parsimony of theory* in explaining and predicting particular outcomes of social events. From the viewpoint of social scientists, "actual historical events" are samples in the probability ranges. In their

view, peculiarities of certain individuals' activities are rather minor. As long as policy outcomes are sufficiently explained and predicted by theories, other things can be treated as "errors." The question is how much is "margin of error" in the probability terms in explaining and predicting outcomes. Therefore, the activities of individual political actors, such as Kaifu, Ozawa, and Kanemaru, are important in terms of their formal position in the overall decision-making structure of the Japanese government and of being partners of transgovernmental coalition making, not in terms of their personal attributes. Here, not individuals but processes of transgovernmental coalition making and overall configuration of such coalitions among key policy-makers who are positioned in the decision-making structure in the government and the party provide us with an opportunity to develop social science theories.

16. The Senate Finance Committee Hearing of January 27, 1989 (SH 1/27/89), pp. 2, 8, 9-10, 64-65. Also refer to Williams, *Daiyamondo* 3/21/92, p. 110; 4/4/92, pp. 12-13.

17. *Nikkei* 1/28/89, p. 1.

18. *Nikkei* 2/3/89, p. 1; *NYT* 2/3/89, p. A5.

19. *WSJ* 2/2/89, p. A3.

20. *NYT* 3/16/89, p. D7; 5/26/89, p. A5; *CQWR* 5/27/89, pp. 1242-1243; *Nikkei* 5/15/89, p. 385; 5/16/89, p. 5. *Asahi* 5/21/89, p. 9. See also the Senate Finance Committee Hearing of 3/1/89, p. 32.

21. *CQWR* 5/20/89, p. 1175; *National Journal* 6/17/89, p. 1566.

22. *Nikkei* 5/3/89, p. 3. The article reports that in another major trade policy dispute, the FSX issue, Sununu and Hills insisted on Japanese's purchase of completed products, rejecting the FSX Memorandum; Mosbacher insisted on agreement on production share, while Baker supported promotion of the Memorandum as it was.

23. *Newsweek* 6/5/89, pp. 48-49.

24. These descriptions are based on the following articles: *Newsweek* 6/5/89, pp. 48-49; *Nikkei* 5/3/89, p. 7; 5/21/89, p. 1; 5/27/89, p. 5; *NYT* 5/16/89, p. 1; *WSJ* 5/26/89, p. A7; NHK, op. cit., p. 79.

25. *Newsweek* 6/5/89, p. 49.

26. These descriptions are based on the following articles: *WSJ* 5/26/89, p. A7; *NYT* 5/26/89, p. A5; *Far Eastern Economic Review* (*FEER*) 6/8/89, pp. 99-100; *Newsweek* 6/5/89, p. 49; *Asahi* 5/21/89, p. 9; *Nikkei* 5/26/89, p. 2; *Tōyō Keizai* 6/10/89, p. 52; *Sekai Shūhō* 3/10/90, p. 52.

27. *U.S. News & World Report* 5/1/89, p. 24.

28. *Nikkei* 1/22/89, p. 3; *NYT* 5/26/89, p. A5. According to one article, it was Brady and Baker that helped tip the scales on Hills and Mosbacher's side for political considerations. See *Washington Post* 6/8/89, p. A23.

29. *Nikkei* 5/26/89, p. 2. Also refer to *National Journal* 6/3/89, p. 1367; *NYT* 5/26/89, pp. A1, A5; *WSJ* 5/26/89, p. A7.

30. *Newsweek* 6/5/89, p. 48. For intense intra-cabinet debate, also refer to Susan MacKnight (1989) "Japan Cited As Super 301 Priority Country."

31. *NYT* 5/26/89, p. D5. Also refer to Matsunaga's memoir article "Seishin seii" for his activities on U.S. administration officials and congressmen (*Asahi* 5/22/94, p.9).

32. *Nikkei* 6/27/89, p. 1.

33. *NYT* 6/27/89, p. D6.

34. Later, Baker's main concern was explicitly expressed to Trade Minister Matsunaga at the time of the Asia-Pacific Economic Cooperation conference in Canberra, Australia. Baker told Matsunaga that "The SII is the real answer to correct persistent trade imbalances" (*Asahi* 11/7/89, p. 1).

35. Refer to Atsushi Odawara (1989), "Kaifu Toshiki: Prime Minister Betwixt and Between."

36. *Nikkei* 9/9/89, p. 2.

37. Refer to *Nikkei* 9/9/89, p. 2; *NYT* 10/3/89, p. A8.

38. *Nikkei* 9/2/89, p. 1; 9/2/89, E.pp. 1, 2; 9/3/89, p. 1.

39. *Nikkei* 9/2/89 pp. 1-2; 9/2/89, E.p. 1-2; 9/3/89, p. 1.

40. *Nikkei* 9/3/89, p. 1.

41. See the summit meeting records and a joint communique of President Bush and Prime Minister Kaifu (*Nikkei* 9/2/89, E.pp. 2-3).

42. *Nikkei* 9/2/89, p. 2; 9/2/89, E.p. 2.

43. *Nikkei* 9/2/89, E.p. 2.

44. On the last day of the first Kaifu cabinet, Matsunaga suggested that a possible repeal of the LSL be considered after the review of law within three years (*Asahi* 2/27/90, p. 1).

45. *Asahi* 9/7/89, E.p. 1.

46. *Nikkei* 9/5/89, E.p. 1.

47. Ibid.

48. *Nikkei* 9/26/89, p. 5.

49. *Nikkei* 10/23/89, p. 1; 3/28/90, p. 3.

50. *Nikkei* 10/23/89, E.p. 1.

51. According to Williams, there were cabinet members who thought some negotiation items of SII were much too interfering, although overall cabinet members were supportive of the SII (*Daiyamondo* 4/11/92, p. 53).

52. *Nikkei* 8/30/89, p. 5.

53. *Nikkei* 10/4/89, p. 5.

54. *Nikkei* 10/5/89, p. 1.

55. *Nikkei* 10/13/89, E.p. 1; *Asahi* 1/26/89; *Japan Economic Survey*, November 1989, pp. 1-2.

56. *Japan Economic Survey*, November 1989, pp.1. Refer to also *Nikkei* 10/13/89, p. 3.

57. For Hills' role as a "presser" and "encourager" for Japanese policy-makers, refer to *Nikkei* 10/5/89, p. 1; 10/13/89, E.p. 1; *Japan Economic Survey* March 1990, pp. 14-15; and her speech before the Japan Society, June 18, 1990, "Japan Must Follow Through on Trade Commitments."

58. *Nikkei* 10/15/89, Sunday Edition (S.), p. 12; 11/6/89, E.p. 1.

59. *Nikkei* 11/11/89, p. 4.

60. *Nikkei* 10/22/89, S.p. 21.

61. *Nikkei* 10/14/89, p. 1.

62. *Asahi* 10/10/89, p. 9.

63. *Asahi* 10/13/89, p. 9; *Nikkei* 11/11/89, p. 4.

64. The conversation between the two leaders was done through translation by the twenty-hour waiting translator in the situation room in the White House (*Nikkei* 2/25/90, p. 1).

65. *Nikkei* 2/28/90, E.p. 1; *NYT* 2/25/90, p. A4.

66. *Nikkei* 2/25/90, p. 1.

67. *Nikkei* 2/25/90, p. 1.

68. NHK, op. cit., p. 303.

69. *NYT* 2/20/90, p. A11; 2/25/90, p. A4.

70. Foreign Ministry official, *Nikkei* 3/5/90, p. 1.

71. Refer to such articles as *NYT* 11/24/89, pp. A1, D7; 2/6/90, p. B7; 2/20/90, p. A11; *Business Week* 3/12/90, pp. 36-37. See also *Newsweek* 10/9/89, pp. 62-70.

72. *Nikkei* 2/24/90, E.p. 1.

73. *Nikkei* 2/25/90, P. 1. Also refer to *NYT* 3/3/90, pp. A31, p. A41; *The Economist* 3/3/90, p. 29.

74. Ordinarily, it takes one month for Foreign Ministry bureaucrats to prepare summit meetings. Setting a summit meeting within a week is "unprecedented" (*Nikkei* 2/25/90, p. 1).

75. *Asahi* 3/5/90, p. 2.

76. *CQWR* 3/10/90, p. 788.

77. *NYT* 3/3/90, p. A41.

78. *Nikkei* 3/5/90, p. 1.

79. *Asahi* 3/5/90, p. 2; *Business Week* 3/12/90, pp. 36-37.

80. Cited in NHK, op. cit., p. 218. High ranking MFA officials later revealed Bush's strong sense of crisis at the Summit, that is, a possible deterioration of U.S.-Japanese bilateral relations because of protectionist sentiment and a "Japan-bashing" atmosphere in the Congress and the nation. See *Asahi* 3/9/90, p. 2.

81. *Asahi* 3/5/90, p. 4.

82. Kaifu's departing remarks in *CQWR* 3/10/90, p. 786. For the Summit meetings, refer to Yabunaka, op. cit., pp. 165-67.

83. *Asahi* 3/5/90, p. 2.

84. *CQWR* pp. 785, 787.

85. See *CQWR* p. 788.

86. Bush's departing remarks (*CQWR* 3/10/90, p. 785). For Kaifu's remarks, see p. 786.

87. *Asahi* 3/4/90, p. 1.

88. Bush departing remarks op. cit., p. 785.

89. Kaifu's departing remarks, op. cit., p. 786.

90. Ibid. Refer to Ministry of Foreign Affairs, *Diplomatic Bluebook 1990*, p. 175, "The two leaders have since fostered a solid relationship of mutual confidence through frequent exchanges of telephone conversations and letters, and through their subsequent meetings."

91. Here I find the parallel point in the economic crisis of the SII case and the military security crisis of the Cuban Missile Crisis with respect to the importance of top-level leaders' personal alliances against the nationalist sentiment to save the destruction of the entire system. In this case, top leaders' personal ties can be seen as "another political structure" or "institution." In time of crisis, the strength of the leaders' personal ties as

an "institution" to resist a nationalist sentiment motivated by narrow domestic interests decides the fate of the entire system, economic or military.

92. *Nikkei* 3/6/90/, p. 2.

93. *Nikkei* 3/5/90, p. 2; 3/6/90, p. 2.

94. *Nikkei* 3/6/90, p. 2.

95. *Nikkei* 3/5/90, p. 2.

96. *Nikkei* 3/6/90, p. 2.

97. *Asahi* 3/6/90, p. 3.

98. *Nikkei* 3/6/90, p. 2.

99. *Asahi* 3/5/90, E.p. 5.

100. *Asahi* 3/6/90, p. 3; *Nikkei* 3/6/90, p. 2.

101. *Asahi* 3/6/90, p. 3. See also *Nikkei* 3/6/90, p. 2.

102. *Asahi* 3/7/90, p. 2.

103. *Asahi* 3/8/90, E.p. 2.

104. *Nikkei* 4/8/90, p. 2.

105. *Nikkei* 3/10/90, p. 1; refer to also 3/14/90, p. 2.

106. *Nikkei* 3/10/90, E.p. 1.

107. *Nikkei* 3/13/90, p. 3.

108. *Asahi* 6/20/90, p. 1. For the time being, Shin Kanemaru was an acting chairman of Keisei-kai. Because of his engagement in the Recruit Stock Scandal, Takeshita was supposed to restrain himself from factional activities.

109. Ibid.

110. *Asahi* 3/14/90, p. 2; 4/6/90, p. 2; 6/20/90, p. 1. Also refer to *Nikkei* 3/5/90, E.p. 3. At the summit meeting of March 2, Bush asked Kaifu to tell his "wish" to meet Takeshita.

111. *Asahi* 3/12/90, E.p. 1; 3/23/90, p. 1; 6/20/90, p. 1. According to the *Asahi* article of 6/20/90, p. 1, Takeshita actually hinted 415 trillion yen over ten years on public works.

112. *Asahi* 3/13/90, E.pp. 1, 2.

113. *Nikkei* 3/13/90, p. 3.

114. *Nikkei* 3/14/90, p. 2; 3/21/90, p. 5. However, Brady later asked Finance Minister Hashimoto for GNP ratio public works spending in the meeting of March 23.

115. *Nikkei* 3/14/90, E.p. 1.

116. *Nikkei* 3/13/90, E.p. 1.

117. *Nikkei* 3/30/90, p. 3; *Asahi* 3/29/90, p. 1; 3/30/90, p. 2.

118. *Nikkei* 3/30/90, E.p. 1.

119. *Nikkei* 3/6/90, p. 2; 3/11/90, S.p. 13; *Asahi* 3/30/90, p. 2.

120. *Asahi* 3/16/90, p. 2; *Nikkei* 3/17/90, p. 5. Okuda was a member of the Takeshita faction. He was originally expected to be Trade Minister. But, strongly backed by Watanabe faction, Muto took the position away from Okuda.

121. *Asahi* 3/30/90, p. 2.

122. *Nikkei* 2/23/90, E.p. 1; *Asahi* 3/9/90, E.p. 2; 3/16/90, p. 2; 3/23/90, E.p. 2.

123. *Nikkei* 3/15/90, p. 5; 3/16/90, p. 5.

124. *Nikkei* 3/14/90, p. 1; 3/15/90, p. 5; 3/16/90, p. 3. The U.S. officials, including Hills and Armacost, gave lectures to the Japanese public from time to time.

125. *Nikkei* 4/8/90, p. 2; *Asahi* 3/29/90, p. 1.

126. *Nikkei* 3/29/90, E.p. 1; 3/30/90, p. 3.

127. *Nikkei* 4/3/90, p. 2.

128. *Nikkei* 3/17/90, p. 5.

129. *Asahi* 4/8/90, p. 1.

130. *NYT* 3/24/90, p. A33.

131. *Nikkei* 4/4/90, p. 1. The pattern of a "direct deal" between Brady and Hashimoto was also reported regarding the Gulf War contribution. Without informing MFA, Hashimoto directly bargained with Brady and decided on Japan's 49 billion dollar contribution to the multinational forces (*Asahi* 11/26/91, p. 9; 7/17/93, p. 8).

132. *Asahi*, 3/9/93, p. 4.

133. *Asahi*, 11/15/91, p. 5; *Nikkei* 3/30/90, p. 5. Armacost attended the plenary meeting of the Palm Springs Summit along with the major cabinet members and presidential aides.

134. *NYT* 11/16/89, p. A4.

135. *Nikkei* 3/30/90, p. 5.

136. *FEER* 4/12/90, p. 57. Also refer to *Asahi* 11/15/91, p. 5, in which Armacost's important role in gaining a large sum of increase for public works after talking with Kanemaru is acknowledged.

137. *Nikkei* 11/8/89, p. 5.

138. *Asahi* 12/13/89, p. 11.

139. *Nikkei* 3/9/90, p. 3.

140. *Nikkei* 3/24/90, p. 2.

141. *Nikkei* 3/30/90, p. 5.

142. Lobbying rank and file of the LDP is important because the rank and file often function like a "pressure source" in the party which can be effectively used but should properly controlled by leaders of the party when they try to realize their own policy agendas. In the view of J. Mark Ramseyer and Frances McCall Rosenbluth, in the face of domestic and foreign pressures for change, the battle lines are often drawn between the party leaders responsible for the party's longer-term electoral prospects and backbenchers concerned with their own immediate survival ([1993], *Japan's Political Marketplace*, p. 193).

143. *Asahi* 3/27/90, p. 1; 3/28/90, p. 2; 3/29/90, p. 1; *Nikkei* 3/27/90, E.p. 1; 6/6/90, E.p. 3.

144. As to Armacost's activities on the media, for example see *Asahi* 3/27/90, E.p. 1. Armacost's interview was the headline article.

145. *Asahi* 3/24/90, p. 2.

146. *Asahi* 11/5/91, p. 5.

147. *Nikkei* 3/28/90, p. 3; *Asahi* 4/2/90, pp. 2-3.

148. *Nikkei* 3/30/90, E.p. 1.

149. *Asahi* 3/28/90, p. 2. Also refer to *Nikkei* 4/7/90, p. 2; *Asahi* 4/7/90, p. 2.

150. *Asahi* 3/28/90, p. 2; 4/3/90, p. 2; *Nikkei* 4/8/90, p. 2.

151. *Asahi* 4/2/90, pp. 2, 3.

152. *Asahi* 4/2/90, p. 2.

153. *Nikkei* 4/5/90, p. 5; 4/5/90, E.p. 1; *Asahi* 4/4/90, p. 2.

154. Watanabe, *Gaikō Fōramu*, May 90, p. 25.

155. *Nikkei* 4/6/90, E.p. 1; 6/25/90, p. 1; 6/17/90, p. 2.

156. *Nikkei* 4/23/90, p. 2. CEA Chairman Boskin, Director of the OBM Darman, and Secretary Baker supported Bush decision.

157. *Asahi* 6/18/90, p. 1.

158. *Asahi* 6/1/90, E.p. 2.

159. *Asahi* 6/1/90, E.p. 2; *WSJ* 6/21/90, p. A11.

160. *Asahi* 6/8/90, E.p. 2; 6/9/90, p. 1; 6/18/90, p. 1.

161. *Ekonomisuto* 6/20/90, p. 7. Also refer to *Asahi* 6/18/90, p. 1.

162. *Asahi* 6/8/90, E.p. 1; *NYT* 6/9/90, p. A 32.

163. *Nikkei* 6/13/90, E.p. 1.

164. *Nikkei* 6/13/90, E.p. 1.

165. See for example, *Asahi* 6/9/90, p. 2; 6/18/90, p. 1; *Ekonomisuto* 6/26/90, p. 7; *WSJ* 6/21/90, p. A11.

166. *Asahi* 6/18/90, p. 1. Also refer to *Nikkei* 5/26/90, p. 5; *Asahi* 6/7/90, p. 9.

167. See *Nikkei* 5/22/90, p. 5. Even before the Hawaii meeting, the U.S. team already requested the Japanese government for not only the total amount but also the GNP ratio public works spending with time tables.

168. Boskin, cited in NHK op. cit., p. 112.

169. *NYT* 6/9/90, p. A32; *Asahi* 6/9/90, p. 1; 6/23/90, p. 1. There was an element of simple "misunderstanding" about the nature of the Interim Report. For U.S. policy-makers, the Interim Report was just an *interim* agreement, *not a final* one. Thus, new demands or requests could be put on the negotiation table. Refer to Armacost's remarks (*Asahi* 6/24/90, p. 1).

170. NHK, op. cit., pp. 112-114.

171. See *NYT* 11/23/89, pp. A1, D7.

172. See *Business Week* 3/12/90, p. 39.

173. Jim Anderson suggests "a White House model of organization under Baker in the State Department in which the traditional formal bureaucracy was generally ignored or downgraded in favor of a trusted inner circle of advisors and confidants." In his view, "the real business" was conducted in the inner circle headed by the collaboration between Baker and Counselor Robert Zoellick (*Foreign Service Journal*, Dec. 1989, pp. 32-33).

174. McCormack, October 30, 1989, "Challenge to the International Economy In the 1990s" (State Department, Current Policy No. 1223), p. 4.

175. *Nikkei* 11/4/89, p. 2; 11/7/89, E.p. 1; 11/9/89, p. 1. See also NHK, op. cit., p. 298. McCormack's concern seemed actually much deeper than a simple worry about the Japanese export drive. McCormack warned Japanese government officials against a "impending Japanese stock market crush" at the SII meetings, which actually began January of 1990 (Interview 10/7/92). Also refer to his paper "The Possible After Shocks of the Multi Trillion Dollar Asset Deflation in Japan's Bubble Economy" (September 14, 1992), "This cycle of industrial over capacity, [export drive], trade tensions, collapse of profits, squeeze on creditors and decline in stock markets, complicated by a belatedly conservative monetary policy is exactly what some 1930's economists, including Kondratieff, identified as contributory causes of periodic depressions" (p. 2).

176. NHK, op. cit., pp. 278.

177. Ibid.

178. I have some clue as to this inference. In his answer to the question of whether or not he actually thought or expected the elimination or significant reduction of the bilateral trade deficit, Under Secretary McCormack said, "No, I didn't. But Secretary Baker expected as much" (Interview 10/7/92).

179. NHK, op. cit, p. 114.

180. Ibid.

181. *Asahi* 6/16/90, E.p. 1; *Nikkei* 6/16/90, p. 1; 6/16/90, E.p. 1.

182. *Nikkei* 6/19/90, p. 1.

183. *Asahi* 6/28/90, p. 2.

184. *Nikkei* 6/19/90, p. 1.

185. Ibid.

186. *Asahi* 4/21/90, p. 9; 6/20/90, p. 22; Nikkei 6/15/90, p. 1; 6/24/90, p. 3.

187. *Asahi* 6/28/90, p. 9.

188. A State Department official in *Asahi* 6/28/90, p. 9.

189. *Nikkei* 6/22/90, p. 1; 6/23/90, p. 5; *Asahi* 6/24/90, p. 2.

190. *Asahi* 6/23/90, E.p. 1.

191. *Nikkei* 6/27/90, p. 3; 6/28/90, p. 1.

192. *Nikkei* 6/27/90, p. 1; *Asahi* 6/30/90, p. 3.

193. For "political decision" of Kaifu, refer to such articles as *Nikkei* 6/23/90, p. 1; 6/26/90, p. 1; *Asahi* 6/28/90, p. 1.

194. *Nikkei* 6/27/90, p. 3; 6/28/90, p. 1; *Asahi* 6/28/90, p. 1.

195. The effect of broadening the policy spectrum may be as important as the effect of the number of policy-makers in the coalition and therefore of the size of the coalition. For example, if Kaifu had not insisted on repeal of the LSL, the spectrum of policy alternatives would have been much narrower, leaning toward more conservative side. This in turn would have affected outcomes of negotiation.

196. See for example *Nikkei* 6/22/90, p. 5.

9 The SII as Part of Transgovernmental Elite Policy Networks of Working-Level Officials

THE MERITS OF THE ELITE POLICY NETWORK MODEL

As seen in the previous chapters, the process of the SII can be described and explained by using the government as a rational unitary actor model, the transgovernmental coalition of subunits model, or the transgovernmental coalition of top-level policy-makers model, each with a different set of assumptions and level of analysis.

The SII processes are also described and explained by the fourth model; the model of the elite policy networks among working-level bureaucrats.[1] This model has several advantages over the other models. First, this model can focus on formal and informal interactions among working-level bureaucrats across the national boundaries through various communication channels.   In today's international political economy, the various activities of macroeconomic policy coordination and day-to-day management of the international finance and monetary markets have been conducted by working-level bureaucrats at many levels in the policy networks of national and international institutions. For example, "The Federal Reserve is in touch with the Bank of Japan almost every day to discuss foreign exchange rates and the possible need to intervene in currency markets."[2] To demonstrate the close communication and cooperation between officials in the Japanese Finance Ministry and those in the Treasury Department, it will suffice to cite a former high-ranking official of the International Finance Bureau (*Kokusai Kinyū-kyoku*) of the MOF: "Senior officials of the U.S. Treasury Department can catch us by telephone wherever we may go on the earth."[3]

This "routine consultation and cooperation" process on international monetary policy and balance of payments matters was already reported and researched by Robert W. Russell in 1973.[4] In his view, interactions among the executive directors of formal international institutions permanently located in Washington,

D.C., was less decisive than interactions among the deputies who met frequently, but remained centrally placed within their own bureaucracies.[5]

Second, this model represents the "problem-solving" aspect of the SII by working-level officials who have expertise in specialized areas. The organizational forms of SII—working group directly responsible for the head of the governments, president and prime minister, can be considered as a "transgovernmental task force" working together to solve structural and balance of payment issues cross-cutting national boundaries. To date, most scholars who study U.S.-Japanese trade relations unconsciously use the assumptions of the first model in seeing and analyzing trade negotiations. In their view, trade negotiations are conducted by officials who represent "national interests" or "departmental/ministerial interests" often related to the interest of domestic industries. However, when the organizational form of trade negotiations is made in a way such as a "multiagency working group" directly responsible for the leaders of the governments, who are also responsible for the fate of the two largest economies in the world, the officials of such organizations simultaneously represent departmental/ministerial interests, national interests, and transnational interests of two economies in the problem-solving process. Representing the transnational interests of two economies is evident in the officials' opening statements of the first SII meeting. The officials in the SII working group shared the common views on the necessity to jointly promote structural reforms in each other's economies with macroeconomic policy coordination in reducing current account imbalances and to counter the rise of revisionist-style managed trade in the effort to maintain and develop the world trading regime of GATT.[6] This is also evident in such Williams' expression as "our dream to integrate the U.S. and Japanese economies" by removing structural impediments in both economies and desire to promote "worldwide partnership" against "economic nationalism" resulting from such practices as exclusionary keiretsu ties.[7] The transnational interests of two economies are also reflected in the notion of "harmonization of economic institutions between two countries" that Japanese officials often used throughout the SII process.[8]

Unlike ordinary trade negotiations in which officials are often divided by national lines directly representing the interests of their own domestic industries, the problem-solving discussions of SII were open and frank, often cross-cutting national boundaries, although there was always room for political bargaining and tactical moves. For example, officials from the Japanese EPA often supported U.S. officials' suggestions about macroeconomic policies by "representing sound economic data."[9] While U.S. officials supported the position of JFTC officials, Japanese patent agency officials agreed to and supported U.S. ideas of streamlining and strengthening the patent examination process.[10] The elite policy networks model highlights the problem-solving process by working-level officials.

The third advantage of the elite policy networks model is that it uses the "perceptions" of working-level officials as a variable in explaining changes in policies. As an empirical reality, one can only speak of the "perceptions" of individuals, not the state (government) or governmental subunits. Think of a policy A1 at the time of t1 and a changed policy A2 at the time of t2. Explaining the policy changes between t1 and t2 in terms of changes in power relations or power balance is one thing; explaining the same policy changes in terms of changes in an individual person's perception is another. Policy-makers change their policies because of changed power balances but without changing their perceptions.

But policy-makers change their policies from time to time because their perceptions change, even though they are not yet forced to move forward by changed power balances among relevant political actors. When the SII talks started, some politicians, such as LDP General-Secretary Ozawa, criticized the U.S. "illusion" that SII issues, which were related to Japanese culture and society, could be solved within a short time. But they ended up arguing that "Japan should harmonize its economic institutions and business practices with the international standard," at the time of the Interim Report.[11] Usually, changes in power balance and those in perceptions occur simultaneously or interactively. But they are *analytically* different processes as explanations.

One can research the "perceptions" of top-level policy-makers, which is important as well. However, the "perceptions" of working-level officials were chosen here because in trade negotiations, specific details of proposals, alternatives, and agreements are often developed by working-level bureaucrats, which in turn depends on their shared specific knowledge, understanding, and information about the issues. The elite policy networks model highlights some interesting aspects of the SII process which the other models do not.

WHY THE U.S. GOVERNMENT INITIATED THE SII: MACROECONOMIC AND STRUCTURAL ADJUSTMENT POLICY COORDINATION NETWORKS OF WORKING-LEVEL OFFICIALS

Congressional Research Services staff William H. Cooper describes the SII as the fourth U.S. trade negotiation after the Yen-Dollar Talks, MOSS, and the Structural Economic Dialogue. Cooper characterizes the SII as if it were created as a new phase of trade negotiations purely developed on a bilateral base by U.S. initiative, not mentioning the influence of multilateral discussions on macroeconomic coordination process or on structural adjustment.[12] However today, few, if any, foreign economic policies are initiated by purely national basis unrelated to the discussions and activities of multilateral trade and macroeconomic policy coordination fora. The SII was no exception. In the very beginning, the SII was initiated and promoted by officials who were in the broad policy milieu of multilateral macroeconomic and structural adjustment elite policy networks of OECD, the G-7 finance ministers and the governors of central banks, and the G-7 economic summit.[13] The bilateral finance and monetary policy networks of Treasury-Finance were considered part of these broad policy networks.

From the perspective of the fourth model, the existence of transgovernmental "consultive and cooperative" policy networks among working-level bureaucrats are important elements for initiating certain policies. Those policy networks are characterized by (1) formal and informal communication channels and (2) the development of common views and collegiality through sharing knowledge and information on substantial economic issues.[14] At the time of SII initiation, officials in the Office of International Affairs (OIA) of the Treasury Department and International Finance Bureau of MOF were connected to each other through various communication channels in the interrelated bilateral and multilateral policy networks, sharing common knowledge and information about the condition of the markets and relevant economic issues. Among those working-level people who were in such bilateral and multilateral policy networks, the most visible were Under Secretary David C. Mulford, Assistant Secretary for International Affairs Charles H. Dallara and Vice Minister for International Affairs Makoto Utsumi. Without them, the SII would not have started as it did.

Until he left from the position at the end of 1992, Mulford had served as the top international economic policy official in the Treasury Department for eight years, "longer than any presidential appointee since the end of World War II."[15] By the time the SII was initiated, he had already played a key role in U.S. foreign economic policy-making. He was the G-7 deputy for the U.S. government and responsible for G-7 macroeconomic policy coordination and exchange market policies. It was he who had developed and implemented the Plaza Accord strategy of exchange rate alignment with Treasury Secretary Baker and Deputy Treasury Secretary Darman in 1985. Since then, Mulford had been the "Administration's leading official in developing the G-7 economic policy coordination process"; a "financial sherpa" for the President in preparation for the Economic Summit of industrial nations.[16] With other Treasury officials, he started the Yen-Dollar Talks to liberalize Japan's capital markets and served as a deputy negotiator from the Treasury Department for MOSS Talks and as co-chairman for the Structural Economic Dialogue. He often worked with financial deputies from other industrialized nations in the Working Party Three of OECD. In short, David Mulford was one of the key persons in the multilateral macroeconomic, finance, and monetary policy networks, which were part of the overall macroeconomic and structural adjustment policy coordination networks of G-7 countries.

As a career bureaucrat in the Treasury Department, Dallara also occupied important positions, becoming part of the macroeconomic, finance and monetary elite policy networks. During his tenure in the Treasury Department, Dallara held many key positions.[17] With Mulford, he played a key role in organizing the Plaza Accord in 1985. Dallara was "instrumental in the development of the international economic policy coordination process."[18] He also worked in the development and implementation of the international debt strategy of the "Brady Plan."

Utsumi, vice minister for international affairs, was also a career bureaucrat working as one of the staff for the G-7 finance ministers and the governors of central banks and G-7 economic summit, and a member of the G-7 deputy finance ministers (G-7D). He had been Director of International Finance Bureau for three years before the SII.[19]

The relevant aspect of their work on the SII initiation was that Mulford, Dallara, and Utsumi all had been original members of the Working Group on Yen-Dollar Exchange Rate Issues and G-7 macroeconomic and structural adjustment policy coordination process since the Plaza Accord. The initial SII ideas were discussed by those officials to restore bilateral and global current account imbalances through promotion of structural reform policies, the basic policies of which were found in the multilateral discussions of the G-7 and OECD.

Before proceeding it is necessary to mention the Yen-Dollar Talks of 1983-1984. These talks were the first broad attempt to liberalize the entire business and industrial sector in Japan, resulting in the internationalization of the yen and the liberalization of Japanese capital markets.[20] The Yen-Dollar Talks had quite interesting features which were succeeded by organizational characteristics of SII. According to Mulford, in contrast to a more conflictual "product-by-product" approach, the "broad-based sector approach" of the Yen-Dollar Talks made it possible to find allies for change in the domestic arena. In the talks, U.S. and Japanese officials as equal partners studied the economic development in the world market and spent equal time examining "dysfunctional" aspects in both the U.S. and Japanese markets. Through discussions during the talks, Mulford stressed that Japanese officials' attitudes changed, taking a "more international outlook." Discussions in the Yen-Dollar Talks sensitized Japanese officials about disadvantages of not opening their market. In Mulford view, the talks eventually succeeded in making the Japanese officials feel that the market liberalization was good for their own interests, that measures were taken not against their will, but rather would improve their life.[21]

After the initial talks of 1983-1984, the follow-up meetings were regularly held for several years. It was the policy milieu of the follow-up process of the Yen-Dollar Talks[22] and the G-7 macroeconomic and structural adjustment policy coordination process that influenced the idea of SII initiation.

According to Mulford, "Our [SII] initiative emerged from the lessons learned from two recent economic policy experiences."[23] These two experiences include the discussions of structural problems on a multilateral and bilateral basis (the agendas of economic summits since 1984, the 1988 Toronto summit's communique, the OECD studies, and the United States-Japan structural dialogue) and macroeconomic policy coordination of the G-7 to address balance of payments imbalances.[24]

Indeed, discussions about structural issues in multilateral fora were going on for years. The OECD has studied structural issues for years. The OECD reports already indicated Japan's poor housing, poor infrastructure, and long working hours as well as structural problems in the Japanese economy, such as regulations in the distribution system and other sectors, resulting in the high living costs and relatively low quality of life among OECD nations.[25] In the spring of 1988, the joint communique of OECD Ministerial Council called for the best mix of macro and "microeconomic" policy coordination in which macroeconomic policies and structural adjustment policies complemented and reenforced each other.[26] According to a former U.S. administration official, the OECD initially had an idea of discussing general structural issues, and the Treasury Department officials were influenced by OECD ideas.[27]

Structural issues have also been on the agendas of G-7 economic summits since 1984. The Toronto economic summit of June 1988 reaffirmed the ideas of OECD communique. In the Toronto summit, G-7 nations agreed to improve the multilateral surveillance system by adding a commodity-price indicator to the already agreed-upon indicators monitored by G-7 countries, and by integrating national structural policies into the macroeconomic policy coordination process. The action program for Japan in the economic declaration of the Toronto summit included reforms in land-use policy, deregulation of the distribution system, and reforms of the tax system in order to promote domestic demand-led growth.[28]

During the same period, to address the global balance of payments imbalances, the macroeconomic policy coordination and foreign exchange rate realignment were orchestrated by G-7 financial and monetary deputies including Mulford and Dallara. In the late fall of 1988, Mulford found that "despite the changes in domestic demand patterns and significant exchange rate realignment, the adjustment in payments imbalances has been less than adequate."[29] Mulford and Dallara were convinced that the substantial appreciation of the yen by 40 percent since 1985 did not work for Japan because the Japanese economy did not respond to the exchange rate change, due to domestic structural rigidities.[30] Then, a new initiative was sought "not as a substitute for the macroeconomic policy coordination, also not only as a U.S.-Japan bilateral problem, but as one of global issues involving other advanced nations."[31] In other words, structural reforms intended by the SII were initiated "to complement" macroeconomic policy coordination in the effort to facilitate adjustment process of global and bilateral current account imbalances.[32]

In the fall of 1988, the first SII ideas were outlined by OIA officials including Dallara and Director C. Robert Fauver and submitted to Mulford.[33] In the early spring of 1989, Dallara informally had contact with his counterpart Utsumi in the Japanese Finance Ministry, suggesting the idea of SII in which structural problems in both countries would be discussed.[34] Utsumi and Dallara were so close that they spoke on the telephone every day.[35] Their personal as well as professional relationship was no secret in the Treasury Department. "They [Dallara and Utsumi] are close friends and know each other very well. They speak by telephone all the time."[36]

Some of the basic ideas of the SII were developed by Dallara and Utsumi, both of whom were original members of the Yen-Dollar Talks and responsible for G-7 macroeconomic policy coordination process.[37]   Their close personal and working relationship and their belief in the SII as a legitimate heir to the Yen-Dollar Talks were demonstrated in the opening statements of the first SII meeting.   Utsumi said, "I remember the Yen-Dollar Talks on which Dallara and I were working together for the past six years.   The Yen-Dollar Talks were the first time Japan and the U.S. together made efforts on structural problems.   The Talks were successful because Japan and the U.S. cooperated with each other and did not conflict with each other."[38]   Dallara also said, "As Vice Minister Utsumi said, the Yen-Dollar Talks was a valuable experience for us.   We should make discussions cooperative, not conflictual."[39]

During the preparation stage, some issues, such as financial keiretsu, were dropped as an independent area by Dallara, because the financial keiretsu issue was already on the agenda for the Yen-Dollar working group.[40]   Perhaps the most controversial issue was a kind of informal consent between Treasury and MOF officials, toward which Dallara and Utsumi were said to take part, that the MOF would accept the SII proposal on the condition that the macroeconomic policies were not directly discussed in the talks; these policies were to be discussed in the G-7 forum or between the Treasure Department and the MOF.[41]   This consent had been kept for a while in the early stage of SII and later was forced to be less than effective, in part, due to criticism from officials from other U.S. and Japanese agencies.

In short, from the perspective of the fourth model, the idea of the SII was initially conceived and promoted by those who were members of the policy networks of the G-7 macroeconomic and structural adjustment policy coordination process and the Yen-Dollar Talks working group.   Those officials contacted each other through daily telephone conversations as well as formal and informal bilateral and multilateral meetings, working for common goals of "facilitating the adjustment of payments imbalances and ensuring that structural impediments do not undermine the development of a more integrated global economy," while sharing a common perspective of an "international outlook."[42]

From the perspective of the fourth model, the policy-making process of April and May, 1989 in the U.S. administration was one of the expanding macroeconomic and structural adjustment elite policy networks over previously separated tracks of product-by-product trade talks of USTR and of political consideration-weighted economic talks of the State Department.   To use one administration official's expression, the SII greatly facilitated interagency communication and coordination.[43]   As the SII proceeded, the deepening interagency communication and coordination among U.S. officials reached the point that "We really have achieved a consensus on what we need to do in the way of results."[44]

A similar situation was found among Japanese officials.   Many Japanese officials from various ministries, such as Labor, Home Affairs, and JFTC, never attended international trade negotiations. Now they began to know how officials of other ministries and foreign government agencies viewed the problems of their own economy. From the perspective of the fourth model, the entire process of SII was one in which an initial transgovernmental macro-economic and structural adjustment elite policy networks gradually expanded and merged with other trade policy tracks and eventually reached broad policy areas that were previously covered by domestic bureaucracies. In the following section, description of expanding macroeconomic elite policy networks begins with a examining the initial intentions of U.S. officials toward the SII.

THE U.S. OFFICIALS' INITIAL INTENTIONS—THE "TWO-WAY STREET" NOTION AND ACCELERATION OF CHANGE IN JAPAN

Unlike previous trade negotiations between the United States and Japan, one of the unique characteristics of the SII talks was its notion of a "two-way street," the recognition that both the U.S. and Japanese economies have structural problems which should be corrected. The definition of structural rigidities in the U.S. and Japanese economies, under the notion of the "two-way street," can be found in the SII agendas. However, the process of how the "two-way street" notion emerged and the actual content of it have not been known and never researched before. Many commentators such as Sasaki simply asserted that the two-way street (TWS) is mere appearance.[45] Fukushima never took the TWS seriously, suggesting that the TWS was agreed upon only for the sake of formality under which the United States expected most changes in Japan as the "true intention."[46] MFA official Yabunaka emphasized the equal nature of the TWS, although he admitted that the depth of the SII commitments are different between the U.S. and Japanese governments because of the different degrees of government regulations in the United States and Japan.[47] As seen above, the interpretation of the TWS is different among commentators.

The view of how the TWS was brought about is also different among commentators. Fukushima mentioned the episode in which the MOF agreed to a Treasury Department proposal on the condition that structural problems in the United States and Japan would be discussed.[48] Yabunaka stated that the United States only wanted to discuss Japanese structural problems at the time of the Super 301 and SII announcement on May 25, 1989. The Japanese officials later insisted on the two-way street nature of the SII talks. Originally, the U.S. officials only had "the ideas of discussing such issues as the Japanese distribution system, dango, and keiretsu, but not discussing the U.S. federal deficit."[49] NHK took the same view as Yabunaka's: "The U.S. side at the preliminary meeting on July 2 insisted that there have been no structural impediments in the U.S.; therefore there is no need to point out problems on both sides."[50] According to one USTR official, the Japanese brought in the two-way street notion.[51] If this is the case, how does one interpret Williams' statement, "We never denied that the U.S. has structural problems. Even before the Japanese said that, we suggested discussing structural issues in both countries."[52]

Perhaps, these contradictory statements are due in part to confusion in the level of analysis. At the level of analysis of working-level bureaucrats, Dallara proposed to Utsumi a discussion of structural problems in both countries,[53] and Utsumi agreed to it, probably after some internal discussions in the MOF. Since both of them were original members of the Yen-Dollar Talks, the two-way street discussions in the SII seemed a natural corollary. In early March 1989, Williams was informed by Dallara about a possible new initiative which was supposed to deal with structural problems in both countries. This is the reason Williams made the previous statement (if that was not an inaccurate recollection). At the level of cabinet-level individuals, Carla Hills' main concern was with Japanese structural issues, which was reflected in her May 25 announcement. There was no expression of the two-way street discussions in her statement.[54] At the level of governmental subunits, although there was already a general agreement to discuss structural issues in both countries between the MOF and the Treasury Department, other ministries such as MFA and MITI did not know the possible nature of the new trade talk and therefore insisted on the TWS to make sure that the U.S. federal deficit issue was included.[55]

From the perspective of the fourth model, the U.S. and Japanese officials did not know exactly "what are structural problems" in the discussions at the preparation meeting at the New York Federal Bank. For example, is the U.S. federal deficit a structural problem? Perhaps, for the U.S. officials, "no" was the answer in the sense that the distribution, dango, and keiretsu were structural problems.[56] This is the reason it took the whole summer for the United States and Japanese officials to identify "what are the structural problems" in the U.S. and Japan.[57]

For the same reason, in the Senate Finance Committee Hearing of July 20, most of Mulford's concern was with Japanese-side issues, just briefly mentioning the "rigidities in both the U.S. and Japanese economies" only a few times. Williams' concern was entirely with Japanese-side issues, except for saying, "Japanese trade practices are not solely responsible for our overall trade deficit. We must look to macroeconomic factors as well."[58] McCormack briefly mentioned U.S.-side issues in the same hearing, however, in general terms such as balancing the budget, increasing savings and investment, and producing competitive products.[59] Therefore, at such an early stage of the SII, the summer of 1989, the U.S. officials accepted the TWS notion mainly as a "tactical" reason as "diplomatic fairness," and perhaps with some consideration of its "strategic" reason, that is, "to educate the public, press, and business about such issues as savings ratio, business planning, and competitiveness," and "to educate Congress about the macroeconomic issues,"[60] while they themselves were not necessarily persuaded in seeing what Japanese officials said were structural problems in the U.S. economy.

Another important notion for the SII at the early stage was the concept of "to accelerate changes" which are already under way in Japan. McCormack cited MITI's "Distribution Vision" to demonstrate his contention that "the Japanese themselves have acknowledged that change is—and should be—taking place. We wish to accelerate or, if necessary, strongly encourage such changes."[61] This notion of "accelerating changes in Japan" is repeated throughout the SII.[62]

Indeed, U.S. officials carefully studied many Japanese government documents, the Provisional Administrative Reform Commission's reports and business organization's reports, such as those of Kiedanren as well as newspaper articles advocating deregulation and reforms in the Japanese system.[63] The Japanese government had already published many reports, drafted law amendments, and issued new guidelines and ordinances, proposing deregulation and reform from the fall of 1988 to the end of 1989. Such policy initiatives included relaxation and normalization of the LSL, the liquor-selling licenses amendment, the transportation law amendment, the Basic Land Law, and a new JFTC guideline and study reports.[64] Many of these reform policies were reflected in the SII agenda prepared by U.S. officials. In sum, the U.S. officials wanted to accelerate change in Japan by pressing many reform policies of deregulation based on market principals that Japanese government officials started thinking necessary.

THE OBSERVED CHANGES IN VIEWS AND ATTITUDE THROUGH INTERACTIONS

When the first round of SII meetings started, it soon became apparent that there was a tremendous "perception gap" or "recognition gap" (*ninshiki no fuitchi*) in seeing the realities of the Japanese economy, although both the U.S. and Japanese officials shared the common goal of countering the revisionist view of Japan.[65] The "recognition gap" between the U.S. and Japanese officials, on such issues as the levels of saving-investment, efficiency in the distribution, keiretsu, and antitrust law enforcement, was so great that both the U.S. and Japanese officials made no effort to hide their differences in viewing the reality of the Japanese economy, in particular, whether or not market mechanisms were working in Japan.[66] While the U.S. officials frequently quoted Japanese government publications and repeated the phrases "consumer interest" and "to improve Japanese living standard," Japanese officials mostly defended and explained their domestic policies.[67] Although the U.S. officials were less defensive about their own system than the Japanese officials and often frankly admitted structural problems in the U.S. economy, they themselves also had to reevaluate those structural problems in their economy in one way or another.[68]

Thus, overall in the first three formal meetings of SII, mostly Japanese officials, but also U.S. officials to a lesser extent, defended their own business practices and economic system, while suggesting many ideas to improve the other's economy.[69] While the discussions in the formal SII meetings seemingly became a "parallel argument" without convergence, there were other developments in conjunction with the formal plenary meetings.

SII officials, including both chief negotiators and their staffs, met each other in many formal and informal bilateral and multilateral meetings on many occasions. According to CEA member John Taylor, he often met his Japanese counterpart, Unno of EPA as well as Ustumi in such meetings as the Working Party Three of OECD and G-7 fora. Through encounters on those occasions, they developed a "professional working relationship" and an "understanding [of] each other on substantive issues."[70] Additionally, Taylor had frequent contact with his counterparts by mail, fax, and telephone, for "considerable amounts of times, for clarification of data and other policy matters."[71] These communication processes are "in a sense, policy-making because of the technical nature of the issues."[72]

JFTC officials also met their counterparts in bilateral and multilateral meetings, such as the OECD sponsored symposium on competition policy and economic development on October 17 and the United States-Japan Antitrust Annual Consultation on November 30, 1989. After attending the first SII meeting, Yoji Sugiyama of JFTC strongly felt that the role of Japanese competition policy was seriously in question. Sugiyama's impression was reenforced by attending the OECD symposium. There, Sugiyama had a strong sense that the concern about competition policies was now becoming a "main trend" in the world and the essence of structural reform policies was to strengthen competition policy.[73]

Another development in conveying the negotiation was informal and secret meetings.[74] Four such meetings were held; some of them were more important than others. The secret meetings usually consisted of principals from "core agencies" (six from the United States and five from Japan) and a few of their staffs. While the interactions between the U.S. and Japanese officials in the large formal plenary session were more "ping-pong-like debate, in part because of the formality," those in the secret meetings were "more like discussion."[75] According to Taylor, "In the informal meetings we get to the heart of the problems much easier, think more freely, [being] exploratory, [therefore] opening further development."[76]

In both the formal and informal meetings, there were many private discussions between counterpart principals during breaks and lunches. Some details of the agreements were developed by counterparts. Private talks between counterparts were often held before and after the formal SII meetings. For example, the issue of the distribution system was discussed by McCormack, Williams, and Suzuki.[77] In Williams' expression, "Real progress [in making agreements] was made by telephone conversations and private discussions."[78]

Through all those formal and informal interactions between working-level U.S. and Japanese officials on a bilateral and multilateral base, some changes in their views and attitudes were observed. While Japanese officials initially "denied structural problems" in their own economy, as time went by they conceded more and admitted that such things as the weak antitrust law was a problem.[79]   Also, even though MITI officials were already aware of the problems of the LSL, such as an unusually long coordination processing period, they now started thinking that the LSL was really a problem and further measures, including repeal of the law, had to be considered.[80]

An example of some of the changes in views and attitudes among the Japanese officials was seen in the issue of the antitrust law.   According to one U.S. official, initially JFTC officials simply presented explanations about the Japanese antitrust law, without any suggestions showing recognition of the problems.   The Japanese officials said that "criminal punishment is too much; penalties are enough."   MITI officials were also not supportive and rather upset with U.S. suggestions.   But, through many informal meetings, the attitude of Japanese officials, including MITI officials, became more positive with more recognition of the importance of the antitrust issue.   Eventually, they came to believe that a strong antitrust law was "good for Japan and the world."[81]

A careful reading of JFTC officials' remarks in newspaper articles confirms the U.S. officials' observation of changing positive attitudes toward antitrust law among Japanese officials, including JFTC Chairman Umezawa.[82]   Initially, JFTC officials rejected U.S. criticism as "domestic interference," defending the merits of keiretsu.[83]   JFTC officials stressed the different methods and purposes of the antitrust law between the United States and Japan.   They said that the surcharge system had been working effectively since its introduction in 1979, reducing the number of cartels; the U.S. system was rather "unique," centering on rigid criminal prosecution.[84]   In Chairman Umezawa's view, "The purpose of the Japanese antimonopoly law is to remove the condition that the law is violated (ihō-jōtai no haijo), while that of the U.S. law is to punish."[85]

By the time of the final SII report, Umezawa showed a very different view, obviously reflecting the internal discussions among working-level officials. According to Umezawa, while JFTC previously exercised its authority by issuing administrative guidance through "warnings" (keikoku shobun), from now on it would rather put weight on "administrative punishment" (gyōsei shobun). He said that JFTC would actively use an administrative punishment of "remonstrance" (kankoku shobun), which is more severe than a simple "warning" on an antimonopoly law violation, and that it would lessen the burden of private damage law suits.   Umezawa pledged JFTC would ask the United States for suggestions at the time of new guideline making, because "international rule-making in the antitrust law is necessary as corporate activities become global."[86]

Meanwhile, there had been some developments in the views and attitudes among U.S. officials.   As the SII talks proceeded, it became apparent that U.S.

officials did not always have clear ideas on structural rigidities and possible remedies for them.[87] For example, at the beginning of the SII, there was some confusion among U.S. officials about what was keiretsu and the different economic effect between "financial keiretsu" and "industrial keiretsu."[88] Although U.S. officials had their own view about the effects of keiretsu, such as slowing foreign investment, hurting the shareholders' rights, and generating conditions for exclusionary business practices, they admitted that the keiretsu issue was "theoretically difficult to explain."[89]

As for the patent issue, U.S. officials' positions became somewhat awkward because in many ways the Japanese patent system was similar to those of the EC and other countries. For example, most countries, including Japan and the EC, had the policy of "first-file," while the United States took the policy of "first-invention." Eventually, the U.S. and Japanese officials agreed that the patent issue should be discussed in the multilateral forum, except for the problem of patent acquisition time (i.e., the average time in Japan is thirty-seven months, whereas, it is eighteen months in the United States).[90]

The Joint Commerce-MITI Price Survey produced even more interesting results. The research results confirmed previous Japanese EPA reports that price levels of commodities in Japan are generally high, 1.6 times higher than those of the United States. The research also found the prices of many Japanese manufacturing goods are higher in Japan than those in the United States, which MITI officials initially denied. On the other hand, in the Japanese officials' view, the research results did not necessarily provide the evidence for the Commerce Department's claim that there was widespread dumping of Japanese goods in the United States.[91] The above-mentioned examples show how the SII processes facilitated communication between the U.S. and Japanese officials in seeing the reality by "clarifying the definition of terms and data,"[92] showing the characteristics of their own country's economic practices in relation to those of other countries, and revealing the real condition of the markets.

The other important development among U.S. officials was how to view their own system as well as the Japanese system. Japanese officials made many suggestions about the importance of a long-term perspective in investment, the level of corporate executive salaries, and raising the savings level in the private sector. According to Taylor, "All participants learned a lot. Each not only learned about the other's system, but also about our own system, and about how the other sees our own system."[93] One USTR official described the SII as a "unique and healthy experience" in which "both [sides] learned a great deal about the others' concern. It educated both sides."[94] Both Watanabe, a chief negotiator from MFA, and Yabunaka reported the seriousness of listening and changes in the views and attitudes among U.S. officials regarding Japanese suggestions.[95]

As the time to create the Interim Report approached, U.S. officials were becoming more serious about not only "educating Congress" but also clarifying their own policies and "accelerating policy-making in the United States." While

Williams had spoken only of the Japanese-side issues in the opening statement of the Senate Hearing of July 20, 1989, he now mentioned the U.S.-side's responsibility in the Senate Hearing of March 5, 1990, however briefly. "It [SII] is also a mutual process. We are responsible ourselves . . . for our own competitiveness. The Japanese participants have fairly identified U.S. practices that may be barriers to exports from the United States, and we have considered and shall continue to consider them carefully."[96]

In the opening statement of the same hearing, Dallara used the explicit term "two-way street" of the SII, asking for U.S. efforts to reduce the federal deficit and boost private savings. He explained how the president's proposals for the Family Savings Accounts and a capital gains tax cut reflected Japanese concerns as well.[97] Taylor asked for congressional support for the president's budget deficit cut proposal, which contained concrete policies, in part reflecting Japanese suggestions to reduce the federal deficit, among others.[98]

Of course, many initial ideas of those policies, such as capital gains tax reduction, enacting a two-year budget, the line-item veto, a balanced budget amendment, and improved education programs, already appeared in the President's Budget Message of February 1989.[99] But these ideas were initially "inclinations," according to a former administration official.[100] "Then, the Japanese made policy suggestions easier. The Presidential Budget Report reflects some of the Japanese suggestions. In this sense, the Japanese suggestions rather accelerated the policy-making process."[101]

The notion of "acceleration of policy-making process" was also expressed by Taylor as a "coincidence of ideas with initiatives": "This is one of the many examples where the ideas put forth by one side coincided with the initiatives underway or coincided with the actual need of the economy and I would say in the case of the President's pro-growth suggestions, there is a coincidence of ideas."[102] In the view of Taylor as well as other U.S. officials, the "coincidence of ideas with initiatives" was true for both the United States and Japan. "On the Japanese side, the distribution system reform was already suggested by EPA, forces were there, SII encouraged the processes. We can't say which forces are more important than the others. It is a matter of degree."[103]

The acceleration of policy-making and changes was even furthered after the Interim Report, as the matching strategy of reducing the federal deficit was intensified. As for Dallara, although there were no discernable changes in the theme and tone of his oral testimony before the Senate Finance Committee, his written testimony showed clear changes. In the March 5 Senate Finance Committee Hearing record, Dallara reaffirmed the U.S.-side's problem, such as a low national savings rate and U.S. firms' competitiveness, which were "already the subject of national concern in the United States, independent of the SII."[104] But in his view, Japanese officials' suggestions "heightened" the issues. "Nevertheless, Japanese concerns have heightened our own awareness of the need to address U.S. economic weakness."[105] In his written testimony for the April 19 House Foreign Affairs Committee hearing, Dallara repeated the "two-way street" of SII and made a stronger statement.

Of course, from the very start, the SII talks have been a two-way street. If they are to be successful, Japanese action on their structural impediments must be complemented by U.S. action on our structural impediments, particularly our inadequate level of public and private savings. The commitments made by the U.S. Government in the interim report reflect the Administration's clear awareness of structural problems in the U.S. economy and our determination to resolve those problems.[106]

We cannot focus only on structural problems in Japan if we are to overcome impediments to balance of payments adjustment. We must also confront our own problems.[107]

In our discussions of the U.S. economy, it has become clear that we and the Japanese agree on the essentials. Foremost among these is the need to boost saving. The surest way to boost savings in the United States is to reduce Federal dis-saving-- that is, to cut, then eliminate the Federal budget deficit. The Japanese argue that we must reduce the budget deficit, and we know that they are right.[108]

Taylor's case is much clearer because of his conscious "matching strategy" as an economist. In the oral statement of the March 5 Senate hearing, Taylor explained more generally the goals of SII and other theoretical issues, such as, "freer markets" in both countries, with the SII being an alternative way to a managed trade approach, the saving-investment gap and its effect on current account balance, and structural barriers. On the other hand, Taylor's oral opening statement of the April 19 House hearing showed more of a policy orientation. He stated that "the SII is economic policy-making in the broadest sense. It covers all sectors of the economy and it involves both domestic and international economic issues."[109]   Therefore, for Taylor, "SII is the most comprehensive and the most sustainable way to reduce our current account and trade imbalances, to increase exports from the United States, and to reduce trade frictions between the United States and Japan."[110]   With respect to the saving and investment initiative, Taylor stressed that for Japan increasing public investment for infrastructure and for the United State reducing the budget deficit would reduce the current account surplus. "Those two operations together, and there is no disagreements among economists on this issue. Those two operations together will result in a reduction in the Japanese current account surplus and in the U.S. current account deficit."[111]   Finally, Taylor again asked congressional members for cooperation and support for the president's pro-growth budget and the saving and education initiatives for "the success of this two-way undertaking."[112]

These statements and descriptions of the sequence of events confirm a former administration official's view that "there are no policies in the final report that the Japanese suggested but the U.S. administration did not want . . . There is nothing that the U.S. side suggested but the Japanese did not want, such as [deregulating] the retail law and public works spending."[113]   In the same official's view, "U.S. pressure accelerated Japanese policy change . . . [while] Japanese suggestions accelerated the policy-making process in the U.S. In this sense, both sides used *gaiatsu* to accelerate policy-making.   But timing is important for policy-making on both sides."[114]

President Bush's tax increase statement on June 26, 1990, eloquently supported this view.   Before the interim reports, U.S. officials denied any possible measures to increase U.S. taxes, because they were tied to Bush's campaign pledge of "no new taxes."[115]   But Bush's changed policy on the tax issue greatly stimulated the SII discussion and helped produce Japanese concessions on the public works spending issue.[116]   U.S. officials later explained that the tax increase was the "most important part of the final report."[117]   McCormack suggested that the SII talks helped the consideration and timing of Bush's announcement of tax increases.[118]

During the year-long SII negotiation process the development of "collegiality" might be observed.   During the interviews, many U.S. officials expressed their personal and professional relationships with their Japanese counterparts through many informal as well as formal meetings.   The sense of collegiality was expressed in such expressions as "close personal relationship," "professional working relationship" (Taylor), "better understanding and personal level of good relationship" (Rill), the feeling of "obligation to consult each other."[119]   McCormack called Japanese negotiators "our Japanese colleagues."[120]

This also seemed true for Japanese officials.   McCormack remembers the scene at the end of the SII meeting, when a Japanese official said with high emotion, "We've found Americans are tough negotiators, but also good friends."[121]   One U.S. administration official, who attended all of the SII meetings, including the secret meetings, said that "the atmosphere [in the meetings] was sometimes intense.   But they [negotiators] became close.   Their relations reached a level of respect for each other."[122]   Of course, these personal and professional relations do not eliminate room for hard bargaining among working-level officials.   But those relations may make the U.S. and Japanese officials reach "agree[ment] on essentials" (Dallara) somewhat easier and faster.   Even Vice Minister of MITI Suzuki, a champion of defending MITI policies, expressed his feeling that "we were able to have substantial discussions which was not always the case [in the past]."[123]

The bottom line is that the U.S. and Japanese officials knew the reality of interdependence between two economies.   In Williams' expression, "Its existence [SII] is a reflection of the interdependence of the two economies and the increased visibility of structural barriers."[124]   On the Japanese side, Watanabe of MFA also had a similar view that "because of economic interdependence, we have to accept domestic interference."[125]   As a former U.S. administration official said, in the SII, "both countries asked the other side for concessions in order to cope with economic interdependence.   It is a mutual compromise."[126]   In other words, the SII was "economic policy-making, a natural complement to the mechanisms for coordination in international macro policy and trade policy," and "policy coordination, a complement to G-7 and other trade talks, coordinating microeconomic policies, such as deregulations and anti-trust laws."[127]

Finally, a seed of "convergence by direct learning" (Taira) among U.S. and Japanese working-level officials might be found through the SII process. As to Japanese officials, when the SII started in September 1989, for example, a chief negotiator from MFA Kunihiro simply stressed the necessity of "structural adjustment" (*kōzō chōsei*) or "structural reform" (*kōzō kaikaku*) by citing the affirmed policies of OECD and the Toronto summit.[128] In November 1989, Kunihiro criticized James Fallow's idea of "containing Japan" and advocated the importance of creating "common rules of economic activities" among nations with different cultures and traditions. It was the interrelated trade and monetary regime of GATT-IMF that Kunihiro had in mind when he spoke of "common rules."[129] In December 1989, a chief negotiator from MFA Watanabe who took over the Kunihiro's position, began to express some notion of "convergence" by saying that the "shapes of branches" of U.S. and Japanese economies were different, although they were both capitalism; therefore these differences should be "trimmed."[130] After the Interim Report, Watanabe much clearly expressed his concern: "The branch shapes of Japanese and U.S. capitalism are quite different. Neither of them is ideal. Through the tasks of SII, I think it is possible that an image of a more ideal form of capitalism, the third type, could emerge, with respect to, for example, the activities of business corporations."[131]

A similar thing seems to be said by some U.S. officials. In the beginning stage of SII, most of U.S. officials' concerns were about the problems of the Japanese way of doing business and their economic structures. However, as the SII proceeded, the U.S. officials became much more aware of the issues of a long-term perspective and a possible economic effect of compensation of executives on corporations' performance and competitiveness when Japanese officials criticized high U.S. CEOs' salaries and short-term business practices of U.S. corporations.[132]

Williams' case is quite suggestive. During the SII, he characteristically stated U.S. officials' concern: "Given our interdependence, what sort of Japan do we want to be doing business with a year from now, two years from now, or five years from now. The answer for us is in our objections and in the specific suggestions of the SII."[133] However, Williams later expressed a clearer view of "convergence" by saying that "We should be more like each other. In the future, in order to continuously participate in the world trade system, Japan should be like the U.S., while in order to maintain the competitiveness, the U.S. should be like Japan."[134] Also refer to Williams' view on macroeconomic policies: "Japan's budget policy has generally put weight on the production at the cost of consumption and export [from other countries]. In contrast, U.S. budget policy has put weight on the consumption at the cost of export and production . . . If there was the best budgeting policy, it would be in the middle between the U.S. and Japan."[135]

In sum, from the perspective of the fourth model, the SII was created and developed by officials in elite policy networks in which U.S. and Japanese officials came together to share knowledge and information and develop collegiality and a common view in order to manage the problems which economic interdependence generated. In this sense, SII can be seen as the activity of creating an epistemic community (a "broad vision of the relationship between the U.S. and Japan") and regime ("fundamental rules of capitalism")[136] by working-level bureaucrats in the transgovernmental elite policy networks.

THE LEVEL OF COMMON VIEWS AND CONCESSIONS

In the forth model, the key variables which condition the degree of agreements in the international trade negotiations are the degree of common views (and collegiality) among working-level negotiation officials.[137] Perhaps, common views are intervening variables between underlying power balance with interest among political actors and bargaining outcomes in the international trade negotiations. Nonetheless, explaining bargaining outcomes based only on power relations ignores another fact of life: policy-makers are also individuals who have certain ways of thinking and viewing economic relations. How policy-makers view particular policy issues makes a difference in policy outcomes. Here, common views or "perception gaps" mean the extent to which working-level officials agree with each other to the basic nature of the problems and possible remedies for them, within available resources.

It is generally assumed that the more common views on the issues (and the nature of the system in general) among policy-makers, the more room for mutually acceptable agreements in international trade negotiations, if other things being equal. From the perspective of the fourth model, the degree of common views or perception gap among trade negotiation officials conditions the levels of agreements reached, because specific details of trade agreements and alternatives are often developed by working-level bureaucrats, which in turn depends on their specific knowledge, understanding, and information about the issues.[138] To examine this hypothesis, the text of the reconstructed records of the three SII meetings in the NHK book were analyzed.

In the saving and investment patterns, U.S. officials' initial suggestions in the first meeting was that the Japanese government make medium-term plans with the priorities in public investment in order to improve the Japanese living standard and reduce current account surpluses.[139] After some discussions about which indicators (e.g. flow or stock) should be used to assess the Japanese public investment level, the Japanese officials admitted that they had recognized the necessity to improve inadequate infrastructures, such as housing, a sewer system, and parks in Japan. In their view, because of that reason, they had been making efforts for a long time to raise the level of the social infrastructure, which had been behind the level of Western industrial nations, although the gap between them was narrowing.[140] From the first to the third discussions, the issue at contention was not whether or not Japan needed to improve the social infrastructure or expand the domestic demands, but how much of the budget from which sources (increased tax, government bonds, or the social welfare funds) the government should spend on public works, especially at the risk of a labor shortage and possible inflation if the massive budget spending was made in the short-term period.[141] In other words, both the U.S. and Japanese officials agreed that balancing savings and investment levels was necessary in Japan as well as in the United States to eliminate current account imbalances. This meant that public investment in Japan needed to be increased, at least in the medium- and long-term.[142]

As to the distribution system issue, the discussions were somewhat difficult to get through. In MITI officials' view, although the Japanese distribution system was somewhat different from that of the United States, both systems were not very much different in terms of efficiency. But MITI officials knew there were problems with the distribution system. Even though the Japanese distribution system was rapidly changing, it could be "rationalized" more from the viewpoint of economic efficiency. For this reason, MITI already published the new policy vision on the distribution system, aiming to clarify procedures and shorten the coordination period for opening new stores, by limiting the scope of the Large Store Law, said MITI officials.[143]

However, for the U.S. officials, MITI officials' assertions appeared as a denial of the problem in the Japanese distribution system. In the U.S. officials' view, the inefficiency of the Japanese distribution system and difficulty in entering the domestic market are common knowledge among foreigners as well as the Japanese. The U.S. officials said that they were amazed to see the grave differences between U.S. and Japanese officials in viewing the reality of the Japanese distribution system. In their view, considering the harmful effects of the LSL on imports and consumers, such "drastic changes as they occurred in Eastern Europe" are necessary; that is, a repeal of the law.[144]

But the perception gap on the exclusionary business practices was much greater than that of the distribution system. From the beginning, U.S. officials severely criticized Japan's lax antitrust enforcement and statutory inadequacy. From the first to third meetings, the U.S. officials continuously pointed out problems of Japanese antitrust law, administrative guidance and industrial policies, and they pressed for change.[145]

Although JFTC officials were forthcoming with the U.S. request, with such new initiatives as more strict operation of the present laws and plans to increase personnel in the third meeting, they made a strong assertion in the first meeting that "there was no difference between the U.S. and Japanese antitrust law." U.S. officials could not agree to JFTC officials' views, and said that "I cannot help thinking that antitrust law is not really working in Japan." In U.S. officials' view, the Japanese antitrust law needs to remedy some "institutional problems" (e.g. lack of private damage remedy system), expand the scope of cartel surcharge application, and strengthen organizational capacity as well as positive enforcement of the law.[146]

MITI officials started not only by defending Japanese corporations' long-term business practices in the first meeting but also positively argued for the "economic rationality" of such practices as the strength of Japanese industry in the second meeting.[147] Even in MITI officials' view, the reasons MITI uses various *shingikai* (government's advisory committee) and "policy vision" were to "maintain the open markets"; and administrative guidance, to "promote competition and not to discriminate against foreign companies."[148] Of course, for the U.S. officials, these are all "market distortion" activities to protect the domestic market.[149]

The perception gap in the keiretsu area was the greatest. In the U.S. officials' view, keiretsu generates many problems such as forging antitrust practices and barring foreign investment, although keiretsu itself may not be necessarily illegal. They said in order for the keiretsu structure to be more open and competitive, the Japanese government should limit the percentage of share-holding, strengthen the disclosure system, abolish the thirty-day examination period for foreigners' investment in Japan, and lower the ceiling of banks' stock holding.[150]

Japanese officials' responses to the U.S. officials' suggestions was brief and cold. In their view, cross-shareholding is a result of free enterprise. Six major keiretsu groups are weakening; there was no need to restrict banks' shareholding. The investment pattern is a matter of private industries' own judgment; and there is no difference in the disclosure system between the U.S. and Japan. Lastly, they said cross-shareholding does not cause any problems for competitive policy; since keiretsu is not illegal, there is no need to exclude it.[151] Listening to these Japanese officials' speeches, the U.S. officials' impression was of "darkness," saying that the Japanese officials were "too cautious" about the keiretsu issue, compared with other issues and underestimated the essence of the problem.[152]

Analyzing the expressions and tones of the U.S. and Japanese officials' speeches in the text of SII meeting records seems to indicate the different degrees of "common views" or "perception gaps" between the U.S. and Japanese officials in four issue areas. The degrees of "common view" in the saving-investment patterns area was high; in the distribution system, medium; in exclusionary business practices, low; and in keiretsu, the lowest. In other words, "perception gaps" in the saving and investment issue area were law; medium, in the distribution system; high, in exclusionary business practices; the highest, in keiretsu. The discussions on land policy in the SII records are brief and complicated and therefore not as ready for assessment as the other issues.

Williams' characterization of the five issue areas supports the above evaluation. According to him, *most* of the U.S. suggestions in the Japanese saving-investment patterns and in the land policy were based on the Maekawa Report and other Japanese documents, in addition to OECD reports, the discussions in the Yen-Dollar Talks, and U.S. official's own experiences.[153] As for the distribution system, since there was little disagreement in Japan about inefficiency of the distribution system, the U.S. ideas were *relatively easily accepted*, except *some innovative (kakushin-teki)* suggestions.[154]   In the exclusionary business practices, the U.S. made the *detailed suggestions* because antitrust law is a extremely specialized area, and Japanese antitrust policy is *very much behind*.[155]   U.S. officials researched and compared the antitrust laws of the United States, Japan, and the EC.   However, finding a proper level of surcharges on illegal cartel is difficult, because the methods of calculation are different among those nations.[156]   In Williams' view, the keiretsu issue caused the *most misunderstanding and confusion* among the issues in SII.[157]   Overall, keiretsu was the "most difficult problem to explain theoretically" even aside from the "initial confusion" on the U.S. side.[158]

According to Williams' characterization, the level of common views in the land policy issue was high because "most" of the U.S. suggestions on the land policy were based on the Japanese government documents (and other sources). In his view, the suggested U.S. policies were the "ones that the Japanese government wanted to do anyway."[159]   However, the level of common views on the land-use issue could be said to be "medium" because there was one important difference in the desired policy between the U.S. officials and Japanese officials, which was the capital gains tax on land sales.   The U.S. officials suggested a "reduction" of the capital gains tax on land sales, while Japanese officials insisted and subsequently realized an "increase" of the capital gains tax on land sales. The "policy direction" was the opposite.[160]   Although the assessment of the level of common views on land use is not definitive, the relatively high level of common views generally support the initial hypothesis. That is, the concessions in the land policy issue area was relatively high because the level of common views was relatively high.[161]

Qualitative text analysis has a weakness. There is room for ambiguity due to subjective judgment on how to interpret the text of speeches, especially if these speeches were made by multiple persons.   Unless analysis results are quantitatively demonstrated by reliable and credible methods, assessment of the level of common views among working-level officials remains necessarily tentative. With this reservation, the overall results of the text analysis seem to support the fourth hypothesis that the greater the level of common views on the issues between U.S. and Japanese officials, the greater the level of Japanese concessions. Or the lower the perception gaps, the higher the concessions. The U.S. officials acquired a high level of concessions from Japanese officials in the issue area of saving and investment patterns because the perception gap was low in that area.   Similarly, the U.S. officials gained medium level Japanese concessions in the distribution system area because of a medium level perception gap; low level concessions in the exclusionary business practices because of a high level perception gap; and the least concessions in the keiretsu area because of the highest level of perception gap.

The above method of text analysis for identifying the perception gaps between U.S. and Japanese officials in each issue area is static and ignores the question of how much the perception gaps were narrowed between the beginning and the ending of the SII negotiation. Strictly speaking, the level of perception gap at one point in time (t1) and the changes in perception gap between one point in time (t1) and the other point in time (t2) are different variables. Thus, the identified perception gaps among SII issue areas in this section are to be interpreted as the "average" perception gaps throughout a year-long SII negotiation.

The overall observations here are as follows. U.S. and Japanese officials came to understand more about the nature of the other system and their own system and therefore their perceptions and attitude somewhat changed. To use Williams expression, "As discussions were repeated, both sides gradually conceded to each other."[162] However, even after a year-long negotiation, perception gaps in some areas were still greater than those in other areas. From the perspective of the fourth model, those differences are reflected in the different degrees of Japanese officials' concessions. In spite of initial differences in their perceptions, some agreement is still possible if Japanese officials understand the nature of the problem and therefore change their views and attitudes in some areas such as antitrust law. However, if there is little or no such change in views and attitudes on issues such as keiretsu, then Japanese officials' concessions are likely to be minimum.

NOTES

1. Here, "working-level bureaucrats" are simply referred to as opposed to "cabinet-level top policy-makers." Different types of interactions among the senior, middle, or lower level bureaucrats across the national boundaries are suspected, but in this chapter, these differences are ignored because of scarcity of data and lack of sufficient theoretical base.

2. *NYT* 3/20/89, p. A8.

3. *Nikkei* 11/8/89, p. 1.

4. Russell, op. cit., p. 432.

5. Ibid., p. 435.

6. See NHK, op. cit., pp. 248-253.

7. Williams, *Daiyamondo* 5/23/92, p. 107; 5/16/92, p. 105.

8. The words "harmonization of economic institutions" first appeared in a study group sponsored by MFA in the late fall of 1988. Refer to Yabunaka, op. cit., pp. 89-92, 194-98.

9. Taylor, telephone interview 1/13/93.

10. Williams, interview 11/7/92.

11. *Asahi* 10/14//89, p. 2; 3/28/90, p. 2. Refer to Kusano, op. cit. (1990), p. 263.

12. Cooper, op. cit., pp. 5-6.

13. Sakai takes this view. In his view, the SII was initiated by the U.S. government to realize the policy mix of macro and "microeconomic" structural reform that were affirmed in the May 1988 joint communique of OECD Ministerial Council and in the declaration of the Toronto Summit of June 1989. See Sakai op. cit., pp. 181-82. According to Hosaka ([1990], "Kōzō chōsei kyōgi no seiji keizaigaku"), the SII was the third attempt to restore global current account imbalances, after the Plaza Accord of 1985 and the Louvre Accord of 1987 in the context of multilateral macroeconomic policy coordination.

14. In reality, these policy networks are often formed by including both governmental and nongovernmental specialists. Indeed, U.S. officials extensively consulted Japanese economists outside the Japanese government, forming sort of "transnational coalitions" with them against some of the Japanese government policies (see NHK, op. cit., pp. 121-127). Takenaka suggests economic specialists as one of four "players" in initiating the SII. See op. cit. (1991), pp. 289-90.

15. *Treasury News* (NB-2055), 11/5/92. Mulford was the Assistant Treasury Secretary for International Affairs from March 1984—March 1989.

16. Ibid.

17. Those positions include the U.S. alternate executive director at the International Monetary Fund (IMF) (1982-82), the deputy assistant secretary of treasury for international monetary affairs (1983-84), U.S. executive director at the IMF and senior deputy assistant secretary for international economic policy (1984-89), assistant secretary for policy development and senior policy advisor to the secretary (October 1988-May 1989), and finally, assistant secretary for international affairs (May 1989-April 1991). See *Treasury News* (4/30/91).

18. Ibid.

19. *Nikkei* 7/19/89, p. 5; *Asahi* 9/4/94, p. 7. Refer to *Nikkei* 11/8/89, p. 1; *Asahi* 11/26/91, p. 9.

20. Mulford, "U.S. & Japan: Forging a New Relation," speech at Johns Hopkins University 12/5/88 (C-SPAN Video, ID:14312 AB).

21. Ibid. Also refer to Mulford's speech before the Japan Society, February 22, 1990, "The impact of the Yen/Dollar discussions in opening and liberalizing the Japanese financial markets marked a major shift in attitude by Japanese officials toward Japan's role in the international financial system. There is no doubt that a more international outlook is now firmly in place in Tokyo," *Treasury News* (NB-680), 1990, p. 4.

22. See Mulford, op. cit. Japan Society Speech of 2/22/90, p. 6, "Treasury's successful formula for the Yen/Dollar Talks inspired us to apply the same framework and philosophy in the U.S.-Japan bilateral trade area, and more recently to structural impediments to external payments imbalances."

23. Mulford, SH 7/20/89, p. 3.

24. Ibid., pp. 3-4.

25. Refer to such reports as *OECD Economic Surveys: Japan* (1987/88), pp. 73-80; (1988/89), pp. 49-65.

26. See *Nikkei* 5/20/88, pp. 1, 3. Refer to Sakai, op. cit., p. 181.

27. Interview, 11/13/92. See also Mulford, SH 7/20/89, p. 3.

28. See *Nikkei* 6/22/88, pp. 1, 4. Also refer to Sakai, op. cit., p. 181; U.S. Department of State, "Economic Summits, 1981-89," p. 2.

29. Mulford, SH 7/20/89, p. 3.

30. Williams, *Daiyamondo* 4/4/92, p. 13.

31. Dallara, cited in NHK, op. cit., p. 71

32. Mulford, SH 7/20/89, p. 4-5. Mulford later clearly stated that "Treasury proposed the SII as a unique approach to identify and remove structural impediments to the adjustment of payments imbalances . . . This [reducing broad structural economic problems] is important for the economic policy coordination process in general, because of relative growth rates and exchange rate realignment have not been enough to promote full adjustment" (op. cit. Japan Society Speech of 2/22/90, p. 6). In the *Nikkei* (6/14/90, p. 5) article, Mulford expressed his understanding that SII was part of policy coordination process among industrialized nations, which included macroeconomic policies, foreign exchange rates, interest rates, and fiscal policies.

33. A Treasury official, interview, 10/7/92, Washington D.C. Refer to also NHK, op. cit., p. 65.

34. NHK, op. cit., p. 71.

35. *Nikkei* 3/21/90, p. 5.

36. A Treasury official, interview 10/7/92. Another Treasury official also said, "Dallara and Utsumi are very close. They often discussed the details of policies by telephone" (interview 10/8/92, Washington D.C.).

37. *Asahi* 11/30/91, p. 1. Refer to remarks of Utsumi and Toyoo Gyoten (then vice minister for International Finance Bureau, *Nikkei* 1/27/89, p. 3; 2/16/89, p. 3.

38. NHK, op. cit., p. 249. Utsumi was the only Japanese official who had been a chief negotiator from the preparation stage to the end of SII negotiations, while the other officials were changed. Refer to Williams *Daiyamondo* 5/16/92, pp. 106-107.

39. NHK, op. cit., p. 251.

40. Ibid., p. 77.

41. Ibid, p. 73. This informal consent was referred to as the "Utsumi-Dallara deal" by the authors of NHK book (p. 57) and was confirmed by Schoppa's interview, see op. cit. (1993), p. 376.

42. Mulford, op. cit., Japan Society Speech of 2/22/90, pp. 4, 7. The preliminary meeting of the SII was held at the meeting room of New York Federal Bank which symbolizes the international macroeconomic, monetary and finance elite policy networks. See NHK, op. cit, p. 83.

43. An administration official, interview 10/6/92, Washington D.C.

44. Farren, SH 3/5/90, p. 22.

45. Sasaki, op. cit., p. 37.

46. Fukushima, op. cit., pp. 210-211.

47. Yabunaka, op. cit., pp. 204-205.

48. Fukushima, op. cit., pp. 205, 206.

49. Yabunaka, op. cit., pp. 149, 150.

50. NHK, op. cit., p. 84.

51. Interview, 10/9/92.

52. Interview, 10/6/92.

53. NHK, op. cit., p. 71.

54. See *Nikkei* 5/26/89, p. 2.

55. See *Nikkei* 5/26/89, p. 2; 5/26/89, E.p. 1.

56. Yabunaka, op. cit., p. 150.

57. Ibid, p. 153

58. SH 7/20/89, pp. 5-7.

59. Ibid, p. 8.

60. Williams, interviews, 10/6/92 and 1/13/93. Also refer to Williams, *Daiyamondo* 5/30/92, p. 828. On "diplomatic fairness," also refer to Yabunaka, op. cit., p. 151.

61. McCormack, SH 7/20/90, p. 9.

62. See for example, Williams, *Tōyō Keizai* 9/30/89, p. 18.

63. A U.S. administration official, interview, 10/9/92, Washington D.C.

64. See *Tōyō Keizai* 9/30/89, pp. 14-16; 12/2/89, pp. 60-61. For the Provisional Administrative Reform Promotion Commission Report, see *Nikkei* 12/2/89, p. 1. Such structural reform policies can be traced back to *The Maekawa Report* of 1986, which first publicly advocated the necessary structural change in Japanese economy.

65. See NHK, op. cit., pp. 248, 249, 250.

66. Ibid,, for example, pp. 262, 265, 267, 269-270.

67. Ibid., pp. 254, 256, 259. Williams, *Daiyamondo* 5/23/92, p. 109.

68. According to a former U.S. official, who attended the first three SII meetings, U.S. officials were defensive of the U.S. economic system too and felt little use in talking about U.S. economic system (interview 11/4/92). Vice Minister of MFA Kunihiro also pointed to the reluctance of U.S. officials to admit their own economic problems in the first meeting. See NHK, op. cit., p. 269.

69. Refer to the reconstructed SII meeting records in NHK, op. cit., pp. 248-304.

70. Taylor, interview 11/7/92.

71. Ibid.

72. Ibid. Frequent consultation between Japanese and U.S. staffs over telephone conversations was reported by a follow-up stage Treasury Department official. "The Japanese Ministry of Construction often consults me about land-use policies over the telephone. I consult Japanese economic experts, too. There is need for constant consultation because the SII commitments require policy changes, which also need legislation" (interview, 10/8/92).

73. *Tōyō Keizai* 12/2/89, pp. 68-69.

74. Such meetings as that in Hawaii on May 23, 1990 were considered "informal meetings" because they were publicly announced and known, while the Bern meeting on January 31 and the meeting held at March 20, 1990 in a suburb of Washington. D.C., were considered "secret meetings" because there was no public announcement of them and those meetings were intended to be secret.

75. Williams, interview 1/13/93.

76. Interview 6/29/93.

77. NHK, op. cit., p. 106.

78. Interview, 10/6/92.

79. Williams, interview 10/6/92. See also Williams, *Daiyamondo* 5/23/92, p. 109. The Japanese negotiators initial denial of the structural problems in the Japanese economy might be part of negotiation tactics.

80. Refer to *Nikkei* 3/21/90, p. 5; *Asahi* 3/26/90, p. 1.

81. An Administration official, interviews 10/8/92 and 10/9/92, Washington D.C. For the responses of JFTC officials, refer to NHK, op. cit., pp. 262, 267, 285, 298.

82. Before becoming chairman of JFTC, Umezawa had been a career bureaucrat reaching a high-rank position in MOF. A position of JFTC chairman is a kind of appointee, not a minister.

83. *Nikkei* 6/14/89, p. 5.

84. *Asahi* 9/2/89, p. 9.

85. *Nikkei* 12/3/90, p. 3. Also refer to *Nikkei* 3/8/90, p. 5; NHK, op. cit., p. 267.

86. *Nikkei* 6/22/90, p. 5. In 1989, JFTC issued 115 warnings while resorting to only seven remonstrances.

87. Refer to Williams, "We ourselves had not yet made the final judgement on many issues [at the time of the first and the second SII meetings]" (*Daiyamondo* 5/23/92, p. 109).

88. See Williams, *Daiyamondo* 5/2-9/92, p. 110. Also refer to Dallara's argument on keiretsu in NHK, op. cit., pp. 285-286.

89. Williams, *Daiyamondo* 5/2-9/92, p 110. A U.S. official commented on keiretsu as "the most complicated issue" (*Tōyō Keizai* 9/30/89, p. 16).

90. Williams, *Daiyamondo* 5/2-9/92, p. 113. Indeed, two sets of multilateral negotiations to reduce the differences among the patent system of all nations ("international harmonization of patent laws") were ongoing that time. These were the Trilateral Conferences among the U.S. Patent and Trademark Office (USPTO), European Patent Office (EPO), and Japanese Patent Office (JPO), and the discussions sponsored by the World Intellectual Property Organization (WIPO) (*Japan Economic Survey*, September 1988, p. 16). The issue of protection of intellectual property including patents was also on the agenda of the Uruguay Round. See *The Final Report*, p. IV-10, "Regarding the patent system, consideration on the harmonization of patent system is under way in multilateral fora such as WIPO and GATT. The Government of Japan, together with the U.S. Government, will actively participate in, and contribute to, the discussions there." Here one will find the interactive processes of bilateral and multilateral discussions in the elite policy networks of the patent issue area.

91. Refer to such articles as *Nikkei* 7/6/89, p. 1; 11/7/89, p. 1; 11/8/89, E.p. 3; *Asahi* 11/8/89, E.p. 1; NHK, op. cit., pp. 97-98, 264-65. Also see Farren's testimony SH 3/5/90, pp. 48-50; "U.S.-Japan Survey Shows Prices Higher There Then Here," *Business America* 2/12/90, pp. 35-36. I consider the joint price research as one of the significant results of the SII, because the research promoted a common understanding about real market conditions. Such joint research between the United States and Japan was never conducted before the SII. Although the Commerce and MITI officials did not completely agree to technical details of research method and how to interpret the results, these differences would be lessened as long as a joint price research continues.

92. Taylor, telephone interview, 11/7/92.

93. Interview, 11/7/92.

94. Interview, 10/9/92, Washington D.C. Several officials expressed such a "learning effect" of SII in my interviews.

95. Watanabe, in *Gaikō Fōramu*, May, 1990, p. 28. Yabunaka, op. cit., pp. 182-89.

96. SH 3/5/90, p. 5.

97. Ibid., p. 10.

98. Ibid, p. 17.

99. Refer to *Vital Speeches of the Day*, 3/1/89, pp. 288-294.

100. Telephone interview, 11/13/92.

101. Ibid.

102. Taylor, SH 4/19/90, p. 132.

103. Taylor, interview, 11/7/92. The other administration officials expressed the view similar to Taylor's, interviews of 10/8/92 and 11/13/92.

104. SH 3/5/90, P. 47.

105. Ibid.

106. HH 4/19/90, p. 100.

107. Ibid., p. 105.

108. Ibid.

109. Ibid., p. 108.

110. Ibid.

111. Ibid.

112. Ibid., p. 109.

113. A U.S. administration official, interview, 11/13/92.

114. Ibid. Watanabe expressed a view similar to this U.S. official that the SII is a catalyst for accelerating changes in both countries. Watanabe revealed U.S. officials' view: "American negotiators said to us, 'We want Japan to have a say in the U.S. economy. This in turn strengthens our positions for policies we want to promote [in the U.S.].'" See *Gaikō Fōramu*, May 1990, pp. 26, 27-28.

115. See Yabunaka, op. cit., p. 185.

116. See Taylor's remarks in "Transcript of Structural Impediments Initiative (SII) Press Conference held at U.S. Embassy in Tokyo on June 28, 1990," pp. 6-7.

117. *WSJ* 6/29/90, pp. A3, A6.

118. *NYT* 6/29/90, p. D2.

119. U.S. officials, interviews 10/7-9/92, Washington D.C.; telephone interview 11/7/92.

120. The April 5 briefing for the press after the fourth SII meeting, in *CQWR* 4/7/90, p. 1180.

121. Interview, 10/7/92.

122. Interview, 10/9/92.

123. *Sekai Shūhō* 3/10/90, p. 27.

124. SH 4/19/90, p. 75.

125. *Gaikō Fōramu*, May 1990, p. 26.

126. Telephone interview, 11/5/92.

127. Taylor SH 4/19/90, pp.108, 109, and interview 11/7/92.

128. *Ekonomisuto* 9/5/89, pp. 10-12.

129. *Chūō Kōron*, November, 1989, p. 98.

130. *Tōyō Keizai* 12/2/89, p. 60.

131. *Gaikō Fōramu*, May 1990, p. 29.

132. Taylor, interview 6/29/93.

133. Williams, HH 4/19/90, p. 75.

134. Williams, *Daiyamondo* 3/14/92, p. 81.

135. Williams *Daiyamondo* 4/18/92, pp. 104-105.

136. Williams, interview 10/6/92.

137. The degree of sharing common views and collegiality may not necessarily go together. Theoretically, it is conceivable that trade negotiators began to share more or less common views on the international economic issues without sharing a sense of collegiality. Also "sharing common views" does not mean international trade negotiations are always "harmonious." Difficult negotiations and hard political bargaining may occur among officials who even share common views on the nature of the system and the issues.

138. If one thinks of the issue of "numeric targets" in the current Clinton Administration's trade talks, one will understand the importance of common views. The "numeric targets" issue is often referred to as a "theological argument." Refer to Yasunori Abe, *This is Yomiuri*, 5, 1994, pp. 64-69.

139. Dallara, in NHK, op. cit., pp. 253-254. See also speeches of Armacost and Taylor, pp. 256.

140. Ibid., Shinozawa of MOF, pp. 274-275, 296.

141. Ibid., Shinozawa, p. 296; Utsumi, p. 296; Unno, p. 276.

142. Ibid., Unno, p. 252; Dallara, p. 253. Refer to Utsumi's remarks in *WSJ* 6/21/90, p. A11. Also refer to remarks of a Japanese mid-level bureaucrat, "With respect to the need to steadily develop social infrastructures, there is consensus in the nation. [Therefore] the difference between two countries' [views concerning public works spending] is, in a sense, its speed" (*Chūō Kōron* 6, 1990, p. 146). According to *Nikkei* 3/11/90, p. 3, "Nonetheless, the Japanese side admitted that there was the necessity to steadily develop social infrastructures. At the bottom line, there was not much difference [in views] between Japan and the United States."

143. Suzuki, in NHK, op. cit., pp. 261, 297, 298. Refer to also Williams' view, "They [Japanese officials] believed the Large Store law was a problem but they could not change" (interview 10/6/92).

144. McCormack in NHK, op. cit., pp. 259-260, 297. See also Suzuki's view "There are differences in recognizing reality, opinion, and evaluation [on the Japanese distribution system between U.S. and Japanese officials]" (ibid., p. 269).

145. Ibid., Rill, pp. 266, 288; Williams, pp. 287-288, 299.

146. Ibid., Itoda of JFTC, pp. 267, 298-299; Rill, pp. 267, 299; Williams, p. 299. Refer to *Nikkei* 3/8/90, p. 5, "Behind the U.S.-Japanese friction was the difference in views on the nature of [antitrust] penalties."

147. Ibid., Suzuki, pp. 267, 289.

148. Ibid., Yokota of MITI, pp. 289, 300.

149. See Williams' remarks, ibid., pp. 287-288. According to Williams, the negotiations on the regulations of the Antitrust law was like a "ground battle without prospect of ending" (*Daiyamondo* 6/13/92, p. 87).

150. Ibid., Dallara, pp. 285-286, 300-301.

151. Ibid., Utsumi, Itoda, Sumiya, Yokota, pp. 286-287, 301-302. According to Williams, Japanese officials did not believe keiretsu was a problem (interview 10/6/92).

152. Ibid., Dallara, p. 302. Also refer to the section of "Basic Recognition" on keiretsu relationship in *the Final Report*. "Certain aspects of economic rationality of Keiretsu relationships notwithstanding, there is a view that certain aspects of Keiretsu relationships also promote preferential group trade, negatively affect foreign direct investment in Japan, and may give rise to anti-competitive business practices. In order to address this concern, the Government of Japan intends to make. . . ." (p. V-1). The

expression indicates that Japanese officials somewhat conceded to U.S. officials' pointing out of effects of keiretsu but did not entirely agree with them for these effects.

153. *Daiyamondo* 5/30/92, p. 830.

154. *Daiyamondo* 5/30/92, p. 830. It is suspected that one of the "innovative" suggestions was a repeal of the LSL which was not proposed by MITI or any governmental agencies.

155. Ibid., p. 830.

156. Ibid., p. 831.

157. *Daiyamondo* 5/2-9/92, p. 110.

158. Ibid.

159. Telephone interview, 6/9/94.

160. The "policy direction" in the other areas are generally the same between U.S. and Japanese officials: that is, "increase" public works spending, "deregulate" the LSL, "strengthen" the Antimonopoly law, and "increase" the openness of keiretsu.

161. If the perception gap explanation is combined with other explanations, the alternative explanation is still consistent with this tentative assessment. That is, the level of common views in the land policy was as high as that in the saving-investment patterns, but because the U.S. team did not put high-level pressure on that issue (or the transgovernmental coalition of governmental subunits is medium), the level of concession in that area is medium.

One thing to keep in mind is that the level of common perception does not necessarily correspond to the level of "political contention." The Japanese public works spending issue was the "most contentious" in the SII. But this does not mean that the U.S. and Japanese officials had a great perception gap. At issue was how much, when, and where the Japanese government would spend the money, not the need to spend such money to eliminate the saving-investment gap, to lead domestic-led growth, or to improve the social infrastructure. On the contrary, repeal of the LSL was controversial because of political sensitivity (the reluctance of LDP to hurt one of its supporters). MITI officials knew the problems of the LSL and wanted to change the way of implementing the law. But they were hesitant to go along with some U.S. requests because those were politically difficult to achieve.

162. Williams, *Daiyamondo* 5/23/92, p. 109.

10   Conclusion: Findings and Implications

This research began by asking why the U.S. administration initiated such an unusual trade negotiation as the SII, a rule-based approach, as opposed to a "result-oriented approach," which was recommended by members of business and some policy-makers, and why the U.S. and Japanese governments reached agreements in the SII. Different conceptual models answer differently. The government as a rational unitary actor model explains in such a way that the U.S. administration proposed the SII to achieve the national trade policy goal of strengthening the GATT world trading regime by countering the congressional initiative of protectionist measures—managed trade and trying to change some of Japanese trade barriers and integrate Japan into the world trading system. In the view of the transgovernmental coalition of subunits model, the SII was initiated because "new comprehensive talks" on structural issues was already an ongoing program involving both U.S. and Japanese agencies as a result of national and transgovernmental turf battles among relevant governmental subunits, such as Treasury and State Departments, USTR, MOF, MITI and MFA, with their own organizational routines. The transgovernmental coalition of top-level policy-makers model explains the SII initiation as a result of pulling and hauling between "free traders" and "pragmatists" in the Bush administration who were variously pressed by congressional leaders with regard to how to implement Super 301 of the 1989 Trade Act. From the perspective of the elite policy networks of working-level officials, the SII idea was initially conceived and developed by officials who were members of the Yen Dollar Talks and multilateral macroeconomic and structural adjustment policy coordination networks of G-7 and OECD, to complement macroeconomic policy coordination process with structural adjustment policies for facilitating global and bilateral current account adjustment.

The answer for the second question also varies, depending on the conceptual models. According to the first model, the U.S. and the Japanese governments reached the SII agreements because the national self-interest of the United States—to promote worldwide partnership with Japan and the Japanese national self-interest—to maintain a good economic as well as military-security relationship with the United States for its own prosperity—converged with each other in certain power relations between them. In the second model, the SII agreements were the result of transgovernmental coalitions among such institutional actors as the White House, Kantei, U.S. departments, Japanese ministries, and the LDP, each with its own organizational goals and programs. The third model explains the SII agreements as a result of the activities of transgovernmental coalition making among top-level policy-makers, such as President Bush, Prime Minister Kaifu, Nakayama, Baker, Takeshita, Brady, Hashimoto, Mosbacher, Kanemaru, Hills, other cabinet and party members, and congressional leaders. In the view of the fourth model, the SII agreements were reached because SII working-level officials came to have some common views about the nature of the problems by sharing information and knowledge on the market conditions and their economic systems in the process of developing specific details and alternatives for agreements.

In international trade negotiations, political power, external pressure, transgovernmental coalitions among subunits and individuals, and policy-makers' perceptions all are influencing each other in complicated interactive processes to produce outcomes. Vertical and horizontal interactions between the units of political actors at different levels work simultaneously. The national governments being positioned in the particular power relations with the supposed national interests compete with each other; governmental subunits with their own departmental goals and organizational routines coalesce with each other; top-level policy-makers with individual concerns and interests as politicians pull and haul with each other; and working-level officials with knowledge and information in transgovernmental elite policy networks contend with each other. But, these processes can conceptually be distinguished from each other and separately systematically analyzed.

The initial proposition for research was that the level of Japanese concessions in the five issue areas of SII were related to at least four factors, which are conceptually distinguished from each other with different levels of analysis: (1) the level of U.S. pressure, (2) the size and strength of the transgovernmental coalitions among the governmental subunits, (3) the size and strength of the transgovernmental coalitions among top-level policy-makers, and (4) the level of common perceptions between the U.S. and Japanese working-level officials. In the research, the different levels of Japanese concessions in five issue areas (i.e., the high level of concessions in the saving and investment patterns, the medium level of concessions in the distribution system and in the land policy, the low level of concessions in the exclusionary business practices, and the lowest level of concessions in keiretsu) were tested by a case study, combined with a content-analysis using different conceptual models.

The research results support the initial proposition. As to the first specific proposition, the level of U.S. pressure explains the negotiation outcomes of three issue areas well. There was a positive relationship between the levels of U.S. pressure and levels of Japanese government concessions: the higher the pressure, the higher the concessions. Specifically, there was a high level of concessions for high-level pressure in saving-investment patterns, a medium level of pressure for medium-level concessions in the distribution system, and a low level of concessions for the low-level pressure in keiretsu.

However, two divergent cases need further explanation. In spite of the medium level of pressure, a low level of concessions was obtained in exclusionary business practices; and a low level of pressure, but a medium level of concessions were achieved in the land policy issue. The explanations for these two cases were provided by other models and empirical research. The low level of concessions in exclusionary business practices was explained by the small size of the transgovernmental coalition of subunits, the small size of the transgovernmental coalition of top-level policy-makers, and the low level of common views among U.S. and Japanese working-level officials. The medium level of concessions in the land policy issue, in spite of a low level of pressure, also was explained by the medium size of the transgovernmental coalition of subunits or a medium level of common views among U.S. and Japanese working-level officials. The explanations by the four models of different levels of Japanese concessions are summarized in Table 10.1.

The explanations by the four models of the different degrees of concessions are not mutually exclusive, but complement each other. For example, the high level of concessions in saving-investment patterns was due to a high level of U.S. pressure. But, it was also due to the large size of the transgovernmental coalition among subunits, and similarly, the large size of the transgovernmental coalition among top-level policy-makers, as well as a high level of common views among U.S. and Japanese officials. However, the same expansionist policy the United States demanded with the high level of pressure in the SII would not have yielded the same high level of concessions, if few or no Japanese top policy-makers, ministries and the party in power had supported the U.S. demands.

Future policy recommendations based on lessons from SII also vary according to conceptional models. Policy recommendations fall in the realm of prediction, in the broad sense. Viewing the government as a unitary actor suggests that more pressure on the Japanese government achieves desirable policy goals, since this model "predicts" that high-level pressures will yield high-level concessions from other governments.

The transgovernmental coalition of subunit model "predicts" that the extent of coalitions of subunits cutting across national lines will result in favorable concessions from Japanese ministries. The rule of the game is "divide and coalesce" with friendly agencies in the other government. The size of transgovernmental winning coalitions is the key variable for achieving desirable

Table 10.1
The Levels of Japanese Concessions in Five Issue Areas and Explanations

The Issue Areas	Level of concessions	Explanations			
		Model I Level of Pressure	Model II Size (& Strength) of Transgovernmental Coalition of Subunits	Model III Size (& strength) of Transgovernmental Coalition of the Top	Model IV Level of Perception-gap among Working-level Officials
1. Saving-Investment Patterns	high	high	large (LDP strongly supported)	large (LDP politicians strongly supported)	low
2. Distribution System	medium	medium	medium (LDP partially supported)	medium (LDP politicians were divided)	medium
3. Exclusionary Business Practices	low	medium	small (LDP opposed)	small (LDP politicians did not support)	high
4. Keiretsu	least	low	-----	-----	highest
5. Land Policy	medium	low	medium (LDP supported)	-----	(medium)

policy outcomes. In the winning coalition, the policy position of the party in power (the LDP) is critically important as to whether and to what extent the basic policy lines are accepted.

The transgovernmental coalition of top-level policy-makers model emphasizes that the extent of top-level policy-makers' personal relationships demonstrated by frequent telephone calls, exchange of letters, summit meetings and the level of joint political intervention in the working-level negotiations are the crucial factors to successfully reaching agreements. The extent of top-level policy-makers' personal relationships, joint political intervention, and the form of coalitions among cabinet-level policy-makers from both governments will "predict" how much progress is made in the negotiation.

The elite policy network model suggests that the development of close consultative policy networks among working-level officials, which include both bilateral and multilateral fora, is important in developing specific policy alternatives and achieving smooth policy coordination. In particular, the level of common perceptions and collegiality, derived from sharing information and knowledge among working-level officials, will "predict" the levels of agreements and their implementation.[1] There are always possibilities that working-level bureaucrats covertly and overtly resist implementation of international agreements made by top-level policy-makers, if these bureaucrats believe that their personal, organizational, or "national" interests are not served by these agreements. Then, promoting transgovernmental collegiality, with increasing common perceptions in the continuous bilateral and multilateral policy networks, is the surest way to achieve implementation of agreements.

Different conceptual models prescribe different policy recommendations focusing different key variables for desirable policy results. For some people, choosing one conceptual model may look like controlling other variables in explaining policy outcomes. Thus, one could make such a statement as "if other things being equal, a higher level of political pressure (or a larger size of transgovernmental coalition of subunits etc.) would yield a higher level of concessions in trade negotiations." In the systematically layered multi-dimensional approach, different conceptual models supplement each other and enhance our understanding of the social events, thereby improving our ability to predict possible policy outcomes. Therefore, this multidimensional approach is more useful than any single model approach.

Hitherto studies of the U.S.-Japanese trade negotiations used the case study method combined with an economic analysis of data, but they did not distinguish those four factors and therefore did not distinguish different explanations with different levels of analysis. The authors of past studies have not been sufficiently self-critical of their conceptual models, the sets of assumptions that are included in them, nor the levels of analysis. Also, they have not conducted systematic research of the relation between the degrees of negotiation success and factors which are supposed to contribute to those successes, using quantitative analysis combined with a case study to empirically test the different explanations (propositions) based on different conceptual models. The authors of past studies did not always have a clear idea that the explanation at one level of analysis did not *falsify* the explanation at another level of analysis.

As a result, past studies of the SII (on U.S.-Japanese trade negotiations in general) suggested different explanations for the different degrees of Japanese concessions, many of which are not only inadequate but also often contradictory. Thus, this research adds to the tradition of trade negotiation/decision-making research. This book has improved and further developed the approach that Allison started, with the emphasis on transgovernmental process and policy positions of political actors, and by explaining policy outcomes using variables that are generated by four conceptual models. By doing so, this book enhances the power of describing, explaining, and predicting the outcomes of international trade negotiations. This research provides a step toward more rigorous study in the field of predicting policy outcomes in international trade negotiations. However, the model and method used in this research can be elaborated further with respect to the needs of a standardized method for the selection of documents for each model, more rigorous content-analysis on multiple newspaper indexes, a quantitatively demonstrable method on "the level of common perceptions," and a more detailed study of elite policy networks. These are items for future research.

In the post-Cold War era in which the economy is becoming more prominent in international relations, policy-makers need a better understanding of the factors and transgovernmental processes which contribute to successful trade agreements. In a world of growing economic interdependence, proper conceptual models and systematically tested empirical knowledge are necessary to enhance the predictive power of policy outcomes in international trade negotiations.

If Clinton administration officials had understood the conditions in which the U.S. government could achieve significant results from trade negotiations with the Japanese government (or any government), they would not have demanded "numeric targets" in recent negotiations. This research points out that when only a few Japanese government subunits, including the party in power, or cabinet-level policy-makers, support the U.S. demands, and common views among U.S. and Japanese working-level officials is low, U.S. pressure, however strong, is unlikely to yield significant concessions from the Japanese government. The "numeric targets" issue happened to be such a case. Throughout the Framework trade negotiation, there were no Japanese cabinet members, politicians in the party in power, working-level officials, or governmental subunits, who support "numeric targets." Without allies in the Japanese government, even the highest level of U.S. pressure is doomed to fail. Policy-makers need to estimate possible negotiation outcomes in international trade negotiations *before* they propose certain policies. Unfortunately, it does not seem that administration officials made such an estimate, thus suggesting that they have great knowledge of neither the Japanese decision-making process nor the transgovernmental process.

This research reveals several other things. The U.S. and Japanese government officials created the SII as another bureaucratic structure (working group) with the organizational characteristic of the "two-way street." U.S. officials initially accepted the "two-way street" notion for mainly "tactical" reasons, diplomatic equality and fairness, but also for "strategic" reasons, to educate the public, press, business, and Congress on such issues as macroeconomic issues, business planning, and competitiveness. Because of the two-way street nature of the SII, the U.S. officials became more aware of the U.S.-side structural problems. After all, not only did the Japanese government for the first time admit, officially on record, that there were structural impediments in the Japanese economy and the need to address these impediments in a comprehensive way,[2] but the U.S. government also, for the first time, recognized structural problems in its own economy and the need to address them on record in bilateral trade talks with Japan.

The SII was an example of transgovernmental policy-making, policy coordination, and policy implementation (follow-up mechanisms) by the national governments, governmental subunits, top-level policy-makers, and working-level bureaucrats, each at a different level. In the SII, "both countries asked the other side for concessions in order to cope with economic interdependence" and "both sides used *gaiatsu* to accelerate [internal] policy-making."[3] In this sense, differences in the Japanese and the U.S. commitments are not in quality but in degree, since the "SII was all coalition because all changes made were ones they [both sides] wanted to change. There is no case in the SII that they both didn't want to change."[4]

The "two-way street" nature of the SII actually contributed to this process. The U.S. officials became more aware of problems in their own system as well as those in the Japanese system. The Japanese officials also clarified issues in their system and began to better understand the need to change some aspects of their economic system and business practices. Many issues are revealed through the SII process. In this sense the SII facilitated the "learning process" among participants about the nature of systemic differences and the need for system change. It thereby contributed to a creation of an epistemic community (a common perception and vision) and international regime (rules).

Based on these findings, several theoretical and practical implications are suggested. The first implication concerns the concept of *gaiatsu*. To date, many scholars have uncritically used the term *gaiatsu* applied only to Japanese policy-making in international trade economic policies. Today, not only Japan but also the United States needs foreign pressures in the form of international policy-making and coordination in the multilateral and, when necessary, bilateral bases, to promote necessary changes against parochial domestic interests, including the legislature, bureaucracy, industries, and interest groups. One of the important issues in our time is how to adjust domestic and local interests with global general interests in the form of a multilateral free trade regime and the growing globalization of production and consumption. The dilemma is that modern democratic institutions, such as legislatures and political parties, which are expected to represent the interests of local districts, may not always be equipped to offer better solutions to deal with issues of globalization of the economy versus domestic interests. The pressure from powerful interest groups often inhibits social reform policies.

Perhaps the national government, located in the intersection of domestic and international interest, will have a better chance to provide a balance between domestic and international interests. But, to achieve these balances, national governments may need foreign governments and international organizations as allies. By the same token, governmental subunits, top policy-makers, and working-level officials may need their foreign counterparts as allies for their own policy goals against other agencies, the domestic bureaucracy, and local interests. As national economies are becoming more and more interdependent, the political process is also becoming international—intergovernmental, transgovernmental, and transnational. Then, it is important for policy-makers to understand these multidimensional processes in the effort to mobilize all forces of all dimensions in order to achieve domestic and international reform policies in balancing local and global general interests.

The above-mentioned conditions may be found in many countries as the world economy becomes more integrated, and thus the *gaiatsu* phenomenon may not be uniquely Japanese, even if it is more visible in Japan. Thus, there is a need for more general models to describe and explain international policy-making and policy coordination processes.[5] *Gaiatsu*, or foreign pressure, is an important part of this model since transgovernmental policy-making and policy coordination by different levels of political actors do not eliminate political bargaining and pressure politics based on different power resources including transgovernmental coalitions. More generalized models of transgovernmental policy-making/coordination/*gaiatsu* can be applied not only to Japan but also to the United States and other countries, since like it or not, the growing interdependence of economies and the problems of economic interdependence faced by the national political institutions are real and have to be jointly dealt with.

In the changing environment of the global economy, both Japan and the United States need to learn how to solve economic friction and adjust their economic systems with each other's, thereby contributing to the development of a rule-based multilateral trade regime. The SII was an attempt in which U.S. and Japanese officials tried to solve trade frictions and adjust their economic systems both by creating an international epistemic community and regime and by accelerating domestic change through a joint bureaucratic structure. Since the adjustment process is mutual, they will be engaging in improving their own system while stimulating the other to modify their system. In a sense, "the Japan Problem" and "the America Problem" are part of the larger problem of growing economic interdependence—globalization of production and consumption. Managing the problems which economic interdependence generates and furthering the "harmonization of economic institutions," are future tasks for the United States and Japan.

For Japan, the task is to integrate itself into the world economic system by opening its market, changing exclusionary business practices, making business-government relations more transparent, and promoting domestic-led growth with fiscal and other measures, while stimulating the United States to modify some negative aspects of cooperate business practices and strengthen fiscal discipline. For the United States, the task will be to reduce the federal deficit and improve its industrial base, while helping Japan to integrate its system into the global system. Both systems can be better if they learn from each other and cooperate with one another. The SII was a institutional framework in which U.S. and Japanese government officials started this process. This mutual system-transforming process will perhaps take years, even decades. But this process and the process of multilateral regime creation in such areas as the antitrust law regime have became easier than before because "We now have a comprehensive platform" and "vision."[6]

NOTES

1. The article of former USTR Director Charles Lake indicates how the level of common views and trust among negotiation officials are important in conducting negotiations to reach mutually acceptable agreements (*Asahi* 2/26/95, p. 11; 3/19/95, p. 11). There are indications that elite policy networks among U.S. and Japanese officials are weakening after the important SII officials left from both governments and as the multilateral G-7 and OECD elite policy networks have somewhat weakened. (Refer to *Asahi* 6/5/93, p. 2; 2/9/94, p. 5).

2. Williams, SH 3/5/90, p. 76.

3. Former administration officials, telephone interviews 11/5/92 and 11/13/92.

4. An administration official, interview of 10/8/92.

5. Richard Rosecrance's "mediative state" is one of the important conceptualizations in this regard. A mediative state is "the intermediary between internal and international pressures—reshaping international forces to make them more hospitable to domestic needs, but at the same time building understanding at home for the intransigent international factors which cannot be altered. Such governments would bargain and balance between their own populations on the one hand and foreign governments on the other. Unless mutual adjustment is possible, international economic conflict will follow" ([1986], *The Rise of Trading States*, p. 40). Gilbert R. Winham's conceptualization about the "mediative role" of working-level officials in policy-making at the international level is quite stimulating in this regard. Refer to Winham (1979-80), "International Negotiation in an Age of Transition," and (1979), "Practitioners' View of International Negotiation."

6. Williams, interview of 10/7/92.

Appendices

Appendix A: The Coding Method for "Performative Structure" Content-Analysis

1. The event-related indexes are coded according to grammatical structure: *who does what to whom*. To enhance reliability, the coding procedure is stylized in the following manner.

(1) The subject *who* can be either Japan (J) or the United States (US).
(2) The subject can be either government (G) or government officials (P).

* Generally, in Japanese the United States and the U.S. government are *"bei," "beikoku," "amerika," "bei-seifu,"* or *"amerika-seifu."* Japan and the Japanese government are *"nichi," "nihon," "nihon-seifu,"* or *"seifu."*

(3) The object *whom* can be either Japan (Japanese government, members of the government, or the Japanese public in general), or the United States (the U.S. government, members of the government, or the American public in general).

(4) The subject-object relation type: There are four types of the subject-object relations.

Type 1:
The United States directs Japan (US→J), or
Japan directs the United States (J→US)

This type is coded as either "Pressure" (P), if the subject wants the object to do what the subject desires, or "Cooperation" (CO), if the subject calls for cooperation or shows a cooperative posture.

"Pressure" includes "Demand" (D), "Criticism" (C), and "Suggestion" (S), depending on the types of verbs in the indexes, which are assumed to reflect the level of intensity of pressure.

* Congress is the subject for 5 indexes, which are coded into "Suggestion" and for 1 index coded as "Criticism." Of course, one can exclude these 6 indexes. Since the general public does not distinguish between the U.S. administration and Congress, they are simply included.

Type 2:
The United States responses to Japan (US←J), or
Japan responses to the United States (J←US)

This type typically is found in the expression "the Japanese governments leaders have endorsed a collection of domestic policy changes in response to U.S. demands." (*WSJ* 3/19/90), and is coded as "Reactive" (R). Furthermore if the index contains two sentences with different subjects, implying one subject does something in response to the other subject's initiative, then the index is also coded as "Reactive."

"Reactive" (Response) is either "Positive" (+) or "Negative" (-). A positive reaction is an accommodating response to the other's demands or suggestions. A negative reaction is a response which does not accommodate the other's demands or suggestions. This includes countercriticism.

Type 3:
The U.S. directs the U.S.(domestic audience) (US→US)
Japan directs Japan (domestic audience) (J→J)

This type is coded into either "policy-making activities" (PM), if the indexes are about the political activities of the government or government officials (speeches, actions, and political moves), or "Policy Initiation" (PI), if the government actually initiates new policies (starts new regulations and laws, drafts new laws, issues guidelines and ordinances, and implements measures, etc.).

Type 4:
Presumably, both the United States and Japan initiated actions together (US↔J)

Thus, this type is thought as Mutual Initiation (M). This type includes indexes in which it is difficult to say which government initiates the first move. Indexes such as "the United States and Japan [*nichi-bei*] reached agreements" and "The Japanese and U.S. officials met," are coded into this type.

* 2 indexes, such as "The U.S. and Japan did not reach agreements" are coded into "Mutual Initiation." 1 index "Japanese and U.S. lawmakers [*nichi-bei giin*] exchanged views on the SII" (*Nikkei* 3/22/90) is coded into "Mutual Initiation". The category "Mutual Initiation" may be less important than the other categories from the theoretical point of view, because it mostly codes "diplomatic formality expressions" cited above.

2. Indexes describing situations and simple facts without subjects (Japan or the United State) are coded into "Description" (D).

3. If the indexes have two sentences with different subjects and themes, they are coded into different categories. Because of this reason, 377 *Nikkei* indexes are coded into 400 entries; therefore about 5 percent of the total indexes are coded into two entries. Also 32 *Wall Street Journal* indexes are coded into 34 entries.

4. Once the coding was done, an inter-coder reliability check was conducted by two independent coders on random samples of 26.5 percent of the total *Nikkei* indexes, and 100 percent of the *WSJ* indexes. The obtained inter-coder reliability coefficients, Pi, between the two coders with higher matching in coding are .81 for *Nikkei* indexes, and .83 for *WSJ* indexes, which are quite robust. (On Pi, refer to William A. Scott, [1955] "Reliability of Content Analysis," pp. 323-324.)

Appendix B: The Coding Method of Key-Word Content-Analysis

1. I checked 153 out of the total 377 SII event-related indexes in the *Nikkei* index which include *the explicit key words*: (1) public works spending (*kōkyō tōshi*), (2) distribution (*ryūtsū*), (3) land use (*tochi riyō*), (4) exclusionary business practices (*haita-teki torihiki kankō*) and antimonopoly law (*dokkin-hō*), including bid-rigging (*dango*), (5) keiretsu (*keiretsu*), including cross-shareholding (*kabushiki mochiai*), or (6) price difference (*naigai kakaku-sa*). The indexes which do not have those explicit topic specifications are not coded, except a few indexes that imply one of six issue areas. For instance, saving (*chochiku*) is a saving-investment issue; "disclosure of the records of executive director meetings (*shachō-kai*)" is a keiretsu issue. Even though this index does not have the explicit key word "keiretsu," it is coded into the keiretsu category.

2. If indexes include two different categories, such as "review of antimonopoly law—dango, keiretsu practices (*Nikkei* 6/6/89), indexes are coded into "exclusionary business practices" and "keirestu." There are several of these types of indexes.

3. Subjects of the indexes were checked, whether they were (1) "the United States" and "U.S. officials," (2) "Japan" and "Japanese officials," or (3) simple descriptive expressions of topics, agendas or schedules that sometimes include the diplomatic prefix of "the U.S.-Japan" (*nichi-bei*). Thus, the index of "The high-ranking U.S. official expresses public investment be 9% of GNP within 5 years" (*Nikkei* 6/15/90) is coded into *U.S.* in *Public Works Spending*. "For the public works investment 10-year plan, the government is reviewing a possible $20-30 trillion addition" (*Nikkei* 6/15/90) is coded into *Japan* in *Public Works Spending*. Likewise, "The SII: GNP ratio will be up—the public investment 10-year plan" (*Nikkei* 5/9/90) is coded into *Misc.* in *Public Works Spending*.

4. Most indexes have a main index and a sub-index. If an index contains one topic and one subject, such index as "In the SII final report, GNP ratio in public works spending is a goal, the U.S. demands again" (*Nikkei* 5/22/90) is coded into *U.S.* in *Public Works Spending*. However, one topic with two subjects like "At the U.S.-Japan foreign minister meeting, harsh exchanges on the public works spending issue—the U.S. demands GNP ratio; Japan is unwilling to concede beyond the total amount" (*Nikkei* 6/16/90) is coded into two entries, *U.S.* and *Japan* in the *Public Works Spending* categories. There are several of this type.

5. This coding operation is to examine the "extent of U.S. concerns and pressure on the Japanese government" in six SII issue areas and the "extent of

Japanese-side concerns" in these six areas. Therefore, the indexes on Japanese demands or suggestions regarding American structural impediments to the U.S. government are not counted (although there are only few indexes of this type). For instance, indexes like "Economic Planning Agency is going to demand that the U.S. increase saving level" are not counted, although this index contains the explicitly mentioned topic, "increase saving level."

Appendix C: Tables

Table C.1
Seven-Category Coding Result of All *Nikkei* Indexes with the Subject the United States, Japan, the United States and Japan, or No Subject
(May 1989-June 1990)

U.S.			5	6	7	8	9	10	11	12	1	2	3	4	5	6	Total			%
1 Pressure	Demand	G	1	1	1	1		3			3	8		2	3	23	39		
		P			1	2	1	2	2		1		4	2		1	16			
	Criticism	G	1	1				3				1				6	10	103	26%
		P						2							2	4			
	Suggestion	G				4	1	4	1		1	2	1	1	5	20	54		
		P	4		3	2		1	1	1	3	10	1		8	34			
2 Reactive	Positive	G						1								1	1		
		P														0		3	1%
	Negative	G						1		1						2	2	P(0%)
		P														0			
3 Policy Making Activities		G	1							1		1	2			5		8	2%
		P		1							1		1			3			
4 Policy Initiation																0		0	0%
5 Cooperation		G						1				2				3		16	4%
		P	1		1	2	1			1		5		2		13			
	(Sub total)		2	7	3	7	10	4	18	2	4	9	26	14	3	21	(130)		(130)	(33%)

Japan			5	6	7	8	9	10	11	12	1	2	3	4	5	6	Total			%
1 Pressure	Demand	G			1		1		1						1	4	4		
		P														0			
	Criticism	G													1	1	2	25	6%
		P				1										1			
	Suggestion	G		1	1	1	1	1			1	3	1	1	11	19		
		P			1	1						3	1		2	8			
2 Reactive	Positive	G	1	2		1		1		2	1	3		6	17	24		
		P				1						4		2	7		33	8%
	Negative	G	1		3					1		1	1	7	9	P(6%)
		P			1	1								2			
3 Policy Making Activities		G	1	1	2	1	2				9	2	1	6	25		65	16%
		P		2		1	1		1	2	20	8	1	4	40			
4 Policy Initiation				1				1		4	4		3	13		13	3%
5 Cooperation		G										1	2	3		20	5%
		P		1		1	2			1	1	5	1	5	17			
	(Sub total)		2	6	6	4	14	3	3	2	1	6	43	28	4	34	(156)		(156)	(38%)
6 Mutual Initiation		G	2		1		3		1			1		4	12		22	6%
		P	1		2		1			1		3	1	1	10			
7 Description			2	6	1	4	8	1	7	1	2	10	13	15	2	20	92		92	23%
Total			8	20	11	17	35	9	29	5	8	25	86	58	9	80	400		400	100%

236

Table C.2
Seven-Category Coding Result of All *Wall Street Journal* Indexes with the Subject the United States, Japan, the United States and Japan, or No Subject (May 1989-June 1990)

Month columns: **'89** = 5 6 7 8 9 10 11 12 ; **'90** = 1 2 3 4 5 6

U.S.		G/P	5	6	7	8	9	10	11	12	1	2	3	4	5	6	Total			%
1 Pressure	Demand	G															0	0		
		P															0			
	Criticism	G					1										1	2	4	12%
		P	1														1			
	Suggestion	G															0	2		
		P											1			1	2			
2 Reactive	Positive	G															0	0		
		P															0		0	0%
	Negative	G															0	0		P(0%)
		P															0			
3 Policy Making Activities		G															0		0	0%
		P															0			
4 Policy Initiation																	0		0	0%
5 Cooperation		G															0		2	6%
		P	1													1	2			
	(Subtotal)		2	0	0	0	1	0	0	0	0	0	1	0	0	2	(6)		(6)	(18%)

Japan		G/P	5	6	7	8	9	10	11	12	1	2	3	4	5	6	Total			%
1 Pressure	Demand	G															0	0		
		P															0			
	Criticism	G					1										1	1	1	3%
		P															0			
	Suggestion	G															0	0		
		P															0			
2 Reactive	Positive	G		1									2	1		1	5	5		
	Negative	P															0		6	18%
		G											1				1	1		P(15%)
		P															0			
3 Policy Making Activities		G															0		1	3%
Activities		P											1				1			
4 Policy Initiation												1	1	1			3		3	9%
5 Cooperation		G															0		2	6%
		P					1						1				2			
	(Subtotal)		0	1	0	0	2	0	0	0	0	1	6	2	0	1	(13)		(13)	(39%)
6 Mutual Initiation		G							1					1		1	3		4	12%
		P														1	1			
7 Description							1	1	1			3	2	2		1	11		11	32%
Total			2	1	0	0	4	1	2	0	0	4	9	5	0	6	34		34	101%

Bibliography

U.S. GOVERNMENT DOCUMENTS

First Annual Report of the U.S.-Japan Working Group on the Structural Impediments Initiative. (May 22, 1991).

Interim Report and Assessment of the U.S.-Japan Working Group on the Structural Impediments Initiative. (April 5, 1990).

The Japanese Ministry of Finance-U.S. Department of the Treasury Working Group. (1984). *Report on Yen/Dollar Exchange Rate Issues*.

Joint Report of the U.S.-Japan Working Group on the Structural Impediments Initiative. (June 28, 1990).

National Trade Policy Agenda. Hearings before the Subcommittee on Trade of the House Committee on Ways and Means, February 28 and April 26, 1989.

The Office of the U.S. Trade Representative. (1989). *The 1989 National Trade Estimate Report*. Washington, D.C.

—————. (1990). *The 1990 National Trade Estimate Report*. Washington, D.C.

Reviewing Structural Impediments Initiative (SII). Hearing before the Subcommittee on International Trade of the Senate Committee on Finance, April 15, 1991.

Second Annual Report of the U.S.-Japan Working Group on the Structural Impediments Initiative. (June 30, 1992).

Structural Impediments Initiative (SII), Key Elements of SII Joint Report. (June 28, 1990). An informal summary in the State Department's file.

Structural Impediments Initiative (SII) Review. Hearing before the Subcommittee on International Trade of the Senate Committee on Finance, March 13, 1992.

"Transcript of Structural Impediments Initiative (SII) Press Conference held at U.S. Embassy Tokyo on June 28, 1990," A State Department file.

United States International Trade Commission. (1988). *Pros and Cons of Initiating Negotiations with Japan to Explore the Possibility of a U.S.-Japan Free Trade Area Agreement*.

United States-Japan Economic Relations: Structural Impediments Initiative. Hearings before the Subcommittees on Asian Pacific Affairs and on International Economic Policy and Trade of the House Committee on Foreign Affairs, February 20 and April 19, 1990.

United States-Japan Structural Impediments Initiative (SII). Hearing before the Subcommittee on International Trade of the Senate Committee on Finance, July 20, 1989, (Part 1 of 3).

United States-Japan Structural Impediments Initiative (SII). Hearings before the Subcommittee on International Trade of the Senate Committee on Finance, November 6 and 7, 1989, (Part 2 of 3).

United States-Japan Structural Impediments Initiative (SII). Hearing before the Subcommittee on International Trade of the Senate Committee on Finance, March 5, 1990, (Part 3 of 3).

The U.S. and Japan MOSS Negotiating Teams. (1986). *Report on Medical Equipment and Pharmaceuticals Market-Oriented, Sector-Selective (MOSS) Discussions*.

U.S. Department of Commerce. (1991). *Destination Japan: A Business Guide for the 90s*. Washington, D.C.

―――. (1993). *U.S. Foreign Trade Highlights, 1992*. Washington, D.C.

U.S. Department of State. (1988a). "U.S. Foreign Economic Policy, 1981-87." Washington, D.C.

―――. (1988b). "U.S. Trade Objectives in the Uruguay Round." Washington, D.C.

―――. (1989). "Foreign Direct Investment in a Global Economy." Washington, D.C.

―――. (1990). "Economic Summits, 1981-89." Washington, D.C.

The U.S. MOSS Negotiation Team. (1986). *Report on Telecommunications Market-Oriented, Sector-Selective (MOSS) Discussions*.

OTHER ENGLISH LANGUAGE SOURCES

Academy for Educational Development. (1971). "Observations on International Negotiations." (Transcript of an Informal Conference). Greenwich, Conn.

Adler, Emanuel and Peter M. Haas. (1992). "Conclusion: Epistemic Communities, World Order, and the Creation of a Reflective Research Program." *International Organization (IO)* 46 (1): 367-390.

Advisory Committee for Trade Policy and Negotiations. (1989). *Analysis of the U.S.-Japan Trade Problem*.

Ahearn, Raymond J. (1982). "Political Determinants of U.S. Trade Policy." *Orbis* 26 (2): 413-429.

Allison, Gary D. and Yasunori Sone, eds. (1993). *Political Dynamics in Contemporary Japan*. Ithaca, N.Y.: Cornell University Press.

Allison, Graham T. (1969). "Conceptual Models and the Cuban Missile Crisis." In G. John Ikenberry (ed.), *American Foreign Policy: Theoretical Essays*. Glenview, Ill: Scott, Foresman and Company: 332-378.

―――. (1971). *Essence of Decision: Explaining the Cuban Missile Crisis*. Glenview, Ill: Scott, Foresman and Company.

Allison, Graham T. and Morton H. Halperin. (1972). "Bureaucratic Politics: A Paradigm and Some Policy Implications." In G. John Ikenberry (ed.), *American Foreign Policy: Theoretical Essays*. Glenview: Scott, Foresman and Company: 378-409.

Altman, Roger C. (1994). "Why Pressure Tokyo?" *Foreign Affairs* 73 (3), pp. 2-6.

Anderson, Jim. (1989). "The President' Man in the State Department." *Foreign Service Journal* December :30-33.

Angel, Robert C. (1988/89). "Prime Ministerial Leadership in Japan: Recent Changes in Personal Style and Administrative Organization." *Pacific Affairs* 61: 583-602.

Armacost, Michael H. (1986). "U.S.-Japan Relations: A Global Partnership for the Future." U.S. Department of State, Current Policy No. 856. Washington, D.C.

——. (1989). "Residual Barriers to Trade Need Discussion," A Transcript: Foreign Press Center Briefing (5290) in the State Department file.

Baker, James A, III. (1991/92). "America in Asia: Emerging Architecture for a Pacific Community." *Foreign Affairs* 70 (5): 1-18.

Baldwin, Robert E. and David A. Kay. (1975). "International Trade and International Relations." *IO* 29 (1): 99-131.

Barnds, William J. (1979). *Japan and the United States: Challenges and Opportunities.* New York: New York University Press.

Bergsten, C. Fred and Marcus Noland. (1993). *Reconcilable Differences?: United States-Japan Economic Conflict.* Washington D.C.: Institute for International Economics.

Bergsten, C. Fred and William R. Cline. (1985). *The United States-Japan Economic Problem.* Washington, D.C.: Institute for International Economics.

Blinder, Alan. (1990). "There are Capitalists, then There are the Japanese." *Business Week* 10/8/90: 21.

Brown, Winthrop G. (1968). "The Art of Negotiation." *Foreign Service Journal* 45 (7): 14-17.

Bull, Hedley. (1977). *The Anarchical Society: A Study of Order in World Politics.* New York, Columbia University Press.

Calder, Kent E. (1988). "Japanese Foreign Economic Policy Formation: Explaining the Reactive State." *World Politics* 40 (4): 516-542.

Cambell, John Creighton. (1977). *Contemporary Japanese Budget Politics.* Berkeley: University of California Press.

Carr, Edward Hallett. (1939). *The Twenty Years' Crisis, 1919-1939.* New York: Harper & Row, Publishers.

Clark, William. (1988). "Trends in U.S.-Japan Economic Cooperation." U.S. Department of State, Current Policy No. 1124. Washington, D.C.

Cohen, Benjamin J. (1990). "The Political Economy of International Trade." *IO* 44 (2): 261-281.

Cohen, Raymond. (1987). "International Communication: An Intercultural Approach." *Cooperation and Conflict* 22 (2): 63-80.

Cohen, Stephen D. (1985). *Uneasy Partnership: Competition and Conflict in U.S.-Japanese Trade Relations.* Cambridge: Ballinger Publishing Company.

——. (1991). "United States-Japanese Trade Relations." *Current History* 90: 152-155, 184-187.

——. (1994). *The Making of United States International Economic Policy.* Westport, Conn.: Praeger.

Conteh-Morgan, Earl. (1992). *Japan and the United States: Global Dimensions of Economic Power.* New York: Peter Lang.

Cooper, Richard. (1972/73). "Trade Policy is Foreign Policy." *Foreign Policy* 9: 18-36.

Cox, Robert W. (1980). "The Crisis of World Order and the Problem of International Organization in the 1980s." *International Journal* 35 (2): 370-395.

Craib, B. Anne. (1994). "The Making of Japan Trade Policy in the Clinton Administration: Institutions and Individuals." *JEI Report* 39A: 1-12.

Cross, John G. (1977). "Negotiation as a Learning Process." *Journal of Conflict Resolution* 21 (4): 581-606.

Curtis, Gerald L., ed. (1993). *Japan's Foreign Policy: After the Cold War, Coping with Change.* Armonk, N.Y.: An East Gate Book, M.E. Sharpe.

Dertouzos, Michael L., Richard K. Lester, Robert M. Solow, and the MIT Commission on Industrial Productivity. (1989). *Made in America: Regaining the Productive Edge.* Cambridge: The MIT Press.

Destler, I. M. (1992). *American Trade Politics*, 3rd ed. Washington, D.C.: Institute for International Economics.

Destler, I.M., Haruhiro Fukui, and Hideo Sato. (1979). *The Textile Wrangle: Conflict in Japanese-American Relations, 1969-1971.* Ithaca, N.Y.: Cornell University Press.

Destler, I. M. and Hideo Sato. (1982). *Coping with U.S. Japanese Economic Conflict.* Lexington: Lexington Books.

Destler, I.M., Hideo Sato, Priscilla Clapp, and Haruhiro Fukui. (1976). *Managing an Alliance: The Politics of U.S.-Japan Relations.* Washington, D.C.: The Brookings Institution.

Deyo, Frederic, ed. (1987). *The Political Economy of the New Asian Industrialism.* Ithaca, N.Y.: Cornell University Press.

Dickerman, C. Robert. (1976). "Transgovernmental Challenge and Response in Scandinavia and North America." *IO* 30 (2): 213-240.

Dore, Ronald. (1986). *Flexible Rigidities: Industrial Policy and Structural Adjustment in the Japanese Economy, 1970-80.* Stanford: Stanford University Press.

Dougherty, James E. and Robert L. Pfaltzgraff, Jr. (1981). *Contending Theories of International Relations.* New York: Harper & Row, Publishers.

Drucker, Peter F. (1986). "Japan and Adversarial Trade." *Wall Street Journal* 4/1/86.

———. (1987). "Japan's Choices." *Foreign Affairs* 65 (5): 923-941.

Druckman, Daniel and Richard Harris. (1990). "Alternative Models of Responsiveness in International Negotiation." *Journal of Conflict Resolution* 34 (2): 234-251.

Dudly, William, ed. (1989). *Japan: Opposing Viewpoints.* San Diego: Greenhaven Press.

Eckstein, Harry. (1975). "Case Study and Theory in Political Science." In Fred I. Greenstein and Nelson W. Polsby (eds.) *Handbook of Political Science Vol. 7: Strategies of Inquiry.* Reading, Mass.: Addison-Wesley Publishing Company: 79-138.

Emmott, Bill. (1989). *The Sun Also Sets: The Limits to Japan's Economic Power.* New York: Times Books, Random House Inc.

Encarnation, Dennis J. and Mark Mason. (1990). "Neither MITI nor America: the Political Economy of Capital Liberalization in Japan." *IO* 44 (1): 25-54.

Endiot, John. (1987). "United State-Japanese Relations: Toward a Security Community." *The Atlantic Community Quarterly* 25 (3): 367-376.

Fallows, James. (1989). "Containing Japan." *The Atlantic Monthly* 263 (5): 40-54.

Fallows, James, Chalmers Johnson, Clyde Prestowitz and Karel van Wolferen. (1990). "Beyond Japan-bashing." *U.S. News & World Report* 5/7/90: 54-55.

Feld, Werner J., Robert S. Jordan and Leon Hurwitz. (1983). *International Organizations: A Comparative Approach.* New York: Praeger Publishers.

Frankel, Jeffrey A. (1984). *The Yen/Dollar Agreement: Liberalizing Japanese Capital Markets*. Cambridge: The MIT Press.

Frieden, Jeffry A. and David A. Lake, eds. (1991). *International Political Economy: Perspectives on Global Power and Wealth*, 2nd ed. New York: St. Martin's Press.

Fukai, Shigeko N. (1992). "The Role of 'Gaiatsu' in Japan's Land Policymaking" (A Paper presented in the 1992 Annual Meeting of APSA in Chicago).

Fukui, Haruhiro. (1970). *Party in Power: The Japanese Liberal-Democrats and Policymaking*. Berkeley: University of California Press.

————. (1978). "The GATT Tokyo Round: The Bureaucratic Politics of Multilateral Diplomacy." In Michael Blaker (ed.), *The Politics of Trade: US and Japanese Policymaking for the GATT Negotiations*. New York: Columbia University :75-170.

Funabashi, Yoichi. (1991/92). "Japan and the New World Order." *Foreign Affairs* 70 (5): 58-74.

Garthhoff, Raymond L. (1977). "Negotiating with the Russians: Some Lessons from SALT." *International Security* 1 (4): 3-24.

George, Aurelia. (1991). "Japan's America Problem: The Japanese Response to U.S Pressure." *The Washington Quarterly* 14 (3): 5-19.

Gilpin, Robert. (1987). *The Political Economy of International Relations*. Princeton: Princeton University Press.

Goodrich, Leland M. and David A. Kay, eds. (1973). *International Organization: Politics and Process*. Madison: The University of Wisconsin Press.

Gourevitch, Peter. (1978). "The Second Image Reversed: The International Sources of Domestic Politics." *IO* 32 (4): 881-911.

Grant, Richard L., ed. *Strengthening the U.S.-Japan Partnership in the 1990s*. Washington, D.C.: The Center for Strategic and International Studies.

Green, Gretchen. (1989). "SII Hearings Run Parallel to Talks." *JEI Report* 438: 7-8.

Haas, Peter M. (1992). "Introduction: Epistemic Communities and International Policy Coordination." *IO* 46 (1): 1-35.

Hart, Jeffrey A. (1992). *Rival Capitalists: International Competitiveness in the United States, Japan, and Western Europe*. Ithaca, N.Y.: Cornell University Press.

Hayashi, Kichiro, ed. (1989). *The U.S.-Japanese Economic Relationship: Can It be Improved?* New York: New York University Press.

Higashi, Chikara and G. Peter Lauter. (1990). *The Internationalization of the Japanese Economy*, 2nd. ed. Boston: Kluwer Academic Publishers.

Hirshman, Albert O. (1970). *Exit, Voice and Loyalty*. Cambridge: Harvard University Press.

Hocking, Brian. (1991). "Japanese Lobbying in the United States: Foreign Threat or Domestic Politics?" *The World Today* April: 64-66.

Holleman, Leon. (1988). *Japan, Disincorporated: The Economic Liberalization Process*. Stanford: Hoover Institution Press.

Hollerman, Leon, ed. (1980). *Japan and the United States: Economic and Political Adversaries*. Boulder: Westview Press.

Holstein, William J. (1990). *The Japanese Power Game: What It Means for America*. New York: Charles Scribner's Sons.

Holsti, K. J. (1980). "Interdependence, Integration, or Fragmentation: Scenarios for the Future." In Charles W. Kegley, Jr. and Eugene R. Wittkopf (eds.), *The Global*

Agenda: Issue and Perspectives. New York: McGraw-Hill Publishing Company: 216-230.

Holsti, Ole R. (1969). *Content Analysis for the Social Sciences and Humanities*. Reading, Mass.: Addison-Wesley Publishing Company.

Hook, Glenn D. and Michael A. Weiner, eds. (1992). *The Internationalization of Japan*. London: Routledge.

Hopkins, Raymond F. (1976). "The International Role of 'Domestic' Bureaucracy." *IO* 30 (3): 405-432.

Hosoya, Chihiro. (1974). "Characteristics of the Foreign Policy Decision-Making System in Japan." *World Politics* 26 (3): 353-369.

Ikenberry, G. John, ed. (1989). *American Foreign Policy: Theoretical Essays*. Glenview, Ill: Scott, Foresman and Company.

Ikenberry, G. John, David A. Lake, and Michael Mastanduno. (1988). *The State and American Foreign Economic Policy*. Ithaca, N.Y.: Cornell University Press.

Inkeles, Alex. (1966). "Models and Issues in the Analysis of Soviet Society." *Survey* (60): 3-17.

Inoguchi, Takashi. (1988/89). "Four Japanese Scenarios for the Future." *International Affairs* 65 (1): 15-28.

———. (1990). "Japan's Politics of Interdependence." *Government and Opposition* 25 (4): 419-437.

———. (1993). *Japan's Foreign Policy in an Era of Global Change*. New York: St. Martin's Press.

Inoguchi, Takashi and Daniel I. Okimoto, ed. (1988). *The Political Economy of Japan Volume 2: The Changing International Context*. Stanford: Stanford University Press.

Iriye, Akira and Warren I. Cohen. (1987). *The United States and Japan in the Postwar World*. Lexington: The University Press of Kentucky.

Islam, Shafiqul. (1990). "Capitalism in Conflict." *Foreign Affairs* 69 (1): 172-182.

Ito, Kan. (1990). "Trans-Pacific Anger." *Foreign Policy* 78: 131-152.

Itoh, Makoto. (1990). *The World Economic Crisis and Japanese Capitalism*. New York: St. Martin's Press.

Janis, Irving L. (1982). *Groupthink*, 2nd. ed. Boston: Houghton Mifflin Company.

Japan Economic Institute. (1986). *U.S.-Japan Economic Relations Yearbook 1984-1985*. Washington, D.C.

Japan External Trade Organization (JETRO). (1990). *White Paper on International Trade, Japan 1990*.

The Japan Foundation. (1988). *An Introductory Bibliography for Japanese Studies, Vol. VI, Part 1, Social Sciences, 1981-85*. Tokyo: Bonjin Co., Ltd.

Johnson, Chalmers. (1982). *MITI and the Japanese Miracle: The Growth of Industrial Policy, 1925-1975*. Stanford: Stanford University Press.

———. (1991). "History Restarted: Japanese American Relations at the End of the Century." A paper for the Fulbright Symposium on December 16-17, 1991 at Australian National University.

Kaifu, Toshiki. (1990). "Japan's Vision." *Foreign Policy* (80): 28-39.

Kaiser, Karl. (1971). "Transnational Politics: Toward a Theory of Multinational Politics." *IO* 25: 790-817.

Keohane, Robert O. (1975). International Organization and the Crisis of Interdependence." *IO* 29 (2): 357-365.

———. (1982). "The Demand for International Regimes." *IO* 36 (2): 325-355.

———. (1984). *After Hegemony: Cooperation and Discord in the World Political Economy*. Princeton: Princeton University Press.

Keohen, Robert O. and Joseph S. Nye. (1974). "Transgovernmental Relations and International Organizations." *World Politics* 27 (1): 39-62.

———. (1977). *Power and Interdependence: World Politics in Transition*. Boston: Little, Brown and Company.

Keohen, Robert and Joseph S. Nye, eds. (1972). *Transgovernmental Relations and World Politics*. Cambridge: Harvard University Press.

Kernell, Samuel, ed. (1991). *Parallel Politics: Economic Policymaking in the United States and Japan*. Washington, D.C.: The Brookings Institution.

Kimmitt, Robert M. (1989). "The U.S. and Japan: Defining Our Global Partnership." U.S. Department of State, Current Policy No. 1221. Washington, D.C.

Kindleberger, Charles P. (1973). *The World in Depression, 1929-1939*. Berkeley: University of California Press.

Kingdon, John W. (1984). *Agendas, Alternatives, and Public Policies*. New York: HarperCollins Publishers.

Kissinger, Henry A. (1969). *American Foreign Policy: Three Essays*. New York: W. W. Norton and Company.

Koh, B. C. (1989). *Japan's Administrative Elite*. Berkeley: University of California Press.

Komiya, Ryutaro. (1990). *The Japanese Economy: Trade, Industry, and Government*. Tokyo: University of Tokyo Press.

Krasner, Stephen D. (1982). "Structural Cause and Regime Consequences: Regimes as Intervening Variables." *IO* 36 (2): 185-205.

Krauss, Ellis S. and Michio Muramatsu. (1988). "Japanese Political Economy Today: The Patterned Pluralist Model." In Daniel I. Okimoto and Thomas P. Rohlen, (eds.), *Inside the Japanese System: Readings on Contemporary Society and Political Economy*. Stanford: Stanford University Press: 208-210.

Krugman, Paul R., ed. (1986). *Strategic Trade Policy and the New International Economics*. Cambridge: The MIT Press.

Kurth, James R. (1979). "The Political Consequences of the Product Cycle: Industrial History and Political Outcomes." *IO* 33 (1): 1-34.

Lanciaux, Bernadette. (1991). "Ethnocentrism in U.S./Japanese Trade Policy Negotiations." *Journal of Economic Issues* 25 (2): 569-580.

Lenart, Silvo and Harry R. Targ. (1992). "Framing the Enemy: New York Times Coverage of Cuba in the 1980s." *Peace & Change* 17 (3): 341-362.

Lincoln, Edward J. (1990). *Japan's Unequal Trade*. Washington, D.C.: The Brookings Institution.

Lipson, Charles. (1971). "Why are Some International Agreements Informal?" *IO* 45 (4): 495-538.

MacKnight, Susan. (1989). "Japan Cited As Super 301 Priority Country." *JEI Report* 22B: 9-12.

———. (1990a). "Interim SII Report Released." *JEI Report* 15B:6-7.

———. (1990b). "Final SII Report: Race Against Time." *JEI Report* 24B:10-12.

———. (1990c). "Tokyo, Washington Hammer Out Final SII Report." *JEI Report* 26B:11-13.

————. (1991a). "U.S.-Japan Economic Relation In 1990: A Look Back." *JEI Report* 8A: 1-14.

————. (1991b). "Mixed Grades on Structural Reforms." *JEI Report* 22B:10-11.

————. (1992). "Washington, Tokyo Examine Ways to Revive SII Process." *JEI Report* 9B:7-8.

Maghroori, Ray and Bennett Ramberg. (1982). *Globalism versus Realism: International Relations' Third Debate*. Boulder: Westview Press.

Manning, Bayless. (1977). "The Congress, the Executive and Intermestic Affairs: Three Proposals." *Foreign Affairs* 55 (2): 306-324.

Mastanduno, Michael. (1992). "Framing the Japan Problem: the Bush Administration and the Structural Impediments Initiative." *International Journal* 47: 235-264.

Maynes, Charles William. (1990). "America without the Cold War." *Foreign Policy* 78: 3-25.

McClelland, Charles A. and Gary D. Hoggard. (1969). "Conflict Patterns in the Interactions among Nations." In James N. Rosenau (ed.), *International Politics and Foreign Policy*. New York: The Free Press: 711-724.

McCormack, Richard T. (1989). "Challenge to the International Economy In the 1990s." U.S. Department of State, Current Policy No. 1223. Washington, D.C.

————. (1990). "Economic Challenge in the U.S.-Japan Relationship." U.S. Department of State, *Dispatch* 1 (11): 255-257. Washington, D.C.

————. (1991). "Japanese Politics and the American Economy." A paper, November 1, 1991.

————. (1992). "The Possible After Shocks of the Multi Trillion Dollar Asset Deflation in Japan's Bubble Economy." A paper, September 14, 1992.

Mulford, David C. (1990). "Statement of the Honorable David C. Mulford, Under Secretary of the Treasury for International Affairs before the Subcommittee on Foreign Operations, Export Financing, and Related Programs of the Committee on Appropriations, U.S. House of Representatives." *Treasury News* NB-714.

————. (1990). "U.S. and Japan: Cooperation in World Economic Leadership." *Treasury News* NB-680.

Murakami, Hyoe and Johannes Hirschmeier. (1979). *Politics and Economics in Contemporary Japan*. Tokyo: Japan Culture Institute.

Nagatani, Iwao. (1992). "Reforming Japanese Capitalism." *Journal of Japanese Trade and Industry* 11 (4): 15-17.

Neff, Robert. (1989). "Rethinking Japan." *Business Week* 8/7/89: 44-52.

Nester, William R. (1991). *Japanese Industrial Targeting: The Neomercantilist Path to Economic Superpower*. New York: St. Martin's Press.

————. (1993). *American Power, the New World Order and the Japanese Challenge*. New York: St. Martin's Press.

Neustadt, Richard E. (1980). *Presidential Power: The Politics of Leadership from FDR to Carter*. New York: John Wiley & Sons, Inc.

Niskanen, William A. (1989). "The Bully of World Tarde." *Orbis* 33 (4): 531-538.

Noguchi, Yukio. (1991). "Budget Policymaking in Japan." In Kernell, Samuel (ed.), *Parallel Politics: Economic Policymaking in the United States and Japan*. Washington, D.C.: The Brookings Institution: 119-141.

Nye, Joseph S. (1990). *Bound to Lead: The Changing Nature of American Power*. New York: Basic Books.

Odawara, Atsushi. (1989). "Kaifu Toshiki: Prime Minister Betwixt and Between." *Japan Quarterly* 36(4): 368-374.

Okimoto, Daniel I., ed. (1982). *Japan's Economy: Coping with Change in the International Environment*. Boulder: Westview Press.

———. (1988). "Political Inclusivity: The Domestic Structure of Trade." In Takashi Inoguchi and Daniel I. Okimoto (ed.), *The Political Economy of Japan Volume 2: The Changing International Context*. Stanford: Stanford University Press: 303-344.

———. (1989). *Between MITI and the Market: Japanese Industrial Policy for High Technology*. Stanford: Stanford University Press.

Okimoto, Daniel I. and Thomas P. Rohlen, eds. (1988). *Inside the Japanese System: Readings on Contemporary Society and Political Economy*. Stanford: Stanford University Press.

Okita, Saburo. (1989). *Japan in the World Economy of the 1980s*. Tokyo: University of Tokyo.

Organization for Economic Cooperation and Development (OECD). (1988). *OECD Economic Surveys, Japan (1987/1988)*. Paris.

———. (1989). *OECD Economic Surveys, Japan (1988/1989)*. Paris.

———. (1990). *OECD Economic Surveys, Japan (1989/1990)*. Paris.

———. (1991). *OECD Economic Surveys, Japan (1991-1992)*. Paris.

Ostrom, Douglas. (1990)."Keiretsu Questions Surface in Merger Announcement, SII Report." *JEI Report* 16B: 1-3.

———. (1991). "SII Followup Talks Focus on Antimonopoly action." *JEI Report* 4B: 5-7.

Pastor, Robert A. (1980). *Congress and the Politics of U.S. Foreign Economic Policy 1929-1976*. Berkeley: University of California Press.

Pempel, T. J., ed. (1977). *Policymaking in Contemporary Japan*. Ithaca, N.Y.: Cornell University Press.

———. (1982). *Policy and Politics in Japan: Creative Conservatism*. Philadelphia: Temple University Press.

———. (1987). "The Unbundling of 'Japan, Inc.': The Changing Dynamics of Japanese Policy Formation." In Kenneth B. Pyle (ed.), *The Trade Crisis: How will Japan Respond?* Seattle: The Society for Japanese Studies: 117-152.

Petri, Peter A. (1984). *Modeling Japanese-American Trade: A Study of Asymmetric Interdependence*. Cambridge: Harvard University Press.

Polachek, Solomon William. (1980). "Conflict and Trade." *Journal of Conflict Resolution* 24 (1): 55-78.

Prestowitz, Clyde V. (1988). *Trading Places: How We Allowed Japan to Take the Lead*. New York: Basic Books, Inc.

Putnam, Robert D. (1988). "Diplomacy and Domestic Politics: The Logic of Two-Level Games." *IO* 42 (3): 427-460.

Putnam, Robert D. and Nicholas Bayne. (1987). *Hanging Together: Cooperation and Conflict in the Seven-Power Summits*. Cambridge: Harvard University Press.

Pyle, Kenneth B., ed. (1987). *The Trade Crisis: How Will Japan Respond?* Seattle: The Society for Japanese Studies.

Ramseyer, J. Mark and Frances McCall Rosenbluth. (1993). *Japan's Political Marketplace*. Cambridge: Harvard University Press.

Rhodes, Carolyn. (1989). "Reciprocity in Trade: The Utility of a Bargaining Strategy."
    IO 43 (2): 273-299.
Richardson, Bradley M. (1974). *The Political Culture of Japan.* Berkeley: University of
    California Press.
Richardson, Bradley M. and Scott C. Flanagan. (1984). *Politics in Japan.* Boston: Little,
    Brown and Company.
Richardson, J. David. (1990). "The Political Economy of Strategic Trade Policy." *IO* 44
    (1): 107-135.
Rix, Alan. (1980). *Japan's Economic Aid: Policy-Making and Politics.* London: Croom
    Helem.
Rosecrance, Richard. (1986). *The Rise of the Trading State: Commerce and Conquest in
    the Modern World.* New York: Basic Books.
Rosecrance, Richard and Jennifer Taw. (1990). "Japan and the Theory of International
    Leadership." *World Politics* 42 (2): 184-209.
Ruggie, John Gerard. (1975). "International Responses to Technology: Concepts and
    Trends." *IO* 29 (3): 557-583.
————. (1982). "International Regimes, Transactions, and Change: Embedded
    Liberalism in the Postwar Economic Order." *IO* 36 (2): 379-415.
Russell, Robert W. (1973). "Transgovernmental Interaction in the International Monetary
    System, 1960-1972." *IO* 27 (4): 431-464.
Sakurai, Masao. (1989). "Formulators and Legislators of International Trade and
    Industrial Policy in Japan and the United States." In Kichiro Hayashi (ed.), *The
    U.S.-Japanese Economic Relationship: Can It be Improved?* New York: New
    York University Press: 160-193.
Samuels, Richard. (1987). *The Business of the Japanese State.* Ithaca: Cornell University
    Press.
Sasaki, Takeshi. (1990). "SII and the Ticking Legacy." *Journal of Japanese Trade and
    Industry* (4): 35-36.
Sato, Ryuzo and Paul Wachtel, eds. (1987). *Trade Friction and Economic Policy.*
    Cambridge University Press.
Scalapino, Robert A., ed. (1977). *The Foreign Policy of Modern Japan.* Berkeley:
    University of California Press.
Scalapino, Robert A. and Junnosuke Masumi. (1964). *Parties and Politics in
    Contemporary Japan.* Berkeley: University of California Press.
Schmiegelow, Henrik and Michele Schmiegelow. (1990). "How Japan Affects the
    International System." *IO* 44 (4): 553-588.
Schmiegelow, Michele. (1985). "Cutting Across Doctrines: Positive Adjustment in
    Japan." *IO* 39(2): 261-296.
Schoppa, Leonard J. (1992). "Gaiatsu and the Japanese Policy Process: The Role of U.S.
    Pressure in Shaping Policy Decisions Related to the Structural Impediments
    Initiative." A paper prepared for the 1992 Annual Meeting of the American
    Political Science Association, Chicago.
————. (1993). "Two-level Games and Bargaining Outcomes: Why Gaiatsu Succeeds
    in Japan in Some Cases but not Others." *IO* 47 (3): 353-386.
Scott, William A. (1955). "Reliability of Content Analysis: The Case of Nominal Scale
    Coding." *Public Opinion Quarterly* 19 (3): 321-325.
Shafigul, Islam. (1990). "Capitalism in Conflict." *Foreign Affairs* 69 (1): 172-182.
Simon, Herbert A. (1976). *Administrative Behavior,* 3rd ed. New York: The Free Press.

Singer, J. David. (1961). "The Level-of Analysis Problem in International Relations." In James N. Rosenau (ed.), *International Politics and Foreign Policy*. New York: The Free Press: 20-29.

Solomon, Richard. (1990). "U.S. and Japan: An Evolving Partnership." U.S. Department of State, Current Policy No. 1268. Washington, D.C.

Sorensen, Theodore C. (1967). "But You Get to Walk to Work." *New York Times Magazine*, 3/19/67: 25, 165-171.

Spector, Bertram I. (1977). "Negotiation as a Psychological Process." *Journal of Conflict Resolution* 21 (4): 607-618.

Spencer, Edson W. (1990). "Japan as Competitor." *Foreign Policy* (78): 153-171.

Spero, Joan Edelman. (1985). *The Politics of International Economic Relations*, 3rd ed. New York: St. Martin's Press.

Stern Robert M., ed. (1989). *Trade and Investment Relations among the United States, Canada, and Japan*. Chicago: The University of Chicago.

Stiles, Kendall W. and Tsuneo Akaha. (1991). *International Political Economy: A Reader*. New York: HarperCollins Publishers.

Stockwin, J. A. A. et al. (1988). *Dynamic and Immobilist Politics in Japan*. Honolulu: University of Hawaii Press.

Strange, Susan. (1975). "What is Economic Power and Who has it?" *International Journal* 30 (2): 207-224.

———. (1982). "Cave! hic dragones: A Critique of Regime Analysis." *IO* 36 (2): 479-496.

———. (1985). "Protectionism and World Politics." *IO* 39 (2): 233-259.

Swanson, Roger F. (1972). "The United State Canadiana Constellation, I: Washington D.C." *International Journal* 27 (2): 185-218.

Taira, Kozi. (1990). "From Americanization of Japan to Japanization of America in HRM/IR." A reprinted paper from *Proceedings of the Forty-Third Annual Meeting*, December 28-30, 1990, Industrial Relations Research Association.

———. (1991). "Japan, an Imminent Hegemon?" *The Annals of the American Academy of Political and Social Science* 513: 151-163.

Takehashi, Hideo. (1990). "Tokyo Promises Changes in Land Policy in SII Report." *JEI Report* 16B: 3-5.

Tasca, Diane, ed. (1980). *U.S.-Japanese Economic Relations: Cooperation, Competition, and Confrontation*. New York: Pergamon Press.

Tetsuya, Kataoka. (1992). *Creating Single-Party Democracy: Japan's Postwar Political System*. Stanford: Hoover Institution Press.

Tsuneishi, Warren M. (1966). *Japanese Political Style: An Introduction to the Government and Politics of Modern Japan*. New York: Harper & Row Publishers.

Tsurutani, Taketsugu. (1977). *Political Change in Japan: Response to Postindustrial Challenge*. New York: David McKay Company, Inc.

Valeo, Francis R. and Charles E. Morrison, eds. (1983). *The Japanese Diet and the U.S. Congress*. Boulder: Westview Press.

Wallace, Michael and J. David Singer. (1970). "Intergovernmental Organization in the Global System, 1815-1964" *IO* 24 (2): 239-287.

Wallis, Allen. (1987a). "Structural Adjustment, Dialogue, and U.S.-Japan Economic Relations." U.S. Department of State, Current Policy No. 924. Washington, D.C.

————. (1987b). "U.S.-Japan Trade Relation." U.S. Department of State, Current Policy No. 942. Washington, D.C.

————. (1988). "American Leadership in International Trade." U.S. Department of State, Current Policy No. 1133. Washington, D.C.

Waltz, Kenneth N. (1954). *Man, the State and War: A Theoretical Analysis.* New York: Columbia University Press.

Weber, Robert Philip. (1990). *Basic Content Analysis*, 2nd. ed. Newbury Park, Calif.: Sage Publications.

Willetts, Peter. (1990). "Transactions, Networks and Systems." In A. J. R. Groom and Paul Taylor (eds.), *Frameworks for International Cooperation.* New York: St. Martin's Press: 255-284.

Williams, David. (1994). *Japan: Beyond the End of History.* London: Routledge.

Williams, Sydney Linn. (1991). "The Outlook for U.S.-Japan Trade Relations: An Interview with S. Linn Williams of USTR." *JET Report* 1A: 1-8.

Winham, Gilbert R. (1979). "Practitioner's Views of International Negotiation." *World Politics* 32 (1): 111-135.

————. (1979/80). "International Negotiation in an Age of Transition." *International Journal* 35 (1): 1-20.

Wolferen, Karel van. (1986/87). "The Japan Problem." *Foreign Affairs.* 65 (2): 288-303.

————. (1989). *The Enigma of Japanese Power: People and Politics in a Stateless Nation.* New York: Alfred A. Knopf.

————. (1990). "The Japan Problem Revisited." *Foreign Affairs* 69 (4): 42-55.

Woodall, Brian. (1993). "The Logic of Collusive Action: The Political Roots of Japan's Dango System." *Comparative Politics* 25 (3): 297-312.

Woronoff, Jon. (1986). *Politics the Japanese Way.* London: Macmillan Press.

Yamamura, Kozo, ed. (1982). *Policy and Trade Issues of the Japanese Economy: American and Japanese Perspectives.* Seattle: University of Washington Press.

————. (1990). *Japan's Economic Structure: Should it Change?* Seattle: Society for Japanese Studies.

Zartman, William I. (1977). "Negotiation as a Joint Decision-Making Process." *Journal of Conflict Resolution* 21 (4): 619-638.

Zhao, Quansheng. (1993). *Japanese Policymaking: The Politics Behind Politics.* Westport, Conn.: Praeger.

JAPANESE GOVERNMENT DOCUMENTS

Keizai Kikaku Chō. (1991). *Keizai Hakusho* (Heisei 3 nen ban). Tokyo.

Kensetsu Daijin Kanbō Seisaku-ka, ed. (1990). *Nichi-bei Kōzō Mondai Kyōgi to Kensetsu Gyōsei.* Tokyo.

Kokusai Kyōchō no tameno Keizai Kōzō Chōsei Kenkyūkai. (1986). "Maekawa Repōto." In Tsūshō Sangyō Shō Seisaku Kyoku, (ed.), *Kōzō Tenkan Enkatsuka-hō no Kaisetsu.* Tokyo: 131-138.

Kōsei Torihiki Iinkai. (1990). *Kōsei Torihiki Iinkai Nenji Hōkoku* (Heisei 2 nen). Tokyo.

Ministry of Foreign Affairs. (1990). *Diplomatic Bluebook 1990: Japan's Diplomatic Activities.* Tokyo.

————. (1991). *Diplomatic Bluebook 1991: Japan's Diplomatic Activities.* Tokyo.

Naikaku Sōri Daijin Kanbō Kōhō Shitsu, ed. (1989). *Seron Chōsa Nenkan* (Heisei Gannen ban). Tokyo.

————. (1990). *Seron Chōsa Nenkan* (Heisei 2 nendo ban). Tokyo.

Nichibei Kōzō Mondai Kenkyūkai, ed. (1990). *Nichibei Kōzō Mondai Kyōgi Saishū Hōkoku*. Tokyo: Zaikai Shōhō-sha.

Nichibei Kōzō Mondai Kyōgi Farōappu, Dai Ikkai Nenji Hōkoku. (1991).

Nichibei Kōzō Mondai Kyōgi Farōappu, Dai Nikai Nenji Hōkoku. (1992).

Sōmu Chō Tōkei Kyoku. (1991). *Nihon Tōkei Nenkan* (Heisei 3 nen). (Japan Statistical Yearbook). Tokyo.

Tsūshō Sangyō Chōsa Kai, ed. (1990). *Nichi-bei Kōzō Mondai Kyōgi Saishū Hōkoku*. Tokyo.

Tsūshō Sangyō Shō. (1988). *Tsūshō Hakusho* (Shōwa 63 nendo ban). Tokyo.

————. (1990). *Tsūshō Hakusho* (Heisei 2 nendo ban). Tokyo.

Tsūshō Sangyō Shō, Sangyō Seisaku Kyoku, ed. (1989). *Nichi-bei no Kigyō Kōdō Hikaku*. Tokyo.

Tsūshō Sangyō Shō, Shōsei-ka, ed. (1989). *90 Nendai no Ryūtsū Bijon*. Tokyo.

OTHER JAPANESE LANGUAGE SOURCES

Akiyama, Kenji. (1990). *Amerika Tsūshō Seisaku to Bōeki Masatsu*. Tokyo: Dōmonkan Shuppan.

Asahi Shinbun Keizai-bu. (1974). *Keizai Seisaku no Butaiura*. Tokyo: Asahi Shinbun-sha.

Awaji, Takehisa. (1990). "Dokkin-hō no unyō kyōka to songai baishō seido." *Jurisuto* 965: 35-40.

Bhagwati, Jagdish and Hugh T. Patrick, eds. (1991). *Sūpaa 301-jō: Tsuyomaru 'Ippō-shugi' no Kenshō*. Tokyo: Saimaru Shuppankai.

Destler, I. M., Haruhiro Fukui, and Sato Hideo. (1980). *Nichi-bei Seni Funsō*. Tokyo: Nihon Keizai Shinbun-sha.

Edo, Yusuke. (1990). *Nichi-bei Kōzō Kyōgi no Yomikata*. Tokyo: Nihon Jitsugyō Shuppan-sha.

Eguchi, Takashi and Manabu Matsuda. (1987). *Bōeki Masatsu, Mienai Sensō*. Tokyo: TBS Buritanika.

Eto, Shinkichi. (1974). "Nihon ni okeru taigai seisaku kettei katei." *Kokusaihō Gaikō Zasshi* March: 30-43.

Ezaki, Masumi. (1983). *Keizai Masatsu Kaishō no Taisaku—Dai-ni no Kaikoku o Mukaeta Nihon*. Tokyo: Sekai Seikei Bunka Kenkyū-kai.

Fukushima, Glen S. (1992). *Nichi-bei Keizai Masatsu no Seijigaku*. Tokyo: Asahi Shinbun-sha.

Funabashi, Yoichi. (1987). *Nichi-bei Keizai Masatsu: Sono Butai Ura*. Tokyo: Iwanami Shoten.

Funada, Masayuki. (1990). "Kakaku mekanizumu to torihiki kankō." *Jurisuto* 965: 41-45.

Furukawa, Eiichi. (1991). *Bei-Nichi Bōeki Hakusho*. Tokyo: Nikkan Kōgyō Shinbun-sha.

Futatsugi, Yusaku. (1989). "Beikoku wa 'mochiai' keitai o tsuki kuzuse nai." *Ekonomisuto* 12/12/89: 10-16.

Fuyushiba, Tetsuzo. (1990). "Nichi-bei giin kōryū ni sankashite." *Kōmei* 341 (6): 84-89.

Hamada, Koichi. (1990). "Nichi-bei masatsu iradachi no kōzu o miru." *Ekonomisuto* 5/8/90: 88-94.

Hanai, Hitoshi. (1982). *Nichi-bei Masatsu no Kenkyū: Kikiteki Kōzō o Saguru*. Tokyo: Gakuyō Shobō.

————. (1990). "Amerika de 'haisha-hō' ga seiritsu suru hi." *Seiron* 9: 44-52.

Harada, Kazuaki. (1990). "Kōzō chōsei o nori kireba tenbō wa akarui." *Ekonomisuto* 4/16/90: 26-34.

Hasumi, Hiroaki. (1991). "Senshin-koku-kan bōeki masatsu to minkan gaikō." *Kokusai Seiji* 97 (5): 134-153.

Higuchi, Kenji. (1990). "Daiten-hō mondai wa chiiki jichi de kaiketsu o." *Ekonomisuto* 6/26/90: 46-47.

Honjo, Noboru. (1994). *Saishin Dokusen Kinshi-hō Kiiwaado*. Tokyo: Zaidan Hōjin Keizai Chōsa-kai.

Hosaka, Naotatsu. (1990). "Kōzō chōsei kyōgi no seiji keizaigaku." *Keizai Hyōron* 39 (4): 2-24.

Hoshino, Takashi. (1991). "Nichi-bei kōzō kyōgi sōron." In Chōgin Sōgō Kenkyū-jo, *Sōken Chōsa* (April) 6: 5-12.

Hoshino, Takashi and Toshiko Igarashi. (1991). "Amerika no saisei ga nichi-bei kankei o hametsu kara sukuu." In Hiroshi Takeuchi and Chōgin Sōgō Kenkyū-jo, (eds.), *Nihon Keizai no Nanmon o Toku*. Tokyo: PHP Kenkyū-jo: 28-103.

Hosoya, Chihiro et al. (1989). *Nichi-bei-ō no Keizai Masatsu o Meguru Seiji Katei*. Tokyo: Sogo Kenkyu Kaihatsu Kikō.

Hosoya, Chihiro and Nagayo Honma. (1991). *Nichi-bei Kankei-shi*. Tokyo: Yūhikaku.

Igarashi, Takeshi. (1990). "Nichi-bei kōzō kyōgi no imi towa nanika." *Gaikō Fōramu* 4: 14-23.

Igarashi, Toshiko. (1991). "Amerika kara mita nichi-bei kōzō kyōgi." In Chōgin Sōgō Kenkyū-jo, *Sōken Chōsa* (April) 6: 13-26.

Inoguchi, Kuniko. (1987). *Posuto Haken Sisutemu to Nihon no Sentaku*. Tokyo: Chikuma Shobō.

Inoguchi, Takashi and Tomoakai Iwai. (1987). *"Zokugiin" no Kenkyū*. Tokyo: Nihon Keizai Shinbun-sha.

Ishida, Hideto. (1994). *Kamitsuita Banken, Dokkin Seisaku Kyōka no Nami o Norikiru*. Tokyo: Chūō Keizai-sha.

Ishii, Kantaro. (1991). "Kokusai kyōchō to kokusai chitsujo." *Kokusai Seiji* 96(3): 143-164.

Ishii, Naoko. (1990). *Seisaku Kyōchō no Keizaigaku*. Tokyo: Nihon Keizai Shinbun-sha.

Ishikawa, Yoshimi. (1990). "'Nichi-bei kōzō kyōgi' zakkan." *Chūō Kōron* 5: 362-370.

Ishizaki, Teruhiko. (1990). *Nichi-bei Keizai no Gyakuten*. Tokyo: Tokyo Daigaku Shuppan-kai.

Itagaki, Hidenori. (1987). *Zoku no Kenkyū: Sei-kan-zai o Gyūjiru Seikai Jitsuryoku-sha Shūdan no Jittai*. Tokyo: Keizaikai.

Itami, Hiroyuki. (1989). "Shijō kyōsō no chigai ga masatsu o jochō suru." *Shūkan Tōyō Keizai* (Rinji Zōkan-go) 6/16/89: 32-37.

Itho, Mitsuharu. (1989). "Nichi-bei kōzō kyōgi ni igi ari." *Sekai* 534: 128-144.

Itho, Motoshige and Kazunori Ishiguro. (1993). *Teigen: Tsūshō Masatsu*. Tokyo: NTT Shuppan.

Itho, Motoshige and Tsūsanshō Tsūshō Sangyō Kenkyū-jo, eds. (1994). *Bōeki Kuroji no Gokai: Nihon Keizai no doko ga Mondai ka*. Tokyo: Tōyō Keizai Shinpō-sha.

JETRO (Nihon Bōeki Shinkō-kai). (1989). *1989 Jetro Hakusho* (Bōeki-hen) and (Tōshi-hen).

Kato, Kyoko and Michael Berger. (1990). *Nihonjin o Shiranai Amerikajin, Amerikajin o Shiranai Nihonjin.* Tokyo: TBS Buritanika.

Kawai, Yoshikazu. (1992). *Iyademo Wakaru Kōtori-i.* Tokyo: Nihon Keizai Shinbun-sha.

Kawata, Tadashi. (1986). "Keizai-teki haken to seisaku tenkan." *Kokusai Seiji* (30 Shūnen-kinen-gō) 10: 67-98.

Kisugi, Shin. (1990). "Dokkin-hō no unyō kyōka—kachōkin." *Jurisuto* 965: 29-34.

Kitada, Yoshiharu, ed. (1983). *Bōeki Masatsu to Keizai Seisaku.* Tokyo: Ōtsuki Shoten.

Kitaoka, Shinichi. (1990). "Rinen-kokka amerika o miayamaruna." *Chūō Kōron* 6: 134-143.

Kojima, Akira. (1990). *Gurobarizeishon* (Globalization). Tokyo: Chūō Kōron-sha.

Komiya, Ryutaro and Tsūshō Sangyō Shō Tsūshō Sangyō Kenkyū-jo, eds. (1989). *Kokusaika Suru Kigyō to Sekai Keizai.* Tokyo: Tōyō Keizai Shinpō-sha.

Konishi, Akiyuki. (1990). "Nichi-bei kōzō kyōgi no igai na shūkaku." *Ekonomisuto* 6/5/90: 14-17.

Koo, Richard. (1994). *Yoi Endaka Warui Endaka.* Tokyo: Tōyō Keizai Shinpō-sha.

Kuribayashi, Yoshimitsu. (1990). *Ōkura-sho Shukei Kyoku.* Tokyo: Kōdan-sha.

Kuroda, Makoto. (1990). *Nichi-bei Kankei no Kangae-kata.* Tokyo: Yūhikaku.

Kuroda, Masahiro. (1990). "Nichi-bei masatsu mō hitotsu no shiten." *Ekonomisuto* 6/25/90: 36-41.

Kusano, Atsushi. (1983). *Nichi-bei Orenji Kōshō.* Tokyo: Nihon Keizai Shinbun-sha.

———. (1984). *Nichi-bei Masatsu no Kōzō.* Tokyo: PHP Kenkyū-jo.

———. (1990). "Kōzō kyōgi go no nichi-bei kankei." *Sekai* 11: 258-269

———. (1991). "Bush seiken-ka no nichi-bei kōzō kyōgi" In *Amerika Gikai to Nichi-bei Kankei.* Tokyo: Chūō Kōron-sha: 97-118.

Maruyama, Masahiro. (1989). "Ryutsū—hi-kanzei-shōheki-ron wa ayamari da." *Shūkan Tōyō Keizai* (Rinji Zōkan-go) 6/16/89: 38-45.

Masamura, Kimihiro. (1990). "Shakai shihon seibi, 90-nendai ga saigo no kikai." *Ekonomisuto* 6/5/90: 108-113.

Matsushita, Mitsuo. (1983). *Nichi-bei Tsūshō Masatsu no Hōteki Sōten.* Tokyo: Yuhikaku.

———. (1990). "Nichi-bei kōzō mondai kyōgi to keizai seido chōsei." *Jurisuto* 965: 15-21.

Matsuzaki, Masahiro. (1988). *Nich-bei Masatsu no Seiji Keizaigaku.* Tokyo: Yachiyo Shuppan.

Minami, Ryoshin et al. (1991). *Gekidō Suru Sekai to Nihon Keizai.* Tokyo: TBS Buritanika.

Miyajima, Hiroshi. (1990). "Sōwaku o osae nagara no jūten ka o." *Shūkan Tōyō Keizai* 3/10/90: 74-76.

Miyazato, Seigen. (1989). *Beikoku Tsūshō Daihyō-bu (USTR).* Tokyo: The Japan Times.

Miyazato, Seigen and Kokusai Daigaku Nichi-bei Kankei Kenkyū-jo, ed. (1990). *Nichi-bei Kōzō Masatsu no Kenkyū.* Tokyo: Nihon Keizai Shinbun-sha.

Morita, Akio and Shintarō Ishihara. (1987). *"No" to Ieru Nihon.* Tokyo: Kōbun-sha.

Motoyama, Yoshihiko, ed. (1983). *Bōeki-masatsu o Miru Me.* Tokyo: Yūhikaku.

Nakano, Minoru. (1986). *Nihon-gata Seisaku Kettei no Henyō.* Tokyo: Tōyō Keizai Shinpō-sha.

Nakao, Shigeo. (1990). "Zai-bei hōgin wa amerika ni totte kyōi ka." *Ekonomisuto* 6/5/90: 70-73.

Nakatani, Iwao. (1989). *Bōdaresu Ekonomi.* Tokyo: Nihon Keizai Shinbun-sha.

———. (1990). "'Yōsai-kokka' nihon no unmei." *Chūō Kōron* 7: 104-110.

———. (1991). "Nichi-bei inbaransu no kihon kōzō." *Chūō Kōron* 1: 50-63.

Namiki, Nobuyoshi. (1989). *Tsūsan-shō no Shūen.* Tokyo: Daiyanondo-sha.

NHK Shuzai-han. (1990). *NHK Supesharu Dokyumento Kōzō Kyōgi, Nich-bei no Shōtōtsu.* Tokyo: Nihon Hōsō Shuppan Kyōkai.

Nihon Keizai Shinbun-sha, ed. (1983). *Jimintō Seichō Kai.* Tokyo: Nihon Keizai Shinbun-sha.

Nikkan Kōgyō Shinbun Tokubetsu Shuzai-han. (1990). *Nichi-bei Keizai Shinjidai: Kecchaku Nichi-bei Kōzō Kyōgi karano Shuppatsu.* Tokyo: Nikkan Shobō.

Ogura, Kazuo. (1984). *Nichi-bei Keizai Masatsu: Omote no Jijō Ura no Jijō.* Tokyo: Nihon Keizai Shinbun-sha.

Okuno, Masahiro. (1990). "Geimu riron to gōri-sei." In Masahiro Okuno, (ed.), *Gendai Keizai-gaku no Furontiya.* Tokyo: Nihon Keizai Shinbun-sha: 151-190.

Omae, Kenichi. (1990). "Kōzō kyōgi wa sokkoku chūshi seyo." *Bungei Shunjū* 5: 122-133.

Ouchi, Hiroshi. (1990). "Masatsu kara kōzō chōsei e." In Miyazato Seigen and Kokusai Daigaku Nichi-bei Kankei Kenkyū-jo, (eds.). *Nichi-bei Kōzō Masatsu no Kenkyū.* Tokyo: Nihon Keizai Shinbun-sha.

Packard, George. (1990). "Ribijonisuto 3 nin shū no gobiyū." *Chūō Kōron* 1: 91-99.

Sakai, Akio. (1991). *Nichi-bei Keizai Masatsu to Seisaku Kyōchō.* Tokyo: Yūhikaku.

Sakaiya, Taichi. (1990). "Kokunan! rinri-kan no henkō o semaru beikoku." *Chūō Kōron* 6: 282-294.

Sakamoto, Masahiro. (1990). *Nichi-bei no Sentaku.* Tokyo: Tōyō Keizai Shinpō-sha.

Sakata, Kazumitsu. (1991). "Daiten-hō to ōgata ten mondai." *Referensu* 6: 48-87.

Sanetaka, Kenji. (1990). "Ryūtsū-seido—ryūtsū keiretsu ka to ryūtsū kankō." *Jurisuto* 965: 22-28.

Sato, Hideo. (1989). *Taigai Seisaku.* Tokyo: Tōkyō Daigaku Shuppan-kai.

Sato, Sadayuki. (1987). *Nichi-bei Keizai Masatsu no Kōzu.* Tokyo: Yūhikaku.

Sato, Seisaburo and Tetsuhisa Matsuzaki. (1986). *Jimintō Seiken.* Tokyo: Chūō Kōron-sha.

Sawa, Takamitsu. (1994). *Heisei Fukyō no Seiji Keizaigaku.* Tokyo: Chūō Kōron-sha.

Shakai Keizai Kokumin Kaigi. (1988). *Kokusai Masatsu o Kiru—Hakyoku Kaihi no Nihon no Sentaku.* Tokyo: Shakai Keizai Kokumin Kaigi.

Shibuya, Eiji, ed. (1990). *Kōzō Kyōgi no Hate o Yomu* (Public Discussion). Tokyo: Zenkoku Asahi Hōsō Kabushiki Kaisha.

Shimada, Katsumi. (1990). *Nichi-bei Keizai no Masatsu to Kyōchō.* Tokyo: Yūhikaku.

Sone, Yasunori and Masao Kanazashi. (1989). *Bijuaru Zeminaru Nihon no Seiji.* Tokyo: Nihon Keizai Shinbun-sha.

Sugiyama, Yoji. (1989). "Nichibei kōzō kyōgi to kyōsō-seisaku." *Shūkan Tōyō Keizai* 12/2/89: 68-71.

Suzuki, Norihiko. (1990). *Nichi-bei Kankei no Shinario to Kiki Kanri.* Tokyo: Dōmonkan Shuppan.

Tahara, Soichiro. (1990). "Nichi-bei ampo ga omocha ni sare dashita." *Bungei Shunjū* 9: 164-181.

Takenaka, Heizo. (1991). *Nichi-bei Masatsu no Keizaigaku*. Tokyo: Nihon Keizai Shinbun-sha.

Tanaka, Naoki. (1990). *Nichi-bei Keizai Masatsu*. Tokyo: Nihon Hōsō Shuppan Kyōkai.

————. (1991). "Kokusai keizai shisutemu tsukuri ni sekkyoku-saku o." *Chūō Kōron* 6: 52-67.

Tanaka, Yoshihiro. (1989). *Nichi-bei Kankei no Gurōbarizeishon*. Tokyo: Keisō Shobō.

Tanaka, Zenichiro. (1981). *Jimintō Taisei no Seiji Shidō*. Tokyo: Daiichi Hōki Shuppan.

Tsurumi, Yoshihiro. (1990), "Nihon no kanryō tōsei keizai o mote amasu amerika." *Sekai Shūō* 71 (10): 20-23.

Tsuruta, Toshimasa and Soshichi Miyachi, eds. (1990). *Posuto Kōzō Kyōgi*. Tokyo: Tōyō Keizai Shinpō-sha.

Watanabe, Koji. (1990). "Chūkan hōkoku torimatome kōshō o oete" (an interview article). *Gaikō Fōramu* May: 22-29.

Watanabe, Satoko. (1990). "Beikoku ni okeru tainichi ishiki to nichi-bei tsūshō masatsu." *Keizai Hyōron* 39 (1): 2-15.

Williams, Sydney Linn. (1992). "Kagami no naka no nichi-bei kōzō kyōgi." *Shūkan Daiyamondo* (series of articles 3/14/92 to 6/20/92, No.1-No.14).

————. (1989). "Kōzō kaikaku o kyohi shite nichi-bei masatsu ni tenbō wa nai" (an interview article). *Shūkan Tōyō Keizai* 10/14/89: 100-102.

Yabunaka, Mitoji. (1990). "Nichi-bei kōzō mondai kyōgi." *Juristo* 965: 46-52.

————. (1991). *Taibei Keizai Kōshō*. Tokyo: Saimaru Shuppan-kai.

Yamaguchi, Asao. (1991). *Dokyumeto Nihon no Kiki Kanri*. Tokyo: Nisshin Hōdō.

Yamamoto, Yoshinobu. (1989). *Kokusai-teki Sōgō-izon*. Tokyo: Tōkyō Daigaku Shuppan-kai.

Yamauchi, Yasuhide. (1991). "Sōgō izon to kokka no yakuwari." *Kokusai Seiji* 96 (3): 165-181.

NEWSPAPERS AND MAGAZINES

Asahi Shinbun
Congressional Quarterly Weekly Report
Economist
Ekonomisuto
Far Eastern Economic Review
Newsweek
New York Times
Nihon Keizai Shinbun
Shūkan Daiyamondo
Shūkan Tōyō Keizai
Time
Wall Street Journal
Washington Post

Index

Abe, Shintaro (former Foreign Minister and General-Secretary of LDP, faction leader), 157
Abe faction, 163, 165, 173, 174, 180
Accelerate changes, 228; in Japan, 200, 206, 228; in the U.S., 203-4, 206
"Add-and-divide-by-two solution," 114-15, 117
Administrative guidance, 18, 140, 209, 210
Aizawa, Hideyuki (EPA General Director), 170, 175, 179, 182
Akers, John, 154
All Japan Retail Stores Development Union Federation (*Zenkoku Shōten Shinkō Kumiai Rengō-kai*), 99
Alliance (relationship), 107, 109
Alliance for Wood Products Exports, National Forest Product, 108
Allison, Graham T., 9, 33, 149; *Essence of Decision*, 9
"Alternative specification," 6-7, 35
American Electronics Association, 108
Analogy of the 1920s, 15, 60
Analytical concepts for four models (table 3.1), 39
"Another bureaucratic structure," 10, 227; joint, 228
Anti-Americanism, in Japan, 57
Anti-Japanese sentiment, in the U.S., 109, 177

Antimonopoly (antitrust) law, 18-19, 40, 90, 119, 120, 161, 163, 169, 174; amending, 115; changing perceptions on, 202, 212; commitments in the final report, 22; Umezawa's view, 161; U.S. criticism on, 108, 140, 161, 209
Antimonopoly Law Special Research Council, of LDP, 168
Areas of responsibility, of U.S. agencies, 137, 139
Armacost, Michael H., 80, 137, 138, 139, 141, 154, 167, 180, 182; transgovernmental lobbying, 172-73
Assessment on the degree of U.S. success in the issue areas, 40; Williams', 46 n.44
Automotive Parts & Accessories Association, 108
Availability, of policy programs and menus, 119-20

"Background condition," support of the media and public as, 5
Baker, James A., III (State Secretary), 57, 104, 152-54 passim, 158-59, 163, 166-67, 174, 180, 181-82, 194; Baker-Nakayama meeting, 178-79; Baker-Takeshita connection, 167-68

Balance of payment adjustment, 16, 105, 191, 192, 196
"Balance of power," among political actors, 5
Bargaining between national governments, 34
Basic features of the second model, 95-99
Basic policy lines, of LDP, 125-26
Baucus, Max (Senator), 153, 174, 176
Bentsen, Lloyd (Senator), 152, 153, 154, 163
Bern, Switzerland, meeting in, 26, 55, 112, 215 n.74
"Billiard ball" model, 67
Border measures, 1
Boskin, Michael J. (CEA Chairman), 15, 154, 160, 177
Brady, Nicholas F. (Treasury Secretary), 104, 153-56 passim, 158, 168, 174, 176, 177, 180; Brady-Hashimoto meeting, 171-72
Budget-making process, Japanese, 5
"Budget summit," 23, 61
Burden sharing, in defense, 59
Bush, George (President), 16, 51, 56, 153-56 passim, 157-58, 162-65 passim, 167-68, 174, 176, 180, 181-82
Bush administration, 3, 15, 48, 49, 50, 51, 150,
Bush-Takeshita Summit, 51, 153

Cabinet members' views on SII issues, Japanese, 159-60, 168-70
Cabinet Secretariat (of Kantei), 99, 101, 113, 118
"Canadiana constellation," Swanson's, 96
Cartel surcharge increase issue, 22, 115, 121, 126, 182, 210; analysis on subunits' policy positions, 118-19
Changed views and attitude, among working-level officials, 200-208, 212
Cheney, Richard (Defense Secretary), 155

Clinton administration, 3, 226
Coalition analysis of subunits, 113-21, 125
Coalition map, transgovernmental, of subunits, 116
Coercive actions, of the stronger state, 90
Cohen, Stephen D., 131 n.94
"Collegiality," among working-level officials, 37, 38, 194, 206, 208, 225
Commerce Department, 103, 104, 111, 139, 203
"Common views," 10, 192, 194, 208, 210, 222, 225; level of, 208-12, 223;
Communication: channels, 32, 36, 191, 194, 212; interagency, 197; order of, 99
Comparative economic institutions approach, 4
Competing initiative-making relationship, 50-51
Competitiveness, U.S. economy, 2, 99 157, 164, 204
"Comprehensive talks," on structural issues, 50-51, 152-53, 154, 212
"Conceptual lens," 33
Conceptual models, 33. See also Models
"Concerns," 68, 83, 84, 137, 138, 140, 147 n.12; U.S. agencies', 137-47
Configuration of coalitions, 43 n.13, 117, 119, 121, 123, 125, 152; among top policy-makers, 177, 179, 181
Congress, 9, 48, 50-51, 55-56, 153-54, 168, 174; in an imperfect three actor game, 60-62
Congressional committees, 100, 104, 108-9, 119, 123, 128 n.31
Congressional committee hearings. See under specific committee's names
Congressional monitoring, 62, 100, 108
Congressional threat, 57, 108
Consultation committee, on cartel surcharge increase issue, 121

Consultation Meeting of Party Dietmen
on Public Investment Promotion (*Tō
Kōkyō Tōshi Suishin Giin Kondan-
kai*), of LDP, 179,
Consumer interest, 6, 157, 189, 161,
200
Consumer-oriented economy, 3, 164
Consumer-oriented liberal economic
system, 2
"Contain Japan," 7, 48, 207
Content-analysis: "performative
structure," 68, 70-81, 232-33; key-
word, 68, 81-89, 234-35; of the SII
meeting records, 137-47
"Convergence by direct learning," 9,
207
Cooper, William H., 193
Council of Economic Advisers (CEA),
103, 111, 116, 121
Crisis, sense of, 57, 113, 163, 166,
174
"Crisis control" (management), 15, 58,
164-65, 168, 169
Cross-shareholding, 19, 22, 84, 140,
210
Current account imbalance, 60, 90,
105, 111, 196, 205

Dallara, Charles H. (Treasury Assistant
Secretary), 15, 54, 80, 140, 141,
180, 194, 196, 197, 199, 204-5
Danforce, John C. (Senator), 153, 176
Dango (bid-rigging), 18, 103, 198
Darman,   Richard   (Office   of
Management and Budget Director),
155, 194
Deadlock, of the SII talk, 26, 55, 162,
176
De facto coalition, 62, 140, 149, 181
De facto jurisdiction, over domestic
issues, of MFA, 146 n.7
Departmental/ministerial interests, 192
Depreciation of the yen, 58, 171
Destabilizing power, Japan as, 57
Direct (or main) dynamics, among
political actors, 99, 100, 105
Distribution system (issue), 86, 107,
125, 162, 198, 204, 211; commit-

ments in the final report, 21; SII
meeting   discussions   on,   209;
structural   impediments   in   the
Japanese economy, 18
Dole, Robert J. (Senator), 159
Domestic demand-led growth, 51, 90,
157, 164, 229
Domestic industries, and local districts,
interest of, 51, 99, 114, 227-28
Duality in a "empirical reality"-level of
abstraction relationship, 32

Economic competition, after the Cold
War, 48, 226
Economic nationalism, 192; sentiment,
57, 163, 165
Economic Planning Agency (EPA),
103, 111, 139, 140, 204; goals of,
109-10, 116
Economic Policy Council (EPC), 36,
150, 154-56, 192, 204
"Economic schizophrenia," 54
Economic Structural Problems Council
(*Keizai Kōzō Mondai Kyōgi-kai*), of
LDP, 160
Economic Subcabinet, U.S-Japan, 103,
104, 178
"Economic threat," from Japan, 48, 57,
162
Edo, Yusuke, 2
Elite policy networks of working-level
officials, 194, 198, 212, 213, 225;
merits of, 191-93; model, 10, 35-38
"Epistemic communities," 38, 44 n.31,
208, 227
Event-related indexes, 68
"Evolutionary phenomenon," of
policies of State and Treasury, 131
n.94
Exclusionary business practices (issue),
83, 86, 107, 126, 140, 182, 211;
commitments in the final report, 22;
SII meeting discussions on, 209-10;
structural   impediments   in   the
Japanese economy, 18

Fallows, James, 207
Falsify explanations, 32, 49, 50

Farren, J. Michael (Commerce Under Secretary), 29 n.23, 94 n.48

Fauver, C. Robert (Director of the Office of Industrial Nations and Global Analysis), 196

Final report, 27, 40, 80, 180; Japanese commitments in, 21-22; U.S. commitments in, 23-24

Five different stages of the SII, 24-28

Foley, Thomas S. (Representative), 159, 168, 174

Follow-up mechanisms, 121, 179, 227

Foreign Affairs Research Council (*Gaikō Chōsa-kai*), of LDP, 173

Four-Cabinet-Member meeting, 166

Framework talks: the Japan-United States Framework for a New Economic Partnership, 3, 226

FSX aircraft issue, 15, 57, 127 n.25, 184 n.22

Fukai, Shigeko, 4, 5

Fukushima, Glen S., 48-49, 50, 60, 150, 198

Gaiatsu (foreign pressure), 8, 9, 34, 67, 169, 206, 227, 228

Gaiatsu politics, 67

GATT Uruguay Round. *See* Uruguay Round

General Agreement on Tariffs and Trade (GATT), 15, 16, 49, 53, 55, 90-91, 106, 192, 207, 212

Gephardt, Richard A. (Representative), 153, 159

Global partnership, 56, 57, 59, 122, 156, 157, 158, 163, 168, 170, 177

GNP ratio public works spending issue, 27-28, 56, 59, 90, 121-24, 167-68, 170-72; Baker and cabinet members, 176-80; Baker-Nakayama meeting, 178-79

Governmental subunits, as institutional actors, 99-101

G-7 Economic Summit, 38, 89, 90, 193-99 passim

G-7 Finance Ministers and the Governors of the Central Banks, 38, 90, 193, 195-97 passim

G-7 macroeconomic policy coordination process, 37-38, 122, 194-97 passim

G-2 relationship, between the U.S. and Japanese governments, 51

Harada, Shozo (Construction Minister), 159, 161

"Hard-liners" ("Pragmatists"), in the Bush cabinet, 154, 155

"Harmonization of economic institutions," 8, 173, 192, 229; approach from the view of, 4

Hashimoto, Ryutaro, 159, 161, 166, 168-69, 170, 176, 177, 179-80, 182; Hashimoto-Brady meeting, 171-72

Hata government, 3

Hawaii meeting, 121, 176-77

Hayashi, Sadayuki (MFA General Director of the Economic Affairs Bureau), 89

Hegemon or leading state, 34, 90, 91

Heinz, John (Senator), 54

Hills, Carla A. (U.S. Trade Representative), 27, 52-53, 54, 80, 83, 90, 104, 106, 158, 168, 174, 176, 180, 199; activities in Japan, 161-62; policy debate in the cabinet on Super 301 designation, 152-56 passim

Hopkins, Raymond, 36

Hosokawa government, 3

"Hot line," between White House and Kantei, 113

House Asian and Pacific Affairs and International Economic Policy and Trade Subcommittees of the Foreign Affairs Committee, 108, 122, 123, 205

House Foreign Affairs Committee, 62

House Ways and Means Committee, 52, 152, 153

Hypothesis on the U.S. level of pressure, 81

Igarashi, Toshiko, 4, 24, 81

"Imperfect three actor game," 9, 60-62

Implications of the first model, 89-91

"Import superpower," 111, 172
"Incrementalism," in Japanese trade concessions, 120
Informal and secret meetings, 201, 215 n.74
Informal barriers, 102, 129 n.49
"Initiation ratio," 74, 76-78
Inkeles, Alex, 32
"Integrate Japan into the world trading system," 53-55, 212, 229
Interagency working group on SII, 16-17; multiagency, 192
Interests, of domestic industries (and local districts), 51, 99, 114, 227-28
Interim report (agreement), 27, 40-41, 56, 80, 117, 119, 175, 205; commitments in, 27
International Finance Bureau (*Kokusai Kinyū-kyoku*), of MOF, 191, 194
International organizations, 36, 37, 228
International regimes, 37, 38, 208, 227; antitrust law regime, 90
Internationally connected markets, 90
Ishihara, Nobuo (Deputy Cabinet Secretary), 166, 169

Japan bashing, 57
Japan Chamber of Commerce (*Nihon Shōkō Kaigisho* or *Nisshō*), 99
Japan Fair Trade Commission (JFTC), 22, 103, 116, 139, 140, 197; policy position on cartel surcharge increase issue, 115, 117-21 passim, 125-26; officials, 201, 202, 209-10
"Japan Money," 177
Japanese antitrust law. *See* Anti-monopoly (antitrust) law
Japanese commitments in the final report: exclusionary business practices, 22; distribution system, 21-22; keiretsu, 22; land policy, 21; pricing mechanism, 22; saving and investment patterns, 21
Japanese government: in an imperfect three actor game, 60-63; as a political actor, 50, 51, 56, 57-59 passim
Joint Commerce-MITI Price Survey,

203
Joint Statement of Bush and Uno on SII initiation (July 14, 1989), 16, 112
Jurisdiction of ministries, over the issues, shown in SII records, 140
Justice Department, 103, 116, 125, 139, 140

Kachō (division chief), 150
Kaifu, Toshiki (Prime Minister), 26, 56, 58, 157-59, 160, 161, 162-64 passim, 169, 172, 175, 179, 181-82; "political decision," 168, 174, 180
Kaikoku (opening of the country), 2
Kanemaru, Shin (former Deputy Prime Minister and Vice President of LDP, faction leader), 157, 162, 166, 170-71, 174-80, 181-82
Kanjichō (Secretary-General), of LDP, 151
Kano, Michihiko (Agriculture Minister), 160
Kanryō shidō gata kyōchō taisei (bureaucrats-led business-government cooperation system), 2
Kantei (the Residence of the Prime Minister), 112, 128 n.35, 113-21 passim, 151, 157; leadership of, 101; policy positions on the LSL, 113; political decision of, 124, 128; on public works spending, 114
Kato, Mutsuki (LDP Policy Affairs Research Council Chairman), 92 n.18, 120, 173
Keidanren (Federation of Economic Organizations), 3, 161, 200
Keiretsu (issue), 16, 83, 84, 86, 140, 162, 172, 182, 198, 202, 210, 211; commitments in the final report, 22; financial, 140, 197, 203; structural impediments in the Japanese economy, 19
Keizai teki sakoku (economic seclusionist, structure of the Japanese economy), 2
Keohane, Robert and Joseph Nye, 33, 36, 132 n.98; *Power and Inter-*

dependence, 33

Key-word content-analysis, 68, 81-89, 234-235

Komoto, Toshio (faction leader), 174

Komoto faction, 157

Kōzō mondai kyōgi (structural problem talk), 47

Kunihiro, Michihiko (MFA Deputy Minister for Foreign Affairs), 60, 207

Kusano, Atsushi, 4

Kyokuchō (general director of the bureau), 150-51

Land policy (issue), 40, 83, 84, 120, 126, 162, 182; assessment on, 40-41; coalition map on, 116; commitments in the final report, 21; level of common views, 211; structural impediments in the Japanese economy, 18; subunits policy positions on, 119

Large Store Law (LSL), 16, 18, 22, 27, 40, 56, 62, 80, 83, 90, 99, 108, 163, 182; "abnormality" of, 94 n.45; amendment of, 107, 118; cabinet members' policy positions on, 169; coalition map on, 116; Kanemaru's influence, 171; LDP policy positions on, 165; normalization of the operational procedure, 113, 117, 169, 200; partial repeal of, 113, 117, 126, 209; repeal of, 26, 55, 112, 117, 169, 170, 174; subunits' policy positions on, 114, 117-18

"Largest common denominator," 50

"Latent support for foreign demands," 6

"Law enforcement," notion of, 94 n.51

League of Japan-U.S. Legislators (*Nichi-bei Giin Renmei*), of LDP, 173

League of Shopping District Dietmen (*Shōten-gai Giin Renmei*), of LDP, 169

Learning process, 9, 203, 227

Level of analysis, 7, 33, 225

Level of analysis problem, and role of models, 31-32

Level of common views, in issue areas, 210-12, 223

Level of (Japanese) concessions, 40-42, 79, 88-89, 125-26, 182-83, 222-23; exclusionary business practices area, 88-89, 125-26, 212; explanations (Table 10.1), 224; distribution system area, 62, 88, 125, 211-12; keiretsu area, 88, 125-26, 212; land policy area, 89, 125-26, 211; saving-investment area, 62, 88, 211; Williams' assessment, 46 n.44

Level of (U.S.) pressure, 5, 79-81, 84, 86, 87-88, 223; exclusionary business practices area, 84-85, 88-89, 146; distribution system area, 62, 84-85,88, 146; keiretsu area, 85, 146; land policy area, 85, 88-89, 146; measured by the number of U.S. agencies with concerns, 141, 146; saving-investment area, 62, 84-85, 88, 141

Level playing field, 56

Liberal Democratic Party (LDP), 5, 99, 101, 117-21 passim, 124-26 passim, 150-51, 160, 224; policy positions on the LSL and public works spending, 114; policy stances of party leaders, 165-66; three top executives, 151

Liberal international economic order, collapsing of, 15

Liberal (free) trade regime, 7, 157

MacArthur, Douglas, 2

McCormack, Richard T. (State Under Secretary), 1, 15, 38, 53, 54, 60, 80, 139, 140, 141, 178, 199, 200, 201, 206; warned stock market crush of 1990, 189 n.175

Macroeconomic adjustment, 109, 110, 212

"Macroeconomic and microeconomic changes," 196, 122

Macroeconomic and structural adjustment elite policy networks, 38, 193-

98 passim, 212

Macroeconomic finance and monetary elite policy networks, 193-94

Macroeconomic measures (issue), to reduce trade deficit, 52, 59, 80, 98 105-6, 107, 109, 110, 197

Macroeconomic policy coordination, 192; "matching strategy," 205. *See also* G-7 macroeconomic policy coordination process

Maekawa Report, 90, 211

Major legal changes, after the SII, 3

Managed trade, 52, 54, 56, 57, 60, 158, 161, 168

Mansfield, Mike, 172

Market-access (issue), 96, 106, 107, 111, 122, 157, 158, 161, 164, 168, 192, 205, 212

Market-Oriented Sector Specific Talks (MOSS), 101-2, 193, 194

Mastanduno, Michael, 4, 15, 47, 49, 50, 96

"Matching strategy," to reduce current account and trade imbalances, 205-6

Matsunaga, Hikaru (Trade Minister), 159, 161

Matsunaga, Nobuo (Ambassador), 156, 174

Media biases, 69

"Mediative state," 229 n.5

Meiji Restoration, 2

"Microcosmic relationship," between MOF and Treasury, 127 n.25

"Microeconomic" issues, 103, 207

Mimura, Yohei, 172

Ministers, in Japanese policy-making process, 151

Ministerial bureaucrats, 35-36, 99, 113, 114, 118, 150, 162, 164

Ministry of Agriculture, Forestry, and Fisheries (MAFF), 98, 116, 119

Ministry of Construction (MOC), 16

Ministry of Finance (MOF), 5, 95, 96, 99, 101-2, 103, 104, 106, 111, 112, 116, 117-21 passim, 123, 176-77, 178, 198, 199; goals of, 110; policy position on public works spending, 114; speeches in SII

meetings, 137-45 passim

Ministry of Foreign Affairs, 103, 110-11, 116, 117-21 passim, 126; goals of, 109; speeches in SII meetings, 137-45 passim

Ministry of Home Affairs, 116, 119, 140, 169

Ministry of International Trade and Industry (MITI), 103, 109, 111, 112, 116, 117-21 passim, 123, 125-26, 169, 199, 203; goals of, 110; officials' view on antitrust law issue, 202, 210; policy position on the LSL, 113; speeches in SII meetings, 137-45 passim

Ministry of Justice (MOJ), 22, 140

Ministry of Transportation (MOT), 16, 140

Mitchell, George J. (Senator), 159

Mitsuzuka, Hiroshi (Trade Minister, Foreign Minister), 52, 156, 157

Miyazawa, Kiichi (former Finance Minister, faction leader), 157, 165-66

Miyazawa faction, 165

Models: elite policy networks of working-level officials, 10, 35-38; government as a unitary rational actor, 9, 34; transgovernmental coalition of subunits, 10, 34-35; transgovernmental coalition of top-level policy-makers, 10, 35

Morita, Akio, 161

Mosbacher, Robert (Commerce Secretary), 154-56 passim, 169, 170, 182

Mulford, David C. (Treasury Under Secretary for International Affairs), 90, 102, 194, 196, 199

Multilateral (free) trade regime (system), 49, 53, 54, 55; demise of, 15, 58, 106, 228; world trade system, 207. *See also* General Agreement on Tariffs and Trade (GATT)

Murayama LDP-Socialist coalition government, policies of, 3

Muto, Kabun (Trade Minister), 166,

169, 170, 172-73, 176, 182

Naikaku kanbō chōkan (chief cabinet secretary), 151
Nakatani, Iwao, 89
Nakayama, Taro (Foreign Minister), 15, 58, 158-59, 161, 166, 168, 169, 170, 180, 182; Nakayama-Baker meeting, 178-79
National Association of Manufacturers, 108
National Forest Products Association, 108
National Land Agency (NLA), 116, 140
National policy outcomes, 34, 98
National self-interest, 48, 59, 192, 222
National Tax Agency, 140
National Trade Estimate Report, 16
National Trade Policy Agenda, 51-52
National trade policy goals (objectives), 34, 51-52, 53, 55, 57, 212
Negative consequences of market forces, 89
Nemawashi (consensus building), by Armacost, 173
NHK Shuzai-han, *NHK Supesharu Dokyumento Kōzō Kyōgi*, 137, 177, 198, 208
"*Nichi-bei kōzō kyōgi gijiroku no kiroku*" (the Record of U.S.-Japan Structural Impediments Initiative Meeting Records), 137
Nihon fūjikome (contain Japan), 7
Nihon kaizō (reform Japan), 7
Nihon Keizai Shinbun (*Nikkei*), 68-86 passim, 141
Nishioka, Takeo (LDP General Affairs Chairman), 92 n.18, 173, 174
Numeric targets, 3-4, 174

"Objectives," "choices," "means," of the government, 34, 49-50, 55, 57
OECD Ministerial meeting, 52, 175
Office of International Affairs (OIA), of the Treasury Department, 194, 196
Official definition of the SII talk, 8

Oishi, Senpachi (Telecommunications Minister), 161
Okuda, Keiwa (Home Affairs Minister), 169, 173, 181
Omnibus Trade and Competitiveness Act of 1988 (the 1988 Trade Act), 15
Organization for Economic Cooperation and Development (OECD), 37-38, 89, 175, 193-95 passim; Working Three of, 194, 201
Organizational goals: Japanese ministries, 109-10; U.S. departments, 105-9
Organizational outputs, 34
Organizational routines, 101, 104, 120, 124
Ouchi, Hiroshi, 4
Outcomes (agreements), of trade negotiation, 34, 35, 88, 98, 182, 208, 226
Ozawa, Ichiro (LDP General-Secretary), 57, 157, 161, 165, 170-71, 173, 174, 181, 193

Palm Springs Summit, 26, 56, 113, 162-64
Paris Economic Summit, 16
Parliamentary system, 181
Parsimony, of theories, 100, 151-52, 183 n.15
"Participation expansion," 5-6, 7, 99
Patent system, 16, 18, 108, 121, 203; intellectual property in Uruguay Round, 52; multilateral discussion on, 216 n.90; patent agency, 192
Pear, Robert, 96
Perception: average perception gaps, 212; gaps, 10, 200, 208, 210-12; of working-level officials, 192-93
Perceptional and attitudinal changes, among policy-makers and business elites after the SII, 3
"Performative structure" content-analysis, 68, 70-81, 232-33
Perry, Matthew C., 2
Personal relationship (ties), between top policy-makers, 10, 158, 163,

164-65, 167, 171, 225; as an institution, 186 n.91
Plaza Accord of 1985, 167, 194
Policy Affairs Research Council (*Seimu Chōsa-kai*, or *Seicho-kai*), of LDP, 151
Policy direction, 211
Policy-making process in the Japanese government, 36, 150-51; "vertical," 183 n.6
Policy-making process in the U.S. government, 150; "horizontal," 127 n.18, 183 n.6; trade policy decisions, 128 n.34
Policy positions, of relevant subunits on issues, 113-15
Policy programs, 34, 104-5, 120
Policy recommendations, 223-24
Policy spectrum, 181
Policy "tribes," of LDP, 128 n.29, 151, 170
Political actors, 34, 35; subunits, 99-101; top-level policy-makers as, 149-52
Political bargaining, between national governments, 89, 90
Political guidance, 100, 112, 113, 119, 163
Political players (Allison's), 35, 44 n.14
Political power relations ratio, 77
Politically powerful government, 68, 89
Pork barrel, 124
Power balance, 193, 208; among subunits, 124-25. *See also* Power relations
Power relations, 193, 222; uneven, 59, 77
"Prediction," 223-24
Presidential system, 181
President's budget, savings and education initiatives, 61, 204, 205
Pressure, political, 57, 68, 86, 140
Prestowitz, Clyde V., 61
Previous research on SII, 4-8
Pricing mechanisms, and price differentials (issue), 19, 83, 140,

159; commitments in the final report, 22
Prime Minister, in Japanese policy making, 151
Principals, subcabinet-level, 36, 150
Principle of capitalist market system, concerning the LSL, 94 n.45
Private damage remedy system, 22, 115, 202, 210
Problem-solving aspect of SII, 192
Product-by-product approach, 102, 103, 105, 195, 197
Professional (working) relationship, 196, 201, 206
Propositions, for research, 41-42, 222
Public works spending (issue), 26, 55, 83, 86, 107, 108, 161, 163, 169, 170, 182; coalition map on, 116; subunits' policy positions on, 114, 117. *See also* GNP ratio public works spending issue
"Pulling and hauling," among top policy-makers, 35, 149, 222
Purpose of research and outline, 8-10

Qualitative text analysis, 208-10, 211
Quantification of interactions, between governments, 67-94

"Radicalization," of State Department, 106, 107, 131 n.94; of Treasury Department, 106, 122, 131 n.94
Rank and file of LDP, 165, 173, 188 n.142
Ratios, political power, 77; pressure, 77; reactive, 77
"Receptivity" of the government, 39, 86
Reduce the trade deficit, 51, 53, 57, 80, 107, 109, 164, 205; as Congress' short-term goal, 62, 123, 159; by "matching strategy," 204-5; as a "principle objective" of the SII, 122
References for policy-outcomes, 35, 43 n.13
Reform Japanese economic structure, 7, 159, 200

Regime. *See* International regimes
Regulatory changes in the U.S. after
    the SII, 3
Relation between U.S. pressure and
    level of Japanese concessions, 79-89
Relevances for policy-outcomes, 35, 43
    n.13
Repertoires, of policy, 34, 120
Research design, 38-42
"Responsiveness," of the government,
    86; gap, 86
Results-oriented approach, 54, 103,
    152, 221
Revisionists, 54, 64 n.31, 192, 200
Rill, James F. (Assistant Attorney
    General), 11 n.8, 38, 140-41, 206
Road Policy Research Council (*Dōro
    Chōsa-kai*), of LDP, 166, 170
Rome Treaty, 1
Rosecrance, Richard, 229 n.5
Rostenkowski, Dan (Representative),
    153
Ruggie, John Gerald, 44 n.31
"Rump group," of the TPRG, 150
Russell, Robert W., 191

Saito, Eishiro, 161, 170
Sakai, Akio, view on the reality of
    international policy coordination, 43
    n.9
Sakaiya, Taichi, 2
Sakamoto, Misoji (Chief Cabinet
    Secretary), 165, 166, 174, 179
Sasaki, Takeshi, 7, 198
Sato, Moriyoshi (NLA Director), 170,
    182
Saving and investment patterns:
    commitments in the final report, 21,
    23; as structural impediments in the
    Japanese economy, 17-18; as
    structural impediments in the U.S.
    economy, 19 *See also* U.S. saving
    and investment patterns
Saving and investment patterns issue,
    40, 62, 88, 125-26, 141, 182, 211;
    SII meeting discussions on, 208-9.
    See also Public works spending
    (issue)

Schoppa, Leonard J, 4, 47, 79, 80;
    criticism on his approach, 4-7
Scowcroft, Brent (National Security
    Adviser), 155, 156, 174
"Second black ship," 2
Second "major foreign policy crisis,"
    15
Second "Smoot-Hawley," 15
Sector-specific trade negotiation, 100
Seichōkaichō (Chairman of the Policy
    Affairs Research Council), of LDP,
    151
Seimu Chōsa-kai (Policy Affairs
    Research Council), of LDP, 151
Semi-feudal militaristic system, 2
Senate Finance Committee, 104, 152,
    153, 107, 108, 122, 139, 199, 204
Senate Finance International Trade
    Subcommittee, 53, 107, 108, 122,
    139
Senate Foreign Relations Committee,
    57
"Shapes of branches," of capitalism,
    207
Shareholders' rights, 19, 140, 203
Shōeki (ministerial interests), 96
SII agenda, 17-20
SII agreement, 21-24
Similarities in coding results, of *Nikkei*
    and the *WSJ*, 76-78
Singer, J. David, 42-43 nn.1, 8
Size and strength of transgovernmental
    coalitions, 41-42; among subunits,
    10, 125-26, 223; among top-level
    policy-makers, 10, 181-82, 223
Sōmukaichō (Chairman of the
    Executive council), of LDP, 151
Sorensen, Theodore, 97
Special Research Commission on
    Economic Adjustment (*Keizai
    Chōsei Tokubetsu Chōsakai*), of
    LDP, 118, 160, 168, 173-74
Stabilize the yen, 58
Standard operating procedures (SOPs),
    organizational programs, repertoires
    (menus), 34
State Department, 83, 99, 103, 104,
    111, 112, 116, 119, 121, 122, 123,

124, 197; goals of, 107-8; policy on the LSL, 113; speeches in SII meetings, 137-45 passim; "white house model" of, 178

State-centric paradigm, 32

Strange, Susan, criticism on the nature of international regimes, 43 n.9

Strategic position: in LDP party politics, 170, 173; among subunits, 125

Structural adjustment, 51, 90, 111, 153, 157, 160, 196, 207, 212

Structural barriers, 52, 106, 108, 205

Structural Economic Dialogue, U.S.-Japan, 101-2, 108, 194, 195

Structural impediments, 1-2, 47, 140, 205, 227; in the Japanese economy, identified by the U.S. government, 17-19; in the U.S. economy, identified by the Japanese government, 19-20

Structural reform, 196, 207

"Structural rigidities," 102, 129 n.49, 196, 198, 199

Sugiyama, Yoji (JFTC Shōgai-tantō Shingikan), 201

Sununu, John H. (Chief of Staff), 154

Super 301 provision, of the 1988 Trade Act, 15-16, 50-53, 79, 108, 152

Super 301 unfair trade practices designation, 15-16, 47-49, 96, 104, 154-56, 212, 221

Surcharges on illegal cartels. See cartel surcharge increase issue

"Surpluses-are-good" argument (kuroji yūyō-ron), 121, 123, 176-77, 178-79

Suzuki, Naomichi (MITI Vice Minister for International Affairs), 60, 201, 206

Systematically layered multidimensional approach, 9, 33, 34-38, 225

Tahara, Soichiro, 7

Takahara, Sumiko (EPA General Director), 159, 161

Takeshita, Noboru (former Prime Minister, faction leader), 51, 57-58,

152, 157, 162, 163, 166, 173, 181, 182; Takeshita-Baker connection, 167-68

Takeshita faction (Keisei-kai), 58, 157, 170, 171

Takuji, Matsuzawa, 161

Taylor, John B. (CEA Member), 38, 54, 141, 201, 203, 204, 206

Telephone conversations, role of, in trade negotiations, 37, 44 n. 30, 112, 113, 162, 175, 176, 180, 196, 201

"Tenuous alliance," between Kennedy and Khrushchev, 149

Theoretical framework, for research, 31-38

Theoretical questions and assumptions, for content-analysis, 67-70

Theoretical shortcomings, of modern economics, 89

Third opening of the country, 2

Three groups, in U.S. trade policy making, 97-98

Three major demands, of the U.S. government, 26, 55

"Three pillars," of the U.S.-Japanese relations, 124

Three requirements, of an analytical models (description, explanation, and prediction), 42-43 n.8

Toronto Summit (June 1988), 90, 195, 196

Toys R Us, 62, 86, 94 n.45, 108, 119, 161, 170, 182

Trade negotiation outcomes. See Outcomes

Trade Policy Review Group (TPRG), 25, 150, 152

Trade Policy Staff Committee (TPSC), 150

"Trade war," 15, 53, 154

Transgovernmental and transnational politics, theoretical discussions and studies, 43 n.10

Transgovernmental coalition, between governments, 61-62

Transgovernmental coalition of subunits, 34, 108, 124, 126, 212,

213, 223; model of, 10, 34-35
Transgovernmental coalition of top-level policy-makers, 35, 212, 213, 225; model of, 10, 35
Transgovernmental policy coordination, policy making, policy implementation, 10, 36, 37, 201, 205, 206-7, 227, 228
"Transgovernmental task force," 192
Transnational coalition, 213 n.14
Transnational interests, of two economies, 192
Treasury Department, 95, 96, 99, 101-2, 103, 104, 111, 112, 116, 119, 121, 123, 124, 178, 194, 198; goals of, 105-6; policy position on public works spending, 114; speeches in SII meetings, 137-45 passim
"Triangular struggle," among Kantei, LDP, and ministries, 129 n.37
"Trifurcated Japan policy," 127 n.19
Trilateral cooperation, among the U.S, Japan, and EC, 57, 163
Turf-battles, 34, 103, 124, 127 n.18
240-item list, 26, 55, 112, 167
Two-pronged trade policy goal, of the SII, 53-55
"Two-way street" notion, of the SII, 8, 9, 25, 62, 157, 158, 164, 175, 198-200 passim
Types of transgovernmental coalition (potential, de facto tacit, explicit), 132 n.98

Umezawa, Setsuo (JFTC Chairman), 161, 182, 202
Uneven Power relations, 59, 77
Unilateral action, 52, 90-91, 156, 158
Unitary rational actor model, 9, 34, 212, 213, 223
Unno, Tsuneo (EPA Vice Minister for Foreign Economic Affairs), 201
Uno, Sosuke (Foreign Affairs Minister, Prime Minister), 16, 152, 157
Unyō kaizen (improving operational procedures), of the LSL, 113,
Uruguay Round, 49, 52, 152, 158, 163
U.S. administration: in an imperfect

three actor game, 60-62; as a political actor, 9, 48, 50, 51, 53-59 passim
U.S. agencies' concerns, 137-47
U.S. antitrust law, 19, 23
U.S. Chamber of Commerce, 108
U.S. commitments in the final report, 22-23
U.S.-Japan Antitrust Annual Consultation, 201
U.S.-Japanese relationship: deterioration, 158, 162; good, 117, 159, 164, 166; stable, 107, 160
U.S.-Japanese security (treaty) relations, 56-58, 109, 180, 222
U.S. pressure, on Japanese government. See Level of (U.S.) pressure
U.S. saving and investment patterns, 19 160, 164, 199, 204-5; commitments in the final report, 23
U.S. structural impediments: corporate behavior, 20, 203, 207, 227; corporate investment activities and supply capacity, 19-20; export promotion, 20; government regulation, 20; research and development, 20; saving and investment patterns, 19; workforce education and training, 20
U.S. Trade Representative (USTR), the Office of, 83, 96, 99, 102, 103, 104, 116, 119, 125, 150; goals of, 106-7; policy position on cartel surcharge increase issue, 115; speeches in SII meetings, 137-45 passim
Utsumi, Makoto (MOF Vice Minister for International Affairs), 35, 194, 196, 197, 199, 201

Vice Cabinet Secretary, 151
"Vicious cycle," of Japanese massive industrial investment and export drive, 59, 178

Wall Street Journal (WSJ), 68, 74-78 passim, 86-88 passim
Washington Treaty of 1922, 7

Watanabe, Koji (MFA Deputy Minister for Foreign Affairs), 203, 206, 207
Watanabe, Michio (faction leader), 174
Watanabe faction, 165
Watanuki, Tamisuke (Construction Minister), 170, 182
White House, 100, 104, 105, 112, 113, 119, 120, 124
Williams, S. Linn (Deputy U.S. Trade Representative), 38, 53, 60, 83, 198-99, 201, 204, 206, 207, 211, 212; assessment of U.S. success in issue areas, 46 n.44; view on budgeting policy, 207-8
Winham, Gilbert R., 229
Winning coalition, 125-26
Working group, 10, 192, 195, 227
Working-level officials (bureaucrats), 35-36, 191, 212 n.1
"World market," 89, 90

World system, 90
World Trade Organization (WTO), 91
Worldwide reform efforts, in 1989-90, 3, 11 n.12

Yabunaka, Mitoji (MFA Director of the Second North America Division), 8, 80, 198, 203
Yamaguchi, Toshio, 160, 165, 174
Yamamura, Kozo, 4, 7; *Japan's Economic Structure: Should It Change?*, 4
Yen-Dollar Talks, 97, 101-2, 111, 193-197 passim, 199
Yeutter, Clayton (Agricultural Secretary), 155

Zoku (policy tribes), of LDP, 128 n.29, 151

About the Author

NORIO NAKA is a visiting fellow at the Center for Japanese Studies, University of California, Berkeley. Until recently, he was a Post-Doctoral Scholar at Purdue University. A specialist in the political economy of U.S.-Japan trade relations and organizational development, Dr. Naka is the author of several journal articles.

ISBN 1-56720-005-2

90000>

EAN

9 781567 200058

HARDCOVER BAR CODE